FROM THE REVIEWERS

"*The Super Health Diet* is a remarkable book. K.C. has done an admirable job of thoroughly covering the topic of obesity, our greatest and most serious health epidemic facing America today. The book has numerous peer-reviewed articles that support his concepts of the Four Corners of Superfood Nutrition and several cutting-edge techniques, including superfoods combined with supplements, high quality plant-based protein smoothies, and micronutrient supplementation to achieve ideal body weight and optimum health. I recommend it to both health care practitioners and everyone else, ranging from those with health challenges to world-class athletes who are interested in achieving super health."

DR. LEONARD SMITH, M.D., F.A.C.S.,
Co-Author of *Gut Solutions*, *Fiber 35 Diet*, and
Detox Strategy

■

"*The Super Health Diet* is an outstanding book for doctors and patients! Following this diet is an excellent educational tool to promote healthy aging and weight optimization."

DR. ROBERT M. GOLDMAN, M.D., PH.D.,
D.O., F.A.A.S.P., Chairman of the Board of A4M

■

"*The Super Health Diet* can revolutionize your health and performance. K.C.'s research and nutrition plan can help you improve your health, increase your resistance to disease, decrease your stress, slow aging, and enjoy life to the fullest. The information on metabolism and the Four Corners of Superfood Nutrition is at the cutting edge of our knowledge of how the human body works. The nutrition plans are based on hard science, and the research evidence is accumulating in support of these principles. I sincerely hope that we are on the verge of a revolution in our understanding of optimal nutrition and how to apply that knowledge to lead healthy happy lives."

DR. GREG WELLS, PH.D., Author of
SuperBodies, Scientist and Human Physiologist

■

"If you're looking for great health and skinnier jeans, I highly recommend *The Super Health Diet*. In this confusing world of dietary information, supplements, and fitness, it is a beacon of light that contains vital, refreshing, and priceless information that could change your life. If you want to feel strong again, lose weight, and regain confidence, the power of transformation is in your hands now. Build the body you've always dreamed of through the powerful principles in this book!"

DR. SUZY COHEN, R.PH.,
Author of *Diabetes Without Drugs* and *Drug Muggers*

■

"Weight gain is a side effect of doing the wrong things just as weight loss is a side effect of doing the right things. Through offering fundamental principles of biochemistry along with well-documented research, K.C. debunks many of the marketing schemes that take advantage of so many consumers, leaving them dissatisfied and unfulfilled. His plan is a well-balanced, focused approach to achieving real success in overcoming the struggles associated with weight loss. Brilliant! A must read for everyone!"

DR. SCOTT HANNEN, D.C.,
Author of *Healing by Design*

■

"Praise for K.C. and his master plan and blueprint for Super Health! He offers hope through knowledge and gracefully teaches the power of food, essential vitamins, minerals, and amino acids. K.C. gives us the uncompromising and searing truth about Super Nutrition, providing a self-empowerment journey with tools on how to discover Super Health. A must read for breaking the vicious cycle of disease."

CHERYL DIANE, B.C.N.,
Integrative Disease Specialist

■

"*The Super Health Diet* is one of only a handful of great, comprehensive diet and nutrition books among the thousands on the market today. K.C. has left no stone unturned when it comes to examining what is right and wrong with the way people eat, lose weight, and aim for optimal health. You will learn why different diets work for some and not for others, as well as why many diets only work short term. Combining personal experience, extensive scientific research, and commonsense guidelines, K.C. takes you on an educational and historical journey that will provide you practical answers to achieving optimal health while increasing your nutritional knowledge way beyond your wildest expectations. This book will be a resource you will return to time and time again."

DR. MARK J. SMITH, PH.D.,
Exercise Physiologist and Nutritionist

■

"K.C. has delivered big time. This isn't another book that just tells you how to be healthy; it actually *shows* you how to be healthy. K.C. walks you through how to change your life one simple step at a time. Healthy living is one of the hardest things to achieve in today's world. It takes knowledge, and it takes a plan. Thanks to Super Health, you now have both!"

DR. GREG ROSE, D.C.,
Co-Founder of the Titleist Performance Institute

■

"Finally, for the first time in my 30 years of practice, a book on diet and health I can completely and enthusiastically recommend without hesitation. *The Super Health Diet* offers the exceptionally rare combination of wit, wisdom, history, science, research, clear and concise explanations, and pure common sense—simply the best book I have read on the subject in 30 years. It cuts through the mass confusion of the myriad of diets and other health myths and offers practical, clinically proven and scientifically supported solutions to help withstand the growing tidal wave of obesity, diabetes, heart disease, cancer, autism, ADHD, and depression that plagues our country."

DR. CINDY COLLINS, D.C., D.A.C.B.N.,
C.C.N., P.T.

■

"Having counseled doctors and patients for 50 years on weight loss, I have seen many books come and go. *The Super Health Diet* is simply the best book I have ever seen on this subject! A must read for anyone interested in reaching a higher level of health and optimal weight."

DR. ROBERT FISHMAN, P.D., Bpharm, C.P., C.N.

■

"Expertise is spelled RESEARCH in the phenomenal case of *The Super Health Diet*. To reach K.C. Craichy's level of discipline involves 20 years of study and investigation in which he has focused on health and nutrition. This God-inspired book is the answer to the world's declining wellness challenges."

DR. PHILLIP GOLDFEDDER, M.D., Neurosurgeon, Author of *Lean God's Way* and *Healing Is Yours*

■

"*The Super Health Diet* is the best resource on weight loss and health that I have seen in my 30 years of practicing Chinese medicine. K.C. uses hundreds of scientific references to validate his approach, and some of his dietary discoveries are nothing short of revelatory. Of particular interest are his 'Four Corners of Superfood Nutrition' and 'The Dynamic Role of Proteins in Weight Loss' and Super Health. A must read for everyone!"

DR. LUKE CUA, PH.D., O.M.D., L.AC., Author of *Chinese Medicine Made Simple*

■

"K.C.'s breadth of knowledge of the field of diet and nutrition is very impressive. There are few doctors who can match his knowledge of nutrition. *The Super Health Diet* is a roadmap to how to survive as closely as possible with the nutritional principles of our Stone Age forebearers only living in our modern age and modern lifestyles, eating delicious foods, and not feel as though one is participating in simply another fad diet. K.C.'s research into how we need to eat to survive well is exceptional, and this is a highly essential read for anyone wanting to move in a healthy direction."

DR. PATRICK PURDUE, D.O.M.

■

"*The Super Health Diet* is an outstanding resource for cutting through the myriad of diets and weight loss approaches. It is a highly informative, research-based analysis of what works and what doesn't, while providing a revolutionary approach to obtaining optimal weight while reaching a higher level of health and wellness. This book is proof that K.C. is one of the industry's most informed and accomplished experts."

ANDY O'BRIEN,
Strength and Conditioning Coach to Elite Athletes

■

"No one can deliver common sense with more enthusiasm or a bigger smile than K.C. Craichy. The best part of his passion is his commitment to his research positioned alongside his honor of our wonderful history. In an age of information gluttony, we need reason, clarity, simplicity, and structure. K.C. has provided this in *The Super Health Diet*. Use some or all of this information to reconsider the things you thought you knew. Enjoy Super Health!"

GRAY COOK, M.S.P.T., O.C.S., C.S.C.S.,
Author of *Movement* and *Athletic Body in Balance*

"As a sports trainer to top professional athletes for more than 20 years, I have learned the importance of proper nutrition and its massive role in sports performance. K.C. Craichy is one of the world's leading nutrition experts, and I trust his wealth of knowledge and expertise when I guide my athletes with their nutritional needs. Through his extensive research and sound principles, K.C. has developed a lifestyle plan that will allow you to achieve your greatest goals, lose weight, and add years to your life. *The Super Health Diet* is truly an inspiration!"

DAVID HERMAN,
Professional Sports Performance Coach

■

"*The Super Health Diet* is the most comprehensive book I've ever read about diet and natural health. I've been involved in martial arts training and instruction for 50 years and thought I knew a lot about health and fitness before K.C. and his family became my students nine years ago and my real education began. This book is truly a 'fountain of youth.' I am approaching my mid 60s and still able to teach martial arts at a high level because of the lessons I've learned in this amazing journey of Super Health!"

MARK McGEE,
Author of *A History of Man's Quest for Immortality*,
Yon Ch'uan Christian Martial Arts

■

"Health conscious people, whether top athletes or simply individuals who are concerned about how they perform, feel, and look, will learn a tremendous amount from *The Super Health Diet*. In a language that is easy to understand, K.C. explains in detail how the body operates and the function of proper nutrition and supplementation to help keep you in peak youthful health. If you care about your health, it is a must read."

DAVID LEADBETTER,
Golf Coach to Many of the World's Top Golfers

■

"*The Super Health Diet* is a motivating book that is jam-packed with clear and concise information about lifestyle, nutrition, and obtaining and maintaining health that everyone needs to know. Buy it and read it; you won't be sorry."

TY BOLLINGER,
Author of *Cancer: Step Outside the Box*

■

"*The Super Health Diet* is a deeply considered and rigorously researched approach to preserving our God-given health. I have worked with K.C. to investigate why his diet actually works. In doing so, we have witnessed the remarkable ability of the Super Health Diet to have therapeutic effects on primary factors—oxidative damage, inflammation, and glycation—that influence all aspects of our health, including weight loss, aches and pains, insulin management, cardiovascular and immune system support. Please accept K.C.'s extraordinary gift!"

DAVID N. BELL, Bell Advisory Services,
Nutrient Analytics

■

"As a clinical nutritionist, biochemist, and environmental toxicologist, I have refused to promote any one type of diet plan. Rather, I have focused on educating my clients on lifestyle eating and choices that fall within a balanced range and are healthy and suitable for the individual, while maintaining principles that create wellness. *The Super Health Diet* has eloquently outlined those principles, and I am so excited to have a resource that is research-based, scientific yet friendly and informative. K.C.'s simple explanation on the complex biochemistry of diet and weight loss is done in an amazing style and with so much clarity. The Four Corners concept captures the most successful working theories in diet and nutrition today. Our office will be recommending this book to everyone who walks through the door on their first appointment."

DR. TAMARA MARIEA, PH.D., C.C.N.,
Founder of Internal Balance, Inc.

∎

"*The Super Health Diet* truly is the last diet book you will ever need. In its pages you will discover everything you need to lose weight quickly, safely, and permanently, while at the same time balancing and maximizing hormone production for Super Health and total well-being."

JOHN PETERSON, Author of *Pushing Yourself to Power* and *Isometric Power Revolution*

∎

THE
SUPER
HEALTH
DIET

THE **LAST DIET** YOU WILL **EVER** NEED!

THE SUPER HEALTH DIET

THE LAST DIET YOU WILL EVER NEED!

K.C. CRAICHY

LIVINGFUEL PUBLISHING
TAMPA, FLORIDA

The information in this book is for educational purposes only. Neither the publisher nor author is engaged in rendering professional advice or services to the individual reader. All matters regarding physical and mental health should be supervised by a health practitioner knowledgeable in treating that particular condition. Neither the author nor the publisher shall be liable or responsible for any loss, injury, or damage allegedly arising from any information or suggestion in this book.

ISBN 978-09827853-1-7

Published by Living Fuel Publishing, a division of Living Fuel, Inc. You can reach us on the Internet at www.livingfuel.com or call 1-866-580-FUEL.

Literary development and cover/interior design by Koechel Peterson & Associates, Inc., Minneapolis, Minnesota.

Manufactured in the United States of America

I DEDICATE THIS BOOK

to my Heavenly Father,

His Son, Jesus Christ,

and the Holy Spirit,

through whom all things

are possible.

The Craichy family from left to right, Austin (16), Monica,
Joshua (4), Sarah (13), KC, Grace (8), and Kyle (17)

ACKNOWLEDGMENTS

To my dearest *Monica*, you are the epitome of what a wife and mother ought to be, a Proverbs 31 woman, and a shining example of the grace of God in my life. You are an amazing role model—when you learn the truth, you do it no matter what. Not only are you the foundation of my success, you are my dream girl, and I love you immeasurably.

To my dear children, *Kyle, Austin, Sarah, Grace,* and *Joshua.* Words cannot describe the love and appreciation I have for each of you. The questions each of you asked me have made this a better book. It has been such a joy to see each of you practice Super Health Diet principles on your own and to see you teach them to your friends. The pages of this book cannot fully describe how proud I am of you and what a blessing and inspiration you are to me. I love you!

To *Leonard Smith*, M.D., you are one of the most brilliant doctors I know, and it is always thought-provoking, stimulating, and educational to work with you. Thank you for your exceptionally detailed review of this book and for challenging some of the Super Health Diet principles so they can stand the test.

To *Lance Wubbels*, for your literary brilliance and invaluable assistance in the writing of this book. Lance, you are as good as it gets! *Dave Koechel*, for your cover design and typesetting skills are the best I have seen. *John Peterson*, for teaching me the "Super Health 7" and "Big 3" exercises presented in this book. Thank you!

To *Jeff Hoening* and *Mark McGee*, God bless you. Thank you for your diligence, keen eyes, and detailed feedback on this book, and thank you for all you do for Monica and me.

To my brother, *John Craichy*, for your interest in this work and your valuable feedback.

Thank you to all who had any part in helping to develop my understanding of this topic, especially the frontline researchers who do the studies that collectively unlock the mysteries of the body, soul, and spirit.

Special thanks to *Mike Adams, Dr. Richard Lippman, Dr. Leonard Smith, Dr. Robert Fishman, Gray Cook, Dr. Scott Hannen, Dr. Robert*

M. Goldman, David Herman, Dr. Patrick Purdue, Andy O'Brien, Cheryl Diane, Dr. Greg Rose, Dr. Phillip Goldfedder, Ty Bollinger, Dr. Suzy Cohen, Mark McGee, Dr. Luke Cua, Dr. Mark J. Smith, David Bell, David Leadbetter, Dr. Greg Wells, Dr. Tamara Mariea, Dr. Cindy Collins, and *John Peterson* for the reviews listed on the cover and inside front cover of this book. You are leaders in your fields, and I greatly appreciate your putting your names on this special work.

In loving memory of my mom, *Sharon S. Craichy,* who passed away during the writing of this book.

TABLE OF CONTENTS

Dangers of Fructose • The Glycemic Index and Glycemic Load •
Metabolic Syndrome or Syndrome X • The Importance of Fiber •
The Glycemic Load
Corner #3—Consume High Antioxidant Superfoods and
Supplements
The Battle Against Degenerative Diseases • The Benefits of Omega-3s
• Availability of Antioxidants • Fruits and Vegetables • Capsaicin
• Measuring a Food's Antioxidant Protection • 20 Common Foods
With the Most Antioxidants
Corner #4—Eat and Supplement with Superfats
Omega-3 Fatty Acids • The Importance of Omega-3s • Not Just Any
Fish Oil
Summary of the Four Corners of Superfood Nutrition
Superfood Nutrition
Regarding the USDA Food Pyramid • Super Health Diet Guide-
lines • Liquid Nutrition Versus Solid Foods
At-a-Glance Foods to Eat and Avoid
Four Corners Shopping List

K.C. CRAICHY

|||||||||||||||||||||||||||||||||||||||||||||||||||||||||||||||||||||||||||||||||

SHARING A VISION FOR OPTIMAL HEALTH

K.C. Craichy is the bestselling author of *Super Health: 7 Golden Keys to Unlock Lifelong Vitality* and Founder and CEO of Living Fuel, Inc.—The Leader in Superfood Nutrition. He is a health advocate, researcher, and recognized expert on natural health and performance nutrition. His extensive study of leading-edge health research and collaborative work with top medical and nutritional practitioners and researchers to solve his wife Monica's health problems—anxiety, depression, and suicidal thoughts—along with the grace of God, led him to the answers for Monica's healing and to the founding of Living Fuel, Inc. As a result of overcoming this health crisis, K.C. and Monica have helped numerous people become overcomers in their own health situations. Together they are now cohosts of the popular Internet TV program called *Living Fuel TV*.

K.C. is committed to changing lives through multimedia, super health lifestyle education combined with super healthy, high impact superfoods. He also serves on the Nutrition Advisory Board for Titleist Performance Institute as well as on the Clinical Nutrition Review Board (the certifying body of the International and American Association of Clinical Nutrition). A frequent natural health and performance nutrition guest on various TV and radio programs as well as a frequent contributor to national magazines and blogs, K.C. lives in Tampa, Florida, with his wife, Monica, and their five children.

FOREWORD

The realm of diet books is a jungle of confusing and conflicting information. As the editor of NaturalNews.com for the last seven years, I've seen it all: Diet fads, weight loss schemes, and celebrity-promoted "miracle" drop-the-pounds programs based on promotional hype rather than real nutritional sense.

That's what makes this book by K.C. Craichy so refreshing. It's not about hype. It doesn't feature an airbrushed photo of a big name celebrity on the cover. And it doesn't promise any miracles other than the ones your body is capable of producing naturally when given the right ingredients.

This is the real secret of *The Super Health Diet*. In this book, K.C. Craichy reveals the truly astonishing "miracles" of health and weight loss your body is naturally capable of producing right now. These miracles don't happen overnight, and they can't simply be wished into existence. Rather, they are revealed step by step through a foundation of superfood nutrition and the Seven Golden Keys to health—all of which are readily attainable by anyone willing to put this wisdom into practice in their own lives.

What's especially noteworthy about this book is that it delivers nutritional know-how based on some of the most exciting breakthroughs in the field while simultaneously making it all so simple and straightforward that it works for first-time superfood dieters, too. Virtually everyone can benefit from reading this book, and I have no doubt that K.C. would strongly agree with the statement that America as a nation would also benefit if the principles of healthy weight loss found in this book were more widely taught.

There's a lot of wisdom to be found in these pages, which is why this book should not merely be read like most other books: It should be absorbed, applied, and used as a blueprint for a lifetime of nutritional trial-and-success that can revolutionize your personal health and help bring your body weight into lifelong balance. It's packed not just with the latest cutting-edge nutritional breakthroughs, but also with valuable wisdom on how to apply it through K.C.'s straightforward approach that I personally know to produce outstanding results.

Enjoy this valuable collection of nutritional wisdom! Your body—and your mind—will thank you for it.

Mike Adams
The Health Ranger, editor of NaturalNews.com

PREFACE

K.C. Craichy has written the most re-markable nutrition book of the twenty-first century. The reader will gain more information from K.C.'s book than from five other nutrition books currently available on Amazon. This book is a must read for everyone who cares about their nutrition and preventative health.

For example, I have attended many academic lectures about the hunger hormones *leptin* and *ghrelin*. These erudite lectures from prominent academics often left me dissatisfied. Then, remarkably, I read K.C.'s hunger hormone explanation in clear, everyday English. He lucidly reveals that the ubiquitous habit of consuming enormous amounts of fructose does not affect leptin. In other words, Americans continue to gorge themselves with fructose without quelling their hunger pains, and subsequently, this behavior leads to ever-increasing obesity and even metabolic syndrome. Thus, we ought to severely reduce our fructose intake, especially "high fructose corn syrup," if we have any hopes of slowing America's current obesity epidemic.

K.C. elucidates that our high fructose diets identified often by increasing belly fat will result in yet another epidemic, namely *inflammation*. Increased belly fat and leptin resistance results in multiple inflammatory cytokines that are responsible for many of the effects of aging one sees, especially in 50- to 80-year-olds. Indeed, inflammation is *the* limiting barrier for living past the age of 80.

Another unhealthy barrier to Super Health that K.C. deals with is *glycation*. Glycation means cross-linking of sugars with amino acids. An example is the eventual hardening of the lens of the eyes leading to cataracts. Anti-glycators, such as N-acetyl carnosine eye drops, reverse these oxidative and free-radical chemical reactions, and eyesight is restored without cataract surgery. Consuming a low sugar diet, such as K.C.'s, also helps since fructose glycates approximately 10 times faster than glucose.

K.C. further elucidates another big problem for professional athletes and their elite trainers. They eat large amounts of junk foods, such as soda, sports drinks, candy bars, so-called energy bars, etc. This I call the "roadkill diet." K.C. quips that "competitive athletes actually comprise one of the fastest growing segments of the malnourished population." In other words, even star athletes and their elite trainers are seduced by the ubiquitous presence of the roadkill diet in America.

K.C. argues that one may counter the craze in unhealthy foods by numerous remedies, such as consuming a high fiber diet filled with free-radical "mopping up" antioxidants. Free radicals are, in fact, the most toxic substances on the planet. They destroy DNA by daily bombarding it with approximately 7,000 hits caused by the virulent *hydroxy* free radical. They also clog our arteries with oxidized cholesterol, and we experience advanced cardiovascular disease as we age. Unfortunately, modern medicine lacks a preventative approach to limiting free radicals, and we are left holding the bag with high blood pressure, atherosclerotic plaques, and expensive statin drugs with serious side effects. K.C. states that "the bottom line is that people with excessive fat tissue are walking *oxidant factories*," whose bodies must cope with enormous loads of these violently destructive molecules.

In later chapters, K.C. further defines the different types of dietary fats, namely the good, the bad, and the ugly (trans fats). He names the highly healthy oils from fish and lamb called "omega-3s." Omega-3s increase the fluidity of our cell membranes and allow nutrients to pass easily through cell membranes. For optimal food health, K.C. recommends eating a diet rich in vegetables and half raw foods. We all need to minimize sugars and high glycemic foods and optimize the God-given treats to good health included in the Super Health Diet, which will significantly improve our health and longevity and starve off the ill effects of the American roadkill diet.

In summary, K.C. raises the alarm for the declining health of all Americans, and only through our personal efforts and prayer can we hope to stem the coming tide of ill health. The government is not going to hand us *preventative* health care on a silver platter. Through the grace of God, we need to empower ourselves with K.C.'s wise understanding of optimal superfood nutrition.

Richard Lippman, M.D.
Author of *Stay 40*, 1996 Nominee for the Nobel Prize in Medicine,
Inventor of the Nicotine Patch

THE
SUPER
HEALTH
DIET

Golden
Keys
to Unlock
Lifelong
Vitality

Introduction

As he thinks in his heart, so is he.

PROVERBS 23:7

I once heard a story about an old Cherokee grandfather who was talking with his grandson about a daily battle that goes on inside people's lives.

The grandfather gazed at his grandson and said, "My son, I feel as though two wolves are fighting in my heart. One is Evil. It is anger, envy, jealousy, sorrow, regret, greed, arrogance, self-pity, guilt, resentment, inferiority, lies, false pride, superiority, and ego. The other is Good. It is joy, peace, love, hope, serenity, humility, kindness, benevolence, empathy, generosity, truth, compassion, and faith."

The grandson thought about it for a minute and then asked his grandfather, "So which wolf wins?"

The old grandfather simply replied, "The one I feed."

Such a simple story, yet how profound! Those words of legendary wisdom mirror a life-changing proverb that King Solomon offered almost 3,000 years ago: "As he thinks in his heart, so is he." We become what we think about. We reap the fruit of the thoughts we sow—positively or negatively.

This principle applies to every aspect of our lives, and especially to our approach to diets and exercise. It's very possible that when you were first introduced to this book you also had the accompanying feeling that you'll never beat your weight and diet problems. Through the years, you may have gotten excited about a new weight loss program, set goals, jumped into it, seen some success, and then saw it collapse and fail. And repeated failure opens the door to a deluge of disappointment, guilt, and condemnation.

I recognize that losing weight and keeping it off might be as much about the psychological struggles as the physical changes. Some people believe they must reach their ideal weight to succeed, or that they've already failed, so why try again. For others, feelings of depression, a loss of control, rationalizing weight gain, and low self-esteem can make losing weight seem like an impossible task. For many people, food is often misused as emotional nourishment and to calm anxieties. They have to find out how to deal with the loss of satisfaction eating provides them by exchanging it with the reward of achieving their goals.

> Beloved, I pray that you may prosper in all things and be in health, just as your soul prospers.
>
> THE APOSTLE JOHN, 3 JOHN 2

Here's some good news for you. If you have failed, it just means you're human. The only person who never failed is Jesus Christ. Determine right now that you will keep reading until you find the keys to your personal success. God not only desires to help you reach your health and fitness goals, but He has a plan that will elevate you from a lifestyle of dieting to a lifestyle of freedom and self-control. He has the power to help you get in the best shape of your life—no matter what your age.

Choose a Positive Approach

As young Michael Jordan dashed down the steps at Laney High School in Wilmington, North Carolina, his heart was pounding as he approached the bulletin board by the gym. Scanning the list of names of the young men who made the varsity basketball team, Jordan felt his heart sink as his name was nowhere to be found, though he read the list over and over. He had not made the cut as a high school sophomore. He wasn't good enough. He failed.

But though his dreams were crushed, he refused to give up. Rather, he used the setback to propel him to action. Jordan said, "I knew I never wanted to feel that bad again. I never wanted to have that taste in my mouth, that hole in my heart."

For the following year, come rain or shine, you could find Jordan practicing in a park near his house for four to six hours a day. He fought through adversity and disappointment, working on every basketball move and every shot that would help him the following season.

Michael Jordan made the team as a high school junior and went on to become the greatest basketball player in the world. *Air Jordan* is arguably one of the best athletes to ever play team sports. Would he have ever achieved his greatness if he had not fought back from defeat? Hard to say definitively, but my guess is no.

He could have thrown in the towel and blamed his failure on the coach or his living situation or his parents, but he didn't. Jordan's motto was "I can accept failure. Everyone fails at something. But I cannot accept not trying." He chose a positive approach at a difficult moment and took control of his life.

> The rest of your life begins today—and what a great day it can be! The power you need to create anything you desire already lies within you.
>
> STU MITTLEMAN

Perhaps you've never started on the right foot in your weight loss efforts. Perhaps your real battle begins where my battle began, and that's with a *mentality* that sabotages every attempt you've ever made. Putting a stake in the heart of this negative attitude is the first step to freedom.

More than a century ago, William James said, "The greatest discovery of this generation is that a human being can alter their life by altering their attitude." I believe that with all my heart, and I've seen it happen countless times during my life. I have had the joy of watching hundreds of people turn their lives around through developing and maintaining a positive approach to health and fitness.

"Thy Food Shall Be Thy Remedy"

Hippocrates spoke those words to his Greek medical students about twenty-five hundred years ago. It seems unbelievable that we have drifted so far from the importance of food as the central component of health. God gave us food as the original source of sustained health, and the various components of the food we eat profoundly influence us either toward health or illness.

For instance, it's a simple fact that eating certain foods raises our risk of heart disease. Some foods help prevent cancer while others seem to contribute to it. Published reports show that improving our diets and lifestyle may reduce the incidence of many types of cancers by 70 to 80 percent. Certain foods trigger hormones and form addictions that act like drugs. Some foods can cause insulin imbalances while others cause neurotransmitter dysfunction that contributes to depression and ADHD.

If we want to enjoy the health God means for us to experience, it begins with an attitude that considers the food we eat as contributing to our long-term health or to our long-term illness. Seeing food for its medicinal value and honoring our bodies with the good foods God meant for us to enjoy are practical decisions that start and stop with us. Making the right decision here has the power to prevent countless illnesses as well as to heal others that may have crept in.

The Super Health Diet

Understanding of diet and nutrition was in its infancy in the 1960s and 1970s. I grew up watching my parents try fad diet after fad diet and exercise gizmo after gizmo to lose weight and get in shape. My grandparents were both almost 300 pounds late in life, and I was a junk food junkie, eating massive amounts of whatever I was craving at the time. The inescapable result was that I became an overweight teenager, experiencing the peer-driven social trauma that only overweight kids can truly understand. During my late teens, I discovered that nutrition (what I ate) made a huge difference in my weight, body fat levels, and ultimately, how I felt. In fact, what I ate determined if I had the energy and motivation to work out.

It was clear that I had both genetic and lifestyle tendencies to be overweight, yet I successfully managed to maintain optimal weight throughout my twenties with periods of fluctuation. I worked out hard but still splurged with fast food, desserts, and sweet tea. It was during the times of fluctuation that I tried so many popular diets and fad diets—Eat to Win, Eat to Succeed, Atkins, Pritikin, and many others. I was fascinated by the various approaches, and

> 82: Percentage of people who know that a poor diet can increase their risk of cancer.
> 15: Percentage of people who have changed their diet to lower that risk.
>
> *HIPPOCRATES* MAGAZINE, JAN.–FEB. 1989

while some worked better than others, many diets worked (for a time) using vastly different approaches. This sparked my lifelong passion for understanding nutrition and health, leading me to read and research thousands of articles, studies, and books on the subject.

Even though I had become an expert in nutrition and health, through time it became more and more difficult for me to maintain optimal weight. Through my research and writings and products, people have been able to achieve and maintain remarkable levels of weight loss. Nevertheless, it just seemed I had a tendency to gain weight throughout my adult life. It took a lot of work and required a lot of mental energy for me to maintain my ideal weight and body fat levels, so I, as have many others, had given in to "genetic and lifestyle" tendencies and became comfortable being fit but still carrying extra pounds. I see this phenomenon happening often in athletics—when an athlete is training for competition they are in tremendous shape, and when not training for competition (the off-season), they stay fit but often carry too much body fat. It's those last few pounds that seem to be the most difficult to lose and maintain.

> I have come that they may have life, and that they may have it more abundantly.
>
> JESUS CHRIST,
> JOHN 10:10

After a few years of being married, my wife, Monica, who was the picture of youth, beauty, and health on the outside, having been Miss Florida and Miss Florida USA and competed in both the Miss America and Miss USA beauty pageants, where she was third runner-up and first in swimsuit competition, started getting panic attacks and became clinically depressed with suicidal thoughts. My book *Super Health: 7 Golden Keys to Unlock Lifelong Vitality* and my company Living Fuel were a direct result of the revelation we received from more than 10 years of research and trial and error that resulted in Monica overcoming that crisis without becoming a lifelong patient. She has not taken a drug in more than 15 years and remains the picture of youth, beauty, and health.

The Super Health 7 Keys are foundational to a lifetime of health, and even though weight loss was not the goal of the book, it has helped thousands of people optimize their weight. The truth is that achieving Super Health results in optimal weight. If you haven't read *Super*

Health, I strongly encourage you to do so because it contains a tremendous amount of important information I won't be able to address within the scope of this book. I will also be touching on the 7 Keys later in the book.

However, with my own personal struggles with weight, it became clear I needed an even deeper understanding of this subject. I was determined to cut through the massive amount of confusing information to discover and write a book on the simplest approach to optimizing weight—*what is the key to a weight optimization lifestyle?*

It was my expectation that this new book would be ready in a few short months of research and writing. One day my now 13-year-old daughter, Sarah, asked me what I was doing. I said, "I'm writing a book on weight loss." She said, "Papa, you are just going to tell people to exercise, eat less, stop eating sugar, and take Living Fuel. Why do you need to write a book about it?"

A lot of truth comes from the mouths of babes. For many people, it's just as simple as following Sarah's program. But for a lot of other people, it seems far more complicated. Modern dietary thinking has been about the Law of Thermodynamics, which states that if a person eats 3,500 calories more than they burn, they will gain one pound of fat. That is an interesting and somewhat useful "theory," but does not stand the test of scientific scrutiny, and thus is not really a law. The reality is there is something going on with the metabolism of many humans that must be addressed.

I discovered in my writing quest that this was not going to be just another diet book, and, as in my book *Super Health*, it will be leading-edge information on weight optimization and healthy aging that is well referenced with scientific studies. During the research and writing of this book, I read countless research studies and personally tried numerous approaches, diet theories, exercise concepts, and supplements, looking for the "magic bullet." I discovered that all these diets had their benefits but were nevertheless flawed, and most were not sustainable through long periods of time for a number of reasons. It seems clear that many of these diet programs have evolved from companies led by passionate founders who solved their own problems with their discoveries, then later sold their companies to become profitable ventures led by professional managers.

The more I experimented with different dietary approaches, the more I realized their limitations and, unfortunately, sometimes their potentially harmful nutritional advice. Many of these diets were difficult to implement, and some advocated food and lifestyle choices that are known to compromise health and undermine performance.

It is now more than two years later, and I am excited to present you with *The Super Health Diet: The Last Diet You Will Ever Need*. Practicing these principles is sure to add years to your life and life to your years!

For the sake of complete transparency, it was my original intention to overtly exclude any mention of Living Fuel products in this book. Nevertheless, it became clear that in certain situations such an omission would be a disservice to the readers, since I know of no comparable alternatives. My only mission is to change lives, so if you have success using the leading-edge techniques presented in this book, using whatever combinations of foods and supplements you choose, my mission is accomplished.

During the writing of this book, my father, who is in his mid 80s and has been in a wheelchair for 15 years since he had a stroke that left him without the use of his left arm and left leg, told me that at 250 pounds he needed to lose 50 pounds. He obviously can do very little exercise and stated he was going to do a total fast and drink nothing but water until he lost the weight. I explained to him that a total fast would result in weight loss, but because of the nutrient and protein deficiency, it would also lead to a severe loss of muscle followed by his regaining all of the lost weight and then some once he stopped the fast. I suggested he instead implement the principles of this book, which he agreed to do. I asked him which of his three meals was his favorite, and he said lunch because it was social time. So we changed his breakfast and dinner to a high protein, nutrient dense Superfood Smoothie instead of a meal, and he continued having his normal lunch. The only supplements he took in addition were an antioxidant omega 3-EPA/DHA/GLA that included vitamins E, D, A and astaxanthan. In eight weeks, without exercise, his weight reduced from 250 to 195 pounds! He has since adopted this program as a lifestyle and has maintained his healthier weight without muscle loss.

Steps Toward Super Health

You are about to embark on an exciting journey—to once and for all take charge of your future and achieve optimal health and vitality for a lifetime. Please realize as you begin that most of our lives have a great deal of imbalance, and it will take time to restore the balance of health God wants you to enjoy. But if you start with a few changes, you'll notice immediate improvements in your physical and emotional well-being. With every step, you'll find yourself increasingly able to reclaim your God-given body to its fullest potential.

Good decisions are the result of choices based on the best information, and on these pages you will learn what works and what doesn't. The truth is that what works for you is the right diet for you.

We live in a rapidly evolving information age, and Monica and I invite you to get connected with us through our social media network. Watch us and other leading health experts on LivingFuel.TV, join or "like" the Living Fuel Page on Facebook, and follow us on Twitter. We would also like to keep you updated and answer your health questions on our blogs and forums, which you can get to through www.livingfuel.com.

The secret to optimal weight and healthy aging is Super Health. As you read this book, please keep in mind that you don't have to do everything at once, and that baby steps in the right direction are monster steps toward Super Health.

THE DIET

PART

ER'S DILEMMA

Chapter 1

How It All Began

*Having good health is very different from only
being not sick.*

SENECA THE YOUNGER (4 *B.C.–A.D.* 65)

If I walked up to you today on the street
and offered you 25 extra years of life…at no cost to you whatsoever,
and I had verifiable proof I could deliver these additional years free of
charge to you, how would you respond?

While that's obviously something I cannot do, if you track life spans
through the course of the twentieth century, that's actually what hap-
pened. In 1900, the average U.S. life expectancy at birth was around
47 years. By 1930, the life spans had increased to 58 for men and 62
for women. By 2001, the average life expectancy was 74 for men and
80 for women, which is an astounding 25-plus years of life.[1]

Through the first half of the twentieth century in the United
States, improved nutrition, sanitation, and the control of infectious
diseases drastically reduced child and infant mortality—developments
that produced astonishing advances in life expectancy. The advent of
flushing toilets and running water in almost every home in America,
rich or poor, and the hauling away of trash had a profound effect on
the quality of health in this land. By 1950, penicillin and sulfa drugs
had yielded the first substantial decrease in U.S. adult mortality. In the
latter part of the century, continued improvements in living standards,
health behaviors, and medical care also lowered mortality from chronic
diseases, especially heart disease and stroke.

While far from perfect and apparently declining with recent leg-
islation, we can be thankful we live in twenty-first-century America!

Through trial and error, research and discovery, we are the recipients of knowledge that has taken generations to discover.

Dieting, for example, is hardly a new concept. It has been part of world cultures for thousands of years, although not in the prolific manner we see today. The word *diet* derives from the Latin *diaeta*, meaning "a way of living." Our diet is the total consumption of what we eat. As time progressed, the concept of dieting came to be defined as a prescribed course of limiting our food intake in kind and in quantity, and of sometimes restricting the very nutrients we need to maintain a healthy lifestyle.

For most people, when the word *diet* is used, it is in relation to losing weight, and for many the "D word" has a negative connotation. This is hardly surprising when we read of prisoners being fed "a diet of bread and water." The connection between diet and punishment is still linked in the minds of some people.

What the Good Book Says

When you study the history of mankind, you quickly realize how food has been an integral part of custom, culture, and religious law. Most religions have dietary instructions, and for centuries many people's dietary practices were in line with their faith persuasion, whether they were Jewish, Christian, Muslim, Hindu, ancient Chinese, etc. In general, religious dietary laws revolve around two restrictive categories: (1) fasting, which involves the abstaining from certain or all foods for a period of time; (2) specific dietary guidelines that are different from the general population.

For example, God instructed Moses to tell the children of Israel how to distinguish between what is clean and what is unclean: "Among the animals, whatever divides the hoof, having cloven hooves and chewing the cud—that you may eat" (Leviticus 11:3). This meant cattle, sheep, goats, and deer were okay, but not pigs, rabbits, camels, or rock badgers (you probably won't have a problem avoiding the latter two animals). And regarding creatures of the sea, "You may eat of all that are in the water: whatever in the water has fins and scales, whether in the seas or in the rivers—that you may eat" (v. 9). An additional list is found in Deuteronomy 14.

To fulfill the Word of God, the Jews have observed the laws of Kashrut (keeping Kosher) for centuries. Foods referred to in the Bible are still the choice of millions today. For instance, on the shelves of major food stores you can buy Ezekiel 4:9 Bread. It's an organic sprouted whole grain product based on the verse: "Also take for yourself wheat, barley, beans, lentils, millet, and spelt; put them into one vessel, and make bread of them for yourself." As you will read in this book, I am not a fan of the regular consumption of breads in general for most people; however, until recently this would have been a good choice for bread eaters. Unfortunately, this company has recently started adding soy to some if not all of their recipes, and I do not recommend daily consumption of soy products unless they are non-GMO soy and fermented, such as tempe, miso, and soy sauce.

Food for Life, the company that produces this bread, found that when the six grains and legumes are sprouted and combined, an amazing thing occurs: A complete protein is created that closely parallels the protein found in milk and eggs. There are 18 amino acids present in Ezekiel 4:9 Bread.

> **Remove far from me falsehood and lies; give me neither poverty nor riches; feed me with the food that is needful for me, lest I be full and deny You and say, Who is the Lord? Or lest I be poor and steal, and so profane the name of my God.**
>
> Proverbs 30:8–9 *AMP*

Several Bible-based diet books have become national bestsellers, including *What Would Jesus Eat?* by Don Colbert, M.D.

The Struggle for Survival

Throughout most of man's history, for the vast majority of people, just getting enough food to survive upon has been a constant struggle. Today, millions are consumed with losing weight, but this was not the problem faced by those who scratched out a living in the deserts, mountains, and plains of an ever-expanding world. In many cases, when food was abundant, people would eat as much as possible—hoping it would give them enough strength and stamina to last through the inevitable times of drought or famine.

For the most part, early man ate whatever he could catch, raise, or grow—or what he could barter for or afford. There was little variety in the diet, and it was generally thought that all foods were the same. Until modern times, there was almost no understanding that certain nutrients are required for life. As long as people had *something* to eat, they believed they would survive. Fortunately for those living prior to the eighteenth century, foods were not refined, and most foods had at least a little protein and little fat. Thus, even for people who ate a very limited diet, they managed to survive.

> Some historians credit William the Conqueror of Britain with starting the first fad diet. Having grown too fat to ride his horse in 1087, William went on a liquid diet of all alcohol in an unsucessful attempt to lose weight.

During these generations, most people were not overweight because they physically toiled from dawn to dusk and exerted tremendous energy. Few people had to wonder about the definition of an "active lifestyle" or concern themselves about whether a certain food might be high on the Glycemic Index. Not all carbohydrate foods are created equal; in fact, they behave quite differently in our bodies. The Glycemic Index or GI describes this difference by ranking carbohydrates according to their effect on our blood glucose levels.

The exception to a "lean" lifestyle was found in those at the highest levels of society. For bankers, judges, clergy, and royalty, it was a status symbol to be fat, because it showed the world you were rich enough to eat well. Lavish banquets lasted for days, even weeks. It seemed the eating never stopped. Take a look at some of the depictions painted during that era and you will see a correlation between gluttony and wealth.

Finding a Cure

Through the centuries, there was precious little or no food science at all. Countless people have died because of diseases for which there were no known cure, but with the proper foods, their lives could have been extended.

Scurvy is a prime example. It was first described by Hippocrates (460–380 B.C.) and was prevalent for *hundreds* of years. Sailors and pirates who sailed the high seas for extended periods of time started getting and dying from this mysterious disease, which had not been known before. It is a condition that leads to the formation of spots on the skin, spongy gums, bleeding from the mucous membranes, and can lead to death. A person with the ailment looks pale, feels depressed, and is partially immobilized.

It wasn't until the 1700s that medical science connected the dots that not all the seafarers got the disease, particularly among those sailors who ate sauerkraut. What was missing in the diets of sailors was fruits and vegetables containing vitamin C. The scurvy mystery was solved!

When Plump Became Popular

In the nineteenth and twentieth centuries, as people began moving up the financial ladder and food production became more abundant, it was only natural for them to overconsume what was previously not available to them. About the same time, fatty, sugary foods were readily accessible, and men and women began to pack on the pounds. Excess eating and drinking became the norm for the masses; and whenever more food is eaten than what is required for immediate energy, growth, or tissue repair, the body stores those calories as fat for use later.

Suddenly, "pleasingly plump" was in fashion. Women padded their clothing and wrote letters to popular magazines for advice on how to gain weight. Words such as "butterball," "porky," and "jumbo" began to creep into the vocabulary.

Let's face it, if given the option between starvation and overeating, we know what most of us would choose! Yet, long ago, King Solomon warned, "When you sit down to eat with a ruler, consider carefully what is before you; and put a knife to your throat if you are a man given to appetite" (Proverbs 23:1–2).

Sounding the Alarm

Even though being fat was popular, there were voices that began to be raised concerning the dangers of excess weight during the late 1700s.

Many point to the dawn of America's focus on dieting to Sylvester Graham, a Presbyterian minister in Philadelphia, who began preaching in the 1830s against the sin of gluttony and that the problems of health (physical, moral, and spiritual) could be solved by making a commitment to a basic vegetarian diet that also eliminated coffee, tea, and other stimulants.

Thousands attended his lectures, and many followers became known as "the Grahamites," although his critics referred to him as "Dr. Sawdust." His popular *Graham Journal of Health and Longevity* also promoted sleeping on hard mattresses with the bedroom windows open, taking cold showers, wearing loose garments, avoiding all alcohol, and practicing chastity.

Graham's name survives today because of the coarsely ground whole wheat flour that he baked into a flat bread he created known as Graham Crackers. He stressed a diet rich in flat bread and strenuously objected to the refined flour used by city bakers to produce bread in his day.

> Graham bread was made from unsifted flour and free from chemical additives. He argued that chemical additives in bread made it unwholesome. The use of additives by bakeries was a common practice during the Industrial Revolution.

About 20 years later, in England, an undertaker named William Banting was so obese he couldn't tie his own shoes and had to descend stairs backward. He tried everything from starvation to diuretics to steam baths in a vain attempt to lose weight—even rigorous exercise did not help him. Nothing worked.

After attempting many cures, a medical doctor suggested that Banting's problem might be solved if he did his best to avoid as much sugar and starch as possible—no sweetened drinks, no pastries, no desserts. His was a high protein, high fat diet that included four meals a day chosen from protein (meat, poultry, or fish) and supplemented with green vegetables, unsweetened fruit, and several glasses of dry wine.

Banting not only lost 50 pounds in the first 12 months, but in 1862 published what many call the first diet book, with the unusual title: *Letter on Corpulence Addressed to the Public*, which became very successful.

Of course, since he wasn't a doctor or scientist, he was scoffed at and condemned in medical circles. The public, however, rushed to try his diet, and Banting's publication quickly spread throughout the English-speaking world and was soon translated into French and German.

Chew! Chew! Chew!

More weight loss advice soon followed. For example, William Gladstone, the British Prime Minister for many of the years between 1868 and 1894, promoted "masticating" as a way to dieting and health. He preached that if a person would chew food 32 times before swallowing, it would lessen the appetite and lead to weight loss and better health. (Thirty-two being the desired number because that's how many teeth there are in the mouth.)

In America, a man named Horace Fletcher took Gladstone's advice one step further. He taught that food should be chewed until it became liquid—and if that were not possible, it shouldn't be eaten! Of course, this meant cutting out fiber, which led to constipation and other unpleasant problems. Known both as the "Great Masticator" and as the "Chew-Chew Man," Fletcher wrote a book called *The A–Z of Our Own Nutrition* and claimed a million Americans were following his plan at one point.

But along came Dr. John Kellogg, who agreed with much of Fletcher's advice but disagreed about fiber, and founded his great American cereal company to make sure people were getting an abundance of fiber in their diets.

In her 1918 book, *Diet and Health,* Dr. Lulu Hunt Peters warned against the use of diet drugs, which contained arsenic and mercury in those days, and she advised dieters to get used to unsweetened food and avoid the "coal tar product" Saccharine.

At the start of the twentieth century, insurance companies began to document a link between obesity and death. This caught the public's attention. After all, who wants to pay higher premiums just for being fat?

The Calorie Counters

In the early 1900s, a chemist named Wilbur Atwater developed a method to count the calories (or energy given off when processed in the digestive system) in various foods, but this research stayed mostly among academic circles. Then, in 1918, Lulu Hunt Peters, a California doctor and syndicated medical advice newspaper columnist, wrote a book, *Diet and Health, With a Key to the Calories*, introducing the notion of how counting calories in a diet leads to weight loss. Dr. Peters was a longtime heavyset woman who topped out at 220 pounds, but who managed to lose 70 of those pounds using the calorie counting system she described in her book. With a message directed mainly to women, she recommended a 1,200-calorie per day limit. Her book sold somewhere between 800,000 and two million copies (depending on who you believe) and was the number four bestselling nonfiction book in 1923, according to *Publisher's Weekly*. It certainly became the first bestselling American diet book.

About the same time, the masses were rushing to the movies, and the stars on the silver screen were glamorous and in terrific shape. After seeing these perfect physiques, the public began to devour anything written on dieting, and the thirst for getting rid of excess fat was in high gear.

Before the Food and Drug Administration got involved in an approval system, there seemed to be a new diet a day—everything including thyroid extracts from animals to exotic herbal medicines and wonder cures.

In many of the early Western movies, there was a traveling "doctor" who came riding into town selling "snake oil" or other medicines he would hype with bogus evidence. He'd usually have a shill in the crowd who would testify to the healing power of the product. They would ride off into the sunset, with money stuffed in their saddlebags, leaving unsuspecting customers with a small bottle of flavor-laden alcohol!

The Diet Crazes

Many practitioners of health and nutrition attracted a large, loyal following. In the 1920s, William H. Hay taught that fruits, proteins, and starches needed to be eaten separately and urged that only one food group per meal be consumed—plus an enema should be employed once a day to "flush out the poisons."

Next on the horizon was Gayelord Hauser with his popular book,

Look Younger, Live Longer. He developed his own line of special foods and supplements, stressing vitamin B and his five "wonder foods"—brewer's yeast, wheat germ, yogurt, powdered skim milk, and especially blackstrap molasses. Movie stars, such as Adele Astaire, Marlene Dietrich, Paulette Goddard, Gloria Swanson, and, most famously, Greta Garbo, promoted Hauser's approach to weight loss.

The only thing that slowed down the diet craze was the Great Depression, which created its own poverty-induced diet! Then following the food rationing and general shortages during World War II, weight loss programs were in vogue once more.

During the 1930s, millions tried the Hollywood Diet (known to the public as the Grapefruit Diet). And in the next decade, people were checking their pounds against "ideal weight" charts that matched a weight with gender, height, and frame.

> Gayelord Hauser believed in the healthful effects of "whole foods" and urged people to avoid starch, gluten, sugar, and excessive consumption of meat. When enriched white breads were introduced in the 1950s, Hauser denounced them as "devitalized."

New Approaches

A major shift in the way people approached their eating habits came in the early 1960s when Jean Nidetch, an overweight woman from Queens, New York, became tired of fad dieting. She invited a few friends to her home to share ideas and form a support group. Weight Watchers was born.

Next, the world was introduced to Dr. Atkins, with his controversial, but immensely popular, high protein, high fat, low carbohydrate diet. This was followed by a wide variety of approaches, including the Pritikin Diet, which was developed by Nathan Pritikin after he learned he had heart disease. His low fat, high fiber regimen, combined with exercise, was not only effective for heart problems, but others turned to it for weight loss.

This brings us to today. In the pages that follow, I will give you an overview of the major diet programs, popular books, medical prescriptions, weight loss clinics, and more. You'll learn the pros and cons of each approach—and the information you need to make the right health decisions.

Most important, I want to share the Seven Keys to Super Health and Optimal Weight. It is based on my lifetime study of health, nutrition, and diet and has transformed the lives of thousands in the U.S. and many nations of the world.

Let's get started.

Chapter 2
Join the Club

> *So Daniel said to the steward whom the chief of the eunuchs had set over Daniel, Hananiah, Mishael, and Azariah, "Please test your servants for ten days, and let them give us vegetables to eat and water to drink. Then let our appearance be examined before you, and the appearance of the young men who eat the portion of the king's delicacies; and as you see fit, so deal with your servants." So he consented with them in this matter, and tested them ten days. And at the end of ten days their features appeared better and fatter in flesh than all the young men who ate the portion of the king's delicacies. Thus the steward took away their portion of delicacies and the wine that they were to drink, and gave them vegetables.*
>
> DANIEL 1:11–16

In the classic 1966 Walt Disney animated featurette *Winnie the Pooh and the Honey Tree*, based upon the book by A. A. Milne, there is a delightful exchange between characters when Pooh gets himself stuck in the honey tree.

After being not able to free Pooh, Christopher Robin says, "Pooh Bear, there's only one thing we can do, wait for you to get thin again."

"Oh bother," Winnie the Pooh responds. "How long will that take?"

Eeyore answers as only Eeyore can answer, "Days, weeks, months, who knows?"

Winnie the Pooh wasn't the first to wonder how long it might take for him to lose some weight, and Eeyore wasn't the last to be negative about it. If you walk down any city street, you'll find an abundance of evidence for the fact that America is in serious…no, make that *desperate*…trouble!

In a January 9, 2009, Reuters' news story titled "Obese Americans Now Outweigh the Merely Overweight," and based upon the most recent numbers posted by the National Center for Health Statistics, the United States has the highest prevalence of obesity among the developed nations of the world. More than 34 percent of all adult Americans over the age of 20 are obese and just under six percent of adults are extremely obese. Another 32 percent of all adult Americans are overweight. The Centers for Disease Control also reported that 32 percent of U.S. children fit the definition of being overweight, 16 percent were obese, and 11 percent were extremely obese.[2]

> **Lucy decided to forget her weight just this once and enjoy herself. This was a decision she made with deplorable frequency.**
>
> JOSEPHINE TEY

So in 2005–2006, more than one-third of America's adults, or a staggering 72,000,000 people, were obese. More than 69,000,000 additional people were overweight besides those who were obese. That means the total number of people either overweight or obese in America exceeds 141,000,000 adults or more than two-thirds (66.7 percent) of the adult U.S. population.

Those numbers are almost unfathomable, but it represents far more than numbers. When you consider that excessive weight can and does cause many serious, potentially life-threatening health problems—diabetes, heart disease, hypertension, some cancers, arthritis, and other conditions—that are almost totally preventable, it's no wonder people are looking for answers.

Where do we search for help? Who can show us how to lose those unnecessary pounds and achieve optimum health?

In this book I will detail many ways to help you with your diet, health, and fitness. One of the ways is to examine a number of programs, but let's begin by looking at the major weight loss centers and those that successfully market specific diet products.

Weight Watchers

This is the granddaddy of the dieting programs, and it has been around since the early 1960s. Weight Watchers was started by New York homemaker Jean Nidetch, when she invited a group of friends to her house to discuss a weight loss plan that had been recommended to her by a dietician. The idea of mutual support struck a chord, and soon about 40 people, all on diets, were gathering to offer encouragement to one another.

A weight loss plan was developed, the company was formed, and franchises began springing up everywhere. It was one of the first dieting programs to recommend walking as exercise.

Weight Watchers was sold to the H. J. Heinz Company in 1978, later acquired in a leveraged buyout in 1999—after which it went public on the stock market. Many companies are licensed to produce their approved products.

How It Works

The basic plan invites members to weekly group sessions that become a support network for those with similar diet goals. After a private weigh-in, a trained meeting leader teaches and motivates members on health, fitness, and nutrition. Instead of telling people exactly what to eat, their goal is to help their members make wise, healthy decisions.

What makes Weight Watchers different is their point system called Flex Plan. They have assigned a point value to each of a comprehensive list of more than 31,000 food items. Points are determined by how much fat, fiber, and calories are in a specific portion of food. Fat free cottage cheese may have one point and a Big Mac about 13 points. You can eat what you like as long as you stay within a daily target number. It's easy to follow and is credited with the success of the plan.

On enrolling in the program, you and your counselor will decide the daily point target (based on your weight, height, gender, activity level, etc.). For example, a person weighing 150 pounds might have a target of 20 points per day. At 200 pounds, the number may be 25 points. No food is prohibited. On the point system, a cup of broccoli is zero points, a three-ounce chicken breast is three points, and one ounce of chocolate is four points.

For those who don't like group sessions, you can enroll in the Core Plan program with no point-counting or tracking. You choose from a list of balanced meal recipes available online for a low monthly fee, and there are thousands of meals to choose from. It also offers exercise guidance. However, the web membership takes away from the social aspect of Weight Watchers meetings.

The company now offers a wide variety of frozen meals.

Comments

Millions of people have had some level of success with this program over the years. While the point system is truly unique, it doesn't really teach about the nutritional value of food. This strategy gives the dieter a false sense of the real nutritional changes they need to make in their lives for long-term success. It is better to focus more on portion control and the quality of food we are eating.

Also, counting points can be rather difficult to maintain once you are no longer active in the program.

The program does not put a priority on exercise, which is essential to long-term success.

Accountability is important in weight loss, so regularly attending classes is a strength of this program.

In March 2010, it was reported that Weight Watchers had officially endorsed Chicken McNuggets as a "healthy meal" in New Zealand, where McDonald's restaurants will begin carrying the Weight Watchers logo on several menu items. Nutritionists, not surprisingly, were shocked at the bizarre and inexplicable announcement. It is ridiculous to think that eating Chicken McNuggets will cause you to lose weight. My point here is to underscore the long list of questionable foods marketed under the "Weight Watchers" brand name. At the minimum you must be willing to read the ingredients lists on food labels and determine what you're actually eating.

Jenny Craig

You've seen their television ads with Valerie Bertinelli and Phylicia Rashad and Kirstie Alley and Queen Latifah, or perhaps you have driven past one of their 600-plus franchise centers and wondered what the Jenny Craig program was all about.

Jenny was raised in New Orleans and married Sidney Craig before moving to Australia and creating a nutrition, fitness, and weight loss program in 1983. Two years later they began operations in the United States. The company was purchased by Nestlé in 2006.

How It Works

When you walk into a Jenny Craig center, you'll meet with a program director who will explain the system, create your profile, give you an initial weigh-in, take your measurements, and recommend a customized program.

There is an enrollment fee, which varies according to the amount you desire to lose. Then, at the start, you are expected to order the frozen packaged meals for breakfast, lunch, and dinner, plus snacks. These foods are chosen to meet a specific caloric target per day.

Nutritionally, the meals have a balance of 50 to 80 percent carbs, 20 to 25 percent protein, and 20 to 35 percent fat. This food is supplemented with fresh foods, vegetables, whole grains, and low fat dairy products you buy at the grocery store.

The emphasis is on eating small but frequent portions, plus your choice of physical activity for 30 minutes, five days a week. In Chapter 13, you'll note that I don't agree with the frequent eating of meals.

There are weekly meetings, where you weigh in and order your food. Plus, phone support is available 24/7. Both the weigh in and phone support are accountability steps that are proven to assist weight loss.

After a few weeks of purchasing their packaged foods, you begin to make the transition to preparing meals on your own (although they certainly don't mind selling you theirs).

If you don't live close to a center, you can enroll in the Jenny Direct program by phone.

Comments

While Jenny Craig is lauded by many for its high level of support, one of the major criticisms is it is difficult to go off the packaged meals and maintain the calorie and nutrition balance with everyday eating. People have lost modest amounts of weight on this program for years. However, as with many of these national programs, this is a system of restricting calories without maximizing nutrition, thus their packaged foods are highly processed, contain questionable ingredients, and are deficient in essential nutrients. They are operating under some valid concepts, but continuing this diet using their processed foods is really not sustainable over the long term.

> It's not what you do once in a while, it's what you do day in and day out that makes the difference.
>
> JENNY CRAIG

NutriSystem

In 1971, Harold Katz, the son of a grocery store owner, opened "Shape Up," a weight loss center in a suburb of Philadelphia. Within five years he was able to franchise the concept under the name Nutri-System.

The initial income came from a setup fee and charges based on the amount of weight loss. The real revenue producer, however, was from the sale of their private-label food that customers were required to purchase weekly.

By 1982, with a booming franchise business, Katz became so wealthy he purchased the Philadelphia 76ers NBA basketball franchise. But after a number of financial and legal setbacks, Katz was forced to sell Nutri-System, and the new owners expanded the operation to more than 1,800 weight loss centers by 1989. However, because of falling profits, in the late 1990s the company decided to abandon the franchise business and turn to selling prepackaged food on the Internet. It succeeded beyond their wildest dreams.

How It Works

The NutriSystem program is based on a specially designed 28-day meal plan that features prepackaged foods with low glycemic "good" carbohydrates and protein to help a person feel full for a longer period of time. In addition, many of the food choices contain omega-3s and soluble fiber designed to promote heart health. Added to the prepared foods, they ask you to include fresh fruits, vegetables, salads, and dairy products.

They encourage their customers to use the online diaries and trackers to keep them on course. Phone counseling and support are also included. There are no membership fees, calories or carbs to count, and no meetings to attend.

You get a breakfast, lunch, dinner, dessert, and two snacks a day for each 28-day purchase. You can let NutriSystem preselect your food, or you can create your own menu. There are 20 options for breakfast, 30 for lunch, and 40 different dinners. Plus 30 dessert and snack options—even chocolate!

There is a 1,200-calorie daily plan for women and a 1,500-daily calorie plan for men. The program can be customized for vegetarians and individuals with diabetes and other special health concerns (www.nutrisystem.com).

Also included is a 12-week "Mindset Makeover" behavioral guide written by a Temple University obesity expert.

Comments

The problem is it does not teach people how to prepare their own healthy meals. And while NutriSystem appeals to those who don't like to cook, many gain their weight back after going off the program and reverting to their old eating habits.

NutriSystem uses two valid weight loss principles—low glycemic foods and calorie restriction but without optimal nutrition. While this approach is better than the diets most people eat, this needs to be seen as another short-term approach to weight loss. Their prepackaged foods are highly processed with questionable ingredients, including artificial flavors, artificial colors, preservatives, and genetically modified ingredients, but because it is based on low glycemic foods and portion control, it works for many for weight loss but not for Super Health. The challenge is to stay motivated and add daily exercise.

LA Weight Loss

As is true of most of the major programs, LA Weight Loss has thousands of success stories on file. The January 13, 2008, edition of *People* magazine featured the account of Sharla Pincock of Sugar City, Idaho, who went from 310 pounds (size 24) to 164 pounds (size 10) on the diet. She then ran a 5K race—her first.

The program, which was started in 1989, has more than 800 centers nationwide.

How It Works

On arriving at a LA Weight Loss Center, you will meet a counselor who will explain the program and create a personal plan for you. The daily menu consists of five to six small meals that include proteins (2 servings), fruits (3 servings), vegetables (3 servings), starches (3 servings), fats (2 servings), plus 2 of the company's "LA Lites" protein nutrition bars or "LA Snacks," with names such as Mini-Cookies and Cheese Curls. Plus, they now offer more than 20 different "Right Portion" entrees for you to choose from.

The diet is 50 to 55 percent carbohydrates, 25 to 30 percent protein, and 20 to 25 percent fat. You can review their program at www. laweightloss.com.

There is no calorie counting, phone consultations, or group meetings. But you will be asked to keep a diary of your food intake and have regular weigh-ins. Journaling is a concept that has proven to enhance weight loss.

You will learn about the three "phases" of the program. *Phase One*—designated weight loss. This is where customers come in two or three times a week. *Phase Two*—stabilization. A six-week program. *Phase Three*—maintenance. Customers check in once a week for a year.

Your personal counselor serves to motivate and keep you on track regarding your diet, exercise, and behavior modification. Strenuous exercise, however, is not part of the program. The good news is no foods are off limits. Rather, the plan is based on balanced nutritional meals eaten in small portions.

Comments

This is a diet system that uses various proven techniques that have resulted in people losing weight. However, the foods they sell are highly processed and are lower in protein and deficient in essential nutrients and contain some questionable ingredients; therefore, this diet is not sustainable over the long term. As you will come to understand as you read this book, I believe in three square meals per day with no snacks. Eating five to six small meals a day is not ideal and can be difficult to manage and prepare for some.

Medifast promotes the fact that a Johns Hopkins University study has shown that Medifast results in significant weight loss (67 pound average loss in males and 57 pound average loss in females). It's worth noting that this study was also funded by Medifast.

Medifast

To its credit, Medifast was created in 1972 by a Johns Hopkins University physician to assist surgery patients to lose weight quickly prior to undergoing an operation. The diet worked so well it expanded nationally.

At first, the plan was only available through participating physicians and required medical supervision. Medifast offered soy-based shakes as meal replacements, and the participants saw rapid weight loss. In some cases, when prescribed by a physician, the cost is covered by insurance. Today, however, it is available both through doctors and to the general public.

How It Works

Medifast is a portion-controlled, low fat diet that includes a combination of prepackaged meals and real food. Instead of breakfast, lunch, and dinner, you'll be eating proportioned, balanced meals every two to three hours.

The company states, "Medifast products are formulated with a

High Fullness Index so you don't get hungry." They claim you lose weight quickly—up to 20 pounds a month—while learning how to eat healthier (www.medifast1.com). And they add, "Medifast Meals are formulated with low fat protein and fiber and fortified with vitamins and nutrients, so you lose pounds and inches without losing out on essential nutrition." What is not mentioned is that they are missing numerous important nutrients and are hardly healthy foods.

There are more than 60 meal choices delivered to your home—from shakes to soups. Their website offers a variety of products geared toward disease management.

On their "5 and 1 Plan," you eat six times a day—five Medifast meals and one "Lean and Green Meal" you prepare yourself. This includes up to seven ounces of chicken, turkey, or fish and up to five ounces of beef, pork, or lamb, plus fresh vegetables.

New products include AntiOxidant Shakes and Flavor Infusions that support cardiovascular health, help balance blood sugar levels, and address other conditions.

One of the major claims of Medifast is it supposedly helps change your eating habits for the better. There are separate plans for men, women, and diabetics. The program emphasizes low key exercise on a regular basis.

The company has established Medifast Weight Control Centers in California, Florida, Texas, and Maryland—with goals for further expansion.

Comments

While this is a system of restricting calorie consumption, which would be a good thing for most people looking to lose weight, their foods are largely soy based, which is a controversial food ingredient as you'll note throughout this book. It is most likely genetically modified (GMO) soy, because they do not say otherwise, and that should always be avoided whenever possible. The foods are highly processed and are missing important nutrients and contain questionable ingredients, including GMOs, preservatives, artificial colors, flavors, etc., and are deficient in the essential nutrients necessary to make it a sustainable diet over a long period of time.

Slim-Fast

Created in 1977 by New York businessman Daniel Abraham, Slim-Fast was so successful that he was on *Forbes* magazine's "richest" list. He sold the worldwide company to Unilever in 2000.

For many years, they used the phrase, "A shake for breakfast, a shake for lunch, then a sensible dinner" to promote their products. Celebrity endorsements have come from Tom Lasorda, Whoopi Goldberg, and others.

How It Works

With a goal of losing one or two pounds a week, the Slim-Fast weight loss program asks dieters to use two meal-replacement shakes, three snacks, and one real meal daily. The plan is to aim for an intake of 1,200 to 1,500 calories per day and add daily exercise of at least 30 minutes.

The objective is to achieve lifestyle changes that will result in permanent weight maintenance after the initial pounds disappear. Their website (www.slim-fast.com) includes online support and an "Ask the Dietitian" feature. Thus they combine portion control with accountability and prepackaged processed foods.

Experts say the real question is whether dieters can continue losing weight when they no longer rely on prepackaged foods. A plan may offer a great jump start to healthier eating, but some dieters stumble right back into their old eating habits afterward.

The company struggled during the low carb diet craze of 2002, but bounced back by introducing Slim-Fast Optima products, which are lower in sugar and carbohydrates, plus they contain healthier fats.

Instead of creating diet centers or selling their products on the Internet, they have made Slim-Fast available through grocery store chains and major retailers. Products include bars, snacks, shakes, smoothies, and more. Fans like the convenience, especially those who live fast-paced lives.

A company-recommended typical day on the plan might look like this: For breakfast, a Slim-Fast Shake with six ounces of fat free yogurt.

Lunch would include a Slim-Fast Shake or Bar, plus a whole wheat English muffin topped with marinara sauce and low fat mozzarella cheese. Dinner will be your own creation containing no more than 500 calories. They ask you to divide your plate into fourths—half should be vegetables, one-quarter protein, and one-quarter starch, along with a salad or fruit.

A typical Slim-Fast Optima Shake contains 20 percent protein, 30 percent fat, and 50 percent carbs. They come in a variety of flavors.

Their Optima Meal Replacement Bars contain about 220 calories, five grams of fat, and 34 carbs. Optima Snack Bars contain even less—120 calories, four grams of fat, and 20 carbs.

Their newer products promote a HC4 formula—a special blend of proteins, fiber, and fats that are intended to provide hunger control.

The plan asks dieters to drink plenty of water and make a commitment to daily exercise.

Comments

This program is based on the proven concept of calorie restriction, but without optimal nutrition. One concern with Slim-Fast is the high amount of sugar in the original formula, which is known to cause a carbohydrate crash. A potentially larger issue is the inclusion of high fructose corn syrup instead of or in addition to sugar.

Slim-Fast has expanded its product line. It now offers Optima, High Protein, and Low Carb variations of the shake, plus the original discussed here, of course. These have somewhat reduced sugar and a little more fiber (four to five grams). Ironically, the "low carb" shakes have more protein (20 grams) than the "high protein" ones (15 grams).

Many people find it difficult to stay on this diet for any length

> **Keep in mind that the weight you've lost while on a diet doesn't tell you how much was fat or muscle. It might be a 50/50 split. If you lose 20 pounds, the loss of 10 pounds of muscle that burn calories at rest means your metabolism has taken a serious downturn. To keep from gaining back the weight requires rebuilding the muscles as well as a focus on burning more body fat.**

of time, not to mention long periods of time, because the shakes are extremely low calorie, at about 240 calories, and not very nutritious, so it leaves them feeling hungry within a couple of hours, which can lead to bingeing. If one could make it through two-thirds of their day with only two shakes and have a reasonably nutritious third meal, they would almost assuredly lose weight. Unfortunately, due to low protein levels, a significant portion of the weight lost would be muscle. (See "The Dynamic Role of Protein in Weight Loss" chapter.)

Their concept is appealing due to its simplicity. However, their shakes and packaged products are highly processed and contain questionable ingredients and not enough nutrients. Therefore, this program is not sustainable over the long term.

Chapter 3

Popular Dieting Plans

I came from a family that considered
gravy a beverage.
ERMA BOMBECK

Popular weight loss approaches and products
to Americans abound to the tune of an estimated $35 billion a year, ac-
cording to a CBS News report given by correspondent Sharyn Alfonsi on
December 1, 2006. Other reputable sources put the industry figure up-
ward of $40 billion a year. And with the seemingly endless diets backed
by slick advertising campaigns bursting with life-transforming testimo-
nies and remarkable promises to those who will follow, doesn't it seem
confounding that the problem of obesity continues to climb? Obviously,
there are problems that today's popular and fad diets aren't fixing.

As the author of *Super Health: 7 Golden Keys to Unlock Lifelong Vitality* and as a health advocate and researcher, I am frequently asked many
questions regarding diets. "Is the Beverly Hills Diet healthy?" "Why
did I end up fatter than I was before I started the No Fat Diet?" "Is the
Atkins' Diet more effective than the South Beach Diet?" "What makes
the Grapefruit Diet work?" With so many diets screaming for our attention, it's easy to see where the confusion and the questions come from.

While one diet promises and delivers weight loss based on a high
fiber vegetarian program, another plan tells you to eat more steaks and
fried bacon than you've eaten in the last five years, and the next one
does the same based on consuming plates and plates full of cabbage.
Most people get lost in the mountain of details and have no idea of
what is best, let alone what is healthy for them.

Many of the people I've met have gotten so frustrated trying to figure it out that they've given up and ended up taking no action while their waistlines continue to expand. Or they've jumped from one diet to another, with varying degrees of initial success, only to fail and end up gaining back whatever they had lost plus a few more pounds on top of it. As a last resort, the extremely obese and desperate get dangerous bariatric surgery and hope that will solve their weight problems. (An astonishing five percent of patients who undergo bariatric surgery die within a year. Another seven to 14 percent will have complications related to the surgery.) Ironically, because of their dramatically reduced capacity for food, all of these patients subsequently have to make such radical changes to their diets that if they would have made those changes before surgery, they may have never needed the surgery in the first place.

> To shed some major pounds for her role in *Dreamgirls,* Beyonce relied on the Maple Syrup Diet and shed 22 pounds in only 14 days. The diet consists of consuming nothing more than water, cayenne pepper, and maple syrup. Not recommended.

All you have to watch is one diet infomercial or even a 30-second ad to understand the appeal of most popular diets—quick, effortless weight loss in exceedingly short windows of time. Given the fact that almost seven out of every 10 Americans are overweight, just about any diet will find a market if it's given the right spin and a couple "before and after" photos. My question isn't whether a significant initial weight loss is possible on a certain diet, but *whether the weight loss is long term or not, is the person left healthy, and have they learned how to stay that way after the diet.* I have long said that most people can have short-term success on just about any of the myriad of diets, because they generally go from totally unstructured eating to some kind of structure.

Sifting through the hundreds or even thousands of diets I've tried, heard, or read about, some weight loss programs have been around for generations, while others have been introduced only recently. Many of the supposed new diets have, in fact, been around for years with various alterations. And many different diets are using the same nutritional approaches, such as ketogenic (a high protein and/or high fat, very low carbohydrate diet), low glycemic, low fat, high protein, etc.

Here are approaches that have made their mark and have attracted many loyal followers.

Bodybuilding Diet

This diet is more about a lifestyle than a diet. Bodybuilders have a long history of maintaining body sculpting diets and are proficient at building lean body mass and reducing body fat. Among bodybuilders is a general acceptance that a diet based on 40 percent carbohydrates, 40 percent protein, and 20 percent fat will support a person's bodybuilding program while still supplying the necessary energy to accomplish their daily tasks and feel their best.

How It Works

While there are many food programs within the Bodybuilding Diet, they are all essentially a method for increasing awareness about one's food intake, which will lead to weight loss. This is an individualistic sport, and many bodybuilders take pleasure in creating the precise diet program that works for them. Many diet programs today follow a few of the basic principles of a Bodybuilding Diet, such as six mini meals, moderate carbohydrate intake, and food journaling. The basic steps are simple and commonsensical.

The Internet provides extensive content regarding activity programs and menu plans. One should use caution, however, and compare any advice given against common medical knowledge of healthy practices. From Hugo Rivera at about.com, for instance, one can find good advice on how to ease into a Bodybuilding Diet during a 10-week period.

A typical program works in this manner. Take an inventory of your current condition, then determine what your target weight is and how long you want to take to get there. Next, you must commit to an exercise program. The key to this diet is to add the exercise that will transform body fat into muscle (you don't have to be a bodybuilder to gain the benefits of a consistent diet and exercise routines!).

Utilizing a basic diet of 40 percent carbohydrates, 40 percent protein, and 20 percent fat, the key components of fat transformation and muscle growth are eating chicken, fish, and turkey for high protein and using complex carbohydrates to change your body along with the exercise workouts. Supplement the good fats in your diet with nuts, flaxseed, fish oil capsules, and essential fatty acid supplements.

> Cheese that is required by law to append the word *food* to its title does not go well with red wine or fruit.
>
> FRAN LEBOWITZ

Reduce the number of calories you are consuming each day. As you make it a habit to eat the right things, you will be making a lifestyle change instead of just maintaining a diet.

Oftentimes, bodybuilders will use protein powders along with additional liquid supplements to round out their program. They will also use food journaling as part of their daily routine.

Comments

While this diet is not nutrient dense enough and thus can lead to multiple nutrient deficiencies and is not sustainable over the long term, you would surely lose weight as you stay on the diet and continue with a serious exercise program. This diet usually recommends eating six smaller meals a day, which I don't recommend.

Additionally, because muscle weighs more than fat, you may not see the fat disappear in weight, but you will see it go down as your body changes. Building lean body mass and reducing body fat is the ultimate goal for anyone seeking to lose and maintain a lower weight.

Total Fasting

For as long as history has been documented, people have fasted for spiritual or religious reasons:

- Moses fasted for 40 days and 40 nights while he was on the mountain with the Almighty (Exodus 34:20).
- The Old Testament Law specifically *required* prayer and fasting for only one occasion, which was the Day of Atonement (Yom Kippur—Leviticus 23:26–32). The sacrifice of the Day of Atonement was repeated annually when the high priest entered the

Holy of Holies to sprinkle blood on the lid of the ark for his sins and for the sins of his people. This became known as "the day of fasting" (Jeremiah 36:6) or "the Fast" (Acts 27:9).

- David fasted when he learned that King Saul and Jonathan had been killed (2 Samuel 1:12).
- Nehemiah prayed and fasted in the Persian capital when he learned that the walls and gates of Jerusalem were still in ruins despite the return of some of the Jewish exiles from captivity in Babylon (Nehemiah 1:4).
- Even Darius, the king of Persia, fasted from food all night and did not sleep after he was forced to put Daniel in the den of lions (Daniel 6:18).
- After Jonah preached in Nineveh, the people fasted to avoid God's judgment (Jonah 3:7).
- Just before Jesus began His earthly ministry, He fasted 40 days and 40 nights (Matthew 4:2).
- The apostle Paul and Barnabas spent time in prayer and fasting for the appointment of elders in the churches (Acts 14:23) that were established during their missionary journey.

The practice of fasting is referred to more than 70 times in the Bible, and many incorporate fasting to this day as part of their prayer life. Some fast for one day, others longer—drinking only water and some without water. Unless you are a very seasoned "faster," I do not recommend total fasts with water for more than a couple of days and NEVER total fasts without water, as these are very dangerous.

There are spiritual and health reasons to fast, and both can be accomplished during the same fast. For many years I have advocated fasting in a way that preserves muscle mass and gives the body everything it needs to thrive without hunger or cravings on a low calorie but nutrient dense liquid diet. (See the FUEL Fast and Micro Fast section within "The Dynamic Role of Proteins in Weight Loss" chapter.)

"Eating," according to Neil Anderson, "is the granddaddy of all appetites." It's hard to argue against that when you look around at today's obesity problems. He goes on to say, "Fasting is a commitment to bring about self-control and overcome every other conceivable temptation." Far too few of us have brought self-control to our eating habits, and fasting is a right step in that direction.

One biblical example of a lack of self-control is Eli, who was the high priest of Israel at the time of Samson and who judged Israel for 40 years. When he toppled over backward and died from a broken neck, we are told he was old and "heavy" (1 Samuel 4:18). Eli had a serious eating problem, so much so that the Lord had asked him, "Why do you kick at My sacrifice and My offering which I have commanded in My dwelling place…to make yourselves fat with the best of all the offerings of Israel My people?" (2:29). Eli's love of eating the fat offerings the people brought to the temple and his lack of discipline concerning food not only caused Eli to become fat, but it spilled over and spoiled the rest of his priestly life.

There are many other reasons for fasting. For example, Socrates and Plato fasted for up to 10 days at a time because they believed it heightened their thinking ability.

Today, in the medical profession, doctors require patients to fast for several hours or longer as part of preparing for surgery. One reason is to avoid complications during anesthesia. You have probably been asked to avoid eating for several hours prior to a blood sample being taken, so there can be a pure baseline.

Most people are unaware that they go on a fast every day or, more specifically, every night. While we are sleeping, our body cleanses and repairs itself. Have you noticed that when you wake up your breath may have a bad odor or your tongue is coated? These can be signs that the body is in a state of detoxification.

The word *breakfast* really means "break the fast."

You may ask, "I know people who fast for various reasons, but what about for dieting and weight loss?"

There are those who preach the benefits of a total fast. Widely read books include *Fasting Made Easy* by Dr. Don Colbert, *The Fasting Diet* by Steven Bailey, and *Fasting—The Ultimate Diet* by Allan Colt.

Of course, you are going to lose weight when you don't eat, but unfortunately typical fasting causes significant muscle loss that is extremely hard to recover. Muscle is a primary key to maintain a fat-burning metabolism. The major reason to fast given by most advocates is to rid the body of environmental toxins, toxins stored in fat, residues from medications, mucus coatings in the intestines, industrial chemicals, buildup of plaque in the arteries, and the "sludge" in our bodies from the junk foods we have ingested through the years. Plus, it is widely held that fasting is the most effective way to eradicate unwanted bacteria, parasites, fungi, and viruses.

Those who recommend total fasting usually prescribe it for short periods of time. Countless people fast one day a week or two days in succession each month.

Comments

Never attempt a total fast without medical supervision and never without water. There are numerous medical conditions that may preclude a person from doing even a one-day total fast, but most people can get significant benefit from fasting. Some doctors will tell you that since glucose is the primary fuel source for the brain to function, long periods of not eating can be dangerous. Consider your health before attempting a fast of any length. You can become weak, faint, dizzy, and nauseous from lack of food and water. While you are on a total fast, you may want to limit your physical activities, including exercise or work. If you want to experience the benefits of fasting without being hungry and without limiting your activities, I strongly encourage you to try the FUEL Fast and Micro Fast within "The Dynamic Role of Proteins in Weight Loss" chapter.

Juice Fasting

In recent years there has been a growing number of people who are sold on juice fasting—not just for dieting, but also for general health. Numerous individuals claim cures for everything

Seven Reasons for Fasting (Isaiah 58:6–7)

1. To loose the bonds of wickedness

2. To undo heavy burdens

3. To free the oppressed and break the yoke of bondage

4. To share food with the hungry

5. To provide shelter for the poor

6. To clothe the naked

7. To provide for one's family

from cancer to nicotine addiction, depression, and arthritis. Others testify to their increased sense of smell and taste, and that they digest their food better and sleep sounder.

Most fans of this diet recommend 32 to 64 ounces of juices, sipped throughout the day. They drink combinations of raw vegetables, including tomatoes, celery, carrots, kale, cabbage, beets, and greens, blended with apples, berries, grapes, and a variety of fruits. Some like to add herbs to their vegetables for flavor, including mint, basil, ginger, garlic, even chili pepper. There are hundreds of recipes available.

Organic fruits and vegetables are considered best. As one juicer asked, "Why take in agricultural chemicals you are trying to eliminate from your body?" Fresh juice is preferable, but you can buy many juice products from a health food store or a juice bar. Keep in mind that fruits and vegetables take a couple of weeks to get from the farm to your kitchen, so the nutrient value has diminished since harvest. The dark green and bright colored vegetables are thought to be the most nutritious, but most people lean toward sweet veggies and fruits, such as carrot juice and apples that contain high sugar levels, which can result in significant weight gain.

Juice fasting is often used to address some particular disease, but many use it to lose weight. Keep in mind that a large portion of the weight lost is muscle mass that is critical to a vibrant metabolism. It is basically a short-term detox diet, also promoted as a good source of antioxidants and vitamins. It is sometimes combined with an enema or a laxative to expel waste from the intestines and colon.

How long should you go on a juice fast? There are about as many answers to that question as there are proponents of the diet. Most schedule it for two or three days at a time, while others recommend a week or even longer. Some people choose to juice fast for one or two days a week and eat normal meals for the other five.

Popular books on the topic include *Juicing, Fasting, and Detoxing for Life* by Cherie Calbom and *The Juicing Bible* by Pat Crocker.

Comments

Juice fasting can be very good for people who are in need of detoxification, but it is not an effective tool for long-term weight loss unless the juice is optimized with essential nutrients, not the least of which is protein and essential amino acids. People wrongly assume they are getting everything they need because they are drinking so many fruits and vegetables. You can overcome that with the FUEL Fast and Micro Fast explained in "The Dynamic Role of Proteins in Weight Loss" chapter.

Juice fasting is not recommended for women who are pregnant or nursing. It is also discouraged for those with diabetes, hypoglycemia, low blood pressure, or who are underweight.

For either total fasting or juice fasting, always check with a physician and proceed under medical supervision. Side effects can include headaches, constipation, bad breath, body odor, diarrhea, and fatigue.

If you experience these symptoms or are taking any prescriptions, it is wise to talk with a health professional specifically trained in detoxification.

> **Fasting confirms our utter dependence upon God by finding in Him a source of sustenance beyond food.**
>
> DALLAS WILLARD

Glycemic Index Diet

The Glycemic Index (or GI) ranks carbohydrates based on their effect on our blood glucose levels. The concept was developed in the early 1980s at the University of Toronto as researchers studied which foods were most advantageous for those with diabetes. As a result of the research, many believe that when you select low GI carbohydrates—those which cause only small fluctuations in insulin and blood glucose levels—you reduce your risk of diabetes and heart disease. Plus, it is lauded as the key to long-term weight loss.

This diet is said to lower blood cholesterol levels, prolong physical endurance, and decrease hunger (keeping you fuller for longer periods of time). Since diabetics need diets that keep blood sugar from swinging up and down too much, this diet has been highly recommended.

How It Works

Those who tout this approach say carbohydrates that break down quickly during digestion—thus sending glucose rapidly into the blood-stream—have a high GI. Those that break down slowly have a slow release (and a low GI) and are considered much better for you.

On the Glycemic Diet you'll be swapping high carbs for low carbs—eating cereals based on oats, barley, and bran. You will be choosing whole grain bread and stone-ground flour and eating fewer potatoes.

The index measures food against pure glucose (which has a GI of 100). It calculates how much a 50-gram portion of carbohydrates raises blood sugar levels compared to pure glucose. Low GI foods are in the range of 55 or less. This includes most fruits and vegetables, fish, eggs, milk, nuts, legumes, and grainy breads. Unrefined breads have a lower GI value than white bread. High GI foods, 70 and above, include white rice, corn flakes, and baked potatoes. Vegetables are generally low in glucose. Foods with lots of sugar are high, but the riper a fruit or vegetable, the higher the number on the index.

What's the link between the Glycemic Index and weight loss? Its advocates believe that controlling blood sugar controls appetite.

It is not necessary to go on a strict GI diet, but when you understand the principles, you will be eating less sugar and more fiber—and that's good!

To learn more, read *The GI Diet* by Rick Gallop, *The Low GI Diet Revolution* by Jennie Brand-Miller, or *The G-Index Diet* by Richard Podell.

Comments

The primary limitation of a GI diet is that the GI is not necessarily relevant to what actually goes into the body, because the GI is not based on a serving of a food. It is based on 50 grams of carbohydrates from each food tested against 50 grams of carbohydrates from another food. Not every food tested has 50 grams of carbohydrates in a serving, so some foods look healthier because they have a lower GI. What really matters is the glycemic response of a food in the body or the Glycemic Load (GL)—an adjusted GI for the actual amount of carbohydrates in a given serving of food. For an understanding of the two, go to the section on "The Glycemic Index and Glycemic Load" in the "Corner #2" chapter.

Also there are sometimes multiple numbers given for the same foods within the index, and they fluctuate according to the particular study. Besides, the index doesn't always take into account the difference in each person's digestive system. According to research reported in the June 2007 issue of *Diabetes Care*, the GI response to a given food varies widely from person to person, and it can even vary within the same person from day to day.

Several popular diets have adjusted their formulas and products to aim for a lower GI, but be careful about the index numbers. There are numerous variables involved, including how food is cooked, its ripeness, and how long it has been stored.

> A cucumber should be well sliced, and dressed with pepper and vinegar, and then thrown out as good for nothing.
>
> Samuel Johnson

Grapefruit Diet

This weight loss program has been around since the 1930s and is also known as the Hollywood Diet or the Mayo Diet (not associated with the Mayo Clinic).

Many believe this is the predecessor to the low carbohydrate diet because it is based on low carbs, moderate protein, and low calories (averaging less than 1,000 calories a day). But let's face it, anyone who consumes this few calories will lose weight, regardless of the diet they are on! And as in most extremely low calorie diets, muscle, which is a primary factor in optimal metabolism, is lost on this diet due to inadequate intake of high quality protein.

Without question, grapefruit is good for you. It has only approximately 75 calories per serving and plenty of vitamin C and fiber (assuming you eat the fruit itself and don't simply drink its juice).

How It Works

The theory behind this diet is that when grapefruit (unsweetened) is eaten with protein, it acts as a catalyst to the fat-burning process. It is promoted as a plan for quick weight loss.

There are many versions of the 12-day grapefruit diet, but here's one example (granted, it is hard to see how this version is 1,000 or less calories):

- Breakfast: two eggs, two slices of bacon, black coffee, half a grape-fruit or eight ounces of grapefruit juice.
- Lunch: Salad with salad dressing, unlimited meat, half a grape-fruit or eight ounces of grapefruit juice.
- Dinner: Red or green vegetables (no starchy foods such as beans or sweet potatoes), salad, unlimited portions of meat or fish. Again, half a grapefruit or eight ounces of grapefruit juice.

You are not to eat between meals, and if you have a snack, this program recommends it should be just before bedtime, which may be the worst possible time to snack. Also, you're asked to cut down on coffee because it interferes with the desired balance.

In addition, you are to drink 64 ounces of water each day. This is always a good idea, whether or not you are on a diet.

The plan is to eat all you want, but just add grapefruit. Fatty meats are okay, and you can even fry vegetables in butter.

Some people go on this diet for 12 days, stop for two days, and repeat the process.

Books on the topic include *The Grapefruit Solution* by Daryl Thompson and *The Grapefruit and Apple Cider Vinegar Combo Diet* by Randall Earl Dunford.

Of course, the Florida, Texas, and California grapefruit industries have always encouraged this diet!

Comments

As is true of the Atkins' Diet, the concept of unlimited types and quantities of meats at each meal is a recipe for health problems. The body can take days to digest certain meats, and digestive congestion is inevitable with back-to-back-to-back meat meals. Also, conventionally raised meats can be extremely toxic when consumed often.

Critics of this approach say the lost weight is primarily from liquids, so the pounds return when you resume normal eating. Also, because of the quick weight loss claims, there are high expectations that aren't always met.

Of major concern to many doctors is the fact that, contrary to most other citrus juices, grapefruit juice contains certain compounds that may cause potentially unhealthy interactions with a wide range of medications (the real problem is the medications not the grapefruit). If you are considering this diet, talk with your physician.

Also, the variety of foods is so restrictive it does little to help dieters improve their eating habits or behaviors. Such a limited variety of foods in small portions is a prescription for boredom, monotony, and taste fatigue—the formula that causes most dieters to throw in the towel, disgusted with trying to lose weight.

Here's the major drawback, though. As far as I can tell, there is no scientific evidence—not a shred—that proves that grapefruit can actually burn fat.

> There is no evidence that grapefruit has fat-burning enzymes nor is it a magic bullet for weight loss.
>
> CONNIE DIEKMAN

Leptin Diet

In 1994, Jeffery Friedman, M.D., and his colleagues at Rockefeller University in New York City, discovered leptin, a hormone that helps regulate body metabolism and appetite.

How It Works

Those who have researched leptin say it is produced by fat tissue and secreted into the bloodstream where it travels to other areas, including the brain. It tells the brain how much fat is in storage. This controls appetite, energy, and metabolic rate.

Proponents say that leptin triggers the message that tells you when to stop eating. Since this hormone is released by fat cells, leptin levels are roughly proportional to body fat.

There are a handful of books written on the subject. For instance, *The Rosedale Diet* by Dr. Ron Rosedale is effectively a high fat, low non-fibrous carb, low protein diet. It deliberately avoids most starchy carbs and sugars, and rather than calorie counting, it advocates eating when you are hungry. Rosedale provides food guidelines regarding leptin and recommends that you eat slowly and not eat within three hours before bedtime.

The Leptin Diet by Byron Richards sets five basic rules for his diet:

1. *Never eat after dinner*—leave 11 to 12 hours between dinner and breakfast to burn fat.
2. *Eat three meals a day*—with a gap of five hours between eating. This is so the body will store the energy from the food.
3. *Don't eat large meals*—because too much food leads to insulin and leptin resistance.
4. *Eat a high protein breakfast*—since a high carb breakfast can cause late afternoon energy crashes.
5. *Reduce the amount and Glycemic Index of carbohydrates you consume*—and fewer starch carbs.

Comments

Since it is a recent discovery, there is not a great deal of research to back up the claims of leptin diets, but it is an important piece of the weight loss puzzle. However, the protein recommendations seem low (between 50 to 75 grams per day). For a male eating 2,000 calories per day, this equates to only 10 to 14 percent of his daily intake. (See "The Dynamic Role of Protein in Weight Loss" chapter.)

Insulin and leptin are two master hormones, and it is wise to optimize them. It seems clear that insulin and leptin resistance are big health issues and do contribute strongly to weight gain and many diseases, including diabetes and metabolic syndrome. It is good advice to avoid snacking and to not eat within three hours of bedtime. Grandma was right! "Eat three square meals per day and don't snack."

Mediterranean Diet

Several decades ago, medical doctors began investigating the fact that people who live in the countries that border the Mediterranean Sea, particularly southern Italy and Greece, had much lower rates of cardiovascular disease and cancer than we have in the West.

Following World War II, people began talking about the benefits of copying the eating habits of those from this region, but it was not until the mid 1990s that the Mediterranean diet was popularized by the research of Dr. Walter Willett of the Harvard University School of Public Health.

A study released on June 23, 2009, in the online edition of the *British Medical Journal*, took aim at what makes this diet so healthy. Researchers from the Harvard School of Public Health in Boston and the University of Athens Medical School in Greece looked at more than 23,000 Greek men and women participating in the European Prospective Investigation into Cancer and Nutrition (EPIC). During the course of eight and a half years, the researchers led by Harvard's Dimitrios Trichopoulous and the University of Athens' Antonia Trichopoulou compared the health of the participants against their adherence to a Mediterranean diet.

> Fake food—I mean those patented substances chemically flavored and mechanically bulked out to kill the appetite and deceive the gut—is unnatural, almost immoral, a bane to good eating and good cooking.
>
> JULIA CHILDS

What they found was that certain foods in the diet, more than others, may offer the bulk of the nutritional benefits of the regimen. The authors note that the analysis "indicates that the dominant components of the Mediterranean diet score as a predictor of lower mortality are moderate consumption of [alcohol], low consumption of meat and meat products, and high consumption of vegetables, fruits, nuts, olive oil, and legumes." In contrast, they noted high consumption of fish and cereals and an avoidance of dairy products in the diet seemed to have little to do with the benefits of the overall diet.[3]

There are numerous books on the benefits of these food choices, including *The Mediterranean Diet* by Marissa Cloutier and Eve Adamson and *The Mediterranean Heart Diet* by Helen V. Fisher.

How It Works

This is a rather simple plan to follow, since it focuses on foods that are not only common in that part of the world, but are readily available everywhere. The traditional Mediterranean diet includes:

- Fruits, vegetables, pasta, and rice.
- Eating fish regularly (three or more times a week) but consuming only small portions of red meat. Poultry is on the approved list.
- Choosing healthy fats, such as those found in olive oil.
- Small portions of nuts each day.
- Dairy products: skim milk, low fat cheese, and fat free yogurt.

If you have ever traveled to this region, you see the locals using olive oil on everything from vegetables to salads, breads, fish, and poultry. Unlike animal fats, olive oil has been shown to lower cholesterol levels in the blood. Virgin and extra-virgin olive oils are the least processed and provide antioxidant effects.

Remember, they eat bread, but not with margarine (which contains hydrogenated oils/trans fats). The breads eaten in this part of the world are usually from whole grains and contain far less trans fats than we consume in the West.

This heart healthy diet doesn't completely eliminate fats, rather it focuses on eating *healthier* fats. In addition, since this style of eating includes generous amounts of fatty fish, which has omega-3 fatty acids, it is said to lower triglycerides. You are to avoid fried fish or those cooked in heavy butter or topped with rich sauces. Instead, grill the seafood in a little olive oil.

Foods are to be lightly cooked and eaten in small portions. In fact, most are raw or unprocessed. Also stay away from corn or corn byproducts and limit packaged and processed foods.

The fruits and vegetables on this diet are usually eaten in season and locally grown. Popular choices include tomatoes, peppers, spinach, eggplant, and chickpeas.

Red wine (in moderate amounts) is part of the Mediterranean lifestyle, and it is said to reduce the blood's ability to clot—thus producing an aspirin-like effect. In addition, red wine may reduce blood vessel damage caused by fat deposits. If you don't drink alcohol, which is best, red grapes and its juice are excellent alternatives, or you can supplement with the super nutrient resveratrol (the secret ingredient of wine) and take fish oil.

A major factor in imitating this lifestyle is that the natives of this region walk much more than Americans do. So don't be a couch potato! Get ready to add plenty of physical activity.

Those who point to the success of the Mediterranean diet say it's not any particular food, rather the combination that makes it so effective.

Comments

This has proven to be one of the better dietary approaches. The three primary keys to this approach are small portion sizes/calorie restriction, high omega-3 and olive oil consumption/healthy fats, and nutrient density, including broad-spectrum antioxidants, such as resveratrol and low sugar consumption. The Four Corners of Super Nutrition have some similarities to this diet. The magic seems to be in the small portions, high omega-3s, resveratrol from wine, and the variety of foods. A lot of people seem to try the Mediterranean diet without the portion control or with types of fish that have little or no omega-3, such as farm-raised fish, and without the variety of vegetables.

One of the biggest concerns is that people use the success of this diet to justify drinking alcohol. Food and drinks can be a double-edged sword. Alcohol is not really a health food, even though a single glass of red wine per day has been shown to offer health benefits, such as lower heart attack risk. So many researchers have focused on the benefits of wine without telling you there are better ways to get the same benefits, such as eating grapes or supplementing with resveratrol, which appears to be the primary benefit to drinking wine.

A final word: Wine has been shown to offer health benefits, but you always have to weigh the benefits against the risks. For some, wine contains nitrites that can trigger migraine headaches and other potential reactions. Additionally, if you're unable to limit your alcohol intake to one glass per day, if you have a personal or family history of alcohol abuse, or if you have heart or liver disease, refrain from drinking wine or any other alcohol.

Paleo Diet

What would happen if we ate the foods of our ancient ancestors—

from the Paleolithic period? It's not just some far-fetched idea, but one that is advocated by many in the health profession. The idea is that since modern humans are genetically adapted to the diet of early man, it's an eating plan we should follow.

It is estimated that more than 70 percent of what we eat comes from what our ancestors did *not* eat, and those who promote this plan say it is the food we consume today that causes cancer, obesity, osteoporosis, acne, arthritis, diabetes, etc.

> **To eat is a necessity, but to eat intelligently is an art.**
>
> LA ROCHEFOUCAULD

Walter L. Voegtlin, a gastroenterologist, first made this diet known in his book *The Stone Age Diet*, published in 1975. Since then, there have been many additional books written on the topic, including *The Paleo Diet* by Loren Cordain, *NeanderThin: Eat Like a Caveman to Achieve a Lean, Strong, Healthy Body* by Ray Audette and Michael Eades, and *Health Secrets of the Stone Age* by Philip J. Goscienski.

How It Works

The idea is to duplicate the food intake of the hunter-gatherer: He hunted meat and seafood and gathered fruit, nuts, mushrooms, herbs, spices, seeds, and vegetables. Called the "Caveman Diet" by some, it consists primarily of fats and proteins, with few carbohydrates. A typical meal might be roast pork with cooked and raw vegetables and fruit.

Regarding vegetables, some supporters state, "If it can't be eaten raw, don't eat it." This doesn't mean you can't cook the food, but make sure it passes the raw test, which means it could be eaten raw.

This diet comes from the pre-agricultural period, which means grains and legumes (which came later) are excluded. Only in more recent history do we find man consuming large amounts of whole grain cereals, alcohol, beans, and dairy products. Then, with the dawn of the Industrial Revolution and the invention of machines that could process foods, we began eating refined cereals, refined vegetables, and refined sugars, which have become a major part of our diets. In the process, nutrients have decreased and we are taking in fewer vitamins and minerals.

Those who follow this eating plan like to point to the "diseases of civilization" that were not around at the time of the caveman. An example is that wheat was not eaten. But we have celiac disease, which comes from the gluten in wheat.

While meat is an essential component, remember that animals in earlier centuries were fed an organic, natural diet, which is not true of commercially raised meats.

Comments

I have colleagues who are huge advocates of this program and have used it successfully with their patients. They generally suggest unlimited meats with more nuts, seeds, fruits, and vegetables than might generally be recommended with this approach. Critics say this is not a healthy diet, since it contains far too much animal fat.

It is important to keep in mind that as in the Atkins' approach, some meats can take days to fully digest and consuming back-to-back-to-back meat meals can cause digestive congestion and even lead to disease. Also, eating non-organic commercially raised meats can cause toxins to build up in the body. Additionally, hunter-gatherers would eat what they killed, and between kills would eat a vegetarian diet—they did not eat three meals every day that contained meat. They unknowingly combined the concepts of fasting between meals and on-and-off vegetarianism.

> Bread that must be sliced with an ax is bread that is too nourishing.
>
> FRAN LEBOWITZ

Pritikin Principle

In the 1950s, Nathan Pritikin was diagnosed with heart disease. His search for an answer led him to a diet that was low in fat and high in unrefined carbohydrates. Plus, he added a regimen of daily exercise. In the process, his cholesterol fell from more than 300 to less than 150. To share with the world what he believed was the perfect way to health, he wrote *The Pritikin Program of Diet and Exercise*. In 1976 he established the Pritikin Longevity Center in Florida.

There are many books available on his plan, including *The Pritikin*

Edge by Robert A. Vogel and *The New Pritikin Program* by Robert Pritikin (son of the founder). More than three millions copies of books by the Pritikins are in print.

How It Works

The original goal was to help diabetics off insulin medication by attempting to normalize their blood sugar and to lower cholesterol. But many found they lost weight in the process.

This comes close to a vegetarian diet, because it centers on eating fruits, grains, and vegetables—with very little fat. The concept is to take in fewer calories than your body burns. Instead of counting calories you are taught which foods are less "calorie dense." You will learn to think of "calories per pound." Examples of foods that are not calorie dense are apples and oatmeal.

The Pritikin goal is to consume foods with fewer than 400 calories per pound. Most vegetables have less than 200 per pound. On the other end of the scale, 16 ounces of chocolate has more than 2,000 calories!

Books detailing the program list the calorie density of various foods. You will learn that highly processed foods have more calories—far more than in their original, natural state.

What can you eat? Fish, chicken, and lean beef. Brown rice, barley, beans, and starches in moderation. Fruits are allowed, plus plenty of water and fiber—to fill you up so you won't feel hungry. You will be eating three meals a day and two snacks.

The Pritikin Principle is high on exercise—at least 30 minutes a day.

Comments

While this diet has its avid fans, it is difficult to stick to, since there are no days off. So no cheating!

It is ideal for individuals who desire to adopt a vegetarian approach to eating, but beware of what you are getting into. This diet is deficient in protein and healthy fats, and therefore is not sustainable over the long term.

Another concern is that since this diet is so low in fat, it can produce hunger pangs or even be problematic to one's health. Some people may need more healthy fats than the Pritikin Principle provides. It inhibits the intake and absorption of fat soluble vitamins and can even limit the amount of essential fatty acids provided by the diet needed for normal cell function, healthy skin and tissue, growth, and development.

Chapter 4

Weight Loss by the Book

You cannot indulge in those foods and liquors that destroy the physique and still hope to have a physique that functions with the minimum of destruction to itself. A candle burnt at both ends may shed a brighter light, but the darkness that follows is for a longer time.

COCO CHANEL

When it comes to understanding the healthiest means to weight loss, most of us feel as overwhelmed as Dorothy when she approached the mighty Wizard of Oz. Medical expressions and nomenclature, such as metabolic syndrome, insulin resistance, low glycemic response, free radicals, antioxidants, omega-3 fatty acids, trans fats, polyunsaturated fats, flavonoids, and tocopherols, thunder and intimidate and make us feel helpless. We need to pull the veil back and expose the Wizard and his fancy words. They only describe basic, commonsense concepts regarding the foods we eat.

Throughout history there has never been a shortage of diet, health, and weight loss advice—good, bad, and even harmful. Everything under the sun has been called a weight loss cure at some time or another. And now, with the seemingly unlimited information accessible through the Internet, snake oil is packaged slicker, backed by testimonials, and more abundant than ever.

Many folks I speak with are so cynical about dietary advice they ignore all of it and simply hope they are one of the few blessed with the genetics to withstand decades of poor diet and little or no exercise. They always point to a heavyset relative who ate like a Trojan and poured sugar over and into everything, laughed his or her way through life, and lived to 100.

The problem with this approach, of course, is they are gambling with their own life, and the stakes couldn't be higher. Even if they have the hardiest, most resilient body in the world, if they eat and live as their relative did, what are the chances they won't drop over from a heart attack at 52 or discover they have colon cancer when they're 63? Unless we've been living with our heads in the sand, we know the profound impact diets have on our health and longevity.

Despite the inundation of dietary advice that we get every day from the media—television, magazines, and bestselling books—as well as from our family and friends, we can pull the curtain back on the Wizard of Oz and sort out the facts from the lies and distortions. And based on that we can improve the quality of our lives by making better decisions about how we treat our bodies without sacrificing our enjoyment of life.

In this chapter we examine a number of diet and health books that have attracted a large and dedicated following. How does the diet work? What makes it unique? Are there any concerns? Is it right for you?

> If you have formed the habit of checking on every new diet that comes along, you will find that, mercifully, they all blur together, leaving you with only one definite piece of information: french-fried potatoes are out.
>
> JEAN KERR

The Biggest Loser by Maggie Greenwood-Robinson, Cheryl Forberg, Michael Dansinger, M.D., and Bob Harper

This book is based on NBC's popular television show by the same name. The subtitle makes this promise: "The Weight Loss Program to Transform Your Body, Health, and Life." If you've watched the program, you know this is simply a healthy diet with an emphasis on lots of exercise. It's a 12-week program developed by obesity clinicians and dieticians at Tufts University.

It has a 4-3-2-1 pyramid (four servings of fruits and vegetables; three of lean protein, two of whole grains; and one "extra" of sweets, oils, or fats of about 200 calories). You'll be eating small, frequent meals (three meals a day and three snacks) with fiber and protein for fullness. The goal is to decrease blood pressure, lower cholesterol, become stronger, and have more energy.

The diet asks you to avoid the "whites" (pasta, potatoes, white bread), because they are said to be what stimulates the appetite. The food choices have plenty of variety, but you will be choosing unprocessed, whole foods, with no added fats, salt, or sugar. So you will eat cherries, but not a toasted cherry pastry tart!

The underlying concept is that the body processes natural foods and uses them more efficiently. A major objective is to burn more calories than you eat each day. How many calories? This diet suggests taking your current weight and multiplying it by seven. So if you weigh 200 pounds, your goal is to take in 1,400 calories a day. If you're at 150 pounds, you would aim for 1,050 daily. As you lose weight, you recalibrate to set your calorie intake lower. For many, this diet is a return to the calorie counting that is deemphasized in many programs.

The daily workouts in "Basic Training" start with 30 minutes a day, six days a week, and increase to an hour. Your exercise regimen will include cardio, strength, and resistance.

You can join the Biggest Loser Club online for support and encouragement (www.biggestloserclub.com). There are animated fitness demos, shopping lists, a progress tracker, and a maintenance plan with motivation from former "biggest losers," and the online program does the calorie counting. You can even set up your own competitions with other members of the online club. The cost is $5 a week.

Comments

This is a program that seems very difficult to do on your own. It does combine several well-known methods of weight loss, including calorie restriction, cardio and resistance exercise, and accountability. But it seems to ignore the increased protein requirements of a low calorie diet and the need for nutrient density, and does not emphasize supplementation. It is important that any diet you do promotes total health in addition to weight loss.

Some people watch the *Biggest Loser* on television and think they can achieve the same results at home. But unless you can afford a personal trainer and devote your entire life to the process, it may not be that easy to stay motivated. Also, you might not like using food scales, measuring cups, and calorie counting to determine the right food portions.

Macrobiotic Diet by Michio and Aveline Kushi

The term *macrobiotic* is found in the writing of Hippocrates, who is called the "Father of Western Medicine." He used it to describe people who enjoyed an extended life and were healthy. The word itself derives from the Greek *macro* and *bios*, which means "long life." This diet was found in cultures from the Incas to the Chinese.

George Ohsawa, a Japanese philosopher, studied this way of eating and brought it to the West—first to Europe, then to North America in the 1950s. Michio and Aveline Kushi, two of his students, became the most noted proponents of his teachings through their book *Macrobiotic Diet*. The Kushis established the Kushi Institute in Boston in 1978.

Gwyneth Paltrow and Madonna are reported to have brought the Macrobiotic Diet into the commercial spotlight as high-profile adherents.

How It Works

The Macrobiotic Diet consists of 30 to 35 percent whole grain cereals, especially brown rice, 30 to 40 percent vegetables, five to 10 percent beans and legumes, five percent miso soup (made from fermented soybeans), and five to 10 percent naturally processed foods. The rest is composed of fish and seafood, seeds, nuts, and fruits. Grains are the basic food, supplemented with vegetables.

You avoid highly processed or refined foods. The Macrobiotic Diet is similar to a vegan diet, but in macrobiotics certain animal foods are eaten. The original diet was extremely rigid in Japan, but has been Americanized and become less restrictive.

On the *not recommended* or *highly restricted* list are "nightshade vegetables"—a popular name for plants in the Solanum family, such as tomatoes, potatoes, peppers, and eggplant, due to the alkaloid content, thought to negatively affect calcium balance.

You are also to avoid over-stimulating foods, such as chocolate, hot spices, chemicals, preservatives, sugar, coffee, and commercial milk.

It's okay to bake, broil, and steam, but no frying.

You are to chew food thoroughly before swallowing and avoid overeating.

Choose local fruit, as fresh as possible, and natural sweets, such as apples. Also use unrefined vegetable oil for cooking. Seasonings are okay, including natural sea salt, grated ginger root, and sliced scallions.

One of the interesting aspects of macrobiotics is the attempt to balance the "yin and yang" factor. In Chinese culture, *yin* is usually characterized as slow, soft, cold, wet, and passive. It is generally associated with the feminine, birth, generation, and with the night. *Yang*, by contrast, is depicted as solid, dry, fast, focused, hot, and aggressive. It is associated with daytime and masculinity. So in this diet you are taught to pair foods according to their balances of sweet, sour, bland, salty, and similar characteristics.

> We never repent of having eaten too little.
>
> THOMAS JEFFERSON

Followers believe the quality of the food affects health and well-being, even happiness.

You adjust foods according to your age, gender, climate, and activity. The advocates say we are to pay close attention to eating certain foods according to the seasons:

- Spring: fresh greens, lighter quality, steam and cook for a short time.
- Summer: more raw foods, lighter grains.
- Fall: root vegetables, pumpkins, beans, heavier grains.
- Winter: root vegetables, pickles, heavier grains.

Many consider the Macrobiotic Diet to be more of a lifestyle than simply a weight control program.

Michio Kushi has also written *The Cancer Prevention Diet* with a basic macrobiotic approach.

Comments

This is an extremely hard diet to follow and involves food combining, which might have some short-term clinical benefit for people with various health conditions. However, the human body is a fantastic creation, and healthy people have the ability to digest numerous food combinations very well. There are many good foods and practices within this diet, but it is too heavy on grains and has too little focus on protein and nutrient density and no supplementation. There is a lot of wisdom in ancient Eastern eating practices, and we may never fully understand it. I do know practitioners of this diet who report success curing disease and in weight loss. The truth is that most people have unhealthy diets, and there is no doubt in my mind they could benefit greatly from changing from their diets to this type of diet as a transition to a new way of eating. Nevertheless, this diet is not sustainable for the vast majority of people, and I believe there are better ways to accomplish the same things.

> To safeguard one's health at the cost of too strict a diet is a tiresome illness indeed.
>
> LA ROCHERFOUCAULD

New Beverly Hills Diet by Judy Mazel

Born into a Jewish home in Chicago, Judy Mazel moved to California with the goal of becoming an actress. But after struggling with weight problems, she turned to finding answers and began writing on diet and health.

After spending several months in Santa Fe, New Mexico, working with a nutritionist, she wrote her first book, *The Beverly Hills Diet*. It was published in 1981 and rose to the *New York Times* bestseller list for more than six months, setting off a diet craze across the nation. She claimed to have lost 72 pounds on the program she created.

She returned to California and opened her successful weight loss clinic, which attracted many high-profile customers.

How It Works

Her first book was a classic starvation crash diet that many would expect runway models or Hollywood starlets to adopt. With a caloric intake of only about 800 calories per day during the initial 42-day phase, the dieter's goal is to lose up to 15 pounds in 35 days. It outlined a diet that includes eating only one type of food at a time. In other words, don't eat proteins and carbs in the same meal. And after the first 10 days of a fruit-rich diet, you are to eat no more fruit. On days 11 to

18, you add bread, two tablespoons of butter, and three cobs of corn. Only on day 19 you can add protein, such as steak and lobster. Great emphasis is given to how you combine the foods you eat.

Mazel's second book, *The New Beverly Hills Diet*, came out in 1996 and had several modifications. It avoids many of the earlier extremes and is less restrictive. Her revised diet separates what you eat in a different way. You start the morning with fruit (not many kinds, but one). A couple of hours later you can eat carbs. Two hours later, you eat a little protein. Once you eat from another group, no more fruit that day.

Also, when you first eat protein during the day (let's say lunch), about 80 percent of everything you eat from that point on should be protein. One meal a day can be "open," meaning you can mix the foods.

Mazel says fruits can become nutrients in your small intestine within 15 or 20 minutes. But it takes three hours for carbs and up to 10 hours for proteins to digest, which requires the help of your stomach's acids. Thus you eat fruit in the morning, followed by carbs, then protein (that keeps being digested through the night).

In her theory, if you eat a steak at noon, it would "trap" the faster digesting food you eat afterward. She believes that what causes weight gain is not the food, but food that is digested inefficiently.

Mazel estimates that you can lose approximately 10 to 35 pounds in the program's initial phase, which lasts about five weeks. After that you stick to a basic, but less limited, program.

Exercise is not compulsory but is recommended.

The book lists 21 open meal choices during the 35-day regimen.

Judy Mazel died in 2007 of complications relating to peripheral vascular disease.

Comments

This diet is a rehash of the Macrobiotic Diet. Some say the weight loss is simply due to low calories. It has been called a fad diet by many, but has been embraced by celebrities from Maria Shriver to Sally Kellerman.

It doesn't have many fans in the medical community and has been criticized by those who say it is nutritionally imbalanced. It is a low calorie diet that is also very low in protein, which will increase the risk of dieters losing muscle mass. The result of this will be a reduced metabolism that will make it highly likely that dieters will regain the weight when they resume normal eating.

> We do not desecrate the dish by serving any other, neither salad nor dessert. We just eat crab Newburg. My friends rise from the table, wring my hand with deep feeling, and slip quietly and reverently away. I sit alone and weep for the misery of a world that does not have blue crabs and a Jersey cow.
>
> MARJORIE KINNAN RAWLINGS

The Atkins' Diet

The low carbohydrate craze hit America in 2003–2004, and it is said that at its peak, one out of every 11 people in the United States were on some form of a low carb diet. Even Pepsi and Coca-Cola were introducing low carb drinks to tap into the market demand. In truth, the diet had been popular for quite a few years, after Dr. Robert C. Atkins, M.D., wrote his 1972 bestseller, *Dr. Atkins' Diet Revolution.*

In 1989, he formed Atkins Nutritionals, Inc., to market the plan and develop a line of health food products. However, after he died in 2003 from a fatal head injury after falling on ice while walking to his office, the company soon went into bankruptcy reorganization, but later emerged selling its branded products to the retail market and on the Internet. Interestingly, because the market had moved from low carbohydrate diets to low glycemic diets, the New Atkins quietly changed its strategy and made that transition.[4]

The program presented at their website is free (www.atkins.com), but you are encouraged to purchase their Atkins Advantage products, including shakes and energy bars.

There have been many studies involving this diet, and the results have varied, but in July 2008 the *New England Journal of Medicine* stated that a low carb diet is more effective than a low fat diet, which once again made the conventional medical critics who largely advocate low fat diets look bad.

How It Works

People relish the idea of eating what they once considered no-no's of weight loss—butter, cream, and even steak! Perhaps this is why so many are drawn to Atkins, where they are told they can eat meat, eggs, and cheese. You can even cook with butter and add olive oil to your salad.

The theory behind the diet is that we burn both carbs and fat to receive energy, but the carbs are used up first. So if we lower the carb intake and eat more fat and protein, we will lose weight, because we are burning off the stored fat far more efficiently.

According to Atkins' theory, when we take in too much sugar, it enters the bloodstream and causes the secretion of excess insulin from the pancreas into our body. When our muscles, liver, etc., can't store any more sugar as glycogen, it converts the excess sugar to fat. That's what we are trying to eliminate.

Fans say it's a rather easy diet to follow. All they have to do is learn to count carbs. Plus, there is plenty of Atkins' information available in books and on the Internet.

With the problem of diabetes escalating, this low carb approach is attractive. Hundreds of thousands, if not millions, have embraced it.

There are four specific phases to the diet:

Phase One: Induction. This is a 14-day quick-start process of burning stored fat by eliminating almost all carbohydrates from your daily intake. The idea is for you to see instant results.

There's a list of acceptable foods, and the carbs and fiber come mostly from salads and leafy greens. Since this lowers energy, you may feel hungry until the fat burning begins to take place—usually in about two days.

Carbohydrates are restricted to approximately 20 grams of net carbs (carbs minus fiber and sugar alcohols) per day. In real terms, we're talking about a cup of cooked vegetables and two cups of salad. Later you can increase the carbs in the form of foods that are rich in fiber. But you can eat all the protein you want, including fish, poultry, even red meat.

Many claim to lose five to 10 pounds per week during this two-week phase, which may not be as incredible as it sounds. When you restrict carbohydrates, the body uses stored carbohydrates in the form of glycogen. Each gram of glycogen holds about three grams of water in the muscles. When the body's 500 to 600 grams of glycogen is depleted, the body releases 1,500 to 1,800 grams of water, resulting in initial weight loss of water and glycogen of approximately five to 10 pounds. This portion of the associated weight loss returns shortly after normal carbohydrate consumption is resumed. So when you do a ketogenic diet, expect that you will lose a few pounds in the beginning and regain a few pounds afterward, so net weight loss can only be determined after returning to normal carbohydrate consumption.

Phase Two: Ongoing Weight Loss. Now you are ready for a longer list of acceptable foods. Actually, those who don't mind slower weight loss start with this phase. The concept is to remain at this level within five or 10 pounds of your goal.

Phase Three: Pre-Maintenance. You'll be eating a few more grams of carbs but will only be losing about one pound each week. This is where you are to find the right balance of carbs and protein that works for you.

Phase Four: Lifetime Maintenance. Here you have a longer list of food choices with the objective of staying at your optimum weight. Complex carbs are recommended instead of simple sugars. If you find you are gaining weight, they suggest you drop back to a previous phase.

You will be told that for the rest of your life you are to avoid (among other things) pasta made with flour, white bread, white potatoes, milk, and white rice.

Some people think the objective is to eat as much protein and as few carbs as possible, but the program attempts to create the right balance. And a positive aspect is that Atkins emphasizes plenty of exercise to keep your heart pumping.

Comments

The biggest problem with Atkins' approach is the unlimited consumption of any kind of commercially raised meats and processed fatty foods without recommending organic foods. Some meats can take days to digest and back-to-back-to-back meat meals every four to six hours can cause digestive congestion and even disease. Additionally, Atkins' highly processed packaged foods contain questionable and even unhealthy ingredients, including hydrogenated oils, artificial colors, artificial flavors, and preservatives.

Another major criticism of the Atkins approach centers on the Induction phase, because of the extremely low amount of carbohydrates. There have been reports of negative physical reactions during the first few days, but this can be expected because most people are addicted to carbohydrates.

Some doctors have cautioned about the disruption of normal metabolic activity if you eat too few carbs, but the vast majority of medical doctors are not trained in nutrition. They say the body needs a minimum of carbohydrates for efficient and healthy functioning—about 150 grams daily. The truth is that carbohydrates are the body's preferred fuel, but it can become very efficient in converting certain amino acids to fuel, as is reflected in the Eskimo population.

> As for butter versus margarine, I trust cows more than chemists.
>
> JOAN GUSSOW

Additionally, the plan doesn't advocate a high intake of fruits and vegetables, which are recommended by most nutrition experts because of the numerous documented health benefits from these foods.

This diet has been controversial in conventional medical circles, especially by those who maintain the approach won't prevent heart disease, stroke, or cancer. They even contend that too much protein and fat can lead to high cholesterol, kidney, and liver problems, which is one of the myths I dispel in "The Dynamic Role of Proteins in Weight Loss" chapter.

With all the program's limitations and controversies, this program has helped numerous people lose weight, even if just for a time. One of the main benefits is that it taught countless people the dangers of overeating carbohydrates.

South Beach Diet by Arthur Agatston, M.D.

As a leading American cardiologist, Dr. Arthur Agatston understood that a low fat diet would lower cholesterol and help prevent heart disease, but found that his patients had an extremely difficult time sticking to the plan. After studying the Glycemic Index and learning what happens when sugar enters the bloodstream, he concluded that low blood sugar leads to hunger pangs and causes people to crave more sugar. He believed that because of this, even those on low fat diets were consuming more calories and gaining weight—and actually increasing their risk of heart disease.

So Dr. Agatston, director of the Mount Sinai Cardiac Prevention Center in Miami, Florida, originally created the South Beach diet to improve his heart patients' health and discovered that his patients also lost significant amounts of weight. In the early 2000s, news of the diet spread and people were using it to lose weight. Three years later, he published *The South Beach Diet*, and now more than 20 million copies of the book and companion publications have been sold worldwide.

In fact, the South Beach Diet is a modification of the Atkins' Diet that evolves into a Glycemic Index Diet. In practice, the diet severely restricts carbohydrates in the first two weeks, then gradually reintroduces those with a low Glycemic Index. It also recommends swapping saturated fats for heart healthy monounsaturates, such as olive oil and nuts.

How It Works

The idea of the South Beach Diet is to replace bad carbs with good carbs and bad fats with good fats. And exercise is encouraged. No counting calories, carbs, or sticking to strict portion sizes. Because foods are chosen with a low Glycemic Index, you are allowed to eat generous portions.

On this diet, trans fats and saturated fats are exchanged for foods that contain plenty of unsaturated fats and omega-3 fatty acid. No more fatty portions of red meat.

Regarding carbs, Dr. Agatston advocates replacing quickly digested carbs with those from whole grains and eating more unprocessed foods. The goal is to stabilize blood sugar levels.

There are three distinct phases to the diet:

The Initial Phase (14 days). Almost all carbs are restricted. You can have helpings of meat, fish, shellfish, chicken, and turkey. Plenty of eggs, vegetables, cheese, and nuts, but no bread, rice, potatoes, pastas, fruits, candy, cake, or alcohol. It is highly restrictive, in an effort to break bad habits. The estimate is that you will lose between eight and 13 pounds during this time.

Phase Two. You stay on this phase (hopefully losing between one and two pounds a week) until you reach your weight goal. This is when you will be reintroduced to carbs, but in a very controlled manner.

The Final Phase. You're encouraged to practice balanced dieting for life using the basic principles you have learned. Individuals are eating at a carb level that allows them to maintain their weight, though they are encouraged to go back and forth between phases as needed. An online program has been developed to help you stay on course (www.southbeachdiet.com). Here you can find a weight tracker, online answers from dietitians, an extensive recipe database, and even find a weight loss partner through the "Beach Buddies" feature. You can also sign up for a daily email newsletter.

The main difference between this diet and the Atkins' Diet is in the amount and type of fatty foods recommended. While the Atkins' Diet advocates unlimited amounts of foods high in saturates, such as cheese, butter, and cream, the South Beach Diet recommends a diet that is low in saturates—lean red meat, skinless chicken, and reduced fat cheeses. The South Beach Diet also places far more emphasis on monounsaturates, such as olive oil.

The Atkins' Diet is also stricter in terms of its carbohydrate restriction, which even extends to limiting fruit and vegetables. In contrast, South Beach fruit, vegetables, and other low Glycemic Index carbohydrates are introduced once you enter Phase Two.

Kraft Foods has licensed the South Beach Diet trademark for a line of packaged products available at major grocery store chains.

Comments

It is a cleaner diet than the Atkins' Diet in terms of advocation of more nutritious foods, but many of the same concerns apply.

Similar to all ketogenic diets, the initial phase is mostly water loss rather than fat loss. The South Beach Diet requires a tremendous amount of discipline, especially at the beginning. Also, be ready to spend time preparing your own food.

You: On a Diet by Mehmet Oz, M.D., and Michael Roizen, M.D.

This weight loss approach created quite a buzz, especially after the authors appeared on the *Oprah Winfrey Show*. Mehmet Oz was born to Turkish parents in Cleveland, Ohio, and is professor of Cardiac Surgery at Columbia University. Michael Roizen is an internist with the Cleveland Clinic in Ohio.

How It Works

Instead of counting calories or getting on the scales, you take out a tape measure and find out how many inches are around your waist. Why? Because the authors believe belly size is linked with so many health risks, which has been demonstrated in multiple studies. The ideal is 32 1/2 inches or less for women and 35 inches or less for men. This should increase proportionally for taller individuals.

According to Oz and Roizen, because of its proximity to vital organs, belly fat is the most dangerous fat you can carry, and it is one of the strongest predictors of health risks (heart disease, diabetes, and more bad stuff) associated with obesity.

This is a light-hearted, often humorous book that gives insight on how the body works and the necessity of physical activity.

The diet begins with a two-week crash program that involves cleaning out your refrigerator for a fresh start. Emphasis is on healthy eating—whole foods to break the cycle of craving refined carbs, such as white bread and sugar. You will also discard foods with high fructose corn syrup. There will be three meals plus snacks throughout the day. But your last snack will be at least three hours before bedtime. Every other day you can have a dessert or special treat.

The authors tell you to walk 30 minutes daily, even if you do it in two or three intervals. And they advocate walking with a friend, so

For her role in *The Devil Wears Prada*, Anne Hathaway stuck to a diet of nothing more than fish, vegetables, and fruit. The actress confessed, "Emily Blunt and I would clutch at each other and cry because we were so hungry."

you'll stick with it, plus five minutes of stretching. Then three times a week you will add 20 minutes of strength exercises. This will help build muscle mass to balance the slowdown in metabolism that occurs with excess body fat.

A unique aspect of this diet is that you are to eat the same things for breakfast and lunch almost every day. That's right, every day! This is because the authors believe that people who minimize food choices lose more weight.

You will eat often throughout the day, so you're constantly satisfied. They believe that if you are hungry, your body wants to store more fat. Oz and Roizen advise eating plenty of fiber in the morning to help control afternoon cravings. They ask you not to have anything with more than four grams of saturated fat or four grams of any sugar (especially high fructose corn syrup) per serving saturated.

> He's got so many love handles he needs a bookmark to find his shorts.
>
> CYNTHIA HEIMAL

In addition, you are to aim for seven or eight hours of sleep a night, because when your body is fatigued, the authors say it makes you hunger for sugar-laden foods. The reasoning behind this is that sugars help release the brain chemicals that are deprived with a lack of sleep.

The book suggests eating a little healthy fat, such as a handful of walnuts, about 20 minutes before a meal. This is supposed to take the edge off, so you won't be tempted to overindulge. Roizen says, "Waist is more important than weight."

Details of the diet are at www.realage.com, the RealAge company website.

Comments

This diet does a great job at explaining the body and why people are overweight but is pretty basic in its dietary approach. There are a lot of sound dietary concepts within this diet, and it is a fun read to help people understand the body.

The Weight Loss Cure by Kevin Trudeau

The reason I have included this diet is not because of its effectiveness, but due to the fact that it has been highly publicized and attempted by a large number of people. The book made the *New York Times* bestseller list.

Kevin Trudeau says he tried every diet out there, but claims to have lost more than 50 pounds because of what he learned from his research. The full name of the book is *The Weight Loss Cure "They" Don't Want You to Know About*. Trudeau is not a doctor, but quite a salesman. His record of overhyping products on television, however, has previously landed him in a heap of trouble.

How It Works

This book is based on what the author says he learned from studying the work of a British physician named Dr. A.T.W. Simeons from the late 1950s, who saw obese people lose significant weight by using something called hCG, which he claimed broke up stored fat. He tells you that Simeons' findings have been suppressed by the medical establishment and food manufacturers who would go broke if everyone were thin.

It is a six-week program of 500 calories a day. You may say, "Wow. That's not enough!" But Trudeau counters that the calories from the stored fat will nourish the person during this period.

What is hCG? The letters stand for human chorionic gonadotrophin—a hormone extracted from purified urine produced by pregnant women. Clinical trials published in *The Journal of the American Medical Association* and *American Journal of Clinical Nutrition* have shown that hCG is ineffective as a weight loss aid.

Trudeau says that obesity is a disorder caused by a malfunctioning hypothalamus in the brain. He blames being fat on a variety of causes, including artificial sweeteners, man-made sugars, bovine growth hormones, antibiotics in meat, trans fats, food additives, lack of sunshine, pasteurization, homogenizing, having too much yeast in your system, and more. And who would argue against that?

During the *initial 30-day phase* of the diet, you can eat all the organic food you want, as long as you do it six times a day. You're supposed to drink a half gallon of water a day, green tea or chamomile tea, plus supplements to cleanse your system and provide calcium. Actually, you will be taking nine different pills daily. In addition, you are to go to a doctor for a colon cleansing every other day, plus liver cleansing and a heavy metal cleansing.

Requirements include walking one hour a day and having a daily sauna. The book promises that you will lose 30 pounds during these 30 days.

The *second phase* lasts for 45 days and in addition to a highly restricted food intake includes a daily injection of hCG—preferably by a doctor, but you can order it online and inject it yourself.

Phase three brings you back to regular eating, but no fast foods or artificial sweeteners. However, if you have gained more than a couple of pounds, the author recommends that you fast until about 6:00 p.m. Then you can have a big steak!

Thankfully, there are no more injections.

> **A fool and his money are soon parted.**
>
> JAMES HOWELL

Comments

I have been asked by various practitioners to review this diet because they are so frustrated with so many diet options and people not losing weight. I even know people who have successfully lost weight on this program. The Simeons' protocol was well studied in the mid 1970s, and experts agree there is no scientific evidence for the hCG claims in this book, and my review came to the same conclusion. The truth is that the author Gary Trudeau is a very controversial individual, and pundits are very quick to criticize anything he does. So in fairness to this diet, it incorporates a lot of valid dietary principles with the addition of the hCG. It is a rather strict program, and it seems clear that people could lose weight on it by following the advice and not even taking the hCG.

You can say a lot of things about a pregnant women—vibrant, beautiful, etc.—but thin is not one of them. Let's face it, hCG for dieting does not pass the commonsense test.

The Zone by Dr. Barry Sears

After his father died of a massive heart attack at age 53, Barry Sears became more than interested in understanding heart disease. In the next few years his father's three brothers all succumbed to heart failure. This spurred Sears to search for a way to fight heart disease.

With a doctorate in biochemistry from Indiana University, his research led through many doors, and finally to a class of hormones called "eicosanoids"—a family of powerful, hormone-like compounds produced in the body from essential fatty acids. They control several systems within the body, including the cardiovascular system. He came to the conclusion that the best way to regulate eicosanoids was through carefully selecting the foods we eat. This evolved into the Zone diet.

How It Works

The name, the Zone, comes from the objective of getting you in a state where the hormones given by the food you eat are not too low or too high—but in the Zone. The ratio is 40 percent carbs, 30 percent fat, and 30 percent protein.

Nothing is totally forbidden. Instead, you limit the kind of foods you eat and balance them with three or four ounces of low fat protein every time you have a meal. The concept is to keep insulin and glucagon levels balanced. By eating a smaller number of calories, your hunger is kept under control.

According to Sears, a portion of low fat protein should be about the size and thickness of the palm of your hand—about three ounces for women and four ounces for men. He preaches that you receive more energy from carbs than from proteins or fats. Each meal is not to exceed 500 calories, and snacks must not surpass 100 calories.

The author says the major benefit is to increase blood flow. This helps eliminate disease and improve your performance and physical well-being. The diet professes to enhance mental clarity, improve energy, and is recommended by many for individuals with type 2 diabetes.

In theory, the human body cannot store fat and burn it at the same time. So if we use stored fat for energy, it causes weight loss.

He seems convinced that a low fat diet increases the production of insulin, causing the body to store more fat. He gives the example of cattle being fed low fat grain to fatten them—and the total amount of calories is rather large. We have been on diets full of low fat grain (but in the form of pasta and breads) and gain weight.

The Zone is a low carb, high protein diet, but not as restrictive as some. Celebrities who have lauded the plan include Tiger Woods, Jennifer Aniston, Cindy Crawford, and Renée Zellweger.

You can check it out at www.zonedietinfo.com.

Comments

To summarize, Sears believes fat consumption is essential for burning fat. It is important to note that no studies demonstrate the type of heart-related claims Sears makes, and some debate if these claims have been exaggerated.

> Vegetables are interesting but lack a sense of purpose when unaccompanied by a good cut of meat.
>
> Fran Lebowitz

This diet is based on many sound dietary principles. Basically, restricting calories and eating about the same amounts of protein, carbohydrates, and fats makes sense if you know which types of proteins, carbs, and fats are good for you versus bad. Also, I am not a fan of snacking between meals as you will read later. My biggest issue is with the processed foods they manufacture and sell, using questionable and even unhealthy ingredients.

Eat More, Weigh Less by Dean Ornish, M.D.

This is known to many as simply "The Ornish Diet." The author is the founder and president of the nonprofit Preventive Medicine Research Institute in Sausalito, California, and is clinical professor of medicine at the University of California, San Francisco. Ornish is well respected in medical circles because of his success in reversing heart blockages without drugs or surgery.

How It Works

The premise is that a diet that is high in fiber, low in fat, and vegetarian will both help you stay healthy and lose weight. It consists of 10 percent fat, 20 percent protein, and 70 percent carbs. He believes it's not just eating fewer calories but wisely choosing the ones we do consume. Ornish claims that eating as much as you want and as often as you are hungry keeps your metabolism the same or increases it. But the high fiber content slows down the absorption of food into the digestive system, thus you feel fuller longer.

You are to avoid meats, fish, and fowl. While Ornish understands that some people will not become total vegetarians, those who don't should consume as little in this category as possible.

Here's what you can have an abundance of whenever you want: beans, legumes, fruits, grains, and vegetables. You can also eat complex carbs, such as fruits and grains.

The following are to be consumed only in moderation: egg whites and nonfat dairy products, including nonfat sour cream, nonfat cheeses, nonfat yogurt, and skim milk.

You are to stay away from oils (and the products that contain them). No olives, seeds, nuts, sugar, alcohol, or anything that contains more than two grams of fat per serving. His goal is for you to take in less than 10 percent of your calories from fat.

This is one of the diets where you eat several little meals each day so you don't get hungry.

Comments

Dr. Ornish has apparently had a lot of success reversing heart disease with his diet, and people lose weight on this vegetarian diet. I like the vegetarian aspect of this diet, but I find it to be generally out of balance, being far too carb-centric, lacking in healthy fats, far too low in protein, and not focused on nutrient density or supplementation.

Some consider this diet to be very rigid. It doesn't allow a lot of food choices for those used to the Western diet; hence, not many people stay on it for the long term.

Dr. Ornish's diet is very low in fat and limits meat and animal product intake to little or none. Many important vitamins and minerals such as zinc and vitamin B12 are acquired from these sources in a normal diet. Without these sources and no recommended supplementation, there is a significant possibility of any number of nutritional deficiencies.

Some criticism in the medical field arises from the fact that the Eat More, Weigh Less system doesn't distinguish between good and bad fats in food. Polyunsaturated and monounsaturated oils actually protect against cardiovascular incidents. Bad fats, such as trans fats, come from margarine, cookies, crackers, and animal fats. The success of this diet with all its deficiencies shows how poor the Western diet has become.

Bible-Based Diets

In recent years there have been several popular weight loss books based on what is found in Scripture. There are specific references to foods mentioned in passages from Genesis to the New Testament. Here are four that have been widely acclaimed:

What Would Jesus Eat?

by Don Colbert, M.D.

As a family physician in Orlando, Florida, Don Colbert believes that faith and prayer are vital parts of the healing process. After people began wearing bracelets with the letters WWJD (What Would Jesus Do), he became curious on another theme: *What Would Jesus Eat?* It resulted in a bestselling book that has impacted the eating habits of millions. Colbert has been featured in *Reader's Digest, Prevention, Newsweek*, and many more publications.

Julianne Moore maintains her slender physique with a super strict diet. The actress has said: "I still battle with my deeply boring diet of, essentially, yogurt, breakfast cereal, and granola bars. I hate dieting. I hate having to do it to be the 'right' size. All actresses are hungry all the time, I think."

How It Works

In many respects, Jesus ate the Mediterranean diet. An example given is that after the resurrection, the disciples thought perhaps they were seeing a ghost, but Jesus asked them, "But while they still did not believe for joy, and marveled, He said to them, 'Have you any food here?' So they gave Him a piece of a broiled fish and some honeycomb. And He took it and ate in their presence" (Luke 24:41–43).

Bread and wine were served at the Lord's Supper (Mark 14:22–25),

Jesus provided wine at the wedding at Cana (John 2:1–10), and He fed the multitudes with bread and fish (John 6:1–14). Colbert documents that Jesus ate fish, olive oil, vegetables, fruits, whole grain bread, and drank plenty of water. He also points out that since Jesus was a Jew, it was natural for Him to follow Old Testament dietary laws.

> **Give us this day our daily bread, but, please, none of the white processed kind.**

As in some other Bible-based diets, this means eating cattle, sheep, and goats, but not pigs. Fish with fins and scales were acceptable, but not hard-shelled seafood.

In New Testament times, fish was easily available, but beef was only eaten on special occasions. For example, at the return of the Prodigal Son, they had a celebration and "killed the fatted calf for him" (Luke 15:30).

Here is Dr. Colbert's message: Since Jesus taught by example, we should follow His eating habits today. This means drinking water instead of sugar or caffeine-laden colas and using olive oil rather than vegetable oil.

You can learn more about this diet at www.drcolbert.com.

Comments

Dr. Colbert is a prolific health author and personal friend. Some theologians contend that the dietary code of the Old Testament was repealed by the coming of Christ and that all foods have been purified because we are no longer under the law but under grace. But God was very specific about which animals are clean foods and which are not, so to ignore this wisdom does not seem prudent. If you look around, you'll note that the general health of today's population seems to indicate that the dietary free-for-all is not working.

The Hallelujah Diet by George Malkmus

At the age of 42, George Malkmus was diagnosed with colon cancer and suffered with a large tumor and several other problems from hemorrhoids to high blood pressure. He was advised by a minister friend to try the diet God gave man in Genesis 1:29. Speaking to Adam in the garden, the Creator said, "See, I have given you every herb that yields seed which is on the face of all the earth, and every tree whose fruit yields seed; to you it shall be for food." This is the essence of a vegetarian diet, and Malkmus embraced it fully. As a result, he claims that in less than one year his baseball-size tumor disappeared.

Today, he and his wife, Rhonda, operate Hallelujah Acres near Shelby, North Carolina. At the center they hold health seminars and sell their products. The diet is promoted as "God's way to optimum health" and claims to have helped people with more than 100 health problems.

How It Works

This is a low calorie vegetarian diet with 85 percent raw organic foods and 15 percent cooked foods. Juicing plants and vegetables is a major emphasis. Beside juices, you will add three servings daily of "Barleymax," other supplements, and one meal of cooked grains and vegetables. That's about it.

The list of prohibited foods is long: no caffeine, coffee, soft drinks, animal products, dairy, white or brown sugar, refined flour. Not even salt or pepper. No canned or sweetened fruits, no breakfast cereal, margarine, shortening, candy, cakes, pies, or vegetables fried in oil.

The theory is that by eating a "living" food diet you will stay away from "addictive" foods mentioned above.

Like many health programs, you are to exercise at least 30 minutes a day, plus get a good dose of sunshine.

The program asks you to use a variety of supplements they sell on their website (www.hallelujahacres.com), such as digestive enzymes and B12 oils.

It is claimed that more than one million people have tried this alternative way of eating.

Comments

Strict vegetarian diets can be very healthy but require a lot of education to follow properly (for more details, see "The Dynamic Role of Proteins in Weight Loss" chapter). This diet has many excellent qualities, such as living foods, supplementation, and avoidance of numerous hazardous foods. But there is far too little emphasis on protein intake. This is the Genesis 1:29 diet without Leviticus 11.

Many health practitioners have placed a "caution" sign on this diet, suggesting users might have nutritional deficiencies because the food and supplement choices are so limited. Critics say it lacks scientific proof and the diet is not in accord with what we know is necessary for human health. It is definitely not recommended for children.

There is a question whether you will get enough calories to satisfy your hunger and adequate levels of protein and other nutrients. Plus, it can be difficult to stay on for any length of time. These are all basically the same criticisms cited by experts regarding vegan diets.

> This was the dawn of plastic eating in America.... We doted on Velveeta. Spam. Canned ravioli. Instant puddings. Instant everything. The further a thing was from texture, flavor, and terrifying unpredictability of real food, the better.
>
> SHIRLEY ABBOTT

Body-for-Life by Bill Phillips

The author comes from a bodybuilding background. In fact, the subtitle of his book is "12 Weeks to Mental and Physical Strength."

Born in Colorado, he moved west and once worked at Gold's Gym in Venice, California (known as the Mecca of bodybuilding). Later he returned to Colorado and began his writing and publishing career. He became involved in promoting products such as METRx and Myoplex, bodybuilding supplements, and being a consultant to celebrities from John Elway to Sylvester Stallone.

His later books include *Eating for Life and Transformation* and *Now and for LIFE*. Today he heads a performance nutritional supplement company.

How It Works

Body-for-Life is a 12-week program of diet and exercise. Phillips holds that a valid program should include weight training to build muscle and increase metabolism. The diet part is easy; exercising is more difficult.

Let's start with the food. On this program you eat every two to three hours, paying attention to the quality of carbs rather than the quantity. The focus is on portion size rather than calorie counting. It is heavy on vegetables, brown rice, fish, and poultry. To make it easy, he recommends a "fist size" portion of protein, same size for carbs. Add at least two portions of vegetables plus supplements and one or two tablespoons of healthy oil.

The diet is 40 to 50 percent protein, the same for carbs, and a small amount of fat. The idea is to graze, not gorge. But you are allowed to cheat one day a week and eat one of your favorite foods. Instead of six or eight glasses of water each day, Phillips recommends 10.

Now comes the hard part. You exercise six days a week, alternating between aerobic (20 minutes, three days a week) and weight training (45 minutes, three days a week). Aerobics can be walking, running, using a treadmill, swimming, or a rowing machine. As you progress, you are to steadily increase intensity. He says that aerobic exercise is more effective when done early before breakfast.

Regarding the use of weights, the author suggests you go back and forth between upper and lower body exercises. This gives the muscles time to recover. Also he says to take one minute rests between sets for a muscle group. He contends that the exercise causes you to burn calories even when you are sleeping.

He also suggests stress-management techniques from meditation to massage. He calls it "food for the soul," so you won't be urged to overeat.

Many doctors recommend this plan, since it is firmly rooted in science. It is said to cut the risk of cancer and help manage hypertension and diabetes. Some followers claim total cures. Thousands have been motivated by this program.

Comments

No doubt this diet can be effective if you follow it closely, but it may require too much exercise for most people. It requires much self-discipline. Because of the great amount of exercise, you would likely lose weight with normal eating.

Since this diet is rigid with limited food choices, it can be difficult to stay on. The problem for many is that it is tough to totally learn new eating habits. Also, by restricting fish (unless you supplement with fish oil), you may be deprived of essential fatty acids, such as omega-3.

The Maker's Diet by Jordan S. Rubin

The idea behind this diet is that if the Jews are God's chosen people, we should pay close attention to the diet they were instructed to follow. The Almighty told them, "If you diligently heed the voice of the LORD your God and do what is right in His sight, give ear to His commandments and keep all His statutes, I will put none of the diseases on you which I have brought on the Egyptians. For I am the LORD who heals you" (Exodus 15:26).

> When you eat the labor of your hands, you shall be happy, and it shall be well with you.
>
> PSALM 128:2

The scriptures from Leviticus 11 are not only the basis for this way of eating, but are used for Kosher food laws of the Jewish people. Remember, in Bible times, Jews lived longer than their neighbors, so this diet is an update of basic Jewish Kosher laws.

How It Works

Rubin's criteria for what we should eat is founded on his belief that since food was placed on this earth by God, it should be eaten in the form He created it. He teaches that since the Bible did not have processed foods, neither should we. Rather, our bodies were designed to eat whole foods in their natural state. This means brown rice instead of white and meat from animals that eat grass instead of those fed on man-made "feed."

Here are a few of the Maker-approved foods from plants he recommends:

- Grains: corn, milled oats, wheat, rye, rice, barley
- Seeds: flax, pumpkin, sunflower, sesame
- Legumes: lentils, peanuts, peas, soybeans, and other beans
- Foods that contain seeds: cucumbers, okra, tomatoes, squash, melons, eggplant, bell peppers
- Nuts: walnuts, cashew nuts, Brazil nuts, pecans
- Fruits: citrus fruits such as lemons and limes, palm fruits, sweet fruits
- Vegetables: artichoke, collard greens, Brussels sprouts, beet greens, broccoli, cauliflower, carrots, beets, potatoes, turnips

Approved foods from animals include:

• Livestock: goat, elk, moose, buffalo, lamb, deer, cow
• Fowl: chicken, turkey, pheasant, quail, grouse
• Fish: trout, sunfish, salmon, pike, perch, bluefish, bass

On the forbidden list are bacon, pork, sausage, ham, and imitation meat. No crab, oysters, lobsters, shrimp, or shellfish (because they don't have scales or fins as required in Leviticus 11:9). In addition, you are to avoid food that has been treated with pesticides or hormones. No partially hydrogenated oil, alcohol, sodas, or starchy foods.

There are three phases of the Maker's Diet to be implemented during a 40-day period. One day a week in each phase there is to be a partial fast. Supplements on these days may be taken, but fluids can include pure water and raw vegetable juices. You are to begin and end each day with prayers of thanksgiving, healing, and petition. One rule is to be in bed by 10:30 each night.

Phase one: During the first two weeks you will be highly restricted regarding foods that many are addicted to: those with sugars, caffeine, preservatives, and those high in carbohydrates. Good-bye junk food! But you can have plenty of protein, healthy oils, and vegetables. This will have a detoxifying effect.

Phase two: Now you'll have far more food options with a goal of helping you establish healthy eating habits that will hopefully last for a lifetime.

Phase three: From day 29 to 40 you will be able to eat some of the foods that were previously eliminated. There is a greater variety of dairy, fruits, certain starches, red meat, and a few saturated fats. Hopefully, your weight should be stabilized. If not, you are to go back to an earlier phase.

Comments

This diet is similar to Dr. Colbert's *What Would Jesus Eat.* Some critics try to debunk the biblical foundations of these diets, but science and millions testify that when faith and belief are added to a weight loss program, the health benefits multiply.

Chapter 5

A Basic Guide to Understanding Diets

A Short History of Medicine

2000 B.C.—"Here, eat this root."

1000 B.C.—"That root is heathen; say this prayer."

A.D. 1850—"That prayer is superstition; drink this potion."

A.D. 1940—"That potion is snake oil; swallow this pill."

A.D. 1985—"That pill is ineffective; take this antibiotic."

A.D. 2000—"That antibiotic is artificial; here, eat this root."

AUTHOR UNKNOWN

Many of us begin a steady march into being overweight during our late twenties. By the time we reach our late twenties, although we're usually not aware of it, we begin to lose muscle mass unless we work hard to retain it. Between the ages of 26 and 28 that loss of muscle mass can represent from three to 10 percent of lean tissue. It's a subtle and unhealthy replacement that's taking place—body fat for muscle mass. If you are athletic, you may not notice that your slim days are behind you for 10 or 12 more years. However, by age 39 the vast majority of us are forced to face the fact that we are overweight.

At that point, many of us begin to experiment with diets and at least tell ourselves we have to get up off the couch and do some sort of exercise. But with so many diets floating around, it's hard to figure out where to start, and there's usually a fair amount of confusion surrounding what approach to take.

Here's a situation you may have experienced and not been able to understand. One of your friends has been on a high protein, low carbohydrate diet for several months and is thrilled to have shed unwanted pounds and dropped several dress sizes. She can't say enough good things about how she's feeling and looking. Meanwhile, another friend decided to go on a high carbohydrate, low fat vegetarian diet, is ecstatic to have lost just as much weight as your other friend, and says she's never had more energy or felt better. How do you explain that such completely opposite approaches to dieting can and often do work equally well…at least as far as initial weight loss?

While I have strong opinions as to how different diet approaches are healthier than others, it has long been my belief that people could lose weight on almost any of the myriad of diets on the market, at least for a while. Having watched hundreds of people experiment with every type of diet imaginable, it seemed to me that when it comes to simple weight loss, common sense tells us that it's not about the nutrients being offered by a diet plan—it's primarily about the fact that on virtually any diet program there is a structure that ultimately limits caloric consumption. When people go from a structureless standard American diet to any structure, they at least get some short-term benefit, particularly if they really believe they will benefit, which involves the placebo effect.

A large piece of the puzzle is the number of calories being consumed versus the amount being burned. Nothing changes the fact that if both your friends are burning more calories every day than they are taking in, they will generally, but not always, lose weight. That's the bottom line, regardless of whether the calories come from protein or fat or carbohydrates. This does not mean that eating less of the wrong calories will maintain weight loss, but studies do confirm that if you eat less of the bad foods you generally eat, you will lose weight. If it were truly that simple, everyone would be able to successfully lose weight and keep it off and be healthy in the process.

Through the years, though, I have not been a stranger to the intense debate about what types of diet are most effective for losing weight. Every day you can find an article somewhere that tells you that a certain diet plan works because it eliminates sugars and refined carbohydrates, while another article stacks up a substantial pile of evidence that points to reduced carbohydrates and increased proteins as the success of a completely different diet. Are they both correct? Neither correct? Does science back them up?

I have read several clinical studies that showed that low carbohydrate, high protein diets resulted in more weight loss during the course of three to six months than conventional high carbohydrate, low fat diets.[5] But I've also read almost as many other research studies that did not concur with these results.[6] A smaller group of studies that extended the follow-up to one year did not show that low carbohydrate, high protein diets were superior to high carbohydrate, low fat diets.[7] In contrast, other researchers found that a very high carbohydrate, very low fat vegetarian diet was superior to a conventional high carbohydrate, low fat diet.[8] I have not found as many studies that extended beyond one year, but the conclusions seem to be all over the map—from one that showed that a low carbohydrate diet was superior to a low fat diet to another that showed no difference between high protein and low protein diets to two studies that showed that a moderate fat, Mediterranean-style diet was superior to a low fat diet.[9]

> Forget about calories—everything makes thin people thinner, and fat people fatter.
>
> MIGNON McLAUGHLIN

Does the Type of Diet Matter?

In the February 26, 2009, edition of *The New England Journal of Medicine*, an article entitled, "Comparison of Weight Loss Diets with Different Compositions of Fat, Protein, and Carbohydrates," details a fascinating two-year study that seems to confirm what I have long believed.[10] Researchers randomly assigned 811 overweight adults to one of four diets. The nutrient goals for the four diet groups were:

• low fat, average protein—20 percent fat, 15 percent protein, and 65 percent carbohydrates

- low fat, high protein—20 percent fat, 25 percent protein, and 55 percent carbohydrates
- high fat, average protein—40 percent fat, 15 percent protein, and 45 percent carbohydrates
- high fat, high protein—40 percent fat, 25 percent protein, and 35 percent carbohydrates.

Two of the diets were low fat and two were high fat, and two were average protein and two were high protein. The primary outcome of the study was the weight loss over a period of two years, and the secondary outcome was the change in waist circumference. Data pooled from the diets were to compare low fat versus high fat and average protein versus high protein. The analysis also included a comparison of two of the four diets, the diet with the lowest carbohydrate content and the diet with the highest carbohydrate content, and included a test for trend across the four levels of carbohydrates. The effects of protein, fat, and carbohydrate levels were evaluated independently.

The amount of weight loss after two years was similar in the participants assigned to a diet with 25 percent protein and those assigned to a diet with 15 percent protein (7.93 and 6.6 pounds, respectively) and among those who completed each of those diets (9.92 and 7.94 pounds, respectively). Weight loss was the same in those assigned to a diet with 40 percent fat and those assigned to a diet with 20 percent fat (7.27 pounds) and was similar among those who completed each of those diets (8.6 and 9.04 pounds, respectively). There was no effect on weight loss of carbohydrate level through the target range of 35 to 65 percent. The change in waist circumference did not differ significantly among the diet groups.

The study concluded that diets that are successful in causing weight loss can emphasize a range of fat, protein, and carbohydrate compositions that have beneficial effects on risk factors for cardiovascular disease and diabetes. Such diets can also be tailored to individual patients on the basis of their personal and cultural preferences and may therefore have the best chance for long-term success.

In November 2010, I came across this extreme example of this similar dieting principle. Kansas State University Professor of Human Nutrition Mark Haub lost 27 pounds during a period of two months while on what he called the Twinkie Diet. He ate one Twinkie every three hours instead of meals, supplementing his diet with other junk food (approximately two-thirds of his daily eating regimen) and vegetables, multivitamins, and protein shakes. He exercised while he was on the diet and carefully monitored his caloric intake, dropping from his normal intake of 2,600 calories to under 1,800 calories per day.

> My doctor told me to stop having intimate dinners for four…unless there are three other people.
>
> ORSON WELLES

No one should be surprised with Professor Haub's results. There have been hundreds of calorie restriction studies in virtually every species you can name that conclusively demonstrate that eating less calories of even unhealthy foods can yield dramatic results. Any thinking person knows the Twinkie "dead food" diet is unsustainable and would eventually lead to significant health consequences. Also, if I didn't think it would kill him, I would challenge Professor Haub to try that diet again without the protein shakes, multivitamins, and vegetables.

There are a lot of ways to "lose weight," but most are not sustainable and just do not result in a healthier you! The bottom line is that these demonstrate that weight loss should not be the goal, but Super Health should be the goal. You really are what you eat.

Don't Believe the Spin Masters

So while one diet marketer will spin their diet plan one way, and another marketer will spin their success rate another way, don't get caught up in the spin or the before-and-after photos. For instance, if you follow the Atkins' Diet and consume between 1,200 and 1,800 calories a day, or if you prepare the Sugar Busters menus and consume about 1,200 calories a day, you will lose weight, provided your body is burning more calories than those rates.

A major concern is that often the weight that is being lost is not necessarily fat. The scale may be going down, and the smiles might be going up, but those increments may only represent water and muscle that's being shed along with some fat. While this is most often true of crash diets, it is a part of many popular diets as well. Without the establishment of a balance of the proper nutrition and exercise, a diet can be far more detrimental in the long term than any temporary celebration through a change in wardrobes.

> Probably nothing in the world arouses more false hopes than the first four hours of a diet.
>
> DAN BENNETT

My question to you is: If it is a fact that you can have success losing weight on almost any diet, why choose one diet over another? And if it is also a fact that most people regain their lost weight and then some, what is the point of dieting in the first place? Why spend your hard-earned dollars on weight loss only to end up worse than you started, then to move on and try another type of diet and start all over again? This is what I call the never-ending, ever-profitable diet merry-go-round or, worse yet, the diet roller coaster.

The answer is to *strive for a higher state of health, wellness, and performance, where optimal weight will take care of itself. This level is called "Super Health."*

How to Recognize a Fad Diet

While there is no absolute definition of a fad diet, I do not mean to imply that "fad" means a popular diet that may or may not fall out of favor in a relatively short period of time. Fad diets come in all shapes and sizes of quick-fix, short-term plans—that's the key for me. The American Heart Association website offers an excellent list of characteristics of fad diets that you will find extremely beneficial.

Here are some red flags that immediately stand out to me as dietary concerns when I hear them:

Diets that promise a quick fix, even though they often defy simple logic and basic biochemistry.

Unusual quantities of only one food group or type of food without covering the spectrum of the body's nutritional requirements, such as eating only tomatoes or beef one day or unusual amounts of cabbage soup or grapefruit. To focus on one food or type of food violates the first principle of good nutrition: Eat a balanced diet that includes a variety of foods. These foods are fine as part of an overall balanced diet, but to eat large quantities of them could lead to unpleasant side effects, such as intestinal gas, bloating, flatulence, and bad breath. When someone stays on this type of diet for a prolonged period of time, he or she may develop nutritional deficiencies that could have a serious impact on their health, because no one type of food has all the nutrients required for good health.

Inflexible, limited menus. Many of these diets set out a very limited selection of foods to be eaten at specific times. Frequently, these limited diets don't address the widely varied taste preferences of our diverse American population.

Specific food combinations. Although some foods taste good together, there is no scientific evidence that eating foods in certain sequences or combinations has any scientific or medical benefit.

Rapid weight loss promises of more than two pounds a week is potentially harmful without sufficient protein, amino acids, and other nutrients to sustain the body and help prevent muscle loss. In order to safely lose more than a couple of pounds per week, the diet must address every nutritional requirement of the body, including adequate protein levels. Claims regarding fast weight loss without properly addressing the body's nutritional requirements appeal to the emotions, because they promise results with little or no effort. However, research has continually proven that these types of nutrient deprived, low calorie, and low protein diets are ineffective at best and, at worst, can actually be detrimental to the health of those who try them.

The diet's explanation as to why it works is overly simplified or beyond quantifying. Promoters may say the complete explanation is too complex for you to understand. Remember, if it sounds too good to be true, it probably is.

No warning for people with either diabetes or high blood pressure to seek advice from the physician or health care provider. Some fad diets can raise blood pressure or blood glucose, even while you are losing weight.

Little or no emphasis of increased physical activity. Simple physical activities, such as resistance exercise, walking, swimming, and high intensity interval training are some of the most important tools to losing and maintaining weight loss. Yet many fad diets never even mention these easy changes. Any increase in physical activity will help you optimize your metabolism.

A Guide to Evaluating Diets

In nutrition circles, diets to promote weight loss are generally divided into four categories: low fat, low carbohydrate, low calorie, and very low calorie. However, Leslie J. Bonci, M.P.H., R.D., L.D.N., sports nutritionist, and the author of *The ADA Guide for Better Digestion*, points out that most diets can be easily categorized into four groups that I think you'll find easier to remember as you evaluate diets in the future. In a previous chapter, I may have made specific comments regarding certain of these diets. My purpose here is simply to help you categorize any diet rather than study them in detail.

Gimmicks or Fad Diets

While the list is lengthy and the promotional material will vary greatly, perhaps the big hitters are the Grapefruit Diet, the Beverly Hills Diet, the Cabbage Soup Diet, and the 5-Day Miracle Diet. What these tend to have in common is the claim that the fat will fall off your body quickly because of the "fat-burning" potential of certain foods in the diet. While the rapid weight loss will be in bold type with exclamation marks, what you probably won't read is that the diet reduces your calorie intake so drastically that it may be unsafe for numerous reasons. Without question, the quick weight loss may be spectacular, but it will consist mainly of water and lean body tissue, so expect an instant weight rebound when you stop the diet that actually packs on additional fat and renders any hope of maintaining the weight loss unachievable. Any weight loss diet that does not address protein and amino acids requirements to preserve muscle will not work in the long term.

Food Combination Diets

Food combining diets focus on stimulating your metabolism to burn fat quickly through eliminating certain foods from your diet while combining others. The theory is that if you burn fat rapidly, you will naturally lose weight. On food combining diets, you are restricted to eating specific foods at certain times, and you must not mix certain foods (for instance, waiting four hours between eating carbohydrates and proteins). Diets such as Fit-for-Life, Suzanne Somers' Get Skinny, The Zone, Sugar Busters, and Eat Right for Your Blood Type are popular among this category.

However, other than protein and certain amino acids, there is no scientific evidence that the food of these food combining diets facilitates substantial fat burning within the body. Always beware of any diet that simply has no scientific research or rationale to support it.

High Protein/Fat, Low Carbohydrate Diets

There is a wide spectrum of low carbohydrate, high protein diets, ranging from the Atkins', South Beach, Protein Power, and Carbohydrate Addict's diets to the general eating pattern recommended for diabetics, who need to be especially careful about foods that affect their blood sugar (primarily carbohydrates), as should everyone. Atkins' and South Beach diets combine ketogenic diets (when the body's sugar stores are depleted and the body makes sugars from amino acids) and low glycemic diets (eating foods that raise the blood sugar more slowly). These diets have been widely promoted in recent years as an effective approach to losing weight. Based upon the notion that most of us are heavy carbohydrate consumers, and carbohydrates (especially refined carbohydrates such as white bread, white rice, white pasta, most crackers, tonics, sweets, jams, and jellies) make us fat, these diets severely restrict refined carbohydrates while putting a major emphasis on foods with high protein and high saturated fat. These diets generally recommend dieters receive 30 to 50 percent of their total calories from protein.

An obvious downside to this type of diet is that in eliminating all or most carbohydrates, you do so at the expense of the nutrient dense "healthier" carbs that are found in fruits and vegetables. People lose remarkable amounts of weight in the first week on ketogenic diets (five to 10 pounds). However, this portion of the weight loss will return within days of the reintroduction of carbohydrates.

While these diets represent varying degrees toward being balanced, the lack of important vitamins and minerals and fiber found in carbohydrates has the potential for long-term health problems. The biggest problem is that these systems tend to allow overconsumption of potentially unhealthy foods, such as factory farmed meats and even fried foods. There are also concerns about digestive congestion and toxicity from continuous back-to-back meat meals and whether the diets promote heart disease (high animal fat is thought to damage arteries), stroke, cancer, and unhealthy metabolic state. People with kidney or liver problems have the potential for troubles with these diets, because high animal protein is thought to cause the organs to work hard to remove the waste products of protein metabolism.

High Carbohydrate, Low Fat Diets

Based upon the premise that calories from fat cause one to become fat, diets such as the Pritikin diet, Dr. Dean Ornish's Eat More, Weigh Less diet, and the F-Plan drop down the fat intake (10 to 15 percent of the total calories) and up the consumption of foods with high fiber, vitamins, and minerals—grains, fruits, and vegetables. While these diets tend to be more highly endorsed as healthy by doctors and nutritionists for their low fat content, the vegetarian slant make these diets less appealing to those reared on a Western diet, and many people don't stick with them. If you go this direction with your diet, don't forget that dietary fat (good fat) is also essential for the transportation of vitamins as well as the simple pleasure of eating. The reality is that most people aren't fat because they eat fat, and healthy fats are essential for numerous functions in the body.

> I have gained and lost the same 10 pounds so many times over and over again my cellulite must have déjà vu.
>
> JANE WAGNER

Body Type, Blood Type, Metabolic Type

There are several dietary approaches that attempt to put people into a small handful of categories—body type, blood type, metabolic type, for example. These diets often point out meaningful correlations that certain types of people sometimes have to certain foods. Unfortunately, it's just not that simple, and these correlations do not apply to all people within a "type." People are far too individualized to fit into these categories and generally have attributes from multiple of these categories, and even those tend to change over time. We are fearfully and wonderfully made, and each of us is a clinical study of one. I have several colleagues who are advocates of some of these diets, including body type diets, blood type diets, and metabolic type diets. Some of these systems may well be beneficial in certain health situations at least for a time, and learning about these different "types" can be helpful, at least in getting started.

For instance, it can be helpful to learn about your body type or *somatotype*. There are three basic body types, and many fitness instructors, doctors, nutritionists, and other health professionals use these types to custom design weight loss and fitness programs for individuals. Knowing your body type can help you understand your body better, so you work with it realistically rather than expecting it to respond in ways it will never be able to achieve. Different body types vary in the degree and rate at which they gain or lose weight, and you may need to adjust your fitness routine and diet according to your body type in order to achieve your weight loss goals and get the best results.

Your body type is a genetically predetermined combination of bone structure, bone density, and musculature. Neither exercise nor diet will lengthen or shorten your arms or legs, change the bone structure of your hips or shoulders, or change your body's natural tendency to put on or take off weight. You probably do not have the long limbs of a model or the natural physique of certain athletes—most of us don't, so you're in good company—so accept the body you have been given by God. However, that doesn't mean you were destined to be overweight. As long as you make the effort it takes to eat properly and exercise regularly, you can work with your body to make it the best it can be (even if you have a friend who is able to get away with looking good with much less effort).

As a body type, *endomorphs* in general are described as having a soft, curvy, and round physique. They often have a larger body frame with hips that are wider than their shoulders, creating a pear-shaped physique. Small shoulders, short arms and legs, a high waist, and large hips accentuate the look. The tendency of an endomorph is to have a slow metabolism, gain weight easily, and have to work hard to lose body fat.

I tend to think of *mesomorphs* as having the "genetically blessed" body type. They are the natural born athletes we tend to idolize with their muscular, compact, and lean bodies that respond quickly to exercise. Typically, their shoulders are wider than their hips, and women tend to have an hourglass figure. Their body fat is evenly distributed over their frame, and we generally describe them as being of "medium" build.

Ectomorphs have a willowy, delicately built body type—slim boned, long limbed, lightly muscled, lithe, with very little body fat. Their shape fills the pages of fashion magazines. With their small joints, small shoulders, chest, and buttocks, they appear fragile. They tend to have accelerated metabolisms and find it difficult to gain weight or add muscle, although that may change as they age.

Most of us have qualities of at least two body types. For example, some of us have the slender upper body of an ectomorph and the heavyset lower body of an endomorph, resulting in a pear shape. Experts tend to label people as a combination of body types, such as ecto-mesomorphs or endo-mesomorphs, where they're mainly mesomorphic but have qualities of the ectomorph (e.g., small joints or a trim waist) or the endomorph (e.g., a tendency to gain fat easily). By the way, height has little to do with body type, despite the fact that we tend to think of skinny people (ectomorphs) as tall and heavyset people (endomorphs) as short.

Again, you can't change your genetics, but you can change your weight, body fat percentage, and muscle tone. You have the potential to develop a wonderful shape, no matter what your dominant body type is. Losing inches, especially off your problem areas, can be accomplished through proper exercise and eating consistently within the Super Health Diet. For instance, endomorphs are said to benefit from a lower carbohydrate diet, which the Super Health Diet is. Your exercise program can be intensified with resistance training that targets different body groups and also downplays other areas you don't want emphasized. You'll see that in my chapter on exercise.

Learn what you can about the different "types," but realize that most people have the same foundational needs that I address in this book. If you stick with my guidelines, you will prevail. Remember, you are fearfully and wonderfully made, and God will help you become the best you can be!

The Set Point Theory

One of the reasons that 95 percent of dieters end up putting back on all the weight they lost during a diet and perhaps additional fat is seldom mentioned in promotional materials for most diets. Here's what typically happens. You jump into a new diet plan and cut your caloric intake to perhaps 1,100 calories, your weight drops quickly and your hunger pains rise, then the pounds begin to come off slower, and eventually your body weight plateaus and any more loss of weight comes at an exceedingly slow rate, although you remain as hungry as ever. Why?

According to the *set point theory*, there is a control system, a built-in biochemical mechanism, in every person whereby "your body weight is naturally regulated to stay within a range of 10 to 20 percent," says Thomas Wadden, Ph.D., director of the Center for Weight and Eating Disorders at University of Pennsylvania Medical School. Some individuals have a high setting; others have a low one. Over the long term, excess food and insufficient exercise will override your body's natural tendency to stay at its set point and lead to a higher, less healthy set point. A slow, gradual weight gain will fool your body into thinking that your set point should be higher—and, in fact, that does reset your set point.

The set point, it would appear, is very good at supervising fat storage and protecting the body against starvation, but it cannot tell the difference between a purposeful diet and a devastating famine. A part of the brain, called the hypothalamus, helps maintain the set point. If you eat less and begin losing weight, the hypothalamus attempts to maintain the set point by increasing your hunger and appetite, so you'll eat more, and by decreasing your metabolism, you'll burn fewer calories. Calories are burned more slowly, so that even a meager diet almost suffices to maintain weight, because your body is in survival mode. Of course, that makes the loss of weight frustrating, discouraging, and often very difficult.

The set point theory was originally developed in the 1982 book *The Dieter's Dilemma* by nutritional researchers William Bennett, M.D., and Joel Gurin to explain why repeated dieting is unsuccessful in producing long-term change in body weight or shape. Going on a weight loss diet, they stated, is an attempt to overpower the set point, and the set point is a seemingly tireless opponent to you, the struggling dieter.

So you tire of your stringent diet and make the move back to your normal caloric intake—say, 2,000 calories. But now that your body's thermostat has been set to burn up 1,100 calories, you have a surplus of 900 calories more than what your metabolism is geared to handle. And where do those calories go? To all the old familiar places as fat. Sure, the metabolism eventually returns to its place of balance and burns faster and hotter, but first you gain back all the fat you lost in your noble attempt and more.

However, the damage should not be measured solely in terms of weight gain. If you did not eat adequate protein and pursue a regular exercise program along with the low calorie diet, you undoubtedly lost muscle and protein tissue plus some fat. In the process, you came out of this as the big loser. *You lost fat, muscle, and other protein, and you gained back fat only.*

Research has shown, and probably your own experience on diets reflects this, that people who continue to gain and lose weight find it ever more difficult to lose weight. Roller-coaster dieting makes a person use food more inefficiently and increases the difficulty in subsequent dieting efforts.

To outwit this compensatory mechanism, don't decrease your caloric intake radically without making certain you optimize your nutrition (see the "Four Corners of Superfood Nutrition"). If you jump into a low calorie diet (1,400 to 1,600 calories per day) without optimal nutrition that includes adequate protein levels, all you will do is set off your body cells' alarm bells, whereas a gradual decrease in food intake will not as readily let the set point know what's going on. It is possible to reset your set point to a lower point. The secret is to work with, not against, your body's natural tendencies and lose weight steadily, one step at a time. Regular exercise is important: A sustained increase in physical activity seems to lower the setting, particularly high intensity exercise. *The secret is to eat less while increasing nutrient density, stop the empty calorie foods such as sugar and white flour, exercise more, and stay with a solid program for the rest of your life.*

Here is my checklist to breaking through a plateau in your weight loss:

1. Eat three square meals per day and keep your per meal calories between 500 and 700.

2. Make sure your protein intake is between 0.75 gram and 1.0 gram per pound of body weight per day.

3. Use my "Stealth Technique" of preloading a meal with essential fatty acids 30 minutes before meals and at bedtime (see "The Dynamic Role of Proteins in Weight Loss" chapter) or alternate the Stealth Technique EAAs with branched-chained amino acids or with 500 milligrams of l-tryptophan before meals and 2,000 milligrams at bedtime.

4. Make sure you are not eating between meals or within three hours of bedtime and do not eat till you are uncomfortably full.

5. Increase the intensity and/or frequency of your exercise. Consider two times per day.

6. Consider a swig of apple cider vinegar or lemon juice at each meal to blunt the glycemic effect of foods eaten. Recent medical research has highlighted the connection between lower levels of insulin and weight loss.

7. Reflect on your emotions and motivations, start journaling everything you eat, and become accountable to someone.

8. Evaluate how you are doing on each of the Super Health 7 Golden Keys and focus on the advanced techniques and information on weight loss impediments presented in this book.

9. Consider a two-meal per day FUEL Fast or an every other day FUEL Fast (see "The Dynamic Role of Proteins in Weight Loss" chapter).

10. If you are still stalled, then change it up. While keeping protein levels at the high end of the range, eat higher fat one day and higher carbs the next.

Fitness Set Point

Interestingly, sports scientist Greg Wells, Ph.D., has discovered that there is also a *fitness set point*. Dr. Wells explained it to me this way: "We all have different genotypes, or genetic codes, that express different phenotypes, or how we actually look. There are two main aspects to our genetics related to how we look athletically. One is that we all have a fitness set point—the level of fitness we hold if we don't train much. Then we also all have a certain amount of trainability or how our bodies respond to training that is determined by a number of genes and physiological markers." This helps to explain why some people perform at higher levels than others and why some respond to training and recover more rapidly than others. Some of us simply have to work harder than others to achieve the results we want. Scientists are now discovering that lifestyle factors, including nutrition and exercise, can have a profound affect on our DNA and RNA. We now know that certain nutrients directly affect positive genetic expression within the body, including fish oil, vitamin D, resveratrol, and others.

Be encouraged, recent advances in the science of epigenetics, the study of inherited changes in phenotype (appearance) or gene expression caused by mechanisms other than changes in the underlying DNA sequence, is opening up a brand-new world of possibilities for all of us. These changes are so profound that they can remain through cell divisions for the remainder of the cell's life and may also last for multiple generations. This phenomenon is without any change in the underlying DNA sequence of the organism. Instead, non-genetic factors cause the organism's genes to behave (or "express themselves") differently. This area of science is so deep and fascinating it could be the subject of another book.

It is exciting that we can positively program our genes to the point they can be passed to future generations; however, it can be a double-edged sword, because we can also program them negatively. The main point here is that even if you have a family history of disease, including obesity, it does not mean you will also have it. We can program or train our genes to work for us or against us through good or bad lifestyle choices. A fascinating book on this subject is called *The Genie in Your Genes* by Dawson Church, Ph.D.

Emotional Eating and Weight Gain

While there are many root causes to weight gain, for many people it is a result of emotional eating, where a person eats to avoid or mask a negative emotion or uncomfortable feeling. It is a symptom of something else that's going on in their lives, a coping mechanism, that needs to change. And it won't be solved through a diet, through dietary supplements, or through exercise—it's crucial that you understand this if you're an emotional overeater.

For example, when a person who hates their job or is involved in a troubled relationship does not deal with the issues, they often turn to a variety of "drugs of choice" to cope with the negative emotions, and food, like tobacco or alcohol, can be addictive and one of those choices. As strange as it may seem to some of us, emotional overeating can be calming; it "works," at least in the short run. Through the distraction of food, repetitive chewing and swallowing, and obsessive food thoughts, intense feelings are redirected into overeating behavior. These behaviors tend to be psychologically safer than confrontations with the real issues, such as a loved one who might cause conflict, arguments, disharmony, or withdrawal.

While the psychological triggers are many, the main ones are depression, loneliness, hurt, boredom, anxiety, fear, fatigue, and anger. Simply put, if a person is eating in response to a difficult situation rather than because of physical hunger and the nourishment of their body, they're eating emotionally. If they turn to food every time their emotions are triggered or they feel out of control, it becomes a destructive habit that takes over their life, both emotionally and psychologically.

Unfortunately, emotional overeaters usually turn to sweets or salty fast foods, the so-called "comfort foods," that are easy to binge on—chips, pizza, chocolate, cookies, cakes, ice cream, and the like. In particular, quick and easy high fat, high sugar foods are addictive, because they numb out feelings. When life gets too stressful, boring, or tense, food can be the emotional anesthetic that makes it feel better temporarily. Some will eat quickly as though they're desperate, while other emotional eaters simply graze on these foods constantly to help them cope with their day. Most will eat well beyond the point of being full, and most feel guilty about their eating and will try to hide it from others.

One such story was a man whose mother would always try to comfort him with his favorite foods after he was regularly abused as a young boy by his father. This resulted in a lifetime of emotional eating, an addiction to comfort foods. This man died in his thirties weighing more than 400 pounds. Emotional eating must be brought into the light and dealt with.

When it comes to taking control of weight gain caused by emotional eating, most people try the traditional methods—dieting, diet supplements, and exercise—and fail repeatedly. As long as the response to an emotional trigger is to reach for food and overeat, it becomes a vicious circle of self-sabotage and mounting guilt for having failed to maintain the diet. No appetite suppressant or exercise program will stop the cycle until the root cause is solved. The only way to break free is to come to terms with the lies and misbeliefs that we have come to accept and refused to challenge.

If you're interested in a Christian-based program that addresses emotional eating, Weight Loss God's Way is one of the most comprehensive programs available (www.weightlossgodsway.com). Created by Dr. Frank Smooth, a Christian weight loss coach and counselor, his program helps you identify the root cause of your emotional problems and then helps you to remove the root cause, resulting in your being able to gain control again. You can be free from these self-sabotaging beliefs and learn the truths that will get you off of the emotional roller coaster. The Weight Loss God's Way program is available as a digital download.

There is an ever growing number of resources. Three other resources for eating disorders, food addictions, anorexia, and bulimia: *God's Tape Measure* DVD series and workbook from Ellel Ministries USA—www.Ellelministries.org/usa, "My First 90 Days" and "Restarting" Conquering Addictions Program by Ed Khouri—www.lifemodel. org, and *Healing Emotional Wounds* by Ruth Hawkey.

THE
SUPER
HEALTH
DIET

Golden
Keys
to Unlock
Lifelong
Vitality

Chapter 6

Pills, Prescriptions, and Procedures

If I'd known I was gonna live this long,
I'd have taken better care of myself.
JAMES HUBERT (EUBIE) BLAKE

If you are looking for a quick and easy way to lose weight, you're not alone. An estimated 50 million Americans will go on diets this year. And while some will succeed in taking off weight, very few (perhaps five percent) will manage to keep all of it off in the long run. Why is that?

One reason, and perhaps the primary reason, for the low success rate is that many of us believe that obesity can be treated the same way as a headache—"just give me a wonder tablet that shreds the pounds away." We find it hard to believe in this age of scientific innovations and medical miracles that an effortless weight loss method doesn't exist.

It is estimated that more than 20 million people purchase some form of diet medication every year. Even though we seldom believe the hype, we nevertheless succumb to quick-fix claims such as "Melt the Fat Away While You Sleep!" We invest our hopes and hard-earned money in all manner of pills and capsules that promise to "burn," "block," "flush," or otherwise eliminate fat from the system. All the while clinging to the promise of a slimmer, happier future.

Despite the promise of incredible profits to the company that comes up with a low risk "magic bullet" for weight loss, science has yet to do so. Even the deep-pocketed pharmaceutical giants have failed in their quest to strike gold with obesity drugs. Some pills may help control the appetite, but they can have serious side effects. Other pills are utterly worthless, and some can be extremely dangerous.

With obesity set to remain a leading health problem for years to come, the anti-obesity drug treatment market offers immense opportunities for drug companies involved in developing weight loss drugs, provided the drug is safe and truly effective. The market for anti-obesity drugs is virtually untapped and continues to hold a glittering allure. Analysts estimate the potential market for obesity drugs ranges from $5 billion to $10 billion per year, and fledgling biotechs have joined in the race. Obviously, the first company to hit the market with a safe and effective weight loss drug will reap astronomical profits.

But the solution may not be so simple, so don't sit around waiting for the magic pill. Long-term treatment is often required, not to mention dealing with associated conditions such as high blood pressure or diabetes.

You need to know, too, that many in the medical community are opposed to using any weight loss drugs. Some even maintain that the obese are "weak willed." But there are those who do understand that certain overweight individuals could have a neurochemical imbalance that is causing their problem. For example, the hormone *leptin,* which is a protein made by fat cells, is said to act like a barometer, sending signals to the brain and acting on receptors in the hypothalamus (the part of the brain that helps regulate appetite) to decrease food intake and increase the amount of calories burned. It is believed that in the obese, this signal is faulty.

Regardless, millions of people are so frustrated and feel so helpless with being obese that they are willing to risk their lives and ignore potential adverse side effects by taking a pill or undergoing dangerous and radical medical procedures for the "possibility" of losing weight.

As you read this section, please pay particular attention to the risks and side effects of these drugs and procedures. I promise you, there is hope and a better way!

Loss at Any Cost

Think back a little more than a decade. Obesity had finally been solved. The miracle drug combination *fen-phen*, an appetite depressant, seemed a magic pill for the national epidemic of obesity and soared to popularity on the basis of a single study involving just 121 patients who lost an average of only 30 pounds in four years. On April 29, 1996, the FDA approved fen-phen, requiring that it be labeled for weight loss and long-term weight maintenance, but cautioning that studies had lasted only one year. Fen-phen sales soared, and it was eventually taken by six million Americans, said Audrey Ashby, a spokeswoman for Wyeth-Ayerst.

Everyone was happy until the FDA began receiving reports of serious cardiac valvular disease in persons who had taken these drugs. This valvular disease typically involves the aortic and mitral valves. It turned out that as many as one-third of patients taking this drug combination had cardio-pulmonary side effects.

As of 2004, fen-phen was no longer widely available. In April 2005, *American Lawyer* magazine ran a cover story on the fen-phen mass tort crisis, reporting that more than 50,000 product liability lawsuits had been filed by alleged fen-phen victims. Estimates of total liability ran as high as $14 billion. As of February 2005, Wyeth was still in negotiations with injured parties, offering settlements of $5,000 to $200,000 to some of those who had sued. At the time, Wyeth announced it had set aside $21.1 billion to cover the cost of the lawsuits.

> He who takes medicine and neglects to diet wastes the skill of his doctors.
>
> CHINESE PROVERB

People accepted risk of dying for the possible benefit of losing 30 pounds!

Now there is a new drug under FDA review that claims to have the benefits of fen-phen without the dangerous cardiac side effects. The most common side effects reported were dry mouth, tingling, constipation, altered taste, and insomnia. Really! Qnexa and Arena Pharmaceuticals Inc.'s *lorcaserin* has individual components similar to those blended to make fen-phen. Orexigen Therapeutics Inc.'s *Contrave*, the third diet drug under FDA review in 2010, contains an antidepressant and addiction drug tied to nausea, vomiting, and dizziness. If the new medicines prove safe, the global diet pill market may reach $10.5 billion by 2018, according to Datamonitor in London.

It is interesting to note that in 1979, Dr. Michael Weintraub, a professor of clinical pharmacology at the University of Rochester who got the idea for the fen-phen combination, was since hired by the FDA to head one of its divisions of new drug approval.

THERE IS A BETTER WAY!

Weight Loss Prescriptions

The FDA guidelines for weight management drug approval is that the product should help people lose at least five percent more weight than a placebo after one year with benefits outweighing the risks. The FDA guidelines say that side effects should be tolerable, but do not say what that means.

Personally, I would not recommend a weight loss drug unless something new and revolutionary becomes available. *Metformin* (glucophage) is the only "weight loss" drug I am aware of whose benefits seem to outweigh the risks. In people with type 2 diabetes, it is a drug on which people seem to lose weight.[11]

A medical prescription for weight loss should only be used *for individuals who are at high risk because of their excess weight and have tried everything else*. It is really a desperate measure. In general, weight loss drugs are only prescribed for people with a body-mass index (BMI) of 30 or higher, or a BMI of 27 along with a condition such as type 2 diabetes, high blood pressure, or high blood lipids (cholesterol and triglycerides). Before taking any kind of weight loss pill, it's important to have a lengthy discussion with your physician about the pros and cons. It should be a final option taken only after traditional diet and exercise programs have been seriously tried and there are no results. Most people who take a drug for weight loss will need to take it long term to be effective, and there is no guarantee that it will ever be effective.

The FDA has become more cautious in approving drugs for obesity, and in the recent past approved diet drugs that have since been recalled from the market, following reports of adverse side reactions, and some of the investigational obesity drugs have gone belly up. For example, several years ago the FDA recalled *Pondimin* and *Redux*, which were linked to potential fatal heart valve abnormalities.

Numerous companies are working on anti-obesity medications. There is a reason that only one prescription anti-obesity drug is approved in the U.S.—these drugs have proven to be dangerous. Any prescription drug carries the potential for side effects, some more serious than others. And many of these drugs can interact with other drugs that you might be taking.

In October 2010 an FDA-approved prescription appetite suppressant drug was removed from the market because it was said that the benefits of modest weight loss did not outweigh the cardiac risks. Pharmaceutical giant Abbott Laboratories voluntarily agreed to pull the drug after an FDA review of data that showed a 16 percent increased risk for heart attack, stroke, and death among people taking *Meridia* (sibutramine), compared with those taking a placebo. It was marketed as a prescription that works by increasing serotonin availability to the brain and was said to short-circuit the cravings for carbohydrates.

Fat Blockers

Only one anti-obesity medication is currently approved by the FDA for long-term use. Roche's ***Xenical***, which is generically prescribed as *orlistat*, is commonly used to treat obesity in patients with high risk factors such as diabetes, high blood pressure, high triglycerides, or high cholesterol. Unlike weight loss drugs that act in the central nervous system and the brain to suppress appetite or to speed up metabolism, *Xenical* works in your digestive system. Its manufacturers claim it blocks about one-third of the fat in the food you eat from being digested. The main problem with this drug is that it interferes with absorption of healthy fats, and eating fat is NOT the primary reason people are obese, so blocking fat is only a piece of the puzzle and potentially dangerous. Eating "bad fats" and then blocking them from absorption is not the answer either.

This is how it works. In your digestive system are enzymes (lipases) that help break down fat. When this drug is taken with meals, it attaches itself to the lipases and blocks fat and prevents them from breaking down a portion of the fat you have consumed. Then, since this undigested fat cannot be absorbed, it is eliminated in your normal bowel movements. Unfortunately, there are some rather unpleasant side effects, including an increased number of bowel movements, increased urgency, gas with oily discharge, and anal leakage. These symptoms are more likely to occur if the user's fat intake exceeds more than 30 percent of his calories; therefore, there's a kind of negative reinforcement that comes along with using this drug.

Xenical can prevent the absorption of some fat-soluble vitamins, so it's recommended that a person take a multivitamin while using this medicine. *Xenical* is taken as a 120-milligram capsule, up to three times per day and is not appropriate for everyone. A long list of disorders often precludes its use. A thorough medical history should be assessed prior to prescribing this medication. Watch out for side effects, including dizziness, anxiety, muscle pain, or stomach cramps.

A Word to the Wise

A good doctor won't prescribe weight loss medication without knowing your physical condition and what other prescriptions you are taking. Existing health issues from allergies to glaucoma may affect the use of these drugs. And remember, these drugs are meant to be used for the time determined by your physician, not as a permanent solution. Since these medications must be used carefully, never take more or less than your doctor prescribes.

Don't expect miracles, and don't buy into the notion that obesity can be solved simply by taking a prescription pill or a supplement. A recent study conducted by Brazilian and Canadian researchers and published in the *British Medical Journal* indicates that weight loss drugs may result only in minor weight loss, even after long-term use. Researchers conducted meta-analyses of a number of studies conducted on the weight loss drugs orlistat (marketed as *Xenical* and *Alli*), rimonabant (marketed as *Acomplia* but not approved in the U.S. or Canada after receiving reports of psychiatric side effects, such as anxiety and depression), and sibutramine (marketed as *Meridia*, which was withdrawn from markets in October 2010), and found that users *lost an average of less than 11 pounds, even after one to four years of use.* For instance, the average long-term user of orlistat lost only seven pounds and had reduced diabetes risk, blood pressure, and cholesterol. Sibutramine was found to reduce patients' weight by an average of only nine pounds. Users of rimonabant lost an average of 11 pounds.

Regarding Serotonin

When the brain is flooded with serotonin, satiety, or a feeling of fullness, normally occurs. A serotonin deficiency has been associated with the carbohydrate bingeing that contributes to the accumulation of excess body fat.[12] Obese individuals have low blood tryptophan levels, which indicate their overeating patterns may be related to a serotonin deficiency in the brain.[13] When obese patients were given 1,000-, 2,000-, or 3,000-milligram doses of l-tryptophan one hour before meals, a significant decrease in caloric consumption was observed. The majority of the reduction in caloric intake was in the amount of carbohydrates consumed and not the amount of protein consumed.[14]

> My fat scares me—it's a ticking time bomb.
>
> CARRIE LATET

For 19 years, tryptophan dietary supplements were restricted. The good news is that pharmaceutical-pure tryptophan supplements are once again available to Americans without a prescription. *Those seeking to embark on a comprehensive weight loss program should consider adding tryptophan (along with nutrients that inhibit tryptophan-degrading enzymes) to their daily program in starting doses of 500 milligrams before meals, two to three times per day.* If you have trouble getting tryptophan itself, you can get the next best thing, which is known as 5HTP.

Diet Supplements

If you've ever stopped to look at the diet supplements shelf of your local drug store, the variety of products is amazing. And when you type "weight control" in a computer search engine, the list of what's being promoted seems endless. So the question becomes, "How do I know what works?" The short answer is that you don't and won't. I address various diet supplements later in this chapter.

In May 2009, one of the most popular dietary supplements, the line of 14 *Hydroxycut* products, was pulled from the market after the

FDA issued a warning based on evidence that it potentially caused irreversible liver damage, heart problems, and a kind of muscle damage that could lead to kidney failure. Its manufacturers had sold more than nine million units of the product in supermarkets and pharmacies in 2008 alone. The original Hydroxycut was introduced as an ephedra product, but ephedra was banned, and they changed their formula to include various other stimulants.

Over-the-Counter Diet Pills

Here are a few of the popular products being marketed today:

Alli, the only FDA-approved, over-the-counter weight loss product, is one-half the strength of *Xenical*, but it's the same drug. It works by blocking the absorption of fat in the gastrointestinal (GI) tract. Again, eating fats is not a primary cause of weight gain, so blocking fat from being absorbed is not the answer.

Alli is taken as a 60-milligram capsule up to three times per day. More than just a pill, the *Alli* program involves a reduced calorie, low fat diet, regular walking and toning exercises, and behavioral changes. If that plan is followed, expectations are that for every five pounds people lose on the low fat diet, *Alli* can help them lose an extra two to three pounds.

Most of the weight lost while taking *Alli* will occur during the first six months. It has some of the same problematic side effects that plagued its prescription-strength predecessor—gas with oily discharge, inability to control bowel movements, oily or fatty stools, and oily spotting. Critics allege that if *Alli* blocks fat so well, it may also block the absorption of important vitamins and minerals. *Alli*'s website recommends working with a registered dietitian for safe and effective weight loss, which is always good advice.

On August 25, 2009, the FDA stated that it is continuing its review of reports of liver damage linked to *Alli*, after receiving additional information from its drug evaluation center as well as the product's manufacturer. The FDA had added orlistat to its drug surveillance list, which includes all products identified as potentially harmful. Orlistat is the drug contained in *Alli*, as well as in *Xenical*, the prescription weight loss product sold by Roche. The FDA said its analysis of the drugs is "ongoing" and advises consumers to continue taking the products. "No definite association between liver injury and Orlistat has been established at this time," it said. It is interesting that *Alli* is on the FDA surveillance list for potential liver damage but the prescription version, *Xenical*, does not appear to be.

Capsaicin, the compound that gives red pepper, chili pepper, and cayenne pepper their heat, generates antioxidant activity that I keep seeing new research on as regards to effectiveness in aiding weight loss. In the "Corner #3—Consume High Antioxidant Superfoods and Supplements" chapter, I go into detail regarding the recent research and why it appears to be effective in weight loss. Although some people who use the product swear by the results, others suggest their outcome was improved because they increased the health of their digestive system.

> The older you get, the harder it is to lose weight, because your body has made friends with your fat.
>
> LYNNE ALPERN AND ESTHER BLUMENFELD

CLA (conjugated linoleic acid) is a naturally occurring polyunsaturated fatty acid found in meat and dairy products and is required to maintain optimal function of the phospholipid membranes of cells. Healthy cell membranes will allow fat, protein, and carbohydrate to flow into active cells, such as muscle, connective tissue, and organ cells, instead of being stored as passive fat cells.

While the human body cannot produce CLA, it is efficiently absorbed in supplement form. It has become a popular dietary supplement that is sold with claims of helping people reduce body fat, maintain weight loss, decrease appetite, retain lean muscle mass, and control type 2 diabetes, which is often associated with obesity. It is also a popular supplement used by bodybuilders who believe it promotes the growth of muscles by pushing glucose into muscle cells and connective tissues instead of letting it turn into fat. CLA has been shown to reduce protein degradation in both humans and animals and to protect against degenerative diseases.

In health food stores, CLA is sold as a pill or as a syrup and comes in varying concentrations. It is recommended that you buy a product containing 80 percent CLA to get maximum weight loss results. I recommend that it be taken at three to six grams per day. It has been shown to be even more effective when taken with caffeine or guarana.

Some experts say CLA might decrease body fat and increase muscle, but isn't likely to reduce total body weight. Clinical studies have not clearly determined its ability for weight loss or decrease in body fat. It can cause diarrhea, indigestion, and other gastrointestinal problems.

I am a fan of CLA because it is an essential fat and has numerous health benefits beyond fat burning.

CortiSlim. This product was designed to decrease the level of cortisol (the "stress hormone") in the body and, as a result, decrease body fat. Cortisol is necessary for proper physical functioning. The makers also state that it helps balance blood sugar levels. Since *CortiSlim* contains stimulants, some users have complained of heart palpitations and nausea. I believe reducing cortisol is a good idea, but not with stimulants. It is better to supplement with *phosphatidylserine* and use stress management, good nutrition, exercise, and sleep.

I have seen some interesting research that suggests that phosphatidylserine is able to reduce cortisol levels when the body experiences stress. Phosphatidylserine is an important chemical with widespread functions in the body. It is part of the cell structure and is key in the maintenance of cellular function, especially in the brain. Although the body is able to produce phosphatidylserine on its own, it must go through a series of reactions that require a substantial investment of energy. This makes supplementation an attractive option. When phosphatidylserine is taken orally, the non-degraded portion is rapidly assimilated and easily crosses the blood-brain barrier. Because it can produce nausea if taken on an empty stomach, it should be taken with meals. It should not be taken just before going to bed, as the neurotransmitters it helps to release could make it harder to fall asleep. Phosphatidylserine does not appear to have any other side effects when taken at the recommended dosages.

Dexatrim. This has been one of the most recognized names in dieting for more than a quarter century. It's an all-natural appetite suppressant that allows your body to burn fat and calories at a quicker rate.

When the FDA banned the ingredient *ephedrine,* it was reformulated and became a drug-free supplement. *Dexatrim* products contain caffeine, known for pulling water from the body, which may result in only temporary weight loss. It is true that stimulants can reduce appetite, but they should be minimized. Additionally, appetite control is not everyone's primary weight loss issue.

Fucoxanthin. As a type of carotenoid found naturally in edible brown seaweed such as wakame (used in miso soup) and hijiki, fucoxanthin is used widely in Asian cuisine. Fucoxanthin is also found in much smaller amounts in red seaweed (the kind typically used in Japanese sushi rolls) and green seaweed.

Fucoxanthin has shown promising possibilities in supplementation for weight loss, although only animal studies have been published regarding it to date. Japanese researchers at Hokkaido University have found that fucoxanthin (isolated from wakame) promotes the loss of abdominal fat in obese mice and rats. Animals lost five to 10 percent of their body weight.[15] Although it's not fully understood how fucoxanthin works, it appears to target a protein called UCP1 that increases the rate at which abdominal fat is burned. Abdominal fat, also called white adipose tissue, is the kind of fat that surrounds our organs and is linked to heart disease and diabetes. Fucoxanthin also appears to stimulate the production of DHA, one of the omega-3 fatty acids found in fatty fish such as salmon.

Up until now, people seeking to boost their resting metabolic rate had to rely on compounds that produced unpleasant stimulating effects. Time and research will tell whether fucoxanthin safely increases resting energy expenditure at the cellular level—with none of the side effects associated with ephedra. I was very impressed with the research on fucoxanthin for weight loss presented by Life Extension Foundation and tried this product for several months at substantially higher dosages than reported without any noticeable results. The research is impressive, but the reality did not work for me.

Because there have been no published research studies on fucoxanthin in humans, the possible side effects aren't known. You have to consider the high amount of iodine in these products, since excess iodine can cause thyroid malfunction. The amount of fucoxanthin in supplementation varies greatly from one product to another. Be careful when you buy a product promoted as fucoxanthin, since you may be, in some cases, basically paying for brown seaweed that floats for free in the ocean.

Green Tea. While I will develop the weight loss benefits and research done on green tea in the "Corner #3—Consume High Antioxidant Superfoods and Supplements" chapter, you may have noticed that green tea is listed as an active ingredient in many weight loss products. Besides enjoying the goodness of a hot or cold cup of flavorful green tea, according to research in the *American Journal of Clinical Nutrition*, "Consumption of green tea produces thermogenesis and increases energy expenditure and fat oxidation." A study in Switzerland found that drinking the equivalent of two to three cups of green tea daily caused the participants to burn 80 extra calories each day, without increasing their heart rates and factoring out the tea's caffeine content.

HCA (hydroxycitric acid) is a close relative of citric acid, the agent that gives citrus fruits their characteristic tart flavor, and is found in many weight loss supplements. HCA is obtained as a 50 percent standardized extract of Garcinia cambogia, a small fruit from southern India, and is a safe, natural supplement for weight management. HCA is a competitive inhibitor of ATP citrate lyase, a key enzyme that facilitates the synthesis of fatty acids, cholesterol, and triglycerides. HCA may reduce the synthesis of fatty acids in humans during a persistent excess of energy intake as carbohydrate. It has also been suggested that HCA promotes weight loss by increasing serotonin levels and reducing hunger and appetite, as well as reducing the increases in oxidative stress and insulin resistance.

> I recently had my annual physical examination, which I get once every seven years, and when the nurse weighed me, I was shocked to discover how much stronger the Earth's gravitational pull has become since 1990.
>
> DAVE BARRY

Hoodia. As a much hyped diet appetite suppressant, hoodia derives from a cactus-like succulent plant found in the semi-deserts of southern Africa. The bushmen of the Kalahari used it for centuries to ward off hunger. Hoodia is sold in capsule, powder, liquid, or tea form in health food stores and on the Internet. The ingredient is also found in the popular diet pill *Trimspa*. Because of the relative scarcity of hoodia, the ingredient is hard for manufacturers to acquire, which makes it hard to understand how dozens of firms now claim to sell weight loss supplements containing hoodia. Scientists at Phytopharm, the only licensed producer of hoodia as a weight loss aid, claim that many firms are fraudulently using their data and claims about hoodia to market their own products. With reports of widespread counterfeit product, it's hard to know if you are actually purchasing a product that truly contains the active ingredient.

Some researchers are concerned about possible unwanted effects on the liver, but no evidence has been presented. According to Oregon State University, true hoodia does not work as a stimulant. Read supplement labels carefully, however, as some hoodia pills may contain stimulants such as ephedrine, caffeine, or guarana. Appetite control is not everyone's primary issue in weight loss.

Irvingia. Irvingia gabonensis is the latest weight loss supplement to hit the marketplace and has been promoted as providing "more weight loss than any other discovery in supplement history." It comes from the nuts of a West African tree commonly known as the wild mango or bush mango. Irvingia gabonensis is high in fat (50 percent) and also comprised of 26.4 percent carbohydrate, 7.5 percent protein, 2.3 percent ash, and 14 percent fiber. Dietary fibers are often recommended to aid with weight loss programs as well as for their health benefits.

While initial studies on the effects of Irvingia were done on humans by a research group based in Cameroon (western Africa) with promising results in 2005 and 2008, indicating that it may circumvent the natural ability of adipocytes (fat cells) to propagate and retain excess fat, questions regarding the quality of the research have flagged enough of a concern for me to wonder about their results. To claim, for instance, "28 pounds of fat loss in 10 weeks with no change in diet or exercise," is way beyond the math possibilities for me. To lose 28 pounds of fat in 10 weeks involves the burning of a total of 98,000 calories, or 9,800 calories per week, or 1,400 calories per day. The notion that this product will raise one's metabolic rate by 1,400 calories per day is astronomical.

Future research might show that Irvingia gabonensis provides significant health benefits, and the proposed anti-obesity benefits may also be confirmed. If it does indeed enhance cellular communication, the results could be impressive. My personal experience is that I could not tell any difference with Irvingia at recommended dosages or even four times the recommended dosage for long periods. Nevertheless, the research is so impressive in terms of enhancing intercellular communication that one might take it anyway.

Natural Appetite Control. This is an oil I recommend from Life Extension that contains pinolenic acid, from the Korean pine nut, which stimulates the release of two of the body's most powerful hunger-suppressing hormones: CCK (cholecystokinin) and GLP-1 (glucagon-like peptide-1). This sends a feeling of satiety or "fullness" to the brain, decreasing the desire to eat and helping to control excessive calorie intake. Hunger is the factor that often precludes most people from even considering a low calorie diet. If appetite is an issue for you, this seems to be a much better approach than stimulants.

Phentermine. This is the name of the active ingredient in a short-term appetite suppressant found in many of the most frequently sold weight loss products. They are marketed under many trade names, including *Fastin, Ionamin, Adipex-P, Phentrol, Redusa,* and *Teramine.* It is said to work by helping to release the chemicals in the brain that control the appetite. Phentermine is no longer marketed in Europe due to a possible association with heart and lung problems. Side effects include diarrhea, dry mouth, constipation, insomnia, palpitations, and high blood pressure, to name a few. It's not typically recommended for anyone with heart problems, especially arrhythmias. Obviously, it is not a magic bullet and has side effects.

SlimQuick. The manufacturers claim this is "the world's first advanced fat burner specifically designed for a woman's body." It was developed to address female hormone imbalances. SlimQuick's herbal, vitamin, and mineral ingredients are promoted to address fat loss, increase metabolism, control appetite, improve muscle tone, and help reduce water retention. Side effects reported by some users include dry mouth, mood swings, and excessive thirst.

White Kidney Bean Extract. Classified as an amylase inhibitor, meaning it interferes with the enzyme responsible for breaking down carbohydrates into glucose, this is a staple of many diet pills. It allows carbohydrates to pass through the body undigested, prohibiting them from eventually converting to fat.

Carb blockers make more sense to me than fat blockers, since carbs are more likely to be the primary reason most people gain weight. Nevertheless, it is better to minimize carbs and enhance digestion, and blocking carbs only works while the supplement is being taken and does not block all carbs. It can also cause people to overeat carbs.

I believe people would be better off just adding a tablespoon or two of apple cider vinegar with their meals. Recent medical research has highlighted the connection between lower levels of insulin and weight loss. That coupled with the fact that vinegar is known to slow the rise of blood sugar after a meal leads to the suggestion that taking apple cider vinegar with a meal reduces the amount of insulin required to process the meal, resulting in weight loss.

Zantrex 3. Used as a fat burner, this product has many fans. This is another stimulant with a couple of good additional ingredients, including green tea extract (a powerful antioxidant), ginseng (to increase energy levels and reduce stress), and maca root (a Peruvian plant that produces physical stamina). But the main ingredient is caffeine. So be careful, since caffeine can elevate your heart rate and increase blood pressure. In this case, the stimulant is intended to enhance metabolism, not suppress appetite, which is possible. Stimulants are just not a good idea, and I would not take this product.

> Matt Damon shed 45 pounds to play a heroin-addicted soldier in *Courage Under Fire* by running 10 miles a day and adhering to a strict diet of egg whites, chicken, vegetables, and dry baked potatoes. The extreme diet took a toll on his health, however, and induced an adrenal gland disorder that made him extremely sick.

Ask Your Doctor

Just because a product is on the market, promoted in the media, and said to have all-natural ingredients doesn't mean it's right for you.

Since these supplements are going into your body, talk with your personal physician regarding what you should or should not use. Tell your doctor everything, including any history of drug or alcohol abuse, eating disorders, pregnancy or breastfeeding, heart disease, high blood pressure, or use of blood-thinning medication. Discuss whether the ingredients in a pill or medication can be habit forming.

Your doctor can provide support and advice on losing weight and can monitor your progress. Just as important, your doctor can talk with you about possible side effects and what to watch out for. Your doctor can help determine if weight loss pills are likely to interact with any prescription drugs you take. Many weight loss pills contain multiple ingredients, such as herbs, botanicals, vitamins, minerals, and even caffeine or laxatives. If you take prescription drugs—or herbal or dietary supplements—adding weight loss pills to the mix can be tricky.

Also avoid herbal laxatives and diuretics. They cause the body to lose water but not fat. Plus, their use can lead to lowering potassium levels and to possible heart and muscle problems.

When talking with one physician about weight loss pills and prescriptions, he told me, "They are good when combined with diet and exercise." Then he added, "But come to think of it, if you diet and exercise, you probably won't need pills and prescriptions!"

I strongly believe for weight optimization and Super Health, one must supplement with essential nutrients, including fish oil with broad-spectrum antioxidants, including resveratrol, essential amino acids, CLA, and broad–spectrum vitamins, especially vitamin D3, minerals, prebiotics, probiotics, and phytonutrients along with superfoods rich in protein, fibrous carbohydrates, and healthy fats. See the Four Corners Shopping List and Smart Meals and SuperSmoothie Recipes for product information.

The following table from the Mayo Clinic website[16] shows common weight loss pills, what the research shows about their effectiveness and safety, and why it is important to do your homework if you're thinking about trying weight loss pills. Read labels and talk with your doctor or pharmacist. Also check the FDA website for alerts about safety concerns and product recalls.

PRODUCT	CLAIM	EFFECTIVENESS	SAFETY
Alli	Decreases absorption of dietary fat	Effective; weight loss amounts typically less for OTC versus prescription	FDA investigating reports of liver injury
Bitter orange	Increases calories burned	Insufficient reliable evidence to rate	Possibly unsafe
Chitosan	Blocks absorption of dietary fat	Insufficient reliable evidence to rate	Possibly safe
Chromium	Increases calories burned, decreases appetite and builds muscle	Insufficient reliable evidence to rate	Likely safe
Conjugated linoleic acid (CLA)	Reduces body fat and builds muscle	Possibly effective	Possibly safe
Country mallow (heartleaf)	Decreases appetite and increases calories burned	Insufficient reliable evidence to rate	Likely unsafe and banned by FDA
Ephedra	Decreases appetite	Possibly effective	Likely unsafe and banned by FDA

PRODUCT	CLAIM	EFFECTIVENESS	SAFETY
Green tea extract	Increases calorie and fat metabolism and decreases appetite	Insufficient reliable evidence to rate	Possibly safe
Guar gum	Blocks absorption of dietary fat and increases feeling of fullness	Possibly ineffective	Likely safe
Hoodia	Decreases appetite	Insufficient reliable evidence to rate	Insufficient information

Medical Procedures

One obstacle to weight loss for many obese individuals is that the signaling between the brain and the gut has become impaired. They feel hungry and a strong urge to eat more because their bodies continually communicate they're not getting enough food. Some individuals will resort to weight loss surgery, which is a serious procedure and should only be considered in cases of severe obesity. These procedures are usually performed only on individuals who have been obese for at least five years. Celebrities such as TV weatherman Al Roker and singer Carrie Wilson have undergone this surgery, and millions of Americans have followed their progress.

While advancements and experience have made these procedures much safer than they used to be, it remains a significant undertaking. All surgeries carry some risk, and these procedures are major, not minor. The likelihood of certain complications—cardiac problems and pneumonia, in particular—increases with patients' obesity levels. Depending on the procedure, there is some risk for surgical complications (bleeding, leaks, and bowel obstructions) as well.

Worth noting: If the significant dietary changes that successful weight loss surgery requires had been implemented prior to surgery, the patient would not have needed the surgery in the first place.

Acupuncture

In November 2010 at the Pacific Symposium, the results of a new study titled "The Effects of Acupuncture on Weight Loss in Overweight and Obese Adults Over 24 Years Old" were announced. It was conducted by Dr. Edward Lamadrid, a doctor of acupuncture and oriental medicine (DAOM), and it reported that 95 percent of its participants lost weight in a six-week period after receiving regular acupuncture treatments. Of those participants, after the treatments stopped, another 50 percent continued to lose weight.

"What's particularly interesting and somewhat shocking about the study's findings is that weight loss occurred across the board without much exercise or dieting, something everyone believes is essential to trimming down," Lamadrid stated. "I certainly don't want to discount the importance of healthy habits such as good fitness and eating nutritionally, but this study confirms that acupuncture is a viable tool for successful weight loss."

Interestingly, 81 percent of participants in Group A, which received three weeks of acupuncture treatments, lost weight, averaging two pounds per week for men and one pound per week for women. After the treatments ceased, 54 percent continued to lose weight. Meanwhile, 79 percent of those in Group B, the control group, which didn't receive acupuncture, gained weight during the three-week period. At the end of those three weeks, this control group then received regular acupuncture treatments, and 77 percent then lost weight at a rate similar to Group A.

While I'm sure more studies will focus on the role of acupuncture and weight loss, I see this as a logical approach that is worth considering. "Patients understand the importance of preventative medicine and a holistic approach to treatment," Lamadrid says. "This body of evidence on the acupuncture-weight loss link is groundbreaking for the worldwide health care and fitness community, considering obesity is now a global epidemic."

Cryolipolysis

This procedure is for the person with some stubborn fat, but not for the obese. Of the medical procedures, cryolipolysis is one of the few promising, safe procedures that makes sense to me. During the procedure, a noninvasive applicator delivers precisely controlled cooling to target and eliminate fat cells in targeted body areas. As they are exposed to cooling, the fat cells begin a process of natural cell death and removal without damage to other tissue. The fat cells in the treated area are gradually eliminated through the body's normal metabolism process. The result is a flattening of fat bulges that is visible in most patients during three to four months. Similar to liposuction, this procedure is not a way to lose weight. The best candidates are people with small areas of unwanted fat, such as the belly, flanks, and back fat pads.

At the May 2010 meeting of the American Society for Laser Medicine and Surgery, Dr. A. Jay Burns, a plastic surgeon in Dallas who is also with the University of Texas Southwestern Medical Center, said regarding a large multicenter study, "There were no reports of serious adverse effects, and all side effects were transient." Ultrasound measurements were available for 41 patients in the study. Patients in this subset achieved a mean fat-layer reduction of 22 percent after a single procedure. This is consistent with smaller, previously published case reports of cryolipolysis.

Pleasanton, California–based Zeltiq currently owns exclusive rights to the technology and markets a cryolipolysis device known as the Zeltiq system, which is cleared in the European Union and Canada for noninvasive fat-layer reduction through cold-assisted lipolysis. It is also cleared by the U.S. Food and Drug Administration for various applications related to skin cooling during dermatologic treatments, with a pending application for noninvasive fat-layer reduction.

Dr. Burns concluded, "Selective cryolipolysis is a very low risk, no-downtime procedure that produces consistent observations of modest, gradual fat-layer reductions in patients. It has a favorable risk/benefit ratio for patients who want to avoid riskier and more invasive procedures."

Comments: This is significant in that every pound of extra fat can have more than one mile of additional blood vessels that were created by the process called angiogenesis, so every pound matters. However, there is a limited scope of people who qualify for this procedure—it is not for the obese, but for those who have enough pockets of fat that can be pinched into a roll. This procedure is in its primitive stages and some patients say it is a very uncomfortable process to go through. Expect advancements in this procedure as it becomes more popular.

Detox Weight Loss

Detoxification is best known to help clear the body of harmful toxins and pollutants that have been building up for years. A detox regimen is also an excellent aid for those who are trying to lose a lot of weight quickly, as it causes all the toxins to be removed from the body in a safe, quick manner. However, talk to your doctor first before you start a detoxification program for weight loss. Those who are pregnant, nursing, or have some medical conditions may not be able to detox.

There are many different detox programs available for men and women to choose from. Water is the only other beverage allowed during a typical detox. One popular detox is the lemonade diet, which is made from a combination of lemon juice, cayenne pepper, organic maple syrup, and water. This drink is consumed every day for a period of three to 14 days and quickly takes off the weight as the body detoxifies itself. Another popular detox follows a fresh organic fruit and vegetable diet eaten all day long, either in raw form or in a liquid state. Some detoxes include a saltwater flush, which is used to speed up the body's elimination process.

Comments: Two extraordinary techniques for detoxification, more rapid weight optimizing, and general well-being are the FUEL Fast and the Micro Fast that I develop in "The Dynamic Role of Proteins in Weight Loss" chapter. These techniques are the most effective ways to accomplish the Four Corners of Superfood Nutrition guidelines out-lined in this book.

The biggest downside to traditional water fasting, juice fasting, and vegetable fasting is significant muscle loss. Muscle loss is extremely unhealthy and hard to replace. It results in an accumulation of body fat that is diametrically opposed to the health benefits of fasting. If you are going to fast, make sure you are obtaining the benefits you are attempting to gain. The key is to do the Four Corners of Superfood Nutrition in your fast, therefore *assuring you are getting everything your body needs while fasting. This can be done without hunger or cravings or a loss of energy.*

Once you are finished with the detox, you must be careful to keep the pounds from coming back on. Those who go back to their old eat-ing habits will most likely gain the weight back. However, many people find they don't need the added toxins they had been consuming in the form of processed foods, junk food, sugar, and the like, and continue on their healthy path.

Gastric Bypass Surgery

This procedure has been around for more than 40 years and is used by approximately 90 percent of the patients who choose surgery for obesity.

Here's how it works. In a normal person, food is digested as it passes through the stomach and into the small intestine. This is the place most of the calories and nutrients are absorbed. From there the food travels into the large intestine—the colon—where the remaining waste material is finally excreted from the body.

In a gastric bypass, the stomach is made smaller by creating a small pouch at the top of the stomach—approximately the size of a walnut. This shrunken stomach can only hold about an ounce of food or liq-uid, which also speeds up the hormonal signals of fullness and satiety, since the undigested food enters the intestine so soon after it is eaten.

Next, the surgeon cuts the small intestine and connects it directly to this pouch. This is achieved by using either surgical staples or a plas-tic band. The procedure can be done either by a large incision in the abdomen or by laparoscopic surgery—by making a small incision and using camera-operated tiny instruments to guide the surgeon.

Most people who have the procedure return to normal activities in about a month.

Many doctors report their patients lose between 60 to 80 percent of their excess weight within one year after surgery. Even after 10 years, 50 to 60 percent weight loss has been maintained by some patients. An estimated 15 percent regain a significant amount, however.

Comments: The risks of gastric bypass include poor absorption of nutrients from foods, particularly of calcium, iron, and vitamin B12. Patients must be vigilant about eating enough protein and will need to take vitamin and mineral supplements. And the side effects can cause nausea, sweating, cramping, or possible diarrhea after eating, especially after eating sweets or fatty foods.

> **In minds crammed with thoughts, organs clogged with toxins, and bodies stiffened with neglect, there is just no space for anything else.**
>
> ALISON ROSE LEVY

This is a radical and dangerous surgery and in my opinion never warranted. This barbaric procedure shows how desperate some people have become. The irony of this procedure is that due to poor digestion post-surgery the patients have to modify their diets due to impaired digestion. If they would have made these diet and lifestyle changes in the first place, they may not have needed the procedure.

Adjustable Gastric Band Surgery

In this procedure (also called Lap-Band surgery) an adjustable band is placed around the uppermost part of the stomach, making it into the form of an hourglass and limiting how much the person can eat and slowing the passage of food into the stomach. Patients feel full after eating less. There is no stapling or cutting involved; therefore, it is less invasive.

The lap band is designed so it can be inflated or deflated to meet the person's weight loss objectives. This is usually done with laparoscopic or "key hole" surgery. It results in lower initial weight loss but has the advantage of being reversible.

With the narrowed opening to the stomach, it makes it hard to digest fibrous foods, pasta, rice, and red meat. All foods must be thoroughly chewed or patients suffer severe discomfort. Fluids are limited—patients cannot drink any liquids within an hour of eating. Also, in as many as half of the patients, the band slips at some point afterward, which requires an additional procedure for adjustment.

While not as radical as the gastric bypass, this is another dangerous procedure that results in the patients having to change their diets and lifestyles to get more nutrients from less food. If they would have done that in the first place, they may not have needed the bands.

Sleeve Gastrectomy

In this procedure, 60 percent of the stomach is surgically removed and the shape is changed to a tube (or "sleeve"), which results in a *permanent* restriction that cannot be undone on how much food you can eat at one time. Also, the portion of the stomach that produces the hunger hormone *ghrelin* is removed, so hunger pangs are diminished. Because this procedure doesn't involve bypass, patients maintain the ability to absorb vitamins and minerals at near-normal levels. But because it leaves a larger portion of the stomach intact, patients can still eat more than they should. If the overeating stretches the stomach, it results in the need for an additional procedure.

Comments: This is another dangerous and radical procedure that requires the patient to make after-surgery changes in diet and lifestyle that may have helped them avoid the surgery in the first place.

Liposuction

Liposuction is a popular type of cosmetic surgery. A plastic surgeon typically performs the medical procedure, using special surgical equipment to suction away unwanted or excess deposits of fat, to improve body appearance, and to smooth irregular or distorted body shapes. The procedure is sometimes called "body contouring." More than 100,000 people go through liposuction surgery every year in the United States.

There are several different liposuction procedures: tumescent liposuction (by fluid injection), a super-wet technique similar to tumescent liposuction, and ultrasound-assisted liposuction. Through a small skin incision, a suction tube with a sharp end is inserted into the fat pockets and swept through the area where fat is to be removed. The dislodged fat is "vacuumed" away through the suction tube.

Similar to the cryolipolysis procedure, liposuction is not a way to lose weight. The best candidates are people with small areas of unwanted fat, such as "love handles," fat bulges, or an abnormal chin line.

Liposuction does permanently remove fat cells, but it is a surgical procedure with significant potential risks and may involve a painful recovery. Risks associated with the procedure include fluid overloads, infections, bleeding, nerve, skin, tissue, or organ damage or burns from the heat or instruments used in liposuction, uneven fat removal, scarring, and occasionally fatal complications.

Though a new procedure, cryolipolysis is a far safer option. The best option is to lose the weight and eliminate any need for the procedure in the first place.

Addressing weight loss issues in century twenty-one gives us a range of weight loss choices our forefathers never dreamed of. If you plan to embark on a medical solution, make your decision based on the best knowledge, the best products, and the best advice you can find.

Surgical procedures are almost never the best option, and if you are morbidly obese and considering these options, there may be deep rooted emotional issues that need to be addressed before going any further with these procedures. I encourage you to read the "Emotional Eating and Weight Gain" section in Chapter 5.

Chapter 7
Spas and Clinics

Now there is in Jerusalem by the Sheep Gate a pool, which is called in Hebrew, Bethesda, having five porches. In these lay a great multitude of sick people, blind, lame, paralyzed, waiting for the moving of the water. For an angel went down at a certain time into the pool and stirred up the water; then whoever stepped in first, after the stirring of the water, was made well of whatever disease he had.

JOHN 5:2–4

Perhaps you've seen the celebrity headline on a supermarket tabloid, "So-and-So Actress Loses 20 Pounds After Fat Farm Torture!" In the past, this has meant munching on lettuce and carrots for a week while going through a military-like regimen of exhausting 4 a.m. physical workouts in a desperate attempt to lose weight ahead of a major appearance, such as the Super Bowl. Typically, the tabloid account will go on to say that the workouts and a bizarre diet left the actress in tears and caused her to have yet another breakdown.

A "fat farm" is a pejorative term that was once widely used for various spas, resorts, and retreats offering weight loss programs for adults. Since the 1950s, there have been large numbers of American weight loss resorts. Unfortunately, some of these achieved their hyped weight loss through forced low calorie diets and exercise and were criticized as "quick fixes" that did not result in long-term weight loss. But they were hardly a new phenomenon.

Before the rush to cure obesity, people from the Babylonians onward have used the waters of hot or cold springs for both spiritual and physical purification. Later, the Greeks began bathing regimens that formed the foundation for modern spa procedures. They established public baths and showers within their gymnasium complexes for relaxation and personal hygiene. Greek mythology specified that certain natural springs or tidal pools were blessed by the gods to cure disease. Around these sacred pools, Greeks established bathing facilities for those desiring healing.

> In 1843, bathing between November 1 and March 15 was outlawed in Philadelphia, Pennsylvania, as a health measure, and in 1845 bathing was banned in Boston, Massachusetts, unless under the direct orders of a physician. The taboos against bathing soon disappeared with advancements in medical science.

The Romans copied many of the Greek bathing practices and developed baths in their colonies, taking advantage of the natural hot springs occurring in Europe to construct baths at many locations, such as Bath and Buxton in England, Aix and Vichy in France, and Aachen and Wiesbaden in Germany. The Romans used the hot thermal waters to relieve their suffering from rheumatism, arthritis, and overindulgence in food and drink. These baths also became centers for recreational and social activities in Roman communities. Libraries, lecture halls, gymnasiums, and formal gardens became part of some bath complexes.

In colonial America, thousands of people traveled to destinations such as Bath, Yellow, and Bristol Springs in Pennsylvania; Saratoga Springs, Kinderhook, and Ballston Springs in New York; and Warm Springs, Hot Springs, and White Sulphur Springs, in Virginia (now in West Virginia). By 1930, it is estimated that more than 2,000 hot- or cold-springs health resorts were operating in the United States.

Most of these resorts have fallen by the wayside, including the twentieth century "fat farms." Taking their place we now have luxurious health spas of all sizes and descriptions. In fact, the word *spa* has been attached to thousands of enterprises—from hotels to small establishments that offer therapeutic massage, facials, or a sauna.

However, there are a handful of health spas, weight loss clinics, and fitness centers whose reputations have risen far above the rest. Let's look at a few that have gained national attention.

Cal-a-Vie Health Spa

If you're ready to lose weight and get fit in the lap of luxury, check out the widely acclaimed Cal-a-Vie Health Spa in Vista, California, located on 200 acres in northern San Diego County. The well-rounded program includes more than 90 fitness classes at all levels, gourmet nutritional cuisine, and an amazing variety of spa treatments—everything from hot stone facials to aromatherapy massage. There is an Olympic-length salt-water pool and an 11,000 square-foot fitness center. Plus, it is the only destination spa in the world that has its own 18-hole golf course.

The food menu includes unprocessed whole grains, fresh fruits and vegetables, essential fatty acids, and lean proteins. Ingredients are carefully prepared and artfully presented. The spa doesn't follow the latest diet trends or recommend quick fixes that are harmful in the long run. Your stay includes cooking demonstrations with tips and recipes to put into practice when you return home.

Learn more at www.cal-a-vie.com.

Canyon Ranch

Located in Tucson, Arizona, this is one of the world's most celebrated health resorts. In fact, it was voted by *Conde Nast Traveler* readers as the number one destination spa.

Your experience will begin with a health and fitness assessment reviewed by a Nurse Educator. There are more than 225 programs to choose from, including private consultations with their team of more than 60 wellness professionals. There are dozens of fitness classes offered each day in the huge spa complex, plus guided hiking and biking excursions in the desert mountains and foothills.

At Canyon Ranch, you choose the program that is right for you—whether it be health-related issues, weight loss, stress management, smoking cessation, or executive health.

Their "Life Enhancement" programs are offered with three diffrent features: (1) *Restoration*—nourishing your mind and body; (2) *Exploration*—stepping out of your comfort zone and focusing on nutrition, preventive medicine, spiritual awareness, and exercise, and (3) *Transformation*—making positive changes and starting a new chapter in your life.

> I had no intention of giving her my vital statistics. "Let me put it this way," I said. "According to my girth, I should be a ninety-foot redwood."
>
> ERMA BOMBECK

Guests rave about the dining experience. It is based on wise choices, with an emphasis on raising your nutritional intelligence and learning healthy cooking techniques that will serve you for a lifetime.

In addition to the original Tucson location, Canyon Ranch has two other facilities: one in Lenox, Massachusetts, the other in Miami Beach, Florida.

All meals—with as many courses and helpings as you wish, plus healthy snacks—are included in your visit, so you never have to consider price or wait for the check. It's a stress-free, no-tipping resort.

Learn more at www.canyonranch.com.

The Cooper Clinic

Kenneth H. Cooper, M.D., is a pioneer in the field of preventive medicine and an international leader in health and wellness research. In fact, he coined the word *aerobics*.

In 1970, he founded the Cooper Clinic in Dallas, Texas, with the objective of helping people achieve optimum health and fitness at every stage of life. Through the years, thousands of men and women have traveled to Texas to be evaluated and enroll in his programs. They learn the "Cooper lifestyle"—a well-balanced approach to weight management, exercise, eating well, supplementation, and stress reduction.

The examination given at the Cooper Clinic has been called by many the "gold standard" in preventive medicine. The detailed results are followed up with staff physicians who specialize in cardiology, dermatology, gastroenology, radiology, and breast health. Nutrition and psychological services are also available.

The founder's son, Tyler Cooper, M.D., has now taken an active role in the organization, which includes more than 650 employees.

Participants have use of the Cooper Aerobics Center in Dallas and Craig Ranch in McKinney, Texas, a major fitness center with multiple programs.

Learn more at www.cooperaerobics.com.

Duke Diet and Fitness Center

This is one of the most highly respected treatment centers in the world for individuals who are overweight or obese. It is located at Duke University in Durham, North Carolina.

The comprehensive programs last from one to four weeks and are designed to empower patients with education, experience, practical behavioral strategies, and ongoing support. The staff includes physicians, nurse practitioners, and other medical personnel, from physical therapists to registered dieticians. It's a multidisciplinary treatment approach that deals with medical problems associated with obesity and inactivity, including high blood pressure, arthritis, and breathing disorders.

On average, the Duke patients lose five percent of their initial body weight and often more during the initial four-week program. Plus, vast improvement is reported in blood sugar, blood pressure, and cholesterol levels. The program claims that after one year, 80 percent of the participants either maintain or continue to lose weight. Emphasis is on making long-term changes.

Those who have completed the residence program are offered free lifestyle group telephone calls to keep them on target.

Learn more at www.dukehealth.org.

When Molly Sims wants to lose weight fast, she visits the We Care Spa in Desert Hot Springs, California, a holistic fasting and spiritual retreat where clients are restricted to eating only 400 calories per day through a natural liquid diet that is primarily wheat grass.

Hilton Head Health Institute

This popular facility has been in operation for more than three decades and has helped thousands of people. It is located in one of the "plantations" on Hilton Head Island, South Carolina.

The program is designed around a unique combination of weight management, healthy diet, and enjoyable exercise. It links the patient's motivation for physical improvement with the staff's expertise in helping people learn the habits of good health. The objective is to assist individuals in building a foundation for healthy weight loss that is sustainable—rather than a lifetime of binge dieting or guilt. Emphasis is on behaviors and choices you can change, control, and build into habits and routines you can keep.

> I am also five three and in the neighborhood of one thirty. It is a neighborhood I would like to get out of.
>
> FLANNERY O'CONNOR

Every participant is given a personally tailored weight loss assessment along with a dieting and fitness plan. Specific programs target managing diabetes, stimulating metabolic rate, practicing new behaviors, and learning to prepare foods in a healthy manner.

The typical program includes accommodations, three healthy gourmet meals, and daily snacks. You also receive a health assessment, blood screening, and a private session focused on goal setting, meal planning, and exercise strategies. There is unlimited participation in all daily fitness classes and nutritional and cooking classes—plus group sessions on stress management, motivation, and self discovery.

Learn more at www.hhhealth.com.

Pritikin Longevity Center and Spa

Earlier, when we discussed popular dieting programs, we reviewed the Pritikin Principle, which was developed by one of the gurus of the dieting revolution, Nathan Pritikin, author of books that have sold millions of copies. In 1976, he established the Pritikin Longevity Center in Aventura, Florida, just north of Miami. It is now directed by his son, Robert Pritikin.

To date, more than 100,000 people worldwide have come to the center for one-week, two-week, or longer programs. For some the goal is to lose weight. Others enroll to prevent and address health issues. Plus, there are those who simply want a spa-health vacation.

The hallmark of this program is its strong medical presence, complete with board-certified physicians. Your stay begins with a comprehensive physical examination, including blood pressure screening, cardiovascular diagnostics, dietary analysis, and weight loss planning. The average Pritikin guest spends about 2.5 hours of private time with a personal physician. Issues addressed include high cholesterol, hypertension, arthritis, pain, smoking, cancer, and both men's and women's health.

The experience is designed to be "transformative"—with a plan you will follow for the rest of your life. There are dozens of educational classes in everything from "Reversing Diabetes" to "Smart Supermarket Shopping" and "Taking Care of Stress."

Learn more at www.pritikin.com.

Medically Supervised Weight Loss Clinics

Some people are desperate to lose weight, but are so confused by the many diet choices that they turn to a doctor to help them. There are many medically supervised weight loss programs that are typically designed for people who are 40 or more pounds overweight. They start out with an evaluation, medical exam, and consultation by a medical professional, including medical history, vital signs, EKG, weight, body fat analysis, and waist circumference.

They provide exercise and nutritional advice, which generally recommends the patient purchase supplements and other nutrition products. They also provide accountability by requiring weekly meetings with a weight loss counselor. These programs are generally extreme calorie restriction diets, which often prescribe stimulants to suppress appetite and offer regular vitamin B12 injections to increase energy.

Unfortunately, most doctors know little about nutrition, and these approaches use the basic theory of calorie restriction without optimal nutrition and use drug stimulants to help people deal with hunger. People do lose weight on these programs; however, once a patient reaches their weight loss goal and returns to life without stimulants and accountability, they generally regain the weight. This has the potential to be a really good system (except the stimulants), because people trust their doctor. However, any diet that does not address the full spectrum of the body's nutritional requirements, including adequate protein, is not likely to sustain long-term weight loss.

A friend of mine in Tampa was doing a local physician weight loss program together with his uncle. A part of the program was to take a medically supervised stimulant. His uncle had such a surge of stimulant energy he decided to do everything he had been putting off around the home in one afternoon—clean the garage, mow the lawn, etc. As a result, he had a massive heart attack and almost died.

Ritz-Carlton—Orlando, Naples Beach, and Bachelor Gulch

These are three of my wife's and my favorite resort/spa combinations. They are all magnificent properties with incredible spas, fully equipped exercise rooms, and professional strength and fitness staff as well as spa restaurants. While these properties are not known for weight loss programs or packages, their facilities are ideal for anyone who is self-motivated enough to use these world-class facilities. If you are familiar with the Ritz-Carlton, you realize that if you let them know you are there to get into shape, they will roll out the red carpet in that direction.

Learn more at www.ritzcarlton.com.

Even though we have highlighted major health spas in the United States, there are many more to choose from worldwide, including:

- Clinique La Prairie Institute in Clarens-Montreux, Switzerland (www.laprairie.ch)
- CuisinArt Resort & Spa in Anquilla, British West Indies (www.cuisinartresort.com)
- Stobo Castle Health Spa in Peeblesshire, Scotland (www.stobocastle.co.uk).

Chapter 8

The Role of the Thyroid and Sex Hormones in Weight Loss

If you never had problems losing or maintaining your weight in your 20s or even in your early 30s, you may not be ready for what happens next. Your metabolism slows by five percent each decade. Compared to age 25, you'll burn about 100 fewer calories a day at 35 and 200 fewer at 45. Do nothing, and you could gain eight to 12 pounds a year.
MADELYN H. FERNSTROM, PH.D.

It happens every day. A middle-aged woman walks into her doctor's office, stating that she is bone-tired and on edge all the time, even after a good night's rest, and often depressed. And no matter what diet she tries, nothing works, and the pounds just keep adding up. If she tries to exercise, she is even more exhausted and feels as though she'll fall apart. She's desperate to lose weight and feel decent again, can't take it anymore. What can be done?

Her doctor should immediately notice that her skin is dry and flaky, her hair is coarse and thin, and her hands feel icy cold. All of which, along with the weight loss problem and nagging fatigue and depression, are symptoms of a low thyroid condition. Unfortunately, often these signals are overlooked.

After more consultation, standard lab tests are taken, which suggest that everything looks normal. All too often she is then told that her complaints are simply common to scores of patients, and she is, in fact, "perfectly normal." However, while it is true that her symptoms are common to hundreds of thousands of people, especially women in her age group, that does not make it *normal*. She is left to think that it must be all in her head or something she's doing wrong, even though she suffers from an underactive thyroid gland that suppresses her metabolism.

Hypothyroidism or Hypometabolic Syndrome

The thyroid gland is located in the front of your neck below the skin and muscle layers and is phenomenally important to your overall health. Every hour approximately five quarts of blood circulate through your thyroid gland, delivering iodide (a compound of iodine) to the gland as well as hormones from the pituitary gland that stimulate the thyroid into its hormone production.

The function of the thyroid gland is to take iodine, found in many foods, and convert it into thyroid hormones: thyroxine (T4) and tri-iodothyronine (T3). These cells combine iodine and the amino acid tyrosine to make T3 and T4, which are then released into the bloodstream and transported throughout the body, where they control metabolism (the rate your body converts oxygen and calories to energy). Every cell in the body depends upon thyroid hormones for regulation of their metabolism, and thus for their health.

Your thyroid gland is under the control of the pituitary gland, which is located at the base of the brain. When the level of T3 and T4 drops too low, the pituitary gland produces Thyroid Stimulating Hormone (TSH), which stimulates the thyroid gland to produce more hormones. Under the influence of TSH, the thyroid will manufacture and secrete T3 and T4, thereby raising their blood levels. The pituitary gland senses this and responds by decreasing its TSH production. Imagine the pituitary gland as your inner thermostat, the thyroid gland as your furnace, and the thyroid hormones as your heat. As the room cools (the hormone levels drop), the thermostat kicks back on (TSH increases), and the furnace produces more heat (hormones), and the cycle continues—if all is normal and functioning correctly.

The hormones the thyroid gland secretes go directly into your bloodstream and enter every cell. Because of the presence of that hormone in your cell, a complex protein molecule binds to DNA in a different manner than it would if that thyroid hormone were not there. This entire process functions like a switch to turn your cellular machinery, or mitochondria, on or off. When thyroid hormone levels increase, thyroid receptors in the cell nucleus increase DNA transcription, which increases both the synthesis of specific mitochondrial proteins and energy production. Decreases in thyroid hormone shut down synthesis of these proteins and lowers mitochondrial energy production. This process determines our absolute intracellular ATP levels (molecules that carry the energy necessary to facilitate all of the processes of human metabolism).

When your body lacks sufficient thyroid hormone, the condition is called *hypothyroidism* or *hypometabolic syndrome*. This can happen when there is inadequate production of T4, poor conversion from T4 to T3, problems with the cells' ability to take up T3, with receptor function, and intracellular transport—obviously, a complex balance is required. Since the main purpose of the thyroid hormone is to drive the body's metabolism, it makes sense that people with this condition experience symptoms associated with a slow metabolism. Decreased mitochondrial energy production reduces the capacity of the cells to function, and a body with insufficient thyroid hormone becomes tired and rundown. As your metabolism slows and burns fewer and fewer calories, it's no surprise if you experience a corresponding gain in weight and numerous other possible symptoms. Your body simply was not meant to operate at such a slow metabolism, and the symptoms are trying to tell you that.

Hypothyroidism is a condition that can occur in both males and females at any age, although middle-aged women are by far the highest percentage of those who are afflicted by the condition. It will often mask its symptoms effectively beneath other common ailments experienced by people without thyroid deficiencies; therefore, it routinely goes undiagnosed. Many doctors note the person's fatigue, weight gain, and/or depression, but some attribute those symptoms automatically to other causes.

Symptoms of Hypothyroidism

The symptoms of low thyroid are often dependent on the amount of decrease in the thyroid hormone and how long the deficiency has existed. For most people, the symptoms are mild and may include the following: weight gain or increased difficulty losing weight, significant fatigue and weakness, rough pale skin, coarse hair and hair loss, dry brittle nails that crack and peel easily, depression, irritability, and mood swings, muscle swelling or cramps, intolerance to cold, frequent bouts of cold and influenza, chronic recurrent infections, loss of appetite, constipation, slowed pulse, low blood pressure, anemia (especially the B12 deficiency type), problems with memory, focus, or concentration, wounds that heal slowly, decreased libido, frequent headaches, and burning and tingling in the fingers. People vary in just what functions are diminished most, and the number of these symptoms can vary with the severity of the deficiency.

> Sometimes your body is smarter than you are.
>
> AUTHOR UNKNOWN

Causes of Hypothyroidism

- *Lack of the Components That Make Up Thyroid Hormones—Iodine* deficiency is somewhat rare within the United States, as extra iodine is put into various food items, including table salt and bread dough, but it is possible. *Tyrosine* is an amino acid that forms the basis for the thyroid hormones and must be in adequate supply.
- *Autoimmune Diseases*—The most common cause of hypothyroidism in the United States is chronic autoimmune thyroiditis, or Hashimoto's thyroiditis, a condition characterized by inflammation and damage to the thyroid tissue. Immune cells that routinely fight off infection and colds attack the body's thyroid tissue instead, leaving a large percentage of the cells of the thyroid damaged or dead and incapable of producing sufficient hormone. If you have other autoimmune diseases, you may also be at risk for

Hashimoto's thyroiditis. Rheumatoid arthritis (where immune cells attack the joints) and diabetes (where immune cells attack the pancreas, which produces insulin) need to be watched. In fact, about 10 percent of patients with type 1 or juvenile diabetes mellitus develop chronic thyroiditis sometime during their life. Diabetics should be checked regularly for thyroid disease.

- *Nutrient Deficiencies*—selenium, chromium, iron, copper, zinc, and vitamins. Low levels of vitamin D, for instance, affect thyroid receptor response. Ferritin is a protein in the body that binds to iron and stores the iron—low ferritin levels restrict the transport of T3 within the cells.

- *Poor Recovery Following Acute Stress*—Stress causes high cortisol levels that increase reverse T3, which actually serves as a mechanism to block the conversion of T4 to T3. It's as though the body knows it is going too fast and overdoing it, so extra reverse T3 lowers energy levels, you get tired, and you're virtually forced to slow down. (Low cortisol can also inhibit T4 to T3 conversion.)

- *Toxins in the Liver*—Whatever inhibits the function of the liver will affect the production of the thyroid, especially heavy metal toxicity. Hormones, such as birth control and estrogen, and steroids inhibit the production of the thyroid hormone as relates to the liver as well. These can cause the thyroid to become sluggish, not necessarily diseased.

- *Surgery*—Whenever the thyroid gland is removed completely by surgery for whatever reason, your doctor will prescribe medication to replace the hormone your body can no longer produce. If only half of your thyroid is removed and the remaining half is normal, you can still produce enough thyroid hormone in order to function normally, but regular blood tests should be made to make certain the remaining portion of the thyroid is continuing to function well.

- *Aging*—Unfortunately, as we age, thyroid function decreases, particularly in women who are 45 to 50 years old.

- *Pregnancy*—Low thyroid is common in the postpartum period and easily confused with postpartum depression. You may require thyroid hormone adjustments. Therefore, thyroid tests are often a routine part of evaluating a patient who has problems with pregnancy.

• *Medications and Radioactive Iodine*—If you are taking a prescription medication that has been shown to cause thyroid disease, such as lithium, you may be at risk for an underactive thyroid. Some thyroid diseases such as Graves' disease are treated with radioactive iodine, which destroys the overactive thyroid cells and eliminates the cause of hyperthyroidism. But sometimes the destruction of these cells goes too far and results in hypothyroidism. If you have been treated with therapeutic doses of radioactive iodine, you should have routine blood tests to monitor it.

• *Secondary Hypothyroidism*—Disorders of the pituitary gland or hypothalamus portions of the brain may cause thyroid hormone deficiency in addition to other hormonal imbalances. This type of rare hypothyroidism can also be treated with thyroid hormone medication.

The Basal Temperature Test

Since the thyroid gland controls your metabolism, one simple measure of your metabolic rate is your body temperature, which can be observed by both you and your physician. The temperature test should be done immediately upon awakening in the morning and before you get out of bed. Here are the specific steps that should be taken:

1. If you are male or a non-menstruating female, take an oral mercury thermometer that has been shaken down below 95°F and placed at the bedside the previous evening. When you wake up, place the thermometer under your arm with the bulb in the armpit and no clothing between it and the armpit for 10 minutes. Readings taken in the armpit are somewhat lower and more accurate than by mouth. Repeat the test five days in a row. Normal temperature ranges from 97.8°F to 98.2°F. If your temperature is low, your thyroid gland may be underactive.

2. If you are a female who menstruates, do the above test on the second and third day of your period in the same manner.

3. If you have a very young child and are unable to take his/her armpit temperature, you can take the rectal temperature for two minutes. Normal would be 1°F higher than the above—that is 98.8°F to 99.2°F.

4. Record your results below and bring this record to your physician.

This temperature test is not part of what is considered the standard diagnosis of low thyroid. Nevertheless, if you consistently get a reading that is well below the normal range, the evidence points toward a sluggish metabolism.

Thyroid Boosters

- *Iodine*—With today's emphasis on staying "off table salt," it's possible to push your iodine intake down too low. Taking kelp, a natural form of iodine, will stimulate the thyroid into producing more thyroid hormone.
- *Tyrosine*—This amino acid is the basis for the thyroid hormones. T3 and T4 are made of three or four atoms respectively of iodine attached to the tyrosine molecule. Tyrosine is a micronutrient found in certain types of protein, such as dairy products, and partners with iodine to help the thyroid manufacture thyroid hormone. Tyrosine supplementation, when health is good and iodide intake is adequate, may increase thyroid hormone levels.
- *Essential Fatty Acids Omega-3 and -6*—1,000 mg to 1,500 mg of combined EPA and DHA from fish oil plus GLA from borage seed oil or evening primrose oil are necessary for optimal hormone production. Cold water fatty fish or fish oils, which provide omega-3 oils, are excellent.
- *Vitamins*—A vitamin is a catalyst that enables other nutrients to work. Vitamin deficiencies can result in low thyroid, especially vitamin D deficiency or insufficiency. It is important to take a

> If you are hypothyroid, your metabolism becomes so efficient at storing every calorie that even the most rigorous diet and exercise programs may not work.
>
> MARY J. SHOMON

complete and high quality multivitamin with minerals as a simple way of getting most of the basic nutrients the body requires. It is vital that you regularly take a balanced "stress" B-complex with meals, which improves cellular oxygenation and energy. Avoid synthetic vitamins.

- *Minerals*—Selenium, copper, chromium, potassium, iron, and zinc are vital to healthy thyroid function. Minerals function, along with vitamins, as components of body enzymes. They are important to the production of hormones and enzymes and in the creation of antibodies. Selenium is thought to support the vital conversion of T4 into T3 and is also found in tuna, mushrooms, and wheat germ.

- *Herbs*—A combination of herbs rich in minerals, such as horsetail, oatstraw, alfalfa, and gotu kola, support thyroid function. Some of the best herbal teas are green tea, black tea, peppermint, spearmint, chamomile, thyme, milk thistle, and licorice. A few herbal stimulants, such as ma-huang, guarana, and excessive caffeine, cause stress to the thyroid and adrenals and should be minimized.

- *Natural Glandular Support*—Many nutrition stores carry what is called a natural thyroid glandular. Although it does not contain the thyroid hormone and is considered a nutritional product, its use borders on the medicinal. They usually come in tablet form and consist of freeze-dried purified animal glands. For some people they apparently provide just enough support to the thyroid gland to stimulate adequate hormone production.

- *Recommended Foods*—Eat high fiber foods, because fiber picks up the slack for a sluggish metabolism, binding to food and moving it quickly through the system so fewer calories are absorbed. Dedicate yourself to the nutrient-rich Four Corners Diet—the Super Health Diet. Eat lots of fresh, whole organic foods, including coconut, eggs, parsley, apricots, dates, prunes, and fish. Raw fresh vegetables and fruits, free of artificial colors, preservatives, or chemicals of any kind are a must. Try to purchase meat from range-fed cattle and poultry raised on an organic diet. It's best to avoid skipping breakfast, especially because the early morning is when certain hormones are at the high point in their daily cycle. Begin your day with a meal that stimulates your metabolic activity, such as a high protein SuperSmoothie.

• *Foods to Minimize or Avoid*—Certain vegetables from the cabbage family, which are normally extremely healthy foods, have been shown to interfere with one's normal thyroid hormone production and should be minimized only in the case of proven thyroid issues—Brussels sprouts, broccoli, cabbage, cauliflower, mustard greens, horseradish, radish, kohlrabi, white mustard, turnips, spinach, rutabaga, and kale. Similarly, eating large quantities of almonds, walnuts, pine nuts, peanuts, sorghum, and millet can also stimulate the release of substances that may cause swelling of the thyroid. Some experts recommend limiting your intake of soy because researchers seem to be linking large doses of soy and thyroid autoimmunity. Avoid as many refined and chemically tainted foods as possible—these disrupt vital organ functions, including the thyroid. Avoid canned and refined foods, drugs, strong spices, sugar, coffee, black tea, and alcohol.

> **Where do you go to get anorexia?**
>
> SHELLEY WINTERS

• *Exercise*—As your thyroid function improves, so will your energy levels. Take advantage of that long-lost energy by starting a mild exercise program such as walking, which will help your thyroid function even better and boost your energy even higher. Low thyroid results in the reduction of the release of serotonin—the feel-good hormone—which can contribute to depression and feelings of lethargy. Exercise helps push the levels of serotonin and improves your mood and energy, *plus* burning calories.

• *Detoxify your liver, gall bladder, and colon.* As mentioned above, toxins from food and the environment can make a person overweight. You can detoxify your body with the right balance of protein, fats, fiber, vitamins, minerals, and phytonutrients found in the Four Corners of Superfood Nutrition, which also are important in detoxing from food intolerances.

Diagnosis of Hypothyroidism

Since hypothyroidism is usually caused by insufficient thyroid hormone being secreted into the bloodstream, its diagnosis is often based exclusively upon the end result—the amount of thyroid hormone present in the blood. Years of testing have established normal ranges for the general population. If your hormone levels drop below the normal range, it's a good indication that you may be suffering from hypothyroidism based on insufficient production of T4 and T3 in the thyroid gland. These tests are routinely available to anyone.

However, be aware that standard lab tests are unable to identify many borderline low thyroid sufferers. H. Jack Baskin, M.D., vice president of the American Association of Clinical Endocrinologists, stated, "While extreme hypothyroidism is rare and is easily identified, mild cases are often not detected in routine blood tests, so subclinical hypothyroidism mostly falls through the cracks. Your doctor might try to convince you that your symptoms are 'a normal part of aging' or 'nothing to worry about.' Don't buy it. It's your quality of life that is being severely compromised, and it is your right to get to the bottom of these 'minor' ailments."

The trick is that in many cases where symptoms of hypothyroidism exist, the cause of the problem may not be the lack of ability to produce an optional amount of thyroid hormone from the thyroid gland. Before initiation of Thyroid Replacement Therapy (TRT), the capacity of the gland to produce optimal levels of the thyroid hormones, primarily T4, should be first determined. If the level is low, it is possible the person does not have sufficient quantities of tyrosine and iodine to make the thyroid hormone.

There may be multiple factors that are causing a person's symptoms of hypothyroidism, and many can be addressed without the need for TRT. If TRT is administered when it is not really needed, the result may be a temporary improvement in symptoms the first few weeks, followed by a return of symptoms. The cause is the body increasing Thyroid Binding Globulin (TBG) in response to the thyroid hormone it doesn't really need, and therefore binding up hormone it considers excessive.

The increase in TBG can take place during two to three months, so the net effect of any initiation or change in TRT is not seen immediately.

If someone has many of the symptoms of hypothyroidism and essentially normal blood work, monitoring basal body temperature may be revealing. (See www.wilsonssyndrome.com for details.) If the basal temperature is less than 97.8°F, it is possible that they have peripheral underconversion hypothyroidism. (In other words, T4 is not efficiently converted to T3 inside the cells.) Several nutrient deficiencies and many other factors will slow and even prevent the conversion of T4 to T3, including selenium and zinc, chromium and iodine, iron, copper, vitamin A, vitamin B2, vitamin B6, vitamin B12, vitamin D3 levels below 40 ng/ml, and vitamin E.

Other factors that block conversion include: Stress with too much or too little cortisol, halogen (chlorine and bromine) toxicity, anti-thyroid peroxidase antibodies, excess reverse T3, excess estrogen, obesity, liver or kidney disease, and starvation. Be sure to check prescription drugs, since many block the T4/T3 conversion, including SSRIs, opiates, beta blockers, and birth control pills. To naturally increase T4/T3 conversion take the above nutrients and an optimum higher protein diet and make all the other lifestyle changes mentioned in this book.

As this chapter has shown, there are many steps you can take on your own that may help your body if it is battling with hypothyroidism. However, if you have the symptoms, I recommend that you go to a doctor. Discuss with your doctor if you've had oral estrogen therapy or used oral contraceptives or any other concerns raised as you read this information. Ask the doctor about the factors that affect transport, receptor density, and receptor response, including chronic high or low cortisol, ferritin, and 25-OH vitamin D. Ferritin should be in a range of 90 to 110 ng/ml and vitamin D in a range of 60 to 80 ng/ml to get optimal thyroid response.

Ask your physician for more than the usual thyroid panel of tests. Ask for the TSH (thyroid stimulating hormone) test, which is a more accurate index of thyroid functions. If your blood tests are normal, but you haven't been tested for thyroid antibodies, insist on this as a next step. Thyroid tests should always include at least one test to check for autoimmune antibodies. These tests include Thyroid Peroxidase antibody (TPO or TPOAb), Thyroglobulin antibody (TgAb), and Thyroid stimulating hormone receptor antibody (TRAb). The TPO test appears to identify a reaction most commonly. If autoimmune reaction is suspected, all three tests can be ordered. Heavy metal toxicity tests can also be ordered if systemic symptoms indicate.

Similar to the relationship of insulin and a diabetic, a small amount of thyroid hormone must be supplied from the outside to make up for the shortfall when a person's thyroid function is truly deficient and the gland is not responding adequately. For the majority of patients with hypothyroidism, taking some form of thyroid hormone replacement returns the thyroid blood tests to the normal range. This process does not always work automatically for everyone, and if you're one of them, it is very important to find a doctor or specialist who will listen and be sympathetic. If thyroid hormone is required, insist on natural or bioidentical hormones.

Special thanks to Leonard Smith, M.D., who provided me research and helpful advice regarding the thyroid and weight loss.

Sex Hormones

Throughout this book, you may notice that all hormones—insulin, leptin, cortisol, serotonin, melatonin, endorphins, testosterone, estrogen, thyroxine, epinephrine, and glucagons—have an effect on our weight. Hormones are chemical messengers that trigger or regulate bodily functions. You've read how when hormones get out of balance, negative effects cascade within the body, including weight gain, and weight gain in turn negatively affects hormones. Hormones can get out of balance as a result of many factors, including stress, poor nutrition, lack of exercise, inadequate rest, and illness—all that my Seven Keys to Super Health specifically deal with. According to Dr. Geoffrey Redmond, director of the Hormone Center of New York and author of *The Good News About Women's Hormones*, you can nutritionally influence your hormones into losing weight by following the principles of the Four Corners of Superfood Nutrition.

Sex hormones, such as estrogen and androgen, affect the growth or function of the reproductive organs, the development of secondary sex characteristics, and the behavioral patterns of mammals. Testosterone and estradiol are the most important human derivatives of androgens and estrogens, respectively. Progesterone is another important sex steroid. In general, androgens are considered "male sex hormones," since they have masculinizing effects, while estrogens and progestagens are considered "female sex hormones," although all types are present in each gender, albeit at different levels.

In a study cited by the Department of Human Nutrition at the Wageningen Agricultural University in the Netherlands, a significant connection was made between sex hormones, visceral fat, and weight loss in women. During the study, women with excessive levels of visceral fat were associated with reduced sex hormones. When the women lost weight (an average of 11 pounds), the visceral fat decreased and the sex hormones increased to normal levels. Clearly, studies show weight control and hormone regulation are key.

In his book *Testosterone for Life,* Abraham Morgentaler, M.D., an Associate Clinical Professor of Urology at Harvard Medical School, shows convincingly the life-enhancing benefits that men with low levels of testosterone can experience when they increase it—increased vitality, better sex, improved health and mental agility, and muscle gain. If you've noticed a decrease in your sex drive, experienced erectile dysfunction, or felt tired, depressed, and unmotivated, this book will help you determine if you have low testosterone—a surprisingly common but frequently undiagnosed condition among middle-aged men—and ways to reverse the effects of it.

There are several health benefits you may experience by taking the steps necessary to regulate your hormones and lose weight. According to Dr. Michael Roizen, chief wellness officer at the Cleveland Clinic, regulating your hormones will not only induce weight loss, but may lower cholesterol levels, reduce blood pressure, improve energy, reduce aches and pains, improve rest, increase oxygen flow to the heart, prevent the development of type 2 diabetes, and stabilize blood sugar.

If you are unsure whether or not your hormones are preventing you from losing weight, you should schedule an appointment with your health care practitioner who will perform a blood test to have your hormone levels checked. For men, it's straightforward to test hormones at any time of the month. Women need to test hormones multiple times during the monthly cycle even if a woman is postmenstrual or has had a hysterectomy. Home saliva testing is best because multiple blood tests during a one-month period are expensive and not practical.

I want to stress the importance of supporting normal hormone production and balance and, when necessary, restoring bioidentical hormones to youthful levels in weight loss and Super Health. Also, I want to stress the importance of bioidentical hormones and that synthetic hormones can be very dangerous. If it has a drug name that sounds similar to the hormone name, you don't want it. If you need testosterone, progesterone, or estrogen, get natural bioidentical testosterone, progesterone, or estrogen hormones from a compounding pharmacy, not a patented drug prescribed by your doctor.

I often recommend people have their doctor contact hormone expert Dr. Robert Fishman of the Robert Fishman Institute for Training and Research (www.askrfi.com). He is a pharmacist who consults and trains doctors to do natural hormone balancing and bioidentical hormone replacement for their patients. Richard Lippman, M.D., for whom I have a great deal of respect, recommends Michael Platt, M.D. of Palm Springs, California, as a leader in this field of medicine (www.plattwellness.com). Additional resources to help you find a physician who is knowledgeable in hormone testing and bioidentical hormone replacement therapy include contacting your local compounding pharmacy and asking for a referral or contacting the American Academy of Anti-Aging Medicine (A4M.org) and Life Extension Foundation (www.lef.org). Home hormone testing kits are also available from Fishman Institute, Life Extension Foundation and ZRT Labs (www.zrtlab.com).

Men and Testosterone Levels

A large percentage of men today suffer from abdominal obesity. As men age, their levels of free testosterone decline and levels of estrogen and insulin increase. This is partly because aging men convert (aromatize) much of their testosterone into estradiol, a form of estrogen. Of the remaining testosterone, much is bound to sex hormone-binding globulin, a protein in the blood, and is not biologically active. It is often difficult, if not impossible for aging men to lose inches off their waist-line if they are deficient in free testosterone, especially in the presence of excess estrogen.[17] Low levels of dehydroepiandro-sterone (DHEA) can also contribute to undesirable fat accumulation in men and women.[18] A comprehensive blood test panel can reveal free testosterone and estrogen (estradiol) levels so that a physician can prescribe a topical testosterone cream and an aromatase-inhibiting drug (if necessary) to restore a man's sex hormone profile to a youthful range. The same blood test panel can also detect DHEA blood levels to enable one to take the proper dose of this over-the-counter dietary supplement.

I need to note that an epidemic problem in aging male members is insufficient free testosterone, i.e., less than 15 to 20 pg/mL of serum. When accompanied by excess estradiol (over 30 pg/mL of serum), this can signal excess aromatase enzyme activity. Optimal estradiol blood levels in men are between 20 to 30 pg/mL. *Elderly males can have much higher estradiol levels that place them at substantial risk for developing coronary atherosclerosis and thrombotic stroke.* Men with even slightly elevated estrogen levels doubled their risk of stroke and had far higher incidences of coronary artery disease.[19] The fact that 99 percent of men today have no idea what their blood estrogen levels are helps explain the epidemic of age-related disease that is bankrupting this nation's medical system.

A study published in the May 2009 *Journal of the American Medical Association* (JAMA) measured blood estradiol (a dominant estrogen) in 501 men with chronic heart failure. Compared to men in the balanced estrogen quintile, men in the lowest estradiol quintile were 317 percent more likely to die during a three-year follow-up, while men in the highest estradiol quintile were 133 percent more likely to die.[20] The men in the balanced quintile—with the fewest deaths—had serum estradiol levels between 21.80 and 30.11 pg/mL. The men in the highest quintile who suffered 133 percent increased death rates had serum estradiol levels of 37.40 pg/mL or above. The lowest estradiol group that suffered a 317 percent increased death rate had serum estradiol levels under 12.90 pg/mL.

In response to overwhelmingly favorable studies, record numbers of aging men are rubbing testosterone creams or gels on to their skin each day to restore this vital hormone to youthful levels. A person needs to be sure to work with a doctor who understands there's more to it than just rubbing on a testosterone cream. If men are prescribed large doses of topical testosterone gel or cream, their estradiol blood levels have to be tested and properly controlled. *Failure to manage estradiol in men receiving high dose testosterone gel or cream can result in a catastrophic estrogen surge that increases vascular disease risk and premature death.*

Testosterone levels can be increased naturally by losing weight, exercising, cleaning up the diet, taking DHEA and natural aromatase-inhibitors such as chrysin or a combination of Chinese herbs (from a traditional Chinese medicine doctor). My recommendation for a natural aromatase-inhibitor is a supplement from Life Extension Foundation called Super MiraForte, which contains high potencies of chrysin and nettle root—plant extracts that naturally reduce the aromatization (conversion) of testosterone to estrogen to enhance free testosterone levels.

Estrogen dominance can be reduced by eating a diet high in fiber, which binds to excess estrogen and removes it from the body as waste and also helps prevent constipation, which exacerbates estrogen dominance. Apple pectin fiber is often used to reduce testosterone levels and should be avoided unless that is the goal. Staying hydrated and exercising regularly encourages healthy hormone balance. Alcohol should be in moderation or not at all—it is an "estrogenic" substance, meaning it causes the body to produce more estrogen. Alcohol is a toxic sugar that damages the liver, promotes insulin resistance, favors fat storage, and thus leads to conversion of testosterone to estrogen in males as well as females.

More Correlation of Low Testosterone and Obesity

In an April 2010 study published in the online version of the journal *Diabetes Care*, researchers at the University at Buffalo showed that obesity, already linked to heart disease and diabetes, may also be associated with low testosterone levels, a condition that affects only men. Forty percent of obese participants in the study had lower-than-normal testosterone readings. For those obese men who also had diabetes, that percent rose to 50 percent. The study also found that as body mass index—the relationship of weight to height—increased in both diabetic and non-diabetic men, testosterone levels decreased.

While past studies have shown a link between diabetes and low testosterone, this study is the largest analysis to look at the association between obesity and low testosterone and the first to compare the prevalence of low testosterone with obesity and diabetes separately and together. The study involved 2,165 men, 45 years or older, who provided blood samples for analysis of testosterone concentrations.

Considering that almost one-third of the U. S. population is considered obese, the findings could have significant medical and public health implications, the authors reported. "The effect of diabetes on lowering testosterone levels was similar to that of a weight gain of approximately 20 pounds," said lead author Dr. Sandeep Dhindsa, an endocrinology specialist at the University of Buffalo, Department of Medicine, and lead author of the study.

The Endocrine Society recommends that all men with type 2 diabetes have their testosterone levels measured. Dhindsa said the new study indicates that physicians also should consider screening obese non-diabetic men, even younger men, for low testosterone.

A separate study published in the December 2008 *Journal of the American College of Surgeons* found that obese men who lost significant weight reported better sexual function, one of several to show the side benefits of slimming down. The research involved 97 men with an average age of 48, all of whom were "morbidly obese." The conclusions are based on the patients' own reporting of sexual function before and again several months after gastric bypass surgery (a smarter strategy for most people would be exercise and good nutrition) that allowed them to shed significant weight. "We estimate that a man who is morbidly obese has the same degree of sexual dysfunction as a non-obese man about 20 years older," the researcher concluded.

Higher testosterone levels slash mortality risk in aging men. Yes, testosterone levels matter in more than just weight loss. I believe it is negligent for conventional medicine to continue to ignore this as a basic health issue.

Additionally, governing authorities over the Olympics, college, and professional sports have taken the matter of steroids too far by including testosterone as a banned substance. It is not just about performance—aging athletes' very lives may depend on restoring youthful levels of this essential hormone.

Chapter 9

14 New Reasons for Losing Weight

*My weight is always perfect for my height—
which varies.*
NICOLE HOLLANDER

If I haven't made it crystal clear by this point in the book, being overweight is not just a cosmetic problem—it is an extraordinary health hazard. Diabetes has already reached epidemic proportions among children, and 70 percent of adults 65 and older are either diabetic or prediabetic, which means they are on their way to being diabetic unless lifestyle changes are undertaken. An estimated 300,000 Americans die prematurely each year of disease caused by being very overweight. Someone who is 40 percent overweight is twice as likely to die prematurely as is an average-weight person. This is because obesity has been linked to several serious medical conditions, including heart disease and stroke, high blood pressure, type 2 diabetes, cancer, gallbladder disease and gallstones, osteoarthritis, gout, and breathing problems, such as sleep apnea and asthma.

Obesity experts believe that overweight people are twice as likely to have high blood pressure as those who are not overweight. A large body of research suggests that chronic inflammation is a major cause of aging and many degenerative diseases, and obesity is a major contributor to chronic inflammation. It can affect your body's ability to fight off infection, cope with stress, digest and metabolize the foods you eat, and affect how hard your heart has to work to keep your body functioning. It can even reduce your ability to reproduce or become pregnant.

Unless we reverse the obesity trend, 43 percent of Americans will be obese by 2018, and it is estimated that the nation will spend $344 billion to address health-related problems. Interestingly, though, in a British study reported in September 2009 *Telegraph*, only one person in 10 identified themselves as being obese, when in fact one in four was obese (roughly 30 or more pounds overweight). British researchers have coined this phenomenon as "the fat gap," referring to the discrepancy between how individuals see themselves and their actual weight. This lack of awareness, which might be due to being surrounded by a majority of other supersized people, unwittingly places the individual at risk for medical problems triggered by obesity.

In the November 2009 issue of the *American Journal of Public Health,* researchers reported that Americans currently in their 60s are going to suffer more disabilities and medical problems than did the preceding generations, thus reversing decades of improvements in the health of seniors. The biggest factor contributing to the decline is the expanding rate of obesity.

There is a steady stream of new research related to obesity and being overweight, and the news is constantly bad. If it's good, don't believe it. If you go to websites such as www.sciencedaily.com, www.natural-news.com, or www.LivingFuel.TV, you'll find reliable updates on why it is essential that you win the battle for the waistline. If you don't have the time to do the research, join the Living Fuel fan page on Facebook or follow me on Twitter. I've assembled just a tiny fraction of the research that was published while writing this book to reiterate to you the wide range of health-related issues that are affected by your weight.

#1—Belly Fat as Well as Fatty Liver Are Big Culprits

A UPI story on August 26, 2009, reported on recently published research in the *Proceedings of the National Academy of Sciences* that suggests liver fat may be the important risk factor for obesity-related metabolic disorders often linked to diabetes, heart disease, and other diseases. As you may be aware, belly fat has long been seen as the major culprit, but that may not be the case.

Researchers were well aware that many people with belly fat also have fatty livers, but when they compared for insulin sensitivity and other factors in obese subjects matched for belly fat but with differing liver fat content, they found lower insulin sensitivity and higher tryglyceride secretion in those with fatty livers. However, these differences were not observed when the subjects differed on amounts of belly fat but were matched on liver fat.

Why does that matter? Fatty liver disease is reversible, and this finding may mean a big health benefit gained through losing just a little body fat, but a lot of liver fat. The senior investigator, Dr. Samuel Klein of the Washington University School of Medicine in St. Louis, stated, "In fact, even two days of calorie restriction can cause a large reduction in liver fat and improvement in liver insulin sensitivity."

Regarding fatty liver, other interesting research continues to come forward. Findings from an animal study published in the October 2009 *Biochemical Pharmacology* showed that supplements of coenzyme Q10 (CoQ10) may protect or retard the development of fatty liver related to obesity. Researchers from the University of Leuven, in collaboration with scientists from the University of Witten/Herdecke in Germany, showed that mice fed a high fat and fructose diet and supplemented with CoQ10 had decreased levels of inflammatory and metabolic stresses markers in their livers than mice just fed the high fat diet. CoQ10 is naturally synthesized in the body and concentrated in the mitochondria—the "power plants" of the cell—and plays a vital role in the production of chemical energy by participating in the production of ATP, the body's so-called "energy currency." The researcher wrote that CoQ10, when given orally, is able to target the liver tissue and to lessen inflammatory stress associated with obesity in mice in this tissue, independent of any action on lipid peroxidation.

However, you shouldn't be feeling relief regarding belly fat. In a study published in the August 17, 2010 *Journal of the American College of Cardiology*, researchers at the Mayo Clinic found that healthy young people who put on as little as nine pounds of fat, specifically in the abdomen, are at risk for developing endothelial cell dysfunction. Endothelial cells line the blood vessels and control the ability of the vessels to expand and contract.

Virend Somers, M.D., Ph.D., a cardiologist at Mayo Clinic, stated, "Endothelial dysfunction has long been associated with an increased risk for coronary artery disease and cardiovascular events. Gaining a few pounds in college, on a cruise, or during the holidays is considered harmless, but it can have cardiovascular implications, especially if the weight is gained in the abdomen.... Patients should know that having a big belly may be more harmful than simply being obese. Letting weight creep on during college or as the result of aging should not be accepted as normal."[21]

Another study released August 23, 2010, in the journal *Archives of Internal Medicine*, linked a large waist, which is associated with a host of potentially serious health issues, such as heart disease, high cholesterol, type 2 diabetes, and inflammation, with death. Researchers from the Epidemiology Research Program of the American Cancer Society in Atlanta looked at data among 48,500 men and 56,343 women ages 50 and older who took part in the study for nine years. Having a very large waist—at least 47 inches for men and 43 inches for women—was associated with about twice the risk of death compared with men with waists measuring 35 inches or less and women with waists measuring 30 inches or less. Having visceral, or intra-abdominal fat, is considered to be a bigger health risk than fat underneath the skin, or subcutaneous fat, because visceral fat surrounds the internal organs.[22]

#2—Obesity and Flu Pandemic

On July 12, 2009, an e-mail newsletter from NaturalNews reported on evidence published by the Centers for Disease Control and Prevention that appears to indicate that obese patients may be most susceptible to death by swine flu. In the CDC's report, researchers documented the case of 10 swine flu patients at a Michigan hospital who became so ill they were put on ventilators, and three of the patients ultimately died. Notably, nine of the 10 were obese, and two of the three who died were severely obese. "What this suggests," said CDC virologist Dr. Tim Uyeki, "is that there can be severe complications associated with this virus infection, especially in severely obese patients." Five of the patients showed evidence of blood clots in their lungs, indicating severe cellular trauma in the lungs. Nine of the patients suffered from multiple organ failure, and six experienced kidney failure.

Obviously, the number of patients reviewed in this study is small, but even so, this could be a warning of things to come. Flu viruses kill through an inflammatory process, and obesity is, itself, an inflammatory condition that intensifies the deadliness of the viruses. With more than 34 percent of all adult Americans over the age of 20 obese and another 32 percent overweight, our American population is highly vulnerable to a flu pandemic.

> **Health is not valued till sickness comes.**
>
> THOMAS FULLER

Make no mistake about it, being overweight or obese compromises your body's immune system, liver, heart, lungs, and kidneys, which lessens your resources for fighting off infections. In an age of threatened pandemics, it's a must to cut any excess body fat and get your immunity system functioning at peak performance.

#3—Longer Hospital Stays

In January 2009, a study by sociologists at Purdue University found obesity leads to more frequent and longer hospital stays. The researchers found that, on average, obese persons stayed one and a half days longer than those with normal weight. Ken Ferraro, Ph.D., a sociologist at Purdue University, also noted that "the longer the person is obese, the longer their stay in the hospital."

Sociologists state the main reason for extra hospitalizations is exactly what one would expect—because of the diseases connected to obesity. In their study, 46 percent of the obese adults had high blood pressure, and those who had been overweight since childhood and carried extra weight into adulthood paid the highest price for being heavy.

Bottom line: Overcoming obesity at a young age is crucial to helping stay out of the hospital later on.

#4—The Association with Periodontal Disease

If you doubt the far-ranging effects of obesity, consider this research presented by investigators from the Harvard School of Public Health and the University of Puerto Rico on April 4, 2009, during the 87th General Session of the International Association for Dental Research. They analyzed data from 36,903 men from the Health Professionals Follow-Up Study for up to 16 years to see if there was an association between different measures of obesity and the risk of periodontal disease. Periodontal (gum) diseases, including gingivitis and periodontitis, are serious chronic bacterial infections that, left untreated, can lead to tooth loss.

By way of general summary from the study, the researchers observed significant associations between all measures of obesity and periodontal disease. Obesity at the beginning of follow-up and during follow-up was significantly associated with a 25 percent and 29 percent increased risk compared with normal weight, respectively. Men with waistlines of 40 or more inches compared with less than 40 inches were associated with a 19 percent increased risk of periodontal disease.

Cut the excess body fat, and cut the risk of periodontal disease.

#5—Childhood Obesity Link to Parents / Genetics

A study published on July 13, 2009, in the *International Journal of Obesity* indicates that girls whose mothers are obese are significantly more likely to struggle with weight problems in childhood, with a similar relationship existing between obese fathers and their sons. The research conducted by the EarlyBird Diabetes Study in the United Kingdom showed that the same trend does not exist between mothers and their sons and fathers and their daughters.

So what does that mean? The study's director, Professor Terry Wilkin, said: "Any genetic link between obese parents and their children would be indiscriminate of gender. The clearly defined gender-assortative pattern which our research has uncovered is an exciting one because it points toward behavioral factors at work in childhood obesity." In other words, *behavioral, rather than genetic, factors could be the key to unraveling the causes of the current obesity epidemic affecting children.*

Wilkin goes on to say, "These findings could turn our thinking on childhood obesity dramatically on its head. Money and resources have focused on children over the past decade in the belief that obese children become obese adults, and that prevention of obesity in children will solve the problem in adulthood. EarlyBird's evidence supports the opposite hypothesis—that children are becoming obese due to the influence of their same-sex parents, and that we will need to focus on changing the behavior of the adult if we want to combat obesity in the child." If that is truly the case, the role of parents becomes that much more important.

In another recent study of genetics, researchers found that the contribution of genetics to the development of obesity is smaller than previously thought. European researchers, led by Ruth Loos from Addenbrooke's Hospital in Cambridge, United Kingdom, performed a genetic survey of more than 20,000 people participating in the European Prospective Investigation into Cancer and Nutrition (EPIC)-Norfolk cohort. The new research, published in the January 2010 *American Journal of Clinical Nutrition*, indicates that *genes for body mass index may be responsible for less than one percent of obesity*. Their research puts the obesity spotlight firmly back on lifestyle and diet.

In an accompanying editorial, Claude Bouchard from the Pennington Biomedical Research Center in Baton Rouge, Louisiana, wrote, "The obesity epidemic we are facing today unfolded during the past few decades and can clearly not be explained by changes in the frequency of risk *alleles*. It is more likely due to a changing social and physical environment that encourages consumption and discourages expenditure of energy, behaviors that are poorly compatible with the genome that we have inherited."

Based upon the same study, the August 2010 *PLoS Medicine* reported that the same research shows that physical activity can reduce the genetic tendency toward obesity by 40 percent. Senior researcher Ruth Loos stated, "Our findings challenge the popular myth that obesity is unavoidable if it runs in the family. We see this as a hopeful message." You can get the benefits without running marathons, she adds. You can walk the dog, bike to work, or take the stairs. "Being active about 30 minutes a day is a good start in reducing the effects of the genes." U.S. experts say the study adds to the data on the importance of exercise for weight control. "This is more evidence that behavior can modify genetic predisposition," says Tim Church, director of preventive medicine research at the Pennington Biomedical Research Center.[23]

#6—Increased Problems During Surgery

According to an American Heart Association scientific advisory published in *Circulation* in June 2009, health care providers must carefully consider the unique risk factors related to severe obesity in patients undergoing all types of surgery. Heart problems in particular are often underestimated during a physical examination in the severely obese patient (body mass index of 40 or higher), according to the advisory.

> The patient should be made to understand that he or she must take charge of his own life. Don't take your body to the doctor as if he were a repair shop.
>
> QUENTIN REGESTEIN

"A severely obese patient can be technically difficult to evaluate prior to surgery," said Paul Poirier, M.D., Ph.D., lead author of the advisory. "For example, severely obese people might feel chest tightness that could be a symptom of their obesity or of an underlying cardiac problem. Doctors need to carefully evaluate severely obese patients before they have surgery."

Conditions associated with obesity that could increase heart risks in surgery include heart failure, atherosclerosis (thickened or narrowed arteries), high blood pressure, heart rhythm disorders, history of blood clots (especially pulmonary embolism), poor exercise capacity, and pulmonary hypertension related to sleep apnea. According to the advisory, it is reasonable to do an electrocardiogram and a chest X-ray in this population, and other noninvasive testing, including exercise testing. Health care providers should be aware that severely obese patients are more likely to stay on a ventilator longer and have a longer hospital stay than patients who are not severely obese.

"Since recovery can be a problem for these patients, we recommend that they take steps to be as healthy as possible before going into surgery," Poirier added.

I say, "Amen. Absolutely. Start this moment."

#7—Increased Risk of Dementia and Abdominal Fat

In a research study published in the March 26, 2008, online issue of *Neurology,* the medical journal of the American Academy of Neurology, people with larger stomachs in their 40s are more likely to have dementia when they reach their 70s. The study involved 6,583 people age 40 to 45 in northern California who had their abdominal fat measured. An average of 36 years later, 16 percent of the participants had been diagnosed with dementia. The study found that those with the highest amount of abdominal fat were almost three times more likely to develop dementia than those with the lowest amount of abdominal fat.

The study's author, Rachel A. Whitmer, Ph.D., a research scientist of the Kaiser Permanente Division of Research, stated, "Considering that 50 percent of adults in this country have an unhealthy amount of abdominal fat, this is a disturbing finding. Research needs to be done to determine what the mechanisms are that link abdominal obesity and dementia." As with all observational studies, it is possible the association of the abdominal obesity and dementia is not driven by the abdominal obesity, but rather by a complex set of health-related behaviors, for which abdominal obesity is but one part.

Interestingly, having a large abdomen increased the risk of dementia regardless of whether the participants were of normal weight overall, overweight, or obese, and regardless of existing health conditions, including diabetes, stroke, and cardiovascular disease. Those who were overweight and had a large belly were 2.3 times more likely to develop dementia than people with a normal weight and belly size. People who were both obese and had a large belly were 3.6 times more likely to develop dementia than those of normal weight and belly size.

Whitmer adds, "Autopsies have shown that changes in the brain associated with Alzheimer's disease may start in young to middle adulthood, and another study showed that high abdominal fat in elderly adults was tied to greater brain atrophy. These findings imply that the dangerous effects of abdominal obesity on the brain may start long before the signs of dementia appear."

A large belly in mid-life has also been shown to increase the risk of diabetes, stroke, and coronary heart disease. Living with the spare tire is no joking matter.

#8—Type 2 Diabetes in Young Adults

In an article in the July 2008 *Archives of Pediatric & Adolescent Medicine*, the University of Michigan C. S. Mott Children's Hospital pediatric endocrinologist Joyce Lee, M.D., M.P.H, warns, "The full impact of the childhood obesity epidemic has yet to be seen because it can take up to 10 years or longer for obese individuals to develop type 2 diabetes. Children who are obese today are more likely to develop type 2 diabetes as young adults." If that is the case, the longer a person has diabetes, the more likely he or she is to develop devastating complications, such as blindness and kidney failure during their lifetimes. Plus, babies born to young women with type 2 diabetes are at greater risk for obesity and type 2 diabetes, creating a vicious cycle.

Dr. Lee adds, "Recent studies suggest that there have been dramatic increases in type 2 diabetes among individuals in their 20s and 30s, whereas it used to be that individuals developed type 2 diabetes in their late 50s or 60s. This may be the first indication of a type 2 diabetes epidemic among young adults who were obese during childhood."

Let's hope she's wrong, but I can't give you a single reason to think that way. Unless trends in childhood obesity are reversed, our society will pay a heavy price in the treatment and management of chronic diseases.

#9—Increase in Disabilities

In the *Journal of the American Medical Association* (2007;298), researchers at the University of Pennsylvania School of Medicine reported that older adults today are much more likely to suffer from disability than those 10 years ago. The study revealed that obesity, which has become more common among older Americans, is having an increasingly profound impact on their day-to-day activities and overall health. By comparing health data from 1988 to 1994 to data from 1999 to 2004, the researchers found that the odds of suffering from functional impairment have increased 43 percent among obese adults age 60 years and older.

Dawn Alley, Ph.D., lead author and Robert Wood Johnson Health and Society Scholar at the University of Pennsylvania School of Medicine, stated, "Obesity is more hazardous to the health of the elderly than we previously suspected. For an older person, suffering from obesity means they are much less likely to be able to walk to the front door or pick up a bag of groceries."

"We believe that two factors are likely contributing to the rise in disability among older obese people," says Virginia Chang, M.D., Ph.D., Assistant Professor of Medicine at Penn and senior study author. "First, people are potentially living longer with their obesity due to improved medical care; and second, people are becoming obese at younger ages than in the past. In both instances, people are living with obesity for longer periods of time, which increases the potential for disability."

> **The greatest wealth is health.**
>
> VIRGIL

Researchers also found that obese people are not benefiting from some of the health improvements that the rest of the population is experiencing. For example, although the odds of ADL (activities of daily living) impairment decreased by 34 percent among the general population, no such improvements were seen in the obese population.

Another significant reason to take your weight seriously.

#10—Loss of Brain Tissue

In the September 15, 2009, online edition of the journal *Human Brain Mapping*, Paul Thompson, senior author and a UCLA professor of neurology, and lead author Cyrus A. Raji, a medical student at the University of Pittsburgh School of Medicine, and their colleagues compared the brains of 94 people in their 70s who were healthy—specifically, not cognitively impaired—five years after original brain scans were taken. The selections involved people who were obese, overweight, and of normal weight. The researchers converted the scans into detailed three-dimensional images using a neuroimaging method that offers high resolution mapping of anatomical differences in the brain.

In looking at both grey matter and white matter of the brain, they found that obese people had eight percent less brain tissue than people with normal weight, while overweight people had four percent less tissue. According to Thompson, "The brains of obese people looked 16 years older than the brains of those who were lean, and in overweight people looked eight years older," having what he describes as "severe brain degeneration…. That's a big loss of tissue, and it depletes your cognitive reserves, putting you at much greater risk of Alzheimer's and other diseases that attack the brain."

Pittsburgh's Raji added, "It seems that along with increased risk for health problems such as type 2 diabetes and heart disease, obesity is bad for your brain: We have linked it to shrinkage of brain areas that are also targeted by Alzheimer's. But that could mean exercising, eating right, and keeping weight under control can maintain brain health with aging and potentially lower the risk for Alzheimer's and other dementias."

#11—Amplified Obesity Through Generations

One question people often ask is why everyone is getting heavier and heavier. One hypothesis is that a mother's obesity before and during her pregnancy affects the establishment of body weight regulatory mechanisms in her baby. Overweight mothers give birth to offspring who become even heavier, resulting in amplification of obesity across generations.

While the following research has not been proven in humans yet, Baylor College of Medicine researchers in Houston found that chemical changes in the ways genes are expressed—a phenomenon called *epigenetics*—could affect successive generations of mice. Dr. Robert A. Waterland, Assistant Professor of Pediatrics at Baylor and lead author of the study that appears in the July 2008 *International Journal of Obesity*, and his colleagues studied the effect of maternal obesity in three generations of genetically identical mice, all with the same genetic tendency to overeat. One group of mice received a standard diet; the other a diet supplemented with the nutrients folic acid, vitamin B12, betaine, and choline. The special "methyl supplemented" diet enhances DNA methylation, a chemical reaction that silences genes.

Dr. Waterland said, "We wanted to know if, even among genetically identical mice, maternal obesity would promote obesity in her offspring, and if the methyl supplemented diet would affect this process. Indeed, those on the regular diet got fatter and fatter with each generation. Those in the supplemented group, however, did not.

"We think DNA methylation may play an important role in the development of the hypothalamus (the region of the brain that regulates appetite)…. Twenty years ago, it was proposed that just as genetic mutations can cause cancer, so too might aberrant epigenetic marks—so called 'epimutations.' That idea is now largely accepted and the field of cancer epigenetics is very active. I would make the same statement for obesity. We are on the cusp of understanding that."

> **A man too busy to take care of his health is like a mechanic too busy to take care of his tools.**
>
> SPANISH PROVERB

Just a theory? Even so, substantial enough to cause us to eat healthy and exercise…if not for ourselves, then for the sake of our children.

#12—Lifestyle Changes Can Prevent or Delay Type 2 Diabetes

With the prevalence of diagnosed diabetes in the United States more than doubling in the past 30 years, due in large part to obesity, there is tremendous need to promote diabetes prevention. Diabetes is a disease in which the body does not produce or properly use insulin, a hormone made by the pancreas that allows glucose, or sugar, from food to be converted to energy. When diabetes is not controlled, glucose and fats build up in the blood and, over time, damage vital organs and lead to potentially fatal complications. Diabetes is the main cause of kidney failure, limb amputations, and new onset blindness in adults and a major cause of heart disease and stroke.

The Diabetes Prevention Program Outcomes Study, published online in *The Lancet* medical journal in October 2009, found that lifestyle changes, such as consuming less fat and calories and increasing regular physical activity to 150 minutes per week, reduced the rate of developing type 2 diabetes by 34 percent and delayed onset of the disease by four years. Researchers also found a 13 percent reduction in the rate of diabetes in those taking metformin, a generic oral medicine used to treat the disease, and a two-year delay in onset.

Honolulu endocrinologist Dr. Richard Arakaki, a professor at the University of Hawaii-Manoa John A. Burns School of Medicine and principal investigator in the 10-year study, said, "This clearly demonstrates we can prevent diabetes by losing weight and increasing physical activity and also by using a common diabetes medication…. If you could just prevent diabetes with simple lifestyle interventions, it could have a tremendous impact. We have to get it across to people right from the get-go, so they can take it to heart, that it's a preventable disease. Just because your mother had it or your father had it, you don't have to get diabetes. You really can do something to reduce your risk."

The outcomes study is a follow-up to a Diabetes Prevention Program clinical trial involving 3,234 overweight or obese adults with elevated blood glucose levels, a precursor to diabetes. The purpose of the Diabetes Prevention Program Outcomes Study was to examine whether the delay in the development of diabetes seen during the initial program could be sustained and to assess the long-term effects of the lifestyle and pharmaceutical interventions. The benefits of intensive lifestyle changes were especially evident in people age 60 and older, who lowered their rate of developing type 2 diabetes during the next 10 years by about half, according to researchers.

#13—Obesity and the Gut Theory

A December 8, 2009, online article at the *Bottom Lines Daily Health News* reported on an interesting theory regarding a possible contributor to obesity. At Washington University School of Medicine in St. Louis, Missouri, scientists found that the intestinal tracts of obese and thin people have different ratios of two types of bacteria that normally predominate in the human gut—*Firmicutes* and *Bacteroidetes*. Obese individuals had higher percentages of Firmicutes and lower percentages of Bacteroidetes bacteria, while the lean group had roughly the opposite balance. After the obese individuals lost weight by following a low calorie diet for one year, the ratio of these two types of bacteria in the obese individuals became more like that of the lean group.

Washington University scientists also bred mice to be free of intestinal flora, then fed them gut bacteria taken from obese mice, and they got fat. In contrast, flora-free mice given gut bacteria from skinny mice gained little weight. The researchers concluded that differences in gut flora *may* contribute to obesity.

The human body hosts trillions of microbes (bacteria), some that support our health and others that threaten it. Problems in the intestinal tract, which is the hub of the body's immune system, quickly lead to problems elsewhere in the body. Beneficial bacteria help your body break down food and absorb nutrients, so it makes sense that having more healthful bacteria helps digestion. Keeping the bacteria of your digestive system in proper balance is essential to maintaining optimal health.

There is a lot of research underway on the connection between obesity and gut bacteria. Contributing editor Andrew Rubman, N.D., states regarding the theory: "Our bodies are programmed to protect us from negative external influences and challenges, so threats (such as inflammation) may lead to an increase in energy storage (i.e., calories) to meet the challenge. If this mistaken attempt at self-protection persists, the ecology of the gut adjusts to favor bacteria that are more proficient at extracting calories from food. Over time, these calorie-hungry microbes contribute to weight gain, making it even harder for overweight people to shed unwanted pounds—an all-too-common complaint. So, the theory goes, people who are already overweight can eat the same meals as lean people, but they'll absorb more calories. Harmful bacteria also slow the passage of food through the digestive tract, and the more time food spends in the body, the more calories you absorb from it."

Fortunately, the Super Health Diet will help restore and maintain a proper microbial balance in your gut, particularly with the emphasis on fresh fruits and vegetables, which encourages the production of friendly microbes. Fiber in fruits and vegetables (especially the skin) helps speed food through the digestive tract. This improves the health of the intestinal lining by nurturing the right bacteria. In contrast, processed foods, such as breads, doughnuts, and cookies, are loaded with starch and simple sugars that harmful bacteria thrive upon. Yogurt with active cultures and a daily probiotic supplement are also excellent aids to the gut.

While there is much more research needed on the influence of gut ecology on weight, it just makes sense to take this initial research seriously and make sure you maintain the right balance of bacteria in your body.

#14—Obesity and Hot Flashes in Women

Through the years, multiple observational studies have reported more frequent or severe hot flashes among women with a higher body mass index (BMI) compared to women with lower BMI. Hot flashes are the most common complaint of women during menopause and perimenopause and persist for five or more years past menopause in up to one-third of women, and they are associated with sleeping problems, anxiety, and depression. As many as three out of four women experience hot flashes as they go through menopause. However, the effect of weight loss on hot flashes has been unknown.

> In health there is freedom. Health is the first of all liberties.
>
> HENRI FREDERIC AMIEL

In findings reported in the online edition of the *Archives of Internal Medicine* on July 12, 2010, a study by the University of California, San Francisco Department of Medicine shows that overweight and obese women who suffer from hot flashes can reduce the severity of their hot flashes if they lose weight through diet or exercise. The study included 338 women aged 30 or older with a BMI of 25 to 50 who were randomly assigned to two groups. One group of women attended weekly one-hour group sessions led by experts in nutrition, exercise, and behavior change, and were encouraged to increase their physical activity to at least 200 minutes per week and asked to follow a reduced calorie diet. A second group of women, the control group, participated in one-hour group sessions that provided general information about weight loss, physical activity, healthy eating, and health promotion. Half of the participants reported being at least slightly bothered by hot flashes. Among these women, reductions in weight, abdominal circumference, and BMI were associated with an improvement in hot flashes.

In fact, women in the active weight loss group were *twice* as likely to see an improvement in their hot flashes after six months compared to women in the control group, according to senior author Deborah Grady, M.D., of the UCSF Department of Medicine and the Veterans Affairs Medical Center, San Francisco. She said, "This gives women who suffer from hot flashes an added option in controlling their symptoms, while also creating a healthier life for themselves."

"We still don't understand the underlying mechanism of hot flashes, or why some women experience flashes and others don't," said Alison J. Huang, M.D., assistant professor of internal medicine in the UCSF Department of Medicine, who was the lead author on the paper. "The good news is that millions of women who are overweight and troubled by hot flashes may be able to reduce their discomfort through diet and exercise."[24]

THE SUPER

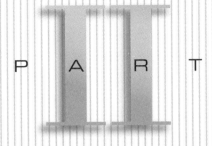

P A R T

HEALTH DIET

Chapter 10

The Four Corners of Superfood Nutrition

> *We are indeed much more than what we eat,*
> *but what we eat can nevertheless help us to*
> *be much more than what we are.*
> ADELLE DAVIS

If we could even begin to grasp how wonderfully our bodies are made, how they are easily the most amazing creation in the entire known universe, and how totally interconnected and complex they are, we would never struggle with our worship of the Creator God. And it is well equipped to keep itself in perpetual health through a powerful immunity and healing system that can meet most challenges without outside help.

God designed that vibrant health reign over every aspect of our body and that we would feel strong physically and emotionally. However, our bodies require that we carefully supply them with all they absolutely require for health through *a combination of nutrition, exercise, hydration, stress management, getting proper amounts of sleep, limiting environmental hazards,* and *practicing meditation and prayer.* And while most of us think the key is to stay physically fit, a study published in the May 2008 edition of *The American Journal of Physiology* states that nutrition may be even more important than exercise.

Here's why. Science has identified 50-plus essential nutrients the human body must have in order to function at its peak. Since the body cannot produce a single one of these nutrients, each one must be obtained by food sources, dietary supplements, and exposure to sunshine.

If we fall short, if we deprive our body of just one of these essential nutrients, we can suffer a breakdown in our health, resulting in dysfunction and disease that negatively affects our whole person. It's inescapable! All of your energies will be burned in trying to cope with the disease, and it will significantly limit all you wish to do as well as the person you'd like to be.

Think of it in these terms. If you were given a brand-new Lamborghini automobile that is designed to run on high octane gasoline, would you even consider using regular low grade fuel? How about diesel fuel instead of gas? How about kerosene? No, of course not. Why? Because we know the result would be many thousands of dollars in repair bills. We would use only the manufacturer-specified gas and motor oil to not risk a catastrophe.

The same is true for the human body, which is far more complex and valuable than any fine sports car. It was designed to be fueled with clean high octane fuel and to use high quality motor oil! Many of the foods we eat are like putting lighter fluid in our gas tank or putting used motor oil in our fine sports car. These foods during the short and long term can cause our bodies to sputter and misfire and lead to disastrous consequences, such as major disease.

Beyond that, most people so overeat that it's like they are filling their gas tank until it runs down the side of the car, then they roll down the back window and fill the back seat. The body has about as much capacity to deal with the constant over fueling as a car does with the gas in the back seat.

Underscoring the nutrient problem is this conclusion of a report published online on August 11, 2010, in the *Journal of Nutrition*: "Nearly the entire U.S. population consumes a diet that is not on par with recommendations." Susan M. Krebs Smith and her colleagues at the National Cancer Institute evaluated data from 16,338 individuals aged two and older who participated in the 2001–2004 National Health and Nutrition Examination Survey (NHANES). With the exception of total grains, meat, and beans, the majority of the sample surveyed failed to consume the minimum recommendations for each of the USDA's food groups. As you will read later in this book, I am no fan of the USDA's food groupings; however, it is important to note that almost all participants failed to consume enough dark green vegetables, orange vegetables, legumes, and whole grains. Total vegetable and milk recommendations were unmet by most people in more than half of the groups. Empty calories, including solid fats, added sugars, and alcoholic beverages were overconsumed by more than 90 percent of those aged 70 and younger. The authors of the study write, "This analysis indicates that nearly the entire U.S. population consumes a diet with fewer vegetables and whole grains than recommended, and that a large majority underconsume fruits, milk, and oils relative to recommendations.... A worrisome state in the context of the obesity epidemic and alarming rates of other diet-related chronic diseases."

It's True for World Class Athletes…and You

As a performance nutrition specialist, I have had the privilege of working with elite trainers and world class athletes in many different sports to help them gain a competitive edge. For athletes in any sport where consecutive days of play are part of the competition, a major problem is that a desire for increased energy levels often causes them to load up on energy bars, drinks, and supplements comprised of cheap ingredients, high sugars, and stimulants, which actually results in a dreaded crash and fatigue after providing only a short peak in energy. Some of these same products can even disrupt a person's sleep pattern, which further decreases the amount of vital energy available to them throughout the course of the day.

One of the biggest mistakes many athletes make is to load up on empty carbohydrates. According to a study published in the May 2008 edition of *The American Journal of Clinical Nutrition*, researchers at the University of Sydney discovered that a single serving of high glycemic/refined carbohydrates (e.g., table sugar, white bread, etc.) given to a lean, healthy young adult is enough to triple their inflammatory response to the surge in blood glucose. This finding reinforces the long-held notion that the refined carbohydrates so prevalent in most people's diets have virtually no nutritional value. These types of foods are actually the enemies of sustained energy, recovery, and performance. In fact, eating such foods can be dangerous to a person's health in the short term and can increase aging and produce disease when consumed over time.

Most of us consume too many of these so-called "filler foods," but I've discovered that professional athletes actually comprise one of the fastest growing segments of the malnourished population. Filling up with soda, sports drinks, cheap protein powders, or candy bars disguised as energy bars can have a negative impact on our levels of energy and concentration.

> "My people are destroyed for lack of knowledge."
>
> HOSEA 4:6

Unfortunately, competitive athletes tend to believe that exercise can override dietary deficiencies and that the consumption of designer sports supplements replaces the need to eat high quality foods or take foundational supplements. Nothing could be further from the truth! Long-term nutrient deficiency is literally a form of silent starvation, and it results in suboptimal performance and shortened athletic careers.

That's why the most powerful way to supply the millions of cells in our body with the right nutrition is by using a system called "The Four Corners of Superfood Nutrition." This is an extremely healthy approach that combines the most nutrient dense superfoods with all the best foundational supplements. You will have unlimited energy to do all the things you want to do and function at optimal levels.

The Fountain of Youth

Thousands of research studies in every species you could name have demonstrated over and over again that Calorie Restriction with Optimal Nutrition (CRON) extends life span, optimizes weight, delays the onset of disease, increases cellular communication, enhances human performance, increases mental clarity, and reduces blood pressure and body temperature. It is the closest we have come to the fountain of youth.

Scientists no longer argue that CRON doesn't work. The debate has turned to *why* it works.

One group of scientists believes the key to CRON is low glycemic response/low sugar intake, and the reason CRON works is because lower caloric intake would seem to result in less glycemic response because less sugar would drive less blood sugar and insulin response. They have successfully done studies to prove their hypothesis.

Another group of scientists believes in the Free Radical Theory of Aging and believes the reason CRON works is because lower calorie intake or higher antioxidant intake results in less oxidation "internal combustion" in the body, and therefore would deliver similar results as CRON. They also have successfully done studies to prove their hypothesis.

Another large and growing body of scientific evidence has demonstrated that adding the right fatty acids, such as fish oil omega-3 EPA/DHA, to one's diet can deliver CRON-like results with no other dietary changes.

The revelation I received almost a decade ago was that there was no reason to argue which of these theories was better, because it was possible and even practical to do all four at the same time. And when combined, these Four Corners of Superfood Nutrition become the most powerful nutritional approach in history with more than three thousand studies behind it.

One study from *Nutrition 2002* profoundly demonstrated this principle. There were four groups of mice that were fed differing amounts of the same food. The control group of mice was fed all they could eat of a high polyunsaturated fat grain diet and lived approximately 232 days. The second group of mice was fed all they could eat, plus they were also fed fish oil, and lived about 100 days longer than the 232-day control group. The third group was fed the same food with the only difference being the calories were cut by 40 percent from the amount fed to the control group, and they lived approximately 200 days longer than the 232-day control group. The last group was fed the same amount of food as the third group, plus they were fed fish oil, and they lived approximately 400 days LONGER than the 232-day control group. This is a dramatic study that demonstrates the power of combining these concepts. Keep in mind that this impact was with calorie restriction but without optimizing the diets with broad-spectrum nutrition.

Imagine what can happen if you combine these Four Corners of Superfood Nutrition and take it to another level by using the latest scientific evidence to optimize your diet with the best forms and right amounts of every known nutrient, including protein, amino acids, fiber, vitamins, minerals, antioxidants, phytonutrients, prebiotics, probiotics, superfoods, etc. As you read on, you will learn about Superfood Nutrition, which is the combining of optimal amounts of high quality essential nutrients together with known superfoods to ensure we get all the nutrients we know about together with the vast amount of nutrients science has yet to discover.

All the information in this chapter is foundationally important to optimizing weight, but please pay particular attention to the discussion later in this chapter about protein and amino acids—understanding this wildly misunderstood subject is a primary key to successful long-term weight optimization and to Super Health.

The Four Corners of Superfood Nutrition was covered extensively with clinical references in my 2005 book, *Super Health: 7 Golden Keys to Unlock Lifelong Vitality*. Back then, I called it the Four Corners of Optimal Nutrition or 4CON, but have since changed it because I believe the concept of Superfood Nutrition, which is combining superfoods with essential nutrients, is a better description of what is really involved.

It is my belief that a comprehensive weight optimization program goes far beyond the removal of excess body fat and the rewards of a leaner physique to the promise of a lengthy, disease-free life. Super Health should be the goal; weight optimization will be one of the many benefits. Being overweight is not just about aesthetics; it is often deadly, increasing the risk for diabetes, cancer, and heart disease. As you will discover, the Super Health Diet includes the reduction of caloric intake followed by the adoption of a lifelong healthy eating plan coupled with the increase of physical activity and energy expenditure rate. It must also improve insulin sensitivity and restore a youthful hormone balance as well as control the rate of carbohydrate absorption and the amount of dietary fat absorption.

The Four Corners of Superfood Nutrition

Simply eating less and exercising more, which is the mantra of medical advice given today, is not enough to help most people remove excess body fat and keep it off. A comprehensive program is necessary to aggressively target the many factors that contribute to excess body fat.

There are more research studies that validate the Four Corners of Superfood Nutrition than any other nutritional approaches in existence. It is a lifestyle approach that provides a comprehensive foundation for new levels of health awareness and life enhancement for everyone from elite athletes to the health challenged, who suffer from conditions such as diabetes, hypoglycemia, obesity, and eating disorders. What is unique about the Four Corners concept as presented here is that the individual four corners have been integrated into a single "unified theory" of nutrition science, including:

1. Eating fewer calories while maintaining optimal levels of all essential nutrients—CRON.
2. Eating and supplementing with generous amounts of broad-spectrum antioxidants.
3. Eating low glycemic impact foods and minimizing sugar.
4. Eating high quality foundational and fuel fats and supplementing with antioxidant essential fatty acids.

Corner #1—Eat Nutrient-Dense, Low Calorie Foods

If you wish to grow thinner,
diminish your dinner.
HENRY SAMBROOKE LEIGH

We eat food for three reasons—to obtain building blocks (for repair, maintenance, and growth) and fuel (for energy) for our bodies, and we eat for fun. Where a lot of people get into trouble is by eating for fun when they should be eating for building blocks and fuel. Food contains foundational nutrients, such as amino acids, fatty acids, vitamins, minerals, and antioxidants for repair and maintenance of the body and contains energy (calories) or fuel for the body to operate and perform its many functions. When we eat, our bodies use the calories to produce energy and to repair and maintain body tissues. If not used, calories are stored as fat in most areas of the body. If we keep adding calories that are not being burned up, we get fat. It makes sense, then, that when it comes to calories, *the key is to pack as much nutrition as possible into the lowest calorie foods that one can comfortably eat.*

The Four Corners of Superfood Nutrition revolve around the Calorie Restriction with Optimal Nutrition (CRON) concept, because more than 2,000 medical studies support the astonishing conclusion that *CRON diets* extend life, delay disease, optimize weight, improve mental clarity, and enhance performance. Researchers first discovered the connection between lean diets and extended life spans in a 1935 study of calorie-restricted rats. Indeed, CRON diets have been shown to greatly enhance the life span of every species in which CRON has been studied.[25]

For instance, in a report published in the July 10, 2009, issue of *Science*, Professor Richard Weindruch and colleagues at the University of

Wisconsin-Madison, the Wisconsin National Primate Research Center, and the William S. Middleton Memorial Veterans Hospital reveal that calorie restriction is successful at improving survival and delaying disease in rhesus macaques, also called the rhesus monkey, whose average life span is 27 years. The study divided 76 macaques aged seven to 14 to receive diets that allowed them to consume as much food as they wanted, or diets that contained 30 percent fewer calories than the unrestricted diets. Thirty of the animals began the diets in 1989 and 46 in 1994.

As of 2009, 80 percent of the monkeys given restricted diets are alive, compared to half of the unrestricted animals. Cancer and cardiovascular disease incidence is more than 50 percent lower in the calorie-restricted animals, and diabetes has not been observed. Additionally, brain volume, motor control, working memory, and problem solving abilities appear to be better maintained in the restricted monkeys. The results come as close as any can to proving that calorie restriction can significantly slow aging in humans.

It is a fact that as people age, their immune response generally declines. However, in a 2009 study, scientists funded by the Agricultural Research Service (ARS), the U.S. Department of Agriculture's principal intramural scientific research agency, found that volunteers who followed either a 30-percent or 10-percent calorie-restricted diet for six months not only lost weight, but also significantly enhanced their immune response. In the study, 46 overweight (but not obese) men and women aged 20 to 40 years were randomly assigned to one of the two groups and all the food was provided to participants. Prior to the study, each volunteer participated in an initial six-week period during which measures of all baseline study outcomes were obtained. For the study, the researchers looked at specific biologic markers. A skin test used called DTH (delayed-type hypersensitivity) is a measure of immune response at the whole body level. The researchers also examined effects of calorie restriction on function of T-cells—a major type of white blood cell—and other factors on the volunteer's immune system. One positive was that DTH and T-cell response, which indicate the strength of cell-mediated immunity, were significantly increased in both calorie-restricted groups. The study may be the first to demonstrate the interaction between calorie restriction and immune markers among humans.[26]

Numerous studies have repeatedly shown that those who eat higher calorie amounts can suffer from a wide range of symptoms, including weight gain, fatigue, sleepiness, hypertension, hypoglycemia, colitis, brain fog, and more. It also affects longevity, seriously enough to subtract years from your life.

Children and young adults up to age 25 should not participate in low calorie diets because it can be dangerous to their health and cause long-term health problems. To summarize the clinical literature regarding the optimal eating pattern for humans, one should eat like an idiot (in terms of volume of healthy foods) until age 25, then switch to a CRON calorie-restricted diet. This is easier said than done, because habits are formed in the young and most people accomplish the first part but never make the transition to a lower calorie lifestyle after 25.

> When it comes to eating right and exercising, there is no "I'll start tomorrow." Tomorrow is disease.
>
> V. L. ALLINEARE

Controlling the Insulin/Blood Sugar Connection

While scientists do not agree on why CRON is the most effective method of life extension and optimal health in history, compelling research suggests the primary mechanism for the success of CRON-based diets may be that it helps to control pancreatic insulin response. Insulin is a powerful hormone produced by beta cells in the pancreas mainly in response to high levels of glucose (sugar) in the blood, playing a critical role in regulating blood sugar levels throughout the body. Insulin also enables the liver to store excess serum glucose and stimulates the liver to form fatty acids that are transported to adipose cells and stored as fat. The net effect of insulin is the storage of carbohydrate, protein, and fat in the body. Many people who struggle with excess weight or who have become diabetic have high levels of insulin in the body.

It is important to understand the nature of this insulin/blood sugar (or glucose) connection. In a normal situation, the blood sugar (or glucose) level is maintained between 85 and 95 mg/dL, with brief increases above these levels for about one to two hours after a meal. Thus there is ideally a tight control between consumed sugar and insulin secreted from the pancreas. Most of the cells of the body are covered with insulin receptors on their cell surfaces. These receptors come in contact with insulin and then open the cell membrane and allow glucose (sugar) to enter the cell, which is then used as a primary fuel for cell functioning.

A poor diet as well as snacking can induce the pancreas to secrete large amounts of insulin. There is also the normal aging that causes the insulin receptors on cell membranes to lose their youthful sensitivity or functionality. In an abnormal situation, too much sugar consumption leads to elevated blood glucose levels, which chronically elevate blood insulin levels. As a consequence, the insulin receptors stop responding to the insulin (medically known as the pathological condition called "insulin receptor resistance" or "insulin resistance"), and the glucose cannot enter the cell. Therefore, the blood glucose continues to increase, which further increases blood insulin, creating more insulin receptor resistance.

The effect of high insulin production is weight gain. As long as insulin is present in the blood, stored fat cannot be mobilized—it is locked in the cell. Insulin not only keeps fat in storage, but insulin also stimulates the production of new fat. It even lowers levels of the amino acid carnitine in the liver. Carnitine is needed to carry fat precursors into the mitochondria, where the fat precursors can be burned as heat to "waste" calories.

So if we eat too much sugar or simple carbohydrates for too long, the insulin receptors stop listening to the increased insulin. In the early stages, too much sugar followed by too much insulin will rapidly drop the blood sugar level. This will cause intense cravings for sugar or simple carbohydrates, since the brain is significantly dependent on glucose to maintain consciousness. When blood sugar levels drop, the brain will virtually demand that sugar or simple carbohydrates be consumed to restore normal glucose levels. I'm sure you know what that feels like—a vicious cycle in which overeating causes more and more body fat to accumulate.

Unchecked, high levels of blood sugar in the body lead to a loss of many vital body chemicals, such as minerals, vitamins, and water. Repeated and chronic elevations of blood sugar can cause other more long-term and potentially fatal problems, such as impairments to cardiovascular, respiratory, and immune functions. Too much insulin harms the kidneys. By acting as a catalyst in promoting cell growth, excess insulin increases the risk and progression of certain cancers. *Hyperinsulinemia*, a condition of high circulating insulin levels, is associated with a significantly increased risk of heart disease. In fact, a recent study showed that patients with heart disease had significantly higher plasma levels of blood sugar and circulating insulin.[27]

Unfortunately, fat free diets (high carbohydrate diets) that have been marketed so heavily in American culture actually encourage people to eat high Glycemic Index (GI) foods, such as bread, cookies, and pretzels, which are quickly converted to sugars in the body. People have assumed that if the product label says "fat free," these foods can be eaten with impunity, as though "fat free" means it has no calories. A close comparison of nutrition labels will show you that fat free or reduced fat products can have just as many, if not more, calories per serving than regular products.

The most effective way of restoring insulin sensitivity is to reduce calorie intake. Calorie restriction to less than 1,500 to 1,800 calories/day significantly enhances insulin sensitivity, as documented by dramatic lowering of fasting glucose and insulin blood levels.[28] Even a moderate cutback of excess calories can markedly improve insulin sensitivity.

In a study published in the June 2006 *Journal of the American Medical Association*, the effects of caloric restriction were measured in a group of overweight adults during a six-month period, after which they were assessed for known markers of aging, such as core body temperature and

> **Fruits are filled with nutrients we need every day, but an eight-ounce glass of orange juice has a whopping eight to nine teaspoons of sugar. All that is in your bloodstream is one teaspoon, so the rest increases your waistline, cholesterol, and triglyceride levels. Eat fruit the way God made it.**

levels of glucose, fasting insulin, and dehydroepiandrosterone sulfate (DHEA-S). Excess insulin, as I have noted, functions as a hormone that devastates virtually every cell and organ system in the body. Decreasing excess insulin by enhancing insulin sensitivity and improving the function of pancreatic beta cells (the cells that produce insulin in the body) is a crucial component in the quest for longevity. In response to the reduced food intake in this study, fasting insulin levels plummeted, while DHEA-S and glucose (blood sugar) levels remained steady.

Core body temperature also fell in the calorie-restriction and calorie-restriction-with-exercise groups. Absolute 24-hour energy expenditure and sleeping energy expenditure decreased in all treatment groups, and the effect was more than could be explained by changes in fat loss. The researchers concluded that caloric restriction induced a "metabolic adaptation"—that is, a reduction in the baseline rate at which the body burns fuel. This adaptation is desirable for the purpose of slowing aging. Also in the *JAMA* study, DNA damage decreased from baseline levels in all the calorie-restricted groups. Accumulating DNA damage is thought to contribute to aging and disease processes such as cancer.

The most exciting finding of this study was the amount of weight lost in the groups that restricted their calorie intake. The moderate calorie-restriction group experienced a 24 percent reduction in body fat mass, while the very low calorie group achieved a 32 percent reduction in fat mass. So, in just six months, taken together, the changes in longevity parameters among all calorie-restriction groups suggest that long-term caloric restriction may extend life span.[29]

You can also aid your body's restoring of insulin sensitivity to your cell membranes with chromium, magnesium, cinnamon, cocoa polyphenols, Irvingia, and fish oil. If you have type 2 diabetes, you may wish to also consult with your physician regarding changing your prescription to a low cost prescription drug called metformin (a.k.a. glucophage) that has been shown to significantly enhance insulin sensitivity.[30]

Optimizing Leptin

Insulin and leptin are master hormones in the body. Along with restoring insulin sensitivity, optimizing the hormone leptin is critical for weight loss and health. Similar to insulin resistance, it appears the cells can also become insensitive to too much leptin, causing it to lose some of its positive effects on fat metabolism. The reason is that fat cells (adipocytes) regulate their size and number by secreting command signals[31] from three sources: leptin, adiponectin, and glycerol-3-phosphate dehydrogenase.

Excess body fat can essentially become the largest endocrine organ in the body. The more fat cells one accumulates, particularly belly fat, the more leptin and multiple inflammatory cytokines are produced, resulting in a state of constant inflammation and high leptin. Another detrimental consequence of belly fat is the production of an enzyme called aromatase that converts testosterone to estrogen. This is a vicious energy-robbing cycle that leads to more accumulation of body fat and the onset of disease.

Released by fat cells, leptin travels to the brain to signal that enough food has been consumed and shuts down one's appetite. Then it depletes bloated fat cells by promoting the burning of stored triglycerides. Leptin is much more abundant in the blood of obese individuals, because leptin receptor sites on cell membranes are inactivated by inflammatory factors in the body. Thus, to optimize leptin must mean to inhibit barriers in the aging body that block the utilization of it.

While I realize this is complex information, what happens in the body is this: With increased levels of insulin, leptin, and cortisol, the cell receptors as well as intracellular mechanisms block the insulin, leptin, and cortisol effect by what is known as negative feedback inhibition (NFI). This is a paradox, because more here means little or no hormonal effect, since the cells have enough intelligence to say no to these three hormones in order to protect the intracellular milieu (pH, hydration, Redox, and more). With insulin not doing its thing on cell surface receptors, blood sugar builds up, and that high blood sugar going to the pancreas causes the release of more insulin to further exacerbate the problem.

Similarly, when excess leptin hits the brain receptors, the receptors stop functioning, and the paradoxical effect is that the hippocampus sends messages through the hypothalamus and pituitary that say "we have no leptin, therefore he is trying to starve us," and the response is to lower thyroid and sex hormones (in other words, it stops anabolism, because we need to conserve energy to survive).

The same thing happens with the cortisol. High chronic stress equals chronically elevated cortisol, and the cortisol receptors in the brain (notably the hippocampus) say "you are screaming at us, so we just won't listen" (another metaphor for negative feedback inhibition). So the hippocampus sends the message to the hypothalamus and then to the pituitary that releases more ACTH because we don't have enough cortisol (when in fact there is too much). So the high cortisol levels break down muscle, store fat, raise blood sugar, and block T4 conversion to T3. Low T3 ultimately lowers nuclear transcription to make mRNA for mitochondrial proteins, resulting in a decrease of mitochondrial numbers and function, which results in a decrease of energetics, promoting further weight (especially fat) gain.

In any case, the main cause of leptin resistance is too much leptin, causing negative feedback inhibition. This is why we should eat three meals per day, not snack, and eat our last meal three hours before bedtime, so we truly "break fast" about 12 to 14 hours later. This meal spacing and overnight fasting is what decreases runaway leptin in a fat person and allows the receptors to get resensitized. The Super Health Diet is a hormone optimizing system that targets the big three negative feedback inhibitions—insulin, leptin, and cortisol!

The key to optimizing leptin is to improve in all 7 Golden Keys, including following the Four Corners of Superfood Nutrition. Also, sleeping at least seven uninterrupted hours per night is a major factor in optimizing leptin.

Quality, Not Quantity

While the benefits of a low calorie diet are high, the most obvious hazard is that as most people lower their caloric intake, they also neglect their nutrition at the same time. I do not advocate the extreme regimens that some practitioners of calorie restriction take. Let's face it: Eating is one of our principal pleasures. To eat well, while restricting caloric intake, is something anyone can do. You merely need a new mindset. *There's never a reason to starve yourself in the pursuit of Super Health.*

Consider, for instance, that a "calorie" is the amount of energy that is required to raise one cubic centimeter of water 1°C. All food contains energy in the form of calories (or more accurately kilocalories) as potential fuel for the body to perform its many functions. The process of energy metabolism within the cell's energy factory, the "mighty mitochondrion," is a highly complex process involving dozens of steps and many biochemical reactions. Consequently, judging the foods you eat simply by counting the number of calories they contain does not account for the amount of energy that is needed to digest the food, nor does it account for the amount of food that is constantly being used in the ongoing bodily processes of breakdown (catabolism) and rebuilding (anabolism).

Calorie counting also doesn't account for food quality, which is so crucial to weight control and overall health. It is foolish to think the 250 calories found in a 20-ounce bottle of a soft drink are equal to the 250 calories found in a delicious salad of dark green vegetables and berries. The calories from the soft drink can deliver more than 60 grams of sugar that go straight into your bloodstream and cause your insulin levels to spike, and the calories you don't burn find their way to your waistline. The fact that soft drinks have no protein, no vitamins, no helpful minerals, no fats, and no fiber also make the calorie comparison to a healthy salad ludicrous.

The Optimal Nutrition component of CRON is about food quality and nutrient density. "Food quality" refers to the actual quality of any given food under consideration. In short, what has it gone through on its way to your plate? Was it radiated, fortified, or heavily processed? Was it stored for inordinate lengths of time in a toxic environment? Has it been "improved" with cosmetic modifications, such as dyes or waxes? Is it covered with pesticides, herbicides, and chemical fertilizers? Are these removable? Is it comprised of genetically modified organisms, even in part? Has it been overexposed to oxygen or heat? These are some of the conditions that could lead to immune imbalance and increased biological toxicity.

Is the food on your plate nutritional building blocks and nutritional "fuel" for the body? And most important…is it a nutritionally healthful food, which is to say, does it contribute to the body's inherent nutritional needs?

"Nutrient density" refers to the number and quality of viable nutrients in any given food, relative to the overall number of calories in it. The more nutrient dense the food is, the better it is, because it enables us to consume the greatest number of health-giving nutrients with the smallest number of overall calories. Optimal nutrition requires that we focus, not on calories alone, but on balancing the correct macronutrients (proteins, fats, fiber, and low glycemic carbohydrates) so as to achieve maximum nutrient density to cover the body's most basic internal requirements.

A Step in the Wrong Direction

While the clinical literature has been clear that most people need to cut their calories by 20- to 30-plus percent and increase nutrient density, during the past 10 years it has gone the opposite direction by 25 percent. Yet on November 16, 2009, in a draft report on recommended energy requirement levels in the United Kingdom, the Scientific Advisory Committee on Nutrition (SACN) said Estimated Average Requirements (EARs) should be increased by up to 16 percent.

> If you want to enhance the quality and extent of your life, here's a simple guide: Whack the calories—max out the nutrition.

Current recommendations put daily calorie intake at 2,000 for women and 2,500 for men, and so a 16 percent increase would give men an extra 400 calories. According to the advisors, previous recommendations, based on research from the Committee on the Medical Aspects of Food and Nutrition Policy in 1991, underestimated average levels of daily exercise. They say the average physical activity level assumed in the 1991 study was lower than the values observed for 90 percent of the subjects in the reference adult population examined for their report. The SACN draft conclusion that EARs should be increased was announced despite the fact that surveys have consistently found energy intake to be below EARs, yet there is a growing obesity problem in the United Kingdom. The report said exercise levels need to be increased in relation to calories consumed to reduce the number of overweight and obese people.

How ridiculous a step in the wrong direction will that be if the Department of Health and the Food Standards Agency were to adopt this policy! *Despite reports that you hear to this effect, remember the right step is to reduce the intake of calories and increase the nutrient-dense foods that you eat.*

Superfoods!

The following is a short list of the top nutrient-dense, low calorie foods that I consider to be some of today's finest superfoods:

- Dark green vegetables (spinach, kale, broccoli, asparagus, green beans, romaine, mixed greens)
- Sea vegetables (spirulina, chlorella, dulse, kelp)
- Grain grasses (wheat grass, barley grass, rye grass)
- Bright colored vegetables (bell and hot peppers)
- Berries (blueberries, strawberries, cranberries, and raspberries)
- Eggs from free range hens
- Grass-fed/grain-free/organic beef, bison, chicken, turkey, lamb, venison
- Rice and yellow pea protein powder blend
- Goat milk protein
- Non-denatured whey protein
- Stabilized brown rice bran
- Sprouted legumes and grains such as quinoa and kasha (buckwheat)
- Fresh squeezed combinations of *vegetable* juices with added protein powder
- Sprouts (broccoli, alfalfa, mung bean)

With any food product, it is very important to buy organic whenever possible. There is an abundance of medical literature referring to the health hazards of pesticides, herbicides, fungicides, and chemical fertilizers. There has been a huge increase in demand for organic foods during the last five years, which will continue. If you are on a budget and cannot afford organic foods, consider focusing on conventional produce that you don't eat the skin, such as avocado, banana, and watermelon, but not peppers, tomatoes, or berries. Another great thing to do is to grow your own organic garden or join a co-op. If space is limited, growing sprouts or vegetables in planters may be an option. At a minimum, you must thoroughly wash your produce.

In the "Golden Key #6—Environmental Hazards" chapter, I have provided a Dirty Dozen™ list of conventionally grown produce that is high in herbicides and pesticides as well as a list of the 15 least contaminated conventionally grown fruits and vegetables. Researchers have found that people who eat five fruits and vegetables a day from the Dirty Dozen™ list consume an average of 10 pesticides a day. Those who eat from the 15 least contaminated conventionally grown fruits and vegetables ingest fewer than two pesticides daily.

THE
SUPER
HEALTH
DIET

Golden
Keys
to Unlock
Lifelong
Vitality

Corner #2—Eat Foods with a Low Glycemic Response

A key to sustainable weight loss, long-term health, and reducing the deadly cascade brought on by high insulin levels in the blood is to choose low GI carbohydrates.

During the 1990s, nutritional scientists mistakenly told us to avoid protein and *all forms of fat*, even the essential fatty acids that are necessary for life and healthy cell function. Meanwhile, food manufacturers were busy marketing their low fat cookies, brownies, and cakes, neglecting to tell us that these processed products were filled with refined sugars and appetite-stimulating chemical additives to make us want to eat more. We see the results today—diabetes and obesity skyrocketed to epidemic proportions and continue to climb. And most of the blame has landed on carbohydrates, so now we're actually afraid to eat carbohydrates.

However, the right amount of carbohydrates, proteins, and fats is absolutely essential for health and overall well-being. Carbohydrates are the major source of energy in our diet and are found in grains, legumes, fruits, vegetables, sugar, and alcohol. In fact, if you starve your body by not fueling it with the right kind of carbohydrates, you'll get to the point where you can't even think straight, and you'll feel edgy all the time. But it's the right kind of carbohydrates—good carbs that are often thought to be simply *complex carbohydrates*, but I prefer to be more specific, calling them *fibrous carbohydrates*—that are essential to good health.

Despite other potential benefits, many of today's diets have us consuming far too many carbohydrates. Indeed, the body's storage capacity for carbohydrates is quite limited. Excess carbohydrates are converted, via insulin, into glycogen, which is stored in the liver and muscles and easily converted to glucose as a source of energy. It is also converted to cholesterol (LDL) and into saturated fat (triglycerides), which is stored in the adipose (or "fatty") tissue. Any meal or snack that is high in carbohydrates can cause blood glucose levels to rise too rapidly. Chronically elevated insulin levels from excess carbohydrates promote fat and block the body's ability to lose that fat. This vicious cycle leads to blood sugar and endocrine issues, including diabetes and metabolic syndrome, or Syndrome X, which leads to virtually every known disease over the long term. The good news is that many of the "degenerative diseases" and "incurable diseases," such as type 2 diabetes, Syndrome X, and other endocrine/blood sugar disorders are often completely reversible through the principles taught in this book.

Carbohydrates

Sugar, starch, and cellulose are carbohydrates. During the digestion of food, carbohydrates in the food are broken down into smaller sugar molecules, such as fructose, sucrose, galactose, and glucose. These are the body's and the brain's favorite fuel, because it helps to maintain concentration, keeps us mentally sharp, and provides the power for the brain's many supremely complex functions. Children also need sufficient levels of carbohydrates, not only because they are so active but also because they need energy to grow.

However, not all carbohydrates break down the same way. Some break down quickly (simple carbohydrates), while the molecular structure of others results in a gradual breakdown into glucose (complex carbohydrates). This breakdown of complex carbohydrates results in slowly released energy that provides longer-lasting sustenance to the body and the brain. These are the carbs we need to make sure are a part of our diet.

Simple carbohydrates, conversely, release sugars quickly. These carbohydrates include refined white starchy foods, sweet drinks, sugars, and alcohol. They deliver a burst of energy by the quick breakdown into glucose, which it then releases into the bloodstream, but the resulting crash soon leaves you exhausted and unable to concentrate. The effect of a drop in blood sugar levels can also include nervousness, hyperactivity, confusion, depression, anxiety, forgetfulness, headaches, palpitations, dizziness, and insomnia. This type of crash can also be a trigger for panic attacks.

Researchers have also discovered that the constant insulin "highs" produced by fluctuating blood sugar levels lead to an increase in body weight. Insulin stimulates an enzyme called lipoprotein-lipase, which directs circulating fatty acids into fat cell storage, which in turn increases body weight. This only reinforces why anyone who snacks on cookies, ice cream, candy, cakes, potato chips, and other simple carbohydrates will pack on the weight.

The extremely high sugar intake in the modern American diet—an average of more than 150 pounds a year per person as compared to an estimated five pounds a year a century ago—has been found to directly relate to numerous degenerative diseases. America is locked into the sugar cycle of destruction. But it isn't just plain table sugar that has this destructive effect on one's health. A high glycemic (or high sugar) biochemical response can also be created in the body by eating foods that rapidly convert to sugar in the bloodstream.

Our blood glucose or blood sugar levels are one of the most important measures of good health. New research has demonstrated that fasting blood glucose levels at about 75mg/dl to 85mg/dl might be ideal[32] and any amount of incremental fasting glucose over 85 mg/dl incrementally increases heart attack risk.[33] Many people are challenged to keep their blood glucose below 100mg/dl, which is a ticking time bomb that should be treated as an emergency with immediate diet and lifestyle changes.

Fruit Juices

Fruit juice can be healthy when consumed in moderation—for instance, in smaller amounts than most people drink (four ounces) with a meal or two to four ounces of juice added to a high protein and fiber SuperSmoothie. Fresh juices are best, but eating the fruit is even better.

Interestingly, drinking high pulp orange juice, lemon juice, or apple cider vinegar has been shown to dramatically reduce the inflammatory response of overeating unhealthy fatty, inflammation-triggering foods.

Orange Juice or Soft Drink?

To show you the importance of understanding the release of carbohydrates into your bloodstream, consider orange juice. Oranges and other fruits are healthy and filled with vitamins and other nutrients we need every day. But did you know there is so much sugar in a glass of orange juice that, in an attempt to justify its sugar levels and even appear healthy, one of the world's largest soft drink companies has compared its sugar content to that found in orange juice? The obvious implication is that their soft drink is not a health risk because of its sugar levels. But just the opposite is true. Too much orange juice is not really a healthy drink because of its high sugar levels.

An eight-ounce glass of orange juice has almost the same amount of sugar in it as a regular soft drink, a whopping eight to nine teaspoons of sugar. Guess how many teaspoons of sugar are necessary in your bloodstream? One. Your brain tightly regulates one tablespoon of sugar in the bloodstream for proper brain function. So where does all that extra sugar go when you drink a soft drink or a glass of fresh orange juice? The pancreas responds by secreting excess insulin to offset the sharp rise in blood sugar, and this results in the liver converting the excess sugar to LDL (or bad) cholesterol and triglycerides (a saturated fat), which in excess is not healthy. Also, the increased insulin levels that result from such a huge inflow of sugar into your bloodstream block your body's ability to burn the newly created triglycerides, which end up as increased blood triglyceride levels and as body fat. Check your waistline—there it is. This is not to say that soft drinks are as healthy as orange juice, because orange juice, particularly fresh squeezed, has many nutrients and soft drinks do not.

Your body simply can't handle the sugar. When you wake up in the morning, your blood sugar level should be around 87. You get to the breakfast table and drink the glass of orange juice and eat a bowl of cereal (both of which convert rapidly to sugar in the body), and your blood sugar level rockets to more than 100. Then your pancreas rises to protect you, secreting high levels of insulin, which then pushes your blood sugar level down into the 70s or low 80s, and you feel exhausted and maybe a little shaky, so you grab a cup of coffee and a doughnut to bring it back up. This just further perpetuates the roller-coaster cycle of blood sugar ups and downs, which, in turn, exhausts your organs. Over time, this roller-coaster ride sets the stage for many diseases to attack and win over a weakened system. Unfortunately, America lives on this health-destroying cycle.

Here's the truth: *Eat fruit the way God made it. Fruit juice is sugar-laden, and fruit juice from concentrate is even worse.*

The Dangers of Fructose

Most of the carbohydrates we eat in "natural foods" are made up of a combination of sugars, including glucose and fructose. As I've stated, when glucose enters the bloodstream, the body increases its production of insulin to help regulate the sugar in the blood so it can be taken to cells and used for energy. This infusion of sugar also increases the production of the hormone leptin (as discussed earlier), which regulates the body's appetite and fat storage, and decreases the production of the hormone ghrelin, which helps regulate your food intake.

Fructose, on the other hand, is processed in the liver. When too much fructose enters the liver, and it can't be processed fast enough for the body to use as sugar, it uses the fructose to produce fats that get sent into the bloodstream as triglycerides. As we'll see, this produces a cascade of bad effects in the body. High blood triglycerides put us at risk for heart disease, but there's a lot more to it than that. Another significant issue with fructose is that it can result in glycation at as much as 10 times the rate of glucose or sucrose (see the Glycation section within Chapter 12).

Fruits and vegetables have relatively small amounts of fructose that most bodies can handle quite well. For example, a cup of chopped tomatoes has 2.5 grams of fructose, which is not a problem. However, due in part to corn subsidies in the United States, fructose has become an incredibly inexpensive and abundant form of sugar added to thousands of packaged food products and soft drinks we eat every day. Check the ingredients on packaged food labels and you'll see the sources of fructose.

The problem is not the fructose itself—all fructose works the same in the body, whether it comes from apples, peaches, corn syrup, cane sugar, or beet sugar. The problem is that the volume of it in our diets has grown exponentially in recent decades. For example, a can of regular soda supplies 23 grams, and a super-size soda has about a whopping 62 grams. If we combine high quantities of fructose, such as these, with the fact that our bodies metabolize it in a different manner than glucose, it can damage our metabolism and is likely fueling the obesity crisis. And, not surprisingly, new research shows that it can increase our tendency to overeat.

Here is why. When our bodies are hungry, ghrelin, the so-called "hunger hormone," is produced mainly by our stomachs. Studies have shown that people who were given ghrelin became so hungry they consumed significantly more than their typical amount of food. Some researchers believe that ghrelin may also act on our brain's "pleasure centers," causing a recall of how good a food tasted and made us feel, which delivers a significant push to take another helping. I'm sure you know that sensation.

Glucose suppresses the hormone ghrelin and stimulates leptin, which suppresses your appetite. In other words, when you eat, your body knows it should feel less hungry and stimulates the production of leptin to signal your brain. *Fructose, however, has no suppressing effect on ghrelin and interferes with your brain's communication with leptin, which naturally leads one to overeat.* Stated in another way, fructose bypasses the appetite-signaling mechanism of the body, so the hormones that regulate the appetite aren't triggered, and you're left feeling hungry. Obviously, this is a recipe for disaster. This is why excess fructose is seen as today's villain that contributes to weight gain, increased belly fat, insulin resistance, type 2 diabetes, and metabolic syndrome—as well as all the other ills related to these conditions. It comes back to balance. In nature, fructose is balanced with other sugars, and when we disrupt that balance with high fructose, problems arise.

Your body's level of ghrelin can be influenced by other factors as well, including your lifestyle habits. For instance, chronic lack of sleep increases ghrelin, making you feel hungry when you don't really need to eat. This is one of the reasons why I emphasize in this book that a lack of sleep can make you gain weight. Any negative emotion, such as anger or stress, can also lead you to use food as a coping mechanism and ultimately overeat.

However, the major step to normalizing your ghrelin, leptin, and insulin levels is to eat a diet consistent with my nutrition plan and exercise program. At the minimum, you must restrict your intake of fructose.

The Glycemic Index and Glycemic Load

The Glycemic Index (GI) is just one of the many tools you have available to you to improve your dietary control. It classifies foods according to how much they raise blood glucose following ingestion of an amount of the food that contains 50 grams of carbohydrates. The GI was devised as a means to help diabetics in their food selections. One of the values of this general index is that it shows that even among carbohydrates, there is a wide variance of values. For instance, the potato is actually a high glycemic food that can spike one's insulin levels.

Glucose (sugar) is the fastest carbohydrate in terms of speed of uptake into the bloodstream and given a value of 100—all other carbs are given a number relative to glucose. For the best health results, consume a diet where most of your foods have a Glycemic Index of less than 45.[34] The impact a food will have on blood sugar levels depends on many other factors, such as ripeness, cooking time, fiber and fat content, time of day, blood insulin levels, and even recent activity.

It is estimated that as much as 40 percent of our supermarket foods contain high fructose corn syrup or HCFS, as the industry calls it.

The Glycemic Index is not the most useful index in terms of a particular food's impact on blood sugar. As mentioned, the GI of a food is based on an amount of that food that contains 50 grams of carbohydrates. However, a single serving of many high GI foods often doesn't contain 50 grams of carbohydrates. For instance, a watermelon has an extremely high Glycemic Index, but one slice has so few carbohydrates that the index is irrelevant. The Glycemic Load, however, takes into account how many carbohydrates are actually in a serving of food rather than a serving of that same food that contains 50 grams of carbohydrates. To calculate Glycemic Load, you simply multiply the Glycemic Index of a food times the number of carbohydrates in a serving of food and divide it by 100. I've put a chart at the end of this chapter to show you a sample of the Glycemic Load for certain foods. A Glycemic Load of 10 or under is considered low. To learn more about Glycemic Index and Glycemic Load, go to www.glycemicindex.com.

> The truth: Coffee (caffeine) is a stimulant that in excess and over the long run actually increases insulin resistance, raises insulin levels, increases diabetes risk, and raises homocysteine.

Low glycemic foods include above-ground dark green vegetables, such as broccoli, kale, and spinach, as well as avocados, nuts, and some fruits, such as blueberries and cranberries. White bread, potatoes, rice, sugary drinks, fruits such as bananas and citrus, and below-ground vegetables such as carrots and beets are high glycemic foods that are known to raise insulin levels into the danger zone. Indeed, many of us have already experienced the severe "low energy letdown" that typically happens when we consume large doses of sugar or other high glycemic foods.

Low Glycemic Foods

- Berries (blueberries, strawberries, cranberries, and raspberries)
- Broccoli
- Kale
- Spinach
- Avocados
- Nuts and seeds
- All meats, most vegetables, and some fruits

High Glycemic Foods

- Grain and grain products
- White breads
- Potatoes
- Rice
- Cooked or juiced carrots and beets
- Soft drinks and sport drinks
- Fruit juices

Benefits of Low Glycemic Response Foods

- Cause a smaller, more gradual rise in blood glucose levels after meals.
- Help you to stay full longer.
- Can improve the body's sensitivity to insulin.
- Can improve blood sugar control in diabetics.
- Help people lose and control weight.
- Reduce blood cholesterol levels.
- Prolong physical endurance and help refuel carbohydrate stores after exercise.

To Reduce the Negative Effect of High GI Foods in a Meal

- Eat high quality fiber, protein, and fats along with GI foods. Include low GI foods such as eggs, meat, or berries.
- Add vinaigrette or other acidic extras, such as lemon juice.
- Cook with or add some extra olive oil or coconut oil.

Metabolic Syndrome or Syndrome X

Metabolic disorders are nearing epidemic proportions in the U.S. as more and more Americans are being diagnosed as diabetic or pre-diabetic. It is my belief that diabetes and Syndrome X are two of the greatest health risks facing the American people today, because these conditions lead to virtually every other "disease of aging."

The combination of a high glycemic diet, high blood insulin levels, and increased body fat reserves is thought to be responsible for creating one of the most deadly health syndromes to surface in the last century—Syndrome X or metabolic syndrome. Syndrome X is the variable combination of obesity, high blood cholesterol, and hypertension (high blood pressure) linked by an underlying resistance to insulin.[35]

In 2001, *Forbes* magazine documented that 70 million Americans are affected by Syndrome X. Only 15 years ago that number was at 43 million. And growing numbers are appearing among children and teenagers, especially in African-American and Hispanic communities.[36] Lifestyle, genetics, and poor nutrition all work together to create this devastating health problem.

Metabolic syndrome and its related conditions all emanate from increased levels of inflammatory molecules called cytokines—and inflammatory cytokines are more prominent in people with excessive stores of body fat.[37] Indeed, physicians now commonly measure certain markers of inflammation such as C-reactive protein (CRP) as a means of screening for people at risk for cardiovascular disease.[38]

Syndrome X owes much of its existence to the massive deterioration in the quality of our food supply in the past 50 years. Prior to World War II, most foods were "whole" in the sense of not being "processed" by high-tech machines. Foods such as whole grain breads were not being stripped of the critical, life-saving nutrients found in the wheat germ. Not only were our foods deprived of one of nature's premier antioxidants, vitamin E, they were also deprived of all the B-complex vitamins that naturally reside within the wheat germ itself. It was at this point in American history that cardiovascular disease became the number-one killer of Americans, seemingly overnight.

As we now know, one of the chief causes of cardiovascular disease is a toxic amino acid called homocysteine, which is produced naturally within the body as the normal product of metabolism. However, the body has a built-in protective shield against homocysteine, which is comprised of the very same B-vitamins that have long since been milled out of whole grains, such as pyridoxine (B6), folate (B9), methylcobalamin (B12), and riboflavin (B2), when the "Age of Refinement" came into being. Moreover, the milling of whole grains into white flour also resulted in the loss of the fat-soluble antioxidant vitamin E, which also has been shown to have a protective effect on the heart.

The processing and refining of whole foods was a kind of "nutritional suicide," resulting in a wave of "empty" foods—full of calories but devoid of almost any nutritional value. Indeed, most refined foods don't even have enough critical nutrients and cofactors to enable them to be properly digested and absorbed into the body. Accordingly, when we consume these nutritionally empty foods, the body has to call upon its critical nutritional reserves just to be able to digest them. This, in turn, leads to a highly destructive cascade of events within the body.

Syndrome X is strongly correlated with the phenomenon of insulin resistance, in that the insulin released by the pancreas is not used efficiently or effectively by the body, which is why progressively greater amounts of insulin are required to metabolize a certain amount of glucose. This increased amount of blood insulin wreaks utter havoc within the body, and additional fat reserves are only the beginning. The resulting health implications are profound: cardiovascular disease, diabetes, thrombosis, female endocrine disorder, acne, abnormal hair growth, infertility, impaired immunity, inflammation, and even cancer.[39]

According to a November 2009 report by the American Institute for Cancer Research, there is a clear correlation between obesity and cancer. It went so far as to link excess body weight to more than 100,000 cancers in the U.S. annually. Some researchers say increased weight causes an increase in the amount of hormones, such as estrogen, or an increase in low-grade inflammation in the body, both of which are theorized to increase cancer risk. Dr. David Euhus, professor of surgical oncology at University of Texas Southwestern Medical Center and director of the Cancer Genetics and Risk Assessment Program at the Simmons Cancer Center, believes the true culprit is insulin resistance, which increases with weight gain and a sedentary lifestyle. He states, "Breast cancer risk increases in the years prior to a diagnosis of diabetes. Women with higher levels of circulating insulin have higher breast cancer rates." His preferred prescription, which he gives to all his patients, is a healthy lifestyle. "Losing weight can decrease breast cancer risk."

People suffering from Syndrome X often show a loss of energy and a general lack of vitality. They tend to lead sedentary lifestyles; they eat larger portions of food than most; and some are substance abusers, in that they consume too much sugar, alcohol, or over-the-counter drugs.

The solution to Syndrome X is mostly lifestyle related. First and foremost, one must focus on eating low glycemic foods as a matter of course.[40] As mentioned before, low glycemic foods are those that slowly and gently produce a gradual increase in blood glucose levels. These foods include nuts, meat, poultry, eggs, and low glycemic complex carbohydrates, such as broccoli, spinach, and berries.

> **Having good health is very different from only being not sick.**
>
> SENECA THE YOUNGER

Several additional nutrients have also been shown to help manage insulin resistance—chromium, vanadium, magnesium, potassium, and cinnamon. Controlled protein intake along with more liberal healthy fats, such as fish oil, olive oil, and coconut oil can have a very positive effect, as does eating a balanced diet that is high in fiber. Regular aerobic exercise is also known to reduce blood insulin levels.[41]

Some lifestyle habits should be avoided. Not only should you refrain from smoking, but also minimize these other addictive substances—caffeine, alcohol, over-the-counter medications, and "hidden" sources of fructose, such as soda and fruit juices. Traditional coffee (caffeinated) can actually increase insulin resistance, raise insulin levels, and increase diabetes risk.[42]

The encouraging news is that many of the "degenerative diseases" and "incurable diseases," such as type 2 diabetes, Syndrome X, and other endocrine/blood sugar disorders, are often completely reversible through the principles taught in this book.

The Importance of Fiber

I've mentioned the importance of fiber in your diet, and here's why as pertains to minimizing the glucose-insulin surge. It's a simple fact that foods with plant fibers will fill you up quickly, which can be very critical in weight management. Another high value of the fiber is that it slows down the digestive process and prolongs the carbohydrate's energy release of insulin into the bloodstream for hours after you've eaten. Fiber comes from the cells' walls and other parts of plants, with fresh, live foods being the best source. It is a key to a low glycemic diet and essential for good health.

A diet rich in fiber can help fight obesity, heart disease, diabetes, and cancer. The Seven Countries Study found that people living in countries with high fiber intake weighed less than those living in countries where fiber intake is low.[43] In the famous Nurses' Health Study, those who ingested more dietary fiber consistently weighed less than those who consumed less fiber.[44] Another study linked higher dietary fiber intake with lower body weight and waist-to-hip ratios, along with a reduction in markers of heart disease risk. Higher fiber consumption predicted less weight gain more strongly than did total or saturated fat consumption.[45]

At the 2004 meeting of the American Diabetes Association, results of two studies using PGX fiber blend (glucomannan with xanthan and alginate soluble fibers in an exact ratio and mulberry concentrate of 20:1 to enhance glycemic-control and lipid-lowering effect) were presented by researchers from the Risk Factor Modification Centre at St. Michael's Hospital and the University of Toronto. Study participants who took three grams of the fiber blend had a 65 percent reduction in post-meal glucose elevation after consuming a 50-gram acute glucose challenge. Study participants who took three grams of the fiber blend (three times a day, before meals) had a 23 percent reduction in post-meal glucose, a 40 percent reduction in post-meal insulin release, and a 55.9 percent improvement in whole-body insulin sensitivity scores. Study participants taking the fiber blend reduced body fat by 2.8 percent from baseline by the end of the three-week study period.

A more recent study, published in the April 2010 *Journal of Nutrition*, sought to investigate the after-meal effects of eating protein and dietary fiber (psyllium) on peptide release and hunger ratings. Sixteen healthy, non-obese study participants were given one of five meals in randomized order on separate days, and serum insulin and plasma glucose, ghrelin, glucagon-like peptide 1 (GLP-1), and peptide YY (PYY) concentrations were determined two hours following the meals. The meals ranged from one that was high in both protein and fiber to one that was low in fiber and protein. *The results revealed that meals containing high amounts of fiber decreased glucose, insulin, ghrelin, and PYY responses.* In addition, PYY secretion, which appears to reduce appetite, was prolonged compared with the other meals. However, they did not find any difference in appetite ratings between the different test meals. These results suggest that meals enriched with psyllium fiber seem to strongly modify postprandial signals arising from the GI tract.[46] While Americans eat an average of 12 to 17 grams of fiber daily, the American Dietetic Association and the National Cancer Institute (NCI) recommend an intake of 30 grams or more of fiber every day, and some experts say that for optimal health a person should get 40 to 50 grams a day.

Before every meal, consume enough soluble fiber to slow the rapid carbohydrate absorption that can cause insulin levels to spike. Fiber comes in two forms: soluble and insoluble. Soluble fiber, which is present in legumes, brans, fruits, vegetables (carrots), rice and oat brans, whole grain products, seeds and nuts, and psyllium seed, helps to reduce cholesterol, helps you feel full quickly, and markedly blunts post-meal elevations in blood sugar and insulin levels. Insoluble fiber, found in whole wheat products, brown rice, kidney beans, skins of fruits, and many vegetables, reduces the risk of constipation as well as helps prevent bowel cancer. After all, fiber speeds the transit time of fecal matter out of the body, which makes it highly valuable. Fiber can also provide prebiotic benefit, helping establish a colony of healthy probiotics.

Psyllium is rich in dietary fiber and has traditionally been used as a bulk-forming laxative; however, recent research points to other uses including the treatment of hypercholesterolemia, irritable bowel syndrome, and ulcerative colitis. In February 1998, the FDA gave permission to allow food manufactures to make this health claim on the packaging of food products regarding psyllium: "Eating soluble fiber from foods such as soluble brown rice fiber, oat soluble beta glucan fiber, and psyllium fiber as part of a diet low in saturated fat and cholesterol may reduce the risk of heart disease." These findings make psyllium a potential agent for reducing the risk of cardiovascular disease.

I recommend soluble fiber at every meal; however, one of the most important times to take fiber is before the highest sugar and fat meal. The objective is to have the fiber slow the release of sugar into the bloodstream and absorb some of the dietary fat to prevent it from absorbing into the bloodstream where it helps contribute to body fat accumulation. *The fiber can absorb these critically important fatty acids before they can reach your cells, so try to take your omega-3/fish oil supplement an hour before a meal whenever possible.* Some people experience unpleasant gastrointestinal side effects when taking high doses of fiber. It is best to begin with a low dose, increasing the dose slowly. Fiber supplements consisting of rice bran, oat bran, guar gum, pectins, and psyllium seed husks are available in capsule form and in powder that can be mixed in liquid and consumed immediately before eating a fatty or high carbohydrate meal. My favorite sources of fiber are brown rice soluble fiber and oat soluble beta-glucan fiber.

The Glycemic Load

A Glycemic Load (GL) of 10 or under is considered low

FOOD	GI	SERVING SIZE	NET CARBS	GL
Peanuts	14	4 oz (113 g)	15	2
Cashew nuts	22	1 oz (30 g)	9	2
Bean sprouts	25	1 cup (104 g)	4	1
Grapefruit	25	1/2 large (166 g)	11	3
Pearled barley	25	1 cup (150 g)	42	11
Kidney beans	28	1 cup (150 g)	25	7

FOOD	GI	SERVING SIZE	NET CARBS	GL
Pizza	30	2 slices (260 g)	42	13
Skim milk	32	8 fl oz (250 ml)	13	4
Low fat yogurt	33	1 cup (245 g)	47	16
Spaghetti, w. wheat	37	1 cup (140 g)	37	14
Apples	38	1 medium (138 g)	16	6
Pears	38	1 medium (120 g)	11	4
All-Bran cereal	38	1 cup (30 g)	23	9
Rye bread	41	1 large slice (30 g)	12	5
Spaghetti	42	1 cup (140 g)	38	16
Oranges	48	1 medium (131 g)	12	6
Bananas	52	1 large (136 g)	27	14
Potato chips	54	4 oz (114 g)	55	30
Snickers Bar	55	1 bar (113 g)	64	35
Brown rice	55	1 cup (195 g)	42	23
Honey	55	1 tbsp (21 g)	17	9
Oatmeal	58	1 cup (234 g)	21	12
Ice cream	61	1 cup (72 g)	16	10

FOOD	GI	SERVING SIZE	NET CARBS	GL
Jelly beans	78	1 oz (30 g)	28	22
Macaroni and cheese	64	1 serving (166 g)	47	30
Raisins	64	1 small box (43 g)	32	20
White rice	64	1 cup (186 g)	52	33
Table sugar (sucrose)	68	1 tbsp (12 g)	12	8
White bread	70	1 slice (30 g)	14	10
Watermelon	72	1 cup (154 g)	11	8
Popcorn	72	2 cups (16 g)	10	7
Soda crackers	74	4 crackers (25 g)	17	12
Doughnut	76	1 medium (47 g)	23	17
Puffed rice cakes	78	3 cakes (25 g)	21	17
Cornflakes	81	1 cup (30 g)	26	21
Baked potato	85	1 medium (173 g)	33	28
Glucose	100	(50 g)	50	50
Dates, dried	103	2 oz (60 g)	40	42

THE
SUPER
HEALTH
DIET

Golden
Keys
to Unlock
Lifelong
Vitality

Corner #3—Consume High Antioxidant Superfoods and Supplements

> *Antioxidants are substances or nutrients in our foods that can prevent or slow the oxidative damage to our body. When our body cells use oxygen, they naturally produce free radicals (byproducts) that can cause damage. Antioxidants act as "free radical scavengers" and hence prevent and repair damage done by these free radicals.*
>
> GLORIA TSANG, R.D.

Compelling research during the past years has demonstrated and raised the public's awareness of the importance of antioxidants in the maintenance of health and even in the prevention of degenerative disease. Indeed, research shows that low oxidative stress or the consumption of large amounts of broad-spectrum antioxidants in fruits, vegetables, some grains, nuts, seeds, legumes, and supplement antioxidants is the other most likely reason CRON diets work. However, what exactly are antioxidants, and why are antioxidants so important for human health?

Appropriately named, *antioxidants* are a group of compounds produced by the body that occur naturally in many foods and in various amounts. They are invaluable substances because they soak up the toxic free radicals that are produced by the oxidation process in our bodies. Free radicals are chemically unstable molecules that attack your cells and damage your DNA. Oxidation is what causes an apple slice to turn brown, fish to become rancid, and a cut on our skin to become raw and inflamed. It happens to all cells in nature, including the ones in our bodies.

The terms *free radicals* and *antioxidants* have become broad terms used by researchers, marketers, and the public to simplify the complex discussion of reactive oxygen species. There are five major classes of free radicals or oxidants, which are more accurately described as reactive oxygen species. The five reactive oxygen species (commonly referred to as *radicals*) that cause oxidative damage in the human body are—hydroxyl, peroxyl, peroxynitrite, singlet oxygen, and superoxide anion. These processes are important biochemical processes within the body, but left unregulated can lead to premature aging, dysfunction, disease, and death.

As we all know, a continuous supply of oxygen is critical for the maintenance of life itself. Oxygen is used to make energy out of the food we eat through a complex biochemical series of reactions called the Krebs Cycle. However, there are toxic byproducts of this energy-making process that are inevitably produced when oxygen is used to produce energy inside the cell's built-in energy factory, the "mighty mitochondria." These toxic byproducts are called free radicals or reactive oxygen species and are dangerous because they tend to wreak all types of biochemical mischief inside the body, in an ever-increasing "domino effect," unless they are "mopped up" by substances designed to stop their toxic spread throughout the body—antioxidants. Think of them as free radical scavengers.

Some free radicals are generated from normal body functions, such as breathing, metabolism, and exercise. Others are created by the immune system to neutralize viruses and bacteria. But it is important to note that not all free radicals are naturally generated within the body in response to normal body metabolism. On the contrary, the vast majority of free radicals come from our toxic environment, whether from pollution in the air and water, radiation, herbicides, cigarette smoke, the ingestion of delicate oils that have been damaged from overexposure to oxygen or heat, charred food, and trans fats. This is one of the many reasons to avoid heat-damaged foods such as deep fried foods.

These externally acquired free radicals then go on to add to the internal damage caused by the body's own pool of naturally produced free radicals. Researcher Jeffrey Blumberg, Ph.D., professor of nutrition at Tufts University in Boston, states, "While the body metabolizes oxygen very efficiently, one or two percent of cells will get damaged in the process and turn into free radicals." These free radicals attack healthy cells, weakening them and making them more susceptible to deterioration and disease. The overall proportion of oxidants to antioxidants within the body has even been shown to be responsible for the vast majority of human diseases.

(Much of the information in this chapter is included for readers who are interested in the scientific details of antioxidant nutrition and how it works.)

The Battle Against Degenerative Diseases

Most people are skeptical of using antioxidants to battle the major degenerative diseases of aging, largely because they don't understand how free radicals themselves can actually cause disease. In the case of cancer, for instance, free radicals attack the genetic machinery inside the DNA molecule, by stealing away electrons from within the DNA. This, in turn, leads to a chain reaction "domino effect," by forcing each newly created free radical to steal yet another electron from among its neighbors. If this terribly destructive process isn't quenched immediately, it goes on to cause catastrophic alterations within the various "base codes" of the DNA molecule.

It is this type of damage to the information content of each DNA molecule that causes the cell to begin to grow wildly, without any control. As 95 percent of all cancers are thought to be caused by the free radicals that are contained in our diet and the environment, it makes sense to consume a protective mixture of broad-spectrum antioxidants, so that self-propagating free-radical reactions can be quenched before they have a chance to alter our DNA and create disease.

Because of its chemical nature, fat is readily oxidized by free radicals—and it is the oxidized form of many lipids that triggers the blood vessel damage and eventual plaque formation that leads to atherosclerosis and its deadly consequences. The propagation of free radicals within the body damages the inner lining of our blood vessels (which is called the *intima*), by stealing electrons from them, causing them to become unstable. These damaged areas of the intima are then plugged with oxidized cholesterol and other fatty deposits, and this process continues unabated until atherosclerotic "plaques" are formed on the inside of our blood vessels. These plaques not only cause the diameter of the blood vessels to shrink (hence leading to a full-scale blockage of blood flow), it also causes the blood to become "hyper-coaguable," by increasing the blood's propensity to clot.

The clots that are formed in this manner contribute to blocking the blood vessels entirely, which in turn leads to the symptoms of ischemia, or low oxygen and nutrient supply to the target tissues that are involved. If this situation is occurring in the brain, a stroke is the typical result. If the target organ is the heart, a classic heart attack is generally the result.

Obesity is closely associated with increased oxidative stress,[47] while loss of body fat is associated with decreasing levels of molecules associated with oxidation.[48] The bottom line is that *people with excessive fat tissue are walking "oxidant factories."* Their bodies must cope with enormous loads of these violently destructive molecules.

While I seldom advocate the use of pharmaceutical drugs, because there is almost always a natural alternative, it is important to point out that natural antioxidants can enhance the benefits of some drugs. Interestingly, the results of a preliminary study released on June 21, 2010, from endocrinology researchers at Catholic University of the Sacred Heart in Rome, show that a diet rich in natural antioxidants improves insulin sensitivity in insulin-resistant obese adults and enhances the effect of the insulin-sensitizing drug metformin. Their study included 16 men and 13 women, ages 18 to 66 years, who were obese and insulin resistant, but not yet diabetic. For three months all participants received a low calorie, Mediterranean-type diet that provided 1,500 calories daily, containing only 25 percent from protein foods, with the rest made up of low glycemic index carbohydrates. Half of the participants' diets contained fruits and vegetables that provide high amounts of antioxidant nutrients. The subjects were further divided into groups that received or did not receive 1,000 milligrams per day of the drug metformin, which improves insulin sensitivity in patients with type 2 diabetes. While all participants experienced similar decreases in weight, only those who received the antioxidant-enriched diet had significant reductions in insulin resistance, with the greatest benefits observed in those who also received metformin. The ability of antioxidants to help reduce oxidative stress may help protect against a number of conditions, including metabolic syndrome. Principal author of the research, Antonio Mancini, M.D., stated, "The beneficial effects of antioxidants are known, but we have revealed for the first time one of their biological bases of action—improving hormonal action in obese subjects with the metabolic syndrome."

> Antioxidants are believed to play an important role in preventing the expansion of such chronic illnesses as heart disease, stroke, cancer, Alzheimer's disease, rheumatoid arthritis, and cataracts.

It seems clear that natural antioxidants did improve the beneficial effects of metformin. *I would be remiss to not mention that there is a natural alternative to metformin called* berberine. *According to clinical double blind crossover studies summarized by Dr. Jonathan Wright in 2008, the nutritional supplement berberine was found to be superior to metformin in controlling type 2 diabetes.*[49]

Fortunately, this degenerative process can also be arrested in the early stages by taking various broad-spectrum antioxidants. By quenching the free radicals that cause the initial damaging of the inner lining of our blood vessels, antioxidants help to stop the original cause of cardiovascular disease. This is good news indeed, for not only does it give us the ability to actually prevent heart disease many years down the road, it also helps to increase the flow of blood throughout the body in the here and now, which in turn leads to a better functioning body today.

You can see how this "free radical theory of aging" and disease can be used therapeutically to help counter the disease process. If disease is simply caused by a significant imbalance of oxidants to antioxidants within the body, it will be of major benefit to introduce a wide variety of antioxidants into the body, in the hope they will help quench the many disease processes initiated by the onslaught of free radicals. This is why the medical use of an intravenous vitamin C drip can be effective in fighting a whole host of different diseases—because all the extra vitamin C goes toward quenching the huge number of disease-causing free radicals within the body.

The Benefits of Omega-3s

New research from the University of Western Australia and the University of Montpellier (France) reported in *Free Radical Research* in June 2010 indicates the heart health benefits of omega-3 fatty acids EPA (eicosapentaenoic acid) and DHA (docosahexaenoic acid) may actually reduce oxidative stress by reducing levels of a compound called F2-isoprostanes. Scientists report that daily supplements of four grams of either EPA or DHA for six weeks were associated with reductions of about 20 percent. Led by Dr. Emilie Mas, the authors of the study wrote, "The data suggest omega-3 fatty acids reduce oxidative stress, which is likely related, at least in part, to their anti-inflammatory actions and the expected reduction in leukocyte activity. These findings give further support for supplementation of the diet with omega-3 fatty acids for cardiovascular risk reduction."[50]

Beyond that research, the September 3, 2010, issue of the journal *Cell* reports the discovery by researchers at the University of California, San Diego School of Medicine of the mechanism used by omega-3 fatty acids in lowering insulin resistance and chronic inflammation. Using cell cultures in mice, Dr. Jerrold Olefsky, a professor of medicine and associate dean of scientific affairs, and colleagues found that exposure to omega-3 fatty acids activates the cellular receptor known as GPR120, which is located on macrophages in mature fat cells and, when activated, prevents the macrophages from causing inflammation. "It's just an incredibly potent effect," stated Dr. Olefsky. "Omega-3s are very potent activators of GPR120 on macrophages—more potent than any other anti-inflammatory we've ever seen.... Our work shows how fish oils safely do this and suggests a possible way to treating the serious problems of inflammation in obesity and in conditions such as diabetes, cancer, and cardiovascular disease through simple dietary supplementation."[51]

It should be noted that the quantity of each person's exposure to environmental poisons is also critical, because antioxidants don't function indefinitely to quell free-radical production. On the contrary, they are used up, and hence become worthless, when they neutralize any given free-radical reaction within the body. This is why *it is imperative to consume enough broad-spectrum antioxidants to effectively neutralize as many toxins and free radicals within the body as possible.*

A good rule of thumb is to try to balance the amount of toxins you are exposed to with the amount of antioxidants consumed on a daily basis. Particularly heavy toxic exposures within the environment should be treated with an even higher dosage of antioxidants, because this will help minimize the free radical-mediated disease process within the body.

Availability of Antioxidants

There are different types of free radicals and reactive oxygen species that are constantly attacking the body. Because only certain kinds of antioxidants quench certain types of radicals, you must get a broad spectrum of antioxidants in your diet. Fortunately, we have available to us today a wide range of very potent antioxidants, which can scavenge and neutralize free radicals before they have a chance to cause disease.

For instance, there are flavonoids, part of a larger group of molecules called polyphenol compounds, that are found in abundance in plants, fruits, vegetables, plant-based beverages, and notably in the pigments of leaves, barks, rinds, seeds, and flowers. Flavonoids:

- Improve memory and concentration and are used to treat attention-deficit disorder.
- Are powerful free radical scavengers that can boost the effectiveness of vitamin C in the antioxidant network.
- Regulate nitric oxide, a potent free radical that is a regulator of blood flow.

- Keep your heart healthy in three important ways. They prevent blood clots, protect against oxidation of LDL cholesterol, and lower high blood pressure.
- Improve sexual function in men.
- Reduce inflammation and bolster immune function.

An online article appearing on August 13, 2009, in advance of publication in the journal *Obesity*, illustrates the power of flavonoids even in weight loss. An average cup of green tea provides 50 to 100 milligrams of catechins, which are natural occurring flavonoids in tea that have strong antioxidant properties. Researchers at Fudan University in Shanghai, China, divided 182 moderately overweight Chinese men and women between the ages of 18 and 55 to receive one of four 90-day regimens: two daily servings of a control drink providing 30 milligrams catechins and 10 milligrams caffeine per day; one serving of the control drink and one serving of a high catechin green tea providing 458 milligrams catechins and 104 milligrams caffeine per day; two servings of a high catechin green tea providing 468 milligrams catechins and 126 milligrams caffeine per day; or two servings of an extra high catechin green tea providing 886 milligrams catechins and 198 milligrams caffeine per day. At the end of the study, lead researcher Dr. Niels Boon stated, "We observed significant decreases in body weight and fat mass. These effects were more pronounced in the group consuming the highest amount of catechins, and the results also suggest the effects were particularly strong on fat located in the abdominal region."

I highly recommend drinking green tea. The green tea polyphenol, epigallocatechin gallate (EGCG), in combination with caffeine (50 milligrams caffeine, 90 milligrams EGCG) has been shown to enhance 24-hour energy expenditure in human test subjects. In this same clinical study, treatment with caffeine alone had no effect on energy expenditure, indicating the effect of green tea in promoting fat burning goes beyond that explained solely by its caffeine content.[52] Other scientific data indicate that green tea polyphenols in combination with caffeine synergistically enhance thermogenesis (fat burning).[53]

An article published online on August 2, 2010, in the journal

Nutrition, Metabolism, & Cardiovascular Disease revealed the results of a clinical trial of overweight and obese individuals that found a benefit for resveratrol, a compound found largely in the skins of red grapes, in improving flow-mediated dilatation (FMD), a biomarker of endothelial function and cardiovascular health. Impaired functioning of the blood vessels' endothelium, or inner lining, occurs in cardiovascular disease and has been associated with high blood pressure and obesity. Rachel H.X. Wong and her colleagues at the University of South Australia stated that consumption of polyphenol-rich foods, including cocoa, tea, grape seed extract, and red wine extract, have been demonstrated to improve FMD. In their discussion of the findings, the authors remark there is evidence that resveratrol could increase blood vessel dilation.[54]

Fruits and Vegetables

Adding more fruit and vegetables of any kind to your diet will improve your health, especially if they are organic, because they limit your exposure to pesticides and herbicides. But some foods are higher in antioxidants than others. To reap the biggest benefit of antioxidants, eat these foods raw or lightly steamed; don't overcook or boil. Three of the most well-known major antioxidant vitamins are beta-carotene, vitamin C, and vitamin E; however, there are many others. It is important to know that a single exotic super fruit, such as acai or pomegranate, or a blend of several like you might find in some of the "wine bottle" antioxidant drinks on the market today, do not cover the full-spectrum of required antioxidants. Remember, there are five major classes of free radicals. You cannot simply take one type of antioxidant and be fully protected. It's like having five holes in a boat with only one or two plugs to keep it from sinking.

Here are the major antioxidant vitamins and their food sources.

Beta-carotene and other carotenoids: apricots, asparagus, beets, broccoli, cantaloupe, carrots, corn, green peppers, kale, mangoes, turnip and collard greens, nectarines, peaches, pink grapefruit, pumpkin, squash, spinach, sweet potato, tangerines, tomatoes, and watermelon.

Vitamin C: berries, broccoli, Brussels sprouts, cantaloupe, cauliflower, grapefruit, honeydew, kale, kiwi, mangoes, nectarines, orange, papaya, red, green, or yellow peppers, snow peas, sweet potato, strawberries, and tomatoes.

Vitamin E: broccoli, carrots, chard, mustard and turnip greens, mangoes, nuts, papaya, pumpkin, red peppers, spinach, sunflower seeds, and rice bran. If you buy a supplement, make sure it is a full-spectrum vitamin E, including tocotrienols and tocopherols.

Vitamins aren't the only antioxidants in food. Other well-known antioxidants are zinc, selenium, manganese, alpha lipoic acid, N-acetyl cysteine, and glutathione. Zinc is found in red meat, poultry, beans, nuts, seafood, whole grains, and dairy products. Selenium is found in Brazil nuts, tuna, beef, poultry, fortified breads, and other grain products.

Capsaicin

Capsaicin, the compound that gives red pepper its heat, generates antioxidant activity that I keep seeing new research on that affects fat metabolism. This is a nutrient I take in supplement form because, as is true of many people, it is too spicy for me to eat enough of to be beneficial. Capsaicin has been shown to provide numerous health benefits and now we can add increased fat metabolism to the list. In the March 2007 *Journal of Agricultural and Food Chemistry*, laboratory researchers from the National Chung Hsing University in Taiwan showed that capsaicin could inhibit the growth of fat cells in mice, by preventing immature fat cells (adipocytes) from developing into mature cells. In the January 2007 *International Journal of Obesity*, a study from Denmark indicated that a combination of catechins, caffeine, capsaicin, and tyrosine were found to boost heat generation and energy expenditure without any adverse effects on blood pressure or heart rate. Findings published in the October 2009 *Obesity* magazine on a study with mice indicated that dietary intakes of capsaicin may prevent the development of diabetes-like symptoms in obese people, lowering blood sugar insulin and leptin levels. In one study, energy expenditure was seen to increase in lean young women after consuming a capsaicin-rich curry.[55] Another study showed that consumption of a cultivar of red pepper increased core body temperature and metabolic rate in test humans.[56]

Until research studies published in April 2010, the underlying molecular mechanism by which the chili pepper compound has been observed to shrink fat tissue, lower fat levels in the blood, and decrease calorie intake has been unclear. Jong Won Yun and colleagues from Daegu University (South Korea) engaged an animal model of obesity and fed high fat diets with or without capsaicin to the study animals. Capsaicin-treated rats were shown to lose eight percent of their body weight and showed changes in levels of at least 20 key proteins found in fat, whereby the altered proteins worked to break down fats. The researcher stated that "these data demonstrate that thermogenesis and lipid metabolism related proteins were markedly altered upon capsaicin treatment in [white adipose tissue]" and urge that "capsaicin may be a useful phytochemical for attenuation of obesity."[57]

> The antioxidants you should care about are the ones God gave you.
>
> DR. ROBERT KELLER

Measuring a Food's Antioxidant Protection

Until recently, the standard way to measure a food's antioxidant protection was with ORAC (Oxygen Radical Absorbance Capacity) scores. ORAC scores are recognized by the USDA as a testing method to assess the antioxidant strength of nutritive compounds. The higher a food's ORAC score, the more potential it has to help protect cells from oxidative damage and fight diseases such as cancer, memory loss, and heart disease.

Total ORAC$_{fn}$ is a new patent-pending test from Brunswick Labs that measures the antioxidant power of a product against five reactive oxygen species (commonly referred to as "radicals") that cause damage in humans—hydroxyl, peroxyl, peroxynitrite, singlet oxygen, and superoxide anion. Total ORAC values are reported in the same standard units as the original ORAC.

1. *Peroxyl* ORAC favors certain antioxidants that work better against the peroxyl radical. For example, compounds such as anthocyanins in the flavonoid family quench peroxyl better than compounds such as lycopene in the carotenoid family.

2. *Hydroxyl* is highly reactive and cannot be eliminated by our endogenous enzymes (such as SOD and glutathione). It can damage virtually all types of macromolecules: carbohydrates, nucleic acids, lipids, and amino acids. In the skin, hydroxyl radicals are created by UV exposure.

3. *Peroxynitrite* is a reactive nitrogen species that is particularly harmful to proteins. It has been implicated in the development of certain cancers, hepatitis, and chronic inflammation. In the skin, peroxynitrite contributes to the breakdown of vital proteins, such as collagen.

4. *Singlet oxygen* is generated in the skin by UV. In vivo, it is linked to the oxidation of LDL cholesterol and cardiovascular disease. Singlet oxygen is highly unstable and durable. Carotenoids are very effective at scavenging singlet oxygen.

5. *Superoxide anion* is a precursor of all other reactive oxygen species—sometimes referred to as "the mother of free radicals." Antioxidants that scavenge superoxide anion also help prevent the formation of radicals such as hydrogen peroxide and hydroxyl. Superoxide anion is highly toxic and contributes to lipid and DNA damage. It has been linked to hypertension and cardiovascular damage.

What natural antioxidants work well against these different free radicals? Research shows that plant-based (botanical) antioxidants can provide broad-spectrum protection against these radicals. However, plant sources of antioxidants seem to "specialize." A botanical source (such as blueberry, tomato, cocoa, or green tea) generally has high concentrations of a particular family of antioxidant compounds (such as anthocyanins, carotenoids, proanthocyanidins, or flavonoids). These compounds tend to perform better against some radicals than others. Here are some general guidelines:

Anthocyanins—peroxyl

Flavonoids—superoxide anion

Carotenoids—singlet oxygen

Proanthocyanidins (PACs)—superoxide anion and hydroxyl

This is why Superfood Nutrition is so important and eating at least nine servings per day of a variety of vegetables and some fruits along with supplementation with broad-spectrum antioxidants. Note: LivingFuel Functional Superfoods are the only foods I am aware of that have been tested to be potent inhibitors of all five of these radical classes. (See page 288 of the Four Corners Shopping List and Smart Meals and SuperSmoothie Recipes.)

20 Common Foods With the Most Antioxidants

United States Department of Agriculture scientists analyzed antioxidant levels in more than 100 different foods, including fruits and vegetables, using Brunswick Lab's standard ORAC score, not the new broad-spectrum Total $ORAC_{fn}$. The standard ORAC measurement only measures antioxidant potential against peroxyl radicals, which is one of the five major radical categories.

Each food was measured for antioxidant concentration as well as antioxidant capacity per serving size using the standard ORAC score. Cranberries, blueberries, and blackberries ranked highest among the fruits studied. Beans, artichokes, and russet potatoes were tops among the vegetables. Pecans, walnuts, and hazelnuts ranked highest in the nut category.

USDA chemist Ronald L. Prior says the total antioxidant capacity of the foods does not necessarily reflect their health benefit. Benefits depend on how the food's antioxidants are absorbed and utilized in the body. Still, this chart should help you add more antioxidants to your daily diet. The key is to eat a wide variety of fruits and vegetables every day along with broad-spectrum antioxidant supplementation.

Food item	Serving size	Total antioxidant capacity per serving
1. Small Red Bean (dried)	Half cup	13,727
2. Wild blueberry	1 cup	13,427
3. Red kidney bean (dried)	Half cup	13,259
4. Pinto bean	Half cup	11,864
5. Blueberry (cultivated)	1 cup	9,019
6. Cranberry	1 cup (whole)	8,983
7. Artichoke (cooked)	1 cup (hearts)	7,904
8. Blackberry	1 cup	7,701
9. Prune	Half cup	7,291
10. Raspberry	1 cup	6,058
11. Strawberry	1 cup	5,938
12. Red Delicious apple	1 whole	5,900
13. Granny Smith apple	1 whole	5,381
14. Pecan	1 ounce	5,095
15. Sweet cherry	1 cup	4,873
16. Black plum	1 whole	4,844
17. Russet potato (cooked)	1 whole	4,649
18. Black bean (dried)	Half cup	4,181
19. Plum	1 whole	4,118
20. Gala apple	1 whole	3,903

THE
SUPER
HEALTH
DIET

Golden
Keys
to Unlock
Lifelong
Vitality

Corner #4—Eat and Supplement with Superfats

The much maligned saturated fats—which Americans are trying to avoid—are not the cause of our modern diseases. In fact, they play many important roles in the body chemistry.... They play a vital role in the health of our bones. For calcium to be effectively incorporated into the skeletal structure, at least 50 percent of the dietary fats should be saturated.

SALLY FALLON

Contrary to popular opinion and despite all the confusing messages and warnings, healthy fats are essential to optimal health and do not make you fat. Essential fats such as omega-3 fatty acids found in cold water fatty fish, grass-fed beef, eggs, some nuts, and chia seeds and flaxseeds are absolutely necessary nutrients for a healthy immune system, heart, skin, endocrine glands, brain function, nervous system, and energy levels. Good fats, known as essential fatty acids, supply the body with its most concentrated source of energy and is lacking in most diets. A University of Buffalo study found that a moderate 33 percent fat diet was equally effective for weight loss as a low fat 18 percent diet, but better at reducing the risk of heart disease and diabetes.

Let's take a quick look at three major types of fat: unsaturated, saturated, and trans.

Good Fats—Unsaturated Fats (usually soft at room temperature and often called oils) are of two varieties—polyunsaturated and monounsaturated—and are found in products derived from plant sources. Polyunsaturated fats are found in high concentrations in chia seeds, flaxseeds, fish oil, and borage seed oil. Monounsaturated fats are found in high concentrations in olives, nuts, and avocados. Omega-3s and omega-6s are types of polyunsaturated fats that are essential for normal growth and may play an important role in the prevention and treatment of coronary artery disease, hypertension, arthritis, cancer, and other inflammatory and autoimmune disorders. Because most of the foods people eat are high in omega-6, most people eat too much omega-6 and are deficient in omega-3s.

Misunderstood Fats—Saturated Fats are mainly animal fats found in meat, dairy products, poultry skin, and egg yolks. Saturated fats are used in the body by muscles for the purpose of providing energy and supporting the body's production of prostaglandins, including those involved in hormone production. Through the years saturated fats have become the dietary scapegoat for almost everything that ails us. They have gotten a bad name because it was once thought that in excess they tend to worsen blood cholesterol levels. However, saturated fats have gotten their bad reputation unfairly, and in fact have many health benefits. Coconut and coconut oil are plant-based medium chain saturated fats that have been shown to provide extraordinary health benefits.

Ugly Fats—Trans Fats exist in nature and are also produced by heating liquid vegetable oils in the presence of hydrogen, in a process known as hydrogenation. This process increases the oils' firmness and resistance to oxidative spoilage. These are fats the body cannot easily break down and often lead to blocked arteries and heart disease. Trans fatty acids damage the body because they displace, and thus supplant, the natural *cis* fatty acids (natural fats and oils contain only *cis* double bonds–e.g., oleic acid, a monounsaturated fatty acid with a *cis* configuration) from the body's various cell membranes, with the tragic result that their essential functionality is profoundly damaged due to the not-found-in-nature "trans"-configuration of *cis* fatty acid called trans fats. This damaged functionality displays itself in the form of a vastly altered permeability of the cellular membrane itself, which in turn results in unwanted molecules making their way inside our cells, while the "right" molecules for optimal health are not absorbed properly. One of the physiological consequences of this is severe and unrelenting inflammation, which leads to all sorts of degenerative diseases within the body.

Most of the trans fats in the American diet are found in foods such as french fries, onion rings, shortening, margarine, doughnuts, partially hydrogenated oils, dressings, puffed cheese snacks, potato chips, tortilla chips, burgers, chicken nuggets, ice cream, candy, cookies, and cakes. Unlike saturated fats, trans fats do not produce any good HDL cholesterol, and they raise bad LDL.

> There is nothing unsafe about butter; quite the opposite, butter contains healthful components that are not found in anything else (other than real cream).
>
> MARY ENIG, PH.D.

Omega-3 Fatty Acids

Natural lipids (fatty acids) of the omega-3 EPA/DHA variety are derived from cold water oily fish as well as from wild animals and plants. Omega-3 fatty acids began to disappear from the typical Western diet in the twentieth century, and only recently have we begun to see the health concerns that their absence has caused. Omega-3 fatty acids are essential for normal growth and may play an important role in the prevention and treatment of coronary artery disease, hypertension, arthritis, cancer, and other inflammatory and autoimmune disorders. They also control many of the most basic functions of the cell, are a major constituent of brain cell membranes, and are converted to critical brain chemicals.

One can see, then, how essential they are for normal nervous system function, and how their deficiency might be linked to mood regulation, attention, memory, and mental health. Omega-3 fatty acids also benefit the body by increasing insulin sensitivity. We tend to think of circulation as the process of flow through arteries and veins; obviously this is the case, but the major part of circulation is what goes into and out of the cell itself, by crossing the all-important cell membrane.

Regardless of what nutrient is delivered to a cell in the blood, it will have no effect at all if it can't get into the cell itself. Cellular circulation is deeply affected by the intake of fatty acids, which in turn affects the fluidity of the cell membrane. *Increasing the omega-3 content of one's diet significantly increases cell-membrane fluidity and allows more nutrients to reach the cells themselves.*

One of the more profound uses of omega-3 fatty acids is in the treatment of a wide range of mental illnesses, including bipolar disorder, unipolar major depression, postpartum depression, schizophrenia, and attention-deficit disorder. The brain does not function well unless adequate amounts of omega-3s are circulating in the bloodstream and are incorporated into cell membranes. It appears that increases in omega-3 dietary intake raise the levels of the neurotransmitter dopamine, which is related to motivation and ambition, qualities often lacking in depressed people.[58]

> **Make a habit of eating wild caught fish, especially cold water deep sea fish, as often as possible. They are rich in omega-3 fatty acids, fat-soluble vitamins, and many important minerals, including iodine, selenium, and magnesium.**
>
> SALLY FALLON

The Importance of Omega-3s

The bottom line is that healthy fats (most importantly, essential fatty acids) are critical to life. The body is designed to manufacture most of the fats it needs. However, there are two major classes of fats the body needs but cannot manufacture on its own; hence they must be obtained through diet alone. These fats are the essential fatty acids (EFAs).

The two EFA classes are called omega-3 and omega-6 fatty acids. There are two categories of omega-3: plant sources, such as flaxseed that contains alpha linolenic acid (ALA), and marine sources, such as salmon, tuna, mackerel, sardines, and anchovies, which contain the most effective forms of omega-3s—EPA (eicosapentanoic acid) and DHA (docosahexaenoic acid). Scientists agree that only 10 to 15 percent of ALA converts to EPA in the body and about five percent converts to DHA. Due to this poor conversion, plant omega-3, such as flaxseed, cannot on its own meet our body's nutritional requirement for EPA and DHA.

Fish oil from cold water fish, such as salmon, herring, and mackerel, is a direct source of EPA and DHA. In fact, fish oil has been shown to significantly increase life span and delay disease where no other dietary changes are made.[59] It favorably influences hormone-like substances in the body known as prostaglandins, specifically PgE1, conferring a protective effect against chronic inflammation and vascular disease, common in overweight individuals. Few people are aware that these omega-3 fatty acids also have beneficial effects on thermogenesis, the process by which energy is converted to heat. They inhibit key enzymes responsible for lipid synthesis, such as fatty acid synthase and stearoyl-CoA desaturase-1, enhance lipid oxidation and fat burning, and inhibit free fatty acids from entering fat cells (adipocytes) for fat storage.[60]

The first reports of the heart health benefits of the marine fatty acids were reported in the early 1970s by Jørn Dyerberg and his co-workers in *The Lancet* and *The American Journal of Clinical Nutrition*. The young Danes sought to understand how the Inuit, or Greenland Eskimos, could eat a high fat diet and still have one of the world's lowest death rates from cardiovascular disease.

A study published in the January 2010 *American Journal of Clinical Nutrition* reported that intakes of omega-3 exceeding levels consumed by the general U.S. population may significantly reduce the risk of chronic disease.[61] High levels of the omega-3 fatty acids EPA and DHA were associated with lower levels of triglycerides, as well as higher levels of HDL cholesterol, according to data from 357 Yup'ik Eskimos in the study. Raised levels of the fatty acids were also associated with decreased levels of markers of inflammation, such as C-reactive protein (CRP). Increased levels of CRP are a good predictor for the onset of both type 2 diabetes and cardiovascular disease.

One would assume that eating fish regularly would be prudent; however, high levels of contaminants such as mercury, PCBs, and dioxins in our environment and waters make eating certain fish regularly a potentially risky dietary choice. This does not mean that fish should be avoided. Published studies clearly show health benefits for those who eat fish. The problem is that some people are overdoing it and eating too much of the wrong kinds of fish. Fortunately, the wealth of health benefits associated with fish consumption can be safely and readily obtained from premium fish oil supplements.

While there is no guarantee that the fish you eat is free of contaminants, the tide has turned when it comes to the safety of omega-3 fish oil supplements. In fact, studies reported in 2005 substantiated that high quality supplements are safer than eating fish. For example, researchers from Brigham and Women's Hospital and Harvard Medical School in Boston analyzed five brands of fish oil supplements and found that levels of PCBs and organochlorine pesticides were below the detectable limit in all five brands tested. The study authors concluded that if a person were to eat fish from the Great Lakes at the optimal recommended amount of about 400 grams per week, he would consume at least 70 times more PCBs and 120 times more organochlorine pesticides than if he were to supplement with the average daily dose of fish oil (1.5 grams) for one week.[62]

Similar to omega-3 EPA/DHA, gamma linolenic acid (GLA) is one of the most powerful forms of omega-6. When GLA (found in borage seed oil and evening primrose oil) is combined with EPA, beneficial prostaglandins (short-lived local anti-inflammatory hormones derived from specialized essential fatty acids) are produced.[63]

Because the American diet is rich in omega-6 foods and salad dressings (sesame, sunflower, corn, peanut, and soy, to name a few) and low in cold water fish, most people tend to eat far too much omega-6 and are dangerously deficient in omega-3. Both the level of omega-3 and the ratio of omega-6 to omega-3 fatty acids are critically important, and a healthy ratio of omega-6 to omega-3 fatty acids is thought to be approximately 3:1. But many Americans have an imbalance of 20:1. The answer is usually as simple as taking fewer omega-6s and adding antioxidant protected fish oil to your diet. It's well worth the price.

High dose fish oil (equivalent to the oil in a serving of fatty fish) has extraordinary health benefits, but is extremely susceptible to oxidation/lipid peroxidation within the body unless therapeutic doses of fat soluble antioxidants (full-spectrum vitamin E, tocotrienols, and tocopherols and the super antioxidant astaxanthin) are taken along with the fish oil. Taking the extra steps of vitamins D and A and balancing it all with GLA (a healthy omega-6 from borage seed oil or evening primrose oil) can be enormously beneficial to your health. Most commercially available fish oils contain miniscule amounts of vitamin E, which addresses the issue of shelf life, but has no protective effect within the body. *Purified antioxidant protected fish oils appear to be the wisest choice; however, this is so important to one's health that lesser quality fish oil appears to be better than none at all.*

Not Just Any Fish Oil

Here is what I consider essential when it comes to the quality of fish oil:

1. The purest forms of fish oil are derived from sardines and anchovies and purified through a flash-molecular distillation process.
2. Fish oil must be rigorously tested to ensure that it is free of unsafe levels of impurities, including PCBs, heavy metals, or oxidized contaminants.
3. The most beneficial omega-3s are EPA and DHA, which can only be found in high concentration in fish oil. Plant-based omega-3 ALA from flaxseed oil cannot give you all the benefits of fish oil.
4. When taking fish oil, also take high quality full-spectrum vitamin E with tocotrienols and tocopherols, vitamin A, vitamin D, and the super antioxidant astaxanthin to protect against lipid peroxidation (essentially unprotected fish oils without antioxidants can spoil inside the body), which can be toxic to every cell in the body. This also provides additional fat soluable antioxidant protection in the body.
5. Along with fish oil consider also taking GLA from borage seed oil or evening primrose oil, which in combination with fish oil helps balance the body's anti-inflammatory pathways.
6. Try to take your fish oil supplement an hour before a meal

> **Low fat diets are associated with greater feelings of anger, hostility, irritability, and depression. These mood changes appear to be biological consequences of inadequate dietary fat in the central nervous system.**
>
> *BRITISH JOURNAL OF NUTRITION*

whenever possible, because the fiber in your meal can absorb these critically important fatty acids before they can reach your cells.

7. Fish oil will retain its original flavor and aroma. If not, the oils have been over-processed.

8. Soon both EPA and DHA will be available from algae sources, which I find exciting because numerous strict vegetarians will finally have access to these essential nutrients.

What to AVOID:

• Every species of commercial fish has been shown to contain unsafe levels of mercury and other contaminants.

• Farm-raised fish are contaminated for different reasons (they are fed toxins).

• Super concentrated fish oils are altered from its natural triglycerides form and reconstructed into an unnatural etherified form (ethyl ester). Fish oil omega-3s in the triglyceride form are better for boosting the omega-3 index than the ethyl ester form, says a new study from Germany, a result which echoes recent Danish findings.[64] Choose fish oil with a maximum of 180 milligrams of EPA and 120 milligrams of DHA per capsule.

• Liquid fish oils due to risk of oxidation. Fish oil should be oxygen protected in a gelatin capsule (buffalo gelatin is best).

• Choose fish oil instead of shellfish oils. Personally, I avoid shellfish and shellfish oils, such as krill oil and green-lipped mussel oils, because of the wisdom behind biblical dietary law and shellfish are the filters of the sea. These oils do contain some omega-3 EPA and DHA, but not nearly as much as fish oils and are far more expensive. Manufacturers claim shellfish oils are better utilized in the body, so one does not have to take as much, and that they also contain some natural antioxidants to help prevent lipid peroxidation. Most researchers do not believe that any enhancement in absorption is enough to offset the dramatically lower amounts of EPA and DHA. The presence of antioxidants is a good thing, but the concentrations are small. However, if you are comfortable with taking shellfish oils or if it happens to be the only EPA/DHA that works for you, by all means take it!

Note: SuperEssentials Omega 3EDA+ is the only antioxidant essential fatty acids supplement that I am aware of that addresses all of these issues. (See Four Corners Shopping List and Smart Meals and SuperSmoothie Recipes.)

THE
SUPER
HEALTH
DIET

Golden
Keys
to Unlock
Lifelong
Vitality

Summary of the Four Corners
of Superfood Nutrition

The Four Corners of Superfood Nutrition can be likened to a team of four players. When all are used in harmony and synergy with the right balance, the results will be greater than the total of the four taken separately. A clinical research study published in *The American Journal of Clinical Nutrition* (June 2002) suggests that the combination of all Four Corners of Superfood Nutrition magnifies the positive results of each corner individually, causing them to work better together. Let's review it for a final time:

1. *Calorie restriction with optimal nutrition* (CRON) decreases free radical damage all the way down to the mitochondria, and thereby allows them to reproduce in a healthy fashion, protecting our energy supply and production.

2. *Consuming low glycemic, low sugar foods* minimizes glycation within the body and helps ensure that blood sugar is not rapidly elevated, forcing the release of excess insulin, promoting insulin resistance, with the negative consequences of inflammation and fat storage.

3. *Broad-spectrum antioxidants* work throughout the cell and even

down into the mitochondria to protect our cells, genes, and energy supply from free radicals.

4. *Healthy fats* are essential to maintain cellular membrane function. This allows cells to efficiently exchange nutrients and wastes and to protect themselves from free radical damage.

Implementing the Four Corners of Superfood Nutrition can add life to your years, and years to your life.

THE
SUPER
HEALTH
DIET

Golden
Keys
to Unlock
Lifelong
Vitality

Superfood Nutrition

*Nature is doing her best each moment to make
us well. She exists for no other end. Do not
resist. With the least inclination to be well,
we should not be sick.*

HENRY DAVID THOREAU

The human body cannot produce any of the more than 50 essential nutrients on its own, thus they must be obtained from food sources and dietary supplementation with the exception of vitamin D, which can be produced by exposure to sunlight. It is interesting that scientists once again are urging people to get more direct sunlight. If a person is deficient in any of these essential nutrients, the result is dysfunction and disease, and complete absence results in death. There are also many well-known nutrients, enzymes, coenzymes, and phytochemicals that are extremely important, but not considered essential, and are found primarily in fruits and vegetables. For this reason, many nutritionists and dietitians advocate obtaining essential nutrients through whole foods rather than supplements. The rise of "Superfood Nutrition" is making it possible to gain the benefits of combining these essential nutrients.

It would be fantastic if we could get all our essential nutrition just by eating food, because there are a lot of junk supplements, including vitamin pills, that use the cheapest available nutrients that have been isolated from their natural cofactors. Unfortunately, getting all essential nutrients from food is virtually impossible. If it were possible, not only would you have to be extremely knowledgeable about nutrition, but you would also have to eat far too many calories to get sufficient amounts of every essential nutrient. This, of course, would be extremely unhealthy and defeat the purpose.

In order to get all of the required nutrition from your diet, you would have to eat only the freshest organic foods, a dozen or more daily servings of vegetables (mostly greens and bright colored vegetables), fruits, and whole foods along with clean, naturally raised protein sources in addition to taking high quality dietary supplements. The majority of our food supply is from over-commercialized farming sources that have been depleted of their nutritional value. Even the biblical Old Testament advocates the cycling and resting of farmland for one full year every seventh year to allow time for the soil to be replenished in minerals and living soil organisms.

Current farming methods do not rotate crops or rest the soil but instead implement fertilizers that contain concentrations of three primary macronutrients NPK: nitrogen (N), phosphorus (P), potassium (K), and various amounts of micronutrients. This repetitive practice produces ever-diminishing nutritional value and requires ever-increasing amounts of herbicides and pesticides that further destroy soil organisms that are responsible for solubilizing minerals so the plant roots can absorb them. Fertilizers may increase growth rates, but the produce has become a hollow food. It is easy to understand that over time this produce becomes less nutritious and is potentially more dangerous to your health because more chemicals are required to grow the produce. It is also important to note that most commercial crops use genetically modified seed, for which we do not know the potential health consequences.

While I see hundreds of websites that quote "Senate Document 264 of the 74th Congress, 2nd Session 1936" on soil depletion as though it is a scientific fact when it is not, a case can be made nevertheless. The March 7, 2005, edition of the *Miami Herald* reported on a study conducted by the University of Texas at Austin, based on U.S. Department of Agriculture data, that has shown that compared to 50 years ago, today's fruits and vegetables contain smaller amounts of some key nutrients, including protein, calcium, phosphorus, iron, riboflavin, and vitamin C. The declines included a six percent dip for protein and 38 percent loss of riboflavin. Dr. Donald Davis, the study's lead author and researcher with the university's Biochemical Institute in the Department of Chemistry and Biochemistry, said the main reason for the fall-off in nutrients is that today's farmers breed higher yielding crops. The study of 43 fruits and vegetables looked at 13 nutrients and found that plants have a fixed amount of energy they can spend and varieties with high yields may have less energy to take minerals from the soil.

Davis said, "When you irrigate and fertilize and control weeds to intensively increase the yield of a crop, it dilutes amounts of some nutrients. By encouraging a plant to grow faster and bigger, it does grow faster and bigger, but it doesn't have the ability to uptake or synthesize the nutrients at the same faster rate." While the results are not indisputable, because the analytical techniques used 50 years ago are not the same as now, it emphasizes the diminished quality of our food supply as well as the need for extra nutritional supplementation.

> To lengthen thy life, lessen thy meals.
>
> BEN FRANKLIN

The average time between when produce is harvested (prior to peak nutritional value) and you purchase it in the grocery store is approximately 14 days or more. This results in further degradation of nutrient value. Canned and frozen foods can be even less nutritious.

Super Health can only be obtained by the regular consumption of every known essential nutrient along with their cofactors and with numerous other vital and beneficial nutrients whose greatest concentrations exist in nutrient-dense superfoods. Since it is virtually impossible to get all of the required nutrition from food, the key to getting everything your body needs is to combine the most powerful superfoods with the most beneficial amounts and most bioavailable forms of all essential nutrients. The result is that you get every essential nutrient we know about plus many nutrients contained in foods that we do not yet even know about without having to eat unhealthy amounts of food. We call this Superfood Nutrition.

Regarding the USDA Food Pyramid

Several years ago, a group known as Physicians for Responsible Medicine successfully sued the USDA to invalidate the long advocated Food Pyramid that we all grew up learning as a fact. They showed the court that the Food Pyramid was formed by lobbyists and lawyers, not by doctors and nutritionists. With all due respect to the many thousands of well-meaning registered dietitians, the USDA and the American Dietetic Association (ADA) are largely responsible for the guidelines that govern the foods served in our schools and hospitals. Any thinking person can understand that school and hospital food does not promote health, quite the contrary. I know many brilliant registered dietitians who have become outstanding nutritionists by taking their educations into their own hands and gaining a deeper understanding of clinical nutrition and supplements.

It is more important than ever for practitioners and patients to take their health into their own hands! Even though the ADA and the educational curriculums of registered dietitians and health care workers in general remain anti-supplement, teaching that you should get your nutrition from food, *the vast majority* of registered dietitians, doctors, and health care workers report they take and recommend supplements to their patients.[65]

For instance, in the July 2009 *Nutrition Journal,* the "Life...Supplemented" Health Care Professionals Impact Study found that 72 percent of physicians and 89 percent of nurses in their sample used dietary supplements regularly, occasionally, or seasonally.[66] Regular use of dietary supplements was reported by 51 percent of physicians and 59 percent of nurses. Physicians and nurses are as likely as members of the general public to use dietary supplements, as shown by comparing the results of this survey with data from national health and nutrition surveys. Also, most physicians and nurses recommend supplements to their patients.

Conventional allopathic medicine is tremendous for diagnostics and for emergency care. However, with little or no knowledge of nutrition and because drugs and surgery are their primary allopathic modalities to treat patients, there usually are better ways to solve most of your family's health issues. I strongly endorse preventative, integrative, and alternative medicine, including clinical nutrition, chiropractic, traditional Chinese medicine, naturopathy, and therapeutic massage as primary and preventative care for the vast majority of health issues we face.

Super Health Diet Guidelines

On this diet you can eat anything you want. The only catch is that I am going to tell you what you are going to want.

It's really important that you make the information in this book your study reference manual. Make a personal evaluation on how you are doing in each of the 7 Keys listed in this book. Correct your metabolism by making improvements in these areas, and your body will want to be active.

Don't necessarily try to do it all at once. Taking baby steps in the right direction are monster steps toward Super Health.

Eat only three meals per day with five to six hours in between. Do not snack or drink caloric beverages in between or eat within two to three hours before sleep. (See the "What About Snacking Between Meals" section in Chapter 13.) The goal is to keep each Four Corners Meal under 600 calories for average-sized individuals while maxing out the nutrition with optimal levels of protein or essential amino acids and virtually every known nutrient, including all essential nutrients such as vitamins, minerals, broad-spectrum antioxidants, phytonutrients, prebiotics, and probiotics. Minimize your intake of sugars and higher glycemic foods. Increase your consumption of healthy fats.

Establish your mealtime windows and make sure you begin to eat your meals as closely as possible within those time windows. For instance, if you generally have your breakfast at 7 a.m., your breakfast window should be plus or minus a half hour or 6:30 to 7:30 a.m. Then calculate your lunch window to be six hours from the middle of your breakfast window or 1 p.m. Your lunch window would be 12:30 p.m. to 1:30 p.m. to start eating your lunch. Your dinner window would be 6:30 p.m. to 7:30 p.m. to start dinner. Try to eat your meal within about an hour from the start of the meal.

Some find it more difficult to get to lunch without snacking, some find it more difficult from lunch do dinner, and others have the most difficulty getting from dinner to bedtime. First, learn to properly fuel your body by adding more protein, fiber, and healthy fats to your meal to help you get five to six hours. Some people find it somewhat difficult to stay within mealtime windows that are spaced five to six hours apart; however, it is really important to learn to properly fuel your body to allow it to work through the complete six-hour meal cycle. If you are flying from Tampa to New York, you don't just fuel the plane to Washington, D.C. As additional landings and takeoffs are hard on an aircraft, so additional endocrine responses from snacking between meals are hard on your body. Second, calculate your mealtime windows by determining your ideal lunchtime window and working backward to breakfast and forward to dinner. This way you can shorten the time between the windows of your most difficult period to avoid snacking. It is okay to have five hours between the breakfast and lunch window and to have six hours between your lunch and dinner window.

> It's difficult to think anything but pleasant thoughts while eating a homegrown tomato.
>
> LEWIS GRIZZARD

Make spring water and lightly caffeinated or non-caffeinated herbal teas your primary beverages. Drink eight to 12 glasses per day with average activity and more on active days.

Minimize or eliminate caloric beverages and artificially sweetened beverages, including juices, soft drinks, coffee (an exception is okay if you only drink organic coffee and drink it black), sports drinks (an exception is to drink only as designed during activities requiring intense exertion), alcohol (an exception is a single glass of wine per day; however, there are better ways to get the same benefits, including omega-3 and resveratrol).

Minimize or eliminate breads, pastries, and desserts.

Minimize high glycemic grains such as corn and white rice. If it's white, it ain't right!

Make greens, instead of grains, a foundation in your diet.

Everyone should have a very good blender instead of a juicer. Invest in a superior blender, such as Blendtec Total Blender (ww.blendtec.com) or Vitamix (www.vitamix.com) and learn to make SuperSmoothies.

Invest in a travel blender, such as the Magic Bullet to Go (www.bullettogo.com). Take a sufficient amount of Functional Superfoods and a travel blender or blender bottle with you when you travel.

Have a Functional SuperSmoothie or Micro SuperSmoothie for breakfast and any other meal you want to maximize your nutrition while minimizing calories for that meal. If a team of organic chefs and nutritionists tried to create a nutritionally equivalent meal, it would be physically impossible to eat the volume of food it would require. (See SuperSmoothie and Micro SuperSmoothie recipes.)

Decide what you are willing to eat and what you are not willing to eat at your next meal before you get hungry.

Eat a variety of nutrient-rich Four Corners foods, a diet rich in vegetables and fruits. Make it a lifestyle to get a minimum 10 servings of mostly vegetables and some fruit per day. Choose high protein, high fiber foods with healthy fats.

Eat fatty fish, such as sardines, anchovies, wild salmon, mackerel, tuna, and herring, at least twice a week.

Supplement with antioxidant protected fish oil, GLA from borage seed or evening primrose oil, full-spectrum vitamin E (tocotrienols and tocopherols), vitamin D, vitamin A, and astaxanthin. (See Four Corners Shopping List for product information.)

Eat fewer meals in restaurants and more meals at home and avoid fast food restaurants.

Have a partial or whole serving of a Functional SuperSmoothie protein fiber shake or Super Micro SuperSmoothie before eating out. Either will help curb your appetite, contribute to the nutrition value of your meal, including increasing protein levels, and help you make better choices in restaurants, such as skipping the bread, sweetened beverages, and desserts.

Avoid back-to-back red meat meals. At least two days in between is best.

Get one or more accountability partners to help you stay on track.

Get a pocket journal or journal in your electronic device and write down absolutely everything you eat and every exercise you do.

Be a physically active person. Don't simply add physical activity to your lifestyle. Rather, plan your life around your physical activities. Have fun and take up a physically demanding hobby, take a spin class or Tai Chi class, play tennis or basketball, start running, swimming, or biking.

Plan in advance when you will exercise and what exercises you will do. Exercise for at least 30 minutes on most days of the week, if not all. Learn to incorporate high intensity interval training (HIIT) into your exercise program two or three days per week. Learn the Super Health 7 Tiger Moves and Big Three. These are tremendous isoflexion exercises that can be done anywhere without equipment. They are also great while rehabilitating a sports injury. (See Chapter 14.)

Learn to read and understand the nutrition facts label and ingredients lists on foods and supplements. A great resource is www.nutritiondata.com.

Choose lean meats and poultry without skin and prepare them without adding saturated and trans fats. Limit your intake of saturated animal fats, trans fats. Plant-based saturated fats, such as medium-chain saturated fats as found in coconut and palm oil, are good for you. Eliminate all foods containing partially hydrogenated vegetable oils to reduce trans fat in your diet.

Replace table salt with Celtic Sea Salt (www.celticseasalt.com).

If you choose to drink alcohol, drink in moderation, one drink per day.

Avoid use of and exposure to all tobacco products.

Do not use unnecessary prescription or over-the-counter pharmaceutical drugs or ever use recreational drugs.

The goal while dieting is to replace two meals of your three meals per day with a SuperSmoothie during your FUEL Fast, then eat a Smart Meal for your third meal of the day. Continue this fast for as long as you feel good or until your reach desired weight. Do extended fasts under the supervision of your health practitioner.

Here are some "fast tips" for proper fasting:

• Replace breakfast or another meal daily with a Functional SuperSmoothie until you're confident that your SuperSmoothie meal will provide five to six hours of sustained energy levels without hunger. Then you're ready to replace another meal. Some people prefer to FUEL Fast just one of their three meals; some replace two of their three meals a day; others replace all three of their meals with a SuperSmoothie. Eat Smart Meals for each meal you do not have a SuperSmoothie. (See Smart Meals and Super-Smoothie and MicroSmoothie Recipes.)

- To extend energy and the time between meals, add fresh vegetables, fruit, nuts, seeds, a splash of juice, or organic coconut milk/oil to your SuperSmoothie.
- Drink plenty of water, lightly caffeinated or caffeine-free herbal teas and SuperCoffee. Minimize caffeine between meals or within three hours of bedtime.
- Advanced weight optimization techniques are the Stealth Technique and Micro Fast. The Stealth Technique can be used 20 minutes before any meal, including a SuperSmoothie meal and at bedtime. The Micro Fast is an ultra low calorie Four Corners Fast, and it can be used to replace any meal, including a SuperSmoothie meal. (See "The Dynamic Role of Protein in Weight Loss" chapter.)

Every meal you replace with a SuperSmoothie or Micro Super-Smoothie will be lower in calories and higher in nutrition than just about anything else with similar nutrients you could eat.

During your FUEL Fast, you should not feel hungry, and you should be able to carry on a regular routine, including exercise and athletic activities, with a high level of energy. Continue the fast for as many days as you feel comfortable or until you reach your desired weight. Athletic activities will increase your need for calories, carbohydrates, and protein.

We produced LivingFuelTV episodes about the FUEL Fast to help you get started. You can see them online at www.LivingFuel.TV.

When you reach your weight loss goal, continue having a Super-Smoothie or Micro SuperSmoothie for one meal per day, preferably breakfast, and continue to eat Smart Meals for the rest of your meals. Continue to make sure your protein and other nutrient intake is at optimal levels.

Continue to regularly monitor your weight and body fat levels, and if you find you have gained more than a couple of pounds or increased body fat levels, go back to being more strict until you return to optimal weight.

There are numerous other strategies in this book that can be incorporated into your program. Try a few things at a time and find out what works for you. How do you know if it is working for you? If you feel good, have high energy levels, show improvements, such as in your focus, sleep, recovery, hair, skin, nails, digestion, and elimination, you are on the path to optimal weight and Super Health.

If you are not seeing the results you were hoping for, try the Advanced Techniques mentioned above and read the "Set Point Theory" section in Chapter 5.

Top 10 Worst Foods

1. Doughnuts
2. French fries and almost all deep fried foods, including anything made with hydrogenated oils or heated vegetable oils
3. Fast food hamburgers, hot dogs, sausages, and all factory farmed meats
4. Produce and meats raised using Genetically Modified Organisms. See www.responsibletechnology.org
5. Corn byproducts
6. Alcoholic beverages
7. Soft drinks, conventional coffee, sports drinks, and fruit juices
8. Sugar and artificial sweeteners (aspartame, sucralose, etc.)
9. Peanut butter (conventional national brands with partially hydrogenated oils and high fructose corn syrup)
10. Foods made from bleached white flower, white bread, pastries, cakes, etc.

Liquid Nutrition Versus Solid Foods

It may come as a surprise that in stressful situations, such as physical performance or the stresses of life, the right liquid nutrition is preferable to solid foods. Solid foods actually can compete with optimal performance. Obtaining nutrients in a liquid form allows the digestive system to absorb them directly into your bloodstream. Hence, we see many of the world's top endurance athletes consume a liquid diet during training and competition. Not only does a liquid diet save time, but it also prevents feeling full or bloated while being active.

The Truth About Juice

Though juicing provides many benefits, there are also more than a few drawbacks. First, anyone who has ever operated a juicer knows the mess they have to clean up, often deterring us from using one in the first place. Since juicers do not preserve the pulp, it also takes quite a few fruits and vegetables to produce just a small amount of juice.

Though juicing does give you a quick boost of energy, you don't get any of the healthy fiber offered by those same fruits and vegetables. Not only is the pulp some of the healthiest part, but the insoluble fiber slows down the sugar's impact on your bloodstream.

Then there's the simple factor of cost. A good juicer can squeeze a few hundred dollars out of your wallet. And that doesn't even touch the cost of all those fruits and vegetables you are going to run through it. Your money is better spent on a very good blender.

> If organic farming is the natural way, shouldn't organic produce just be called "produce" and make the pesticide-laden stuff take the burden of an adjective?
>
> YMBER DELECTO

Are Smoothies the Answer?

There is a liquid nutrition solution that is both simple to make and cost effective. Smoothies can be made with whole fruits and vegetables and provide a great source of fiber, vitamins, minerals, and antioxidants. Thanks to a high fiber content, smoothies provide a sustained release of nutrients over time. By helping you feel fuller longer, smoothies are an acceptable choice for breakfast or lunch. Unfortunately, traditional smoothies contain far too much sugar and are deficient in protein and both macronutrients and micronutrients.

Add the power of Superfood Nutrition to your diet. Instead of relying on the nutritional myth of "carbo-loading" with all kinds of carbohydrates, start the day with a complete and balanced superfood smoothie breakfast. A high protein superfood smoothie is highly digestible, plant-based liquid nutrition with balanced amounts of protein, carbohydrates, fiber, fats, and the full spectrum of essential nutrients. Superfood smoothies are just packed with vitamins, minerals, and antioxidants that, because it is in liquid form, are efficiently delivered into the bloodstream to boost performance, energy, mental clarity, and recovery.

You can build a basic SuperSmoothie by starting with your favorite smoothie recipe and using mostly water (with or without ice) in a blender. Cut the amount of high sugar fruits and juices by 80 percent. Now, add 25 to 50 grams of a high quality protein powder along with five to 10 grams of a plant-based soluble fiber powder. The result will be a lower calorie, low glycemic, highly nutritious meal that will stabilize your blood sugar levels and help control your appetite. There are plenty of other high impact healthy ingredients that are important to add later—but this is a super healthy start. (See the SuperSmoothie Recipes.)

It is a well-known fact in athletics that digestion competes with performance, so consider having a superfood smoothie instead of a burger or deli sandwich for lunch. Make superfood nutrition your competitive edge to Super Health and your quality of life will skyrocket.

THE
SUPER
HEALTH
DIET

Golden
Keys
to Unlock
Lifelong
Vitality

At-a-Glance Foods to Eat and Foods to Avoid

Beverages

- Drink eight to 12 glasses of spring water a day.
- Drink lightly caffeinated or caffeine-free organic herbal teas and SuperCoffee.
- Minimize fruit juices (except when mixed with high protein/fiber).
- Eliminate all soft drinks.
- Minimize coffee, alcoholic beverages, and artificial sweeteners.

Foods

- Eat a variety of organic salads, green vegetables, and bright colored, above-ground vegetables. Some good choices include broccoli, spinach, kale, mixed greens, asparagus, green beans, peppers, cucumbers, barley greens, radishes, garlic, and onions.
- Eat organic, free-range eggs.
- Eat berries (cranberries, strawberries, raspberries, and blueberries).
- Eat organic chicken, turkey, and wild game, such as grass-fed beef, venison, buffalo, lamb, and deer.
- Take antioxidant protected fish oil and eat certified mercury-free and wild salmon, summer flounder, haddock, anchovies, and sardines. See www.vitalchoice.com.
- Use virgin coconut oil, virgin olive oil, GLA, conjugated linolenic acid (CLA), and raw organic butter.
- Use Celtic Sea Salt or Real Salt brand mineral sea salts.

- Eat nuts (almonds, cashews, and macadamia) and organic coconut.
- Minimize all grains (bread, rice, and cereal); avoid junk foods, anything deep fried, such as french fries, and pizza.
- Minimize pasteurized dairy products, such as milk, cheese, and cream.
- Minimize unfermented, genetically modified soy products.
- Minimize factory farmed, grain-fed commercial beef, pork products, and shellfish.
- Avoid farm-raised fish, such as catfish or salmon, and other fish with high mercury levels, such as tuna.
- Avoid hydrogenated oil found in commercially prepared baked goods, margarines, snacks, and processed foods.
- Minimize all sugars (candy, cookies, cakes, and syrups) and chips.
- Avoid produce and meats grown using Genetically Modified Organisms. See www.responsibletechnology.org.

THE
SUPER
HEALTH
DIET

**Golden
Keys**
to Unlock
Lifelong
Vitality

Four Corners Shopping List

Vegetables

Asparagus
Avocado
Beets
Bell peppers
Broccoli
Brussels sprouts
Cabbage
Carrots
Cauliflower
Celery
Collard greens
Cucumber
Eggplant
Fennel bulb
Garlic
Green beans
Green peas
Kale
Leeks
Mustard greens
Olives
Onions
Parsley
Romaine lettuce
Root vegetables
Sea vegetables
Spinach
Squash, summer
Squash, winter
Sweet potato, with skin
Swiss chard
Tomato, fresh
Turnip greens
Yam

Fatty Fish (wild caught)

Anchovies
Fish oils with antioxidants
Herring
Mackerel
Salmon
Sardines
Tuna

Fruits

Apple
Apricot
Banana
Blueberries
Cantaloupe
Cranberries
Fig
Grapefruit
Grapes
Kiwi fruit
Lemons and limes

Orange
Papaya
Pear, Bartlett
Pineapple
Plum
Prune
Raisins
Raspberries
Strawberries
Watermelon

Dairy and Eggs
Cheeses, soft raw milk
Organic eggs, free-range
Milk, raw goat or cow
Yogurt, raw goat or cow

Beans and Legumes
Black beans
Dried peas
Garbanzo beans
Kidney beans
Lentils
Lima beans
Miso
Navy beans
Pinto beans
Tempeh

Poultry and Lean Meats
(organic)
Beef, lean, grass-fed, grain-free
Chicken, free-range
Lamb
Turkey, roast
Venison

Nuts and Seeds
Almonds
Cashews
Chia seeds
Coconut
CocoChia
Extra Virgin coconut oil
Flaxseed
Olive oil
Macadamia
Pumpkin seeds
Walnuts

Healthy Grains
Barley
Oats
Quinoa
Rye

Sprouts
Quinoa
Spelt

Other Acceptable Grains
Brown Rice
Buckwheat

Spices and Herbs
Basil
Black pepper
Cayenne pepper
Chili pepper, red, dried
Cinnamon, ground
Cloves
Coriander seeds
Cumin seeds

Dill weed, dried
Ginger
Mustard seeds
Oregano
Peppermint leaves, fresh
Rosemary
Sage
Thyme, ground
Turmeric, ground

Natural Sweeteners
Blackstrap molasses
Brown rice syrup
Erythriol
Mannitol
Raw honey
Stevia
Tagatose
Therasweet
Xylitol

Beverages
Almond milk
Green/white/red/black teas
Oat milk
Rice milk
SoDelicious coconut milk
SuperCoffee

Other
Celtic Sea Salt or Real Salt
Soy sauce (tamari), organic

Functional Superfoods
Whole Meal Superfoods
LivingFuel SuperGreens
LivingFuel SuperBerry Original
LivingFuel SuperBerry Ultimate

Protein Supplements
LivingFuel LivingProtein
IMUPlus non-denatured whey
    protein
Rice protein
Yellow Pea Protein
Hemp Protein

Foundational Supplements
Antioxidant complex
Carnosine
CLA (conjugated linoleic acid)
CoQ-10 (ubiquinol)
Creatine
LivingFuel Super Essential
    Omega 3 EDA+
LivingFuel SuperEssentials Multi
LivingFuel SuperEssentials
    Aminos
LivingFuel Pure D&A
Phosphatidylserine

LIVING FUEL PRODUCTS VS POPULAR ANTIOXIDANTS

Total ORAC Values for Comparative Antioxidant Products

Antioxidant Product	Peroxyl	Hydroxyl	Peroxynitrite	Superoxide anion	Singlet oxygen	Total ORAC
LFSB Ultimate	23,500.0	3,700.0	3,000.0	61,000.0	28,000.0	119,200.0
LFSB Original	17,500.0	2,900.0	2,300.0	52,000.0	24,000.0	98,700.0
LF Super Greens	15,500.0	2,300.0	2,000.0	28,600.0	34,400.0	82,800.0
LF Living Protein	4,800.0	800.0	900.0	12,400.0	-	18,900.0
Cocoa powder	7,800.0	1,200.0	600.0	9,200.0	1,700.0	20,500.0
100% grape juice	4,200.0	600.0	400.0	7,000.0	5,500.0	17,700.0
Grape seed extract	4,300.0	900.0	300.0	8,300.0	1,300.0	15,100.0
V8 Juice	1,300.0	300.0	200.0	2,500.0	9,800.0	14,100.0
Green tea	2,300.0	400.0	400.0	8,300.0	-	11,400.0
Vitamin C	2,600.0	100.0	1,400.0	3,500.0	1,100.0	8,700.0
Acai powder	1,800.0	300.0	200.0	1,300.0	-	3,600.0

Chapter 11

The Dynamic Role of
Proteins in Weight Loss

*Our research shows that people may have a better
outcome losing weight if they increase their
intake of lean protein.*
DR. OSAMA HAMBY

This strategic use of proteins and amino acids
is a foundational principle in the implementation of the Four Corners of
Superfood Nutrition for weight optimization and Super Health. Of all
the chapters in this book, this is an absolute must read.

Ask one hundred sports trainers and strength athletes what the single most important nutrient is and you might get universal agreement
that protein is that nutrient. However, within conventional health care
circles, you will probably hear warning after warniwng that too much
protein is dangerous, causes kidney problems, deteriorates bones, and
that excess protein turns to fat. Protein is one of the most important, yet
least understood, nutrients in the human diet, and especially as it relates
to weight loss and general health. This chapter will dispel many long
held beliefs about the dynamic role of protein and essential amino acids
play in weight optimization and in Super Health. You will learn the best
sources of protein, the best types of protein and amino acids powders, as
well as leading-edge nutrition techniques on how and when to best take
them to accomplish your goals.

The bioactivity of proteins and amino acids remains one of the great
mysteries in science, and our understanding continues to evolve through
research. We eat protein because it is a miraculous raw material comprised

of amino acids and is a primary source of nitrogen. Our body digests the protein, breaking it down into the building blocks of life called free-form amino acids, then the body repackages the free-form amino acids for a wide range of complex roles in the body—one of the main functions being protein synthesis (the making of proteins such as muscle from ingested amino acids, for instance) and for numerous different functions.

Amino acids are the building blocks for proteins. Enzymes, hormones, neurotransmitters, connective tissue, cell membranes, and blood cells, for example, are all made up of proteins, which require amino acids as the raw material for their synthesis (manufacture). Additionally, many amino acids have other roles, such as being converted to energy production in a process called "gluconeogenesis," where certain amino acids are converted to glucose in the absence of carbohydrates and stored muscle glycogen. Amino acids can provide five to 10 percent of the total energy during prolonged endurance training or competition, which can be much higher with depleted glycogen stores.

Regular consumption of essential amino acids is required for life, since the body cannot produce them. However, the body can produce nonessential amino acids. More on amino acids later.

The Power of Protein

Proteins are the basic foundation of the human body. Proteins are complex molecules that are made up of smaller units called amino acids and help build muscles, blood, skin, hair, nails, and internal organs. As discussed earlier, amino acids play central roles both as building blocks of proteins and as intermediates in metabolism. Proteins not only activate all (or most) of the reactions in living cells, they control virtually all cellular process.

Next to water, protein is the most plentiful substance in the body, and most protein molecules (around 60 to 70 percent) are located in the skeletal muscles. Unlike fat and glucose, our body has little capacity to store protein. If we stop eating protein, our body will begin to break down muscle tissue for its protein needs within a day or so.

Protein comes from the Greek word *proteos*, which means "the first," suggesting its primary importance. The human body can survive and thrive without carbohydrate intake, and even go very long periods of time without dietary fats; however, protein deficiency during longer periods of time leads to death. In my book *Super Health: 7 Golden Keys to Unlock Lifelong Vitality*, I discuss that food is either a building block or fuel, and protein can be both. Protein is primarily a structural nutrient, or a building block,[67] but can also be converted by the body to fuel during low to no carbohydrate intake or low caloric intake through "gluconeogenesis." Certain populations, such as some Eskimo communities, eat very little carbohydrates in their diets and thus are fueled by the conversion of amino acids to fuel.

Thus, excess protein intake is otherwise used or excreted by the body, not stored as fat.

The Amino Acids of Protein

Dietary protein is raw material from which amino acids are derived through the digestion process. There are 20+ amino acids that are derived from the diet and numerous others that are made within the human body. Dietary amino acids are called *essential amino acids* (EAAs) or *indispensible amino acids* if the body cannot make them from other amino acids, and they are called *nonessential amino acids* (NEAAs) or *dispensable amino acids* if the body can make them from other amino acids. Regardless of the type of amino acid, the reality is that all 20+ dietary amino acids are essential. However, EAAs must be derived from the diet, while the body can manufacture NEAAs.

Humans cannot produce eight to 10 of the 20 dietary amino acids. The others must be supplied in the food we eat and supplements we take, and all of which must be present at the same time to synthesize muscle. Failure to obtain enough of even one of the eight to 10 EAAs, those that we cannot make, results in degradation of the body's proteins—muscle, tissues, and so forth—to obtain the one amino acid that is needed. Unlike fat and starch, the human body does not store significant excess amino acids for later use—*the EAAs must be obtained in the diet every day*. Not only can you not physically thrive without EAAs, you cannot live without them.

The 10 amino acids that we can produce are alanine, asparagine, aspartic acid, cysteine, glutamic acid, glutamine, glycine, proline, serine, and tyrosine. Tyrosine is produced from phenylalanine, so if the diet is deficient in phenylalanine, tyrosine will be deficient as well. The essential amino acids are arginine and histidine (conditionally essential because they are required for the young, but not always for adults), isoleucine, leucine, lysine, methionine, phenylalanine, threonine, tryptophan, and valine. These amino acids are required in the diet. Plants, of course, must be able to make all the amino acids. Humans, on the other hand, do not have all the enzymes required for the biosynthesis of all of the amino acids.

Weight Optimization and Protein

A major key to Super Health and lifelong weight optimization is to obtain and maintain muscle, which requires protein and the strategic use of EAAs. As we point out in Chapter 14, resistance exercise and High Intensity Interval Training is important, and we highly advocate it as the stimulus that sends the signal to the brain to maintain and grow muscle, but there is evidence that muscle can be grown with the strategic use of EAAs. In this respect, nutrition is as important as exercise, and we should utilize both to obtain Super Health.

Protein should be the foundation of effective weight loss and for healthy weight gain. The amount of quality protein and balance of EAAs in your diet is one of the most important nutrients that help optimize your metabolic rate, sustain fat loss, fuel muscle growth, enhance internal antioxidant function and immunity, optimize HDL cholesterol, and endocrine function—all of which contribute toward weight optimization. Adequate amounts of high quality protein help to preserve, maintain, and grow muscle even while dieting. *The more active you are, the more protein you require to build and maintain the body; the lower your calorie intake, the more protein you require to avoid muscle loss.*

Sarcopenia, or muscle catabolism (loss), is a major but largely ignored health issue until it becomes critical (usually in the aging population, but the same process happens to everyone to some degree). Maintaining and increasing lean muscle mass is vital to health and is key to successful weight optimization and maintenance. People generally lose muscle mass as they age with poor nutrition, lower protein intake, and decreased physical activity. In an ever-increasing spiral, lean body mass is replaced with body fat, which in turn produces inflammatory cytokines (small cell-signaling protein molecules) and aromatase, which converts testosterone to estrogen, leading to low testosterone levels, particularly in men. This leads to increased body fat, decreased levels of testosterone, reduced hormone production, low energy levels, and numerous diseases of aging.[68]

Dr. Robert Wolfe, to whom I am indebted for his research and willingness to answer my questions on this topic, gives this summary: "Improved lean body mass along with a reduction of obesity should decrease inflammatory cytokines, and thus diminish the body's signal for continued muscle catabolism [breakdown].

"The fundamental mechanism by which dietary protein affects muscle and other physiological processes is the stimulation of muscle protein synthesis [manufacture] by the absorbed amino acids."[69]

> **Today at the supermarket, one dozen large eggs can cost as little as $1. One egg contains the protein equivalent of one ounce of meat—that's a great value for the money.**
>
> Andrea Dunn

Dietary Sources of Protein

Not all protein is alike, and just because you get a lot of protein does not mean you are necessarily getting an ideal amount of EAAs. Foods that contain sufficient amounts of all of the EAAs are called *complete proteins*. These foods include beef, chicken, fish, eggs, milk, cheese, and just about any other food derived from animal sources. Animal protein has long been thought to be the standard; however, optimized plant proteins now have taken center stage. Recent studies have shown that plant protein that has been optimized (i.e., combination of brown rice protein powder with yellow pea protein powder with specific amino acids added to strengthen the amino acids profile) can replicate the amino acids profile of animal protein without the acidity and potential allergic reactions commonly associated with some of the most popular animal protein powders.

Keep in mind that dietary sources of complete protein vary widely.

Most meats contain virtually no carbohydrates but can vary widely in their percentages of protein and fat. Lean meats, such as skinless chicken breast that contain mostly protein and very little fat, are a great protein source. On the other hand, prime rib or rib eye steak might contain as much fat as protein. The same is true for dairy products, which can contain wildly differing levels of protein, carbohydrates, and fats. For instance, certain cheeses can be half protein and half fat while others are almost all protein. When calculating daily protein intake, it is critical to also consider the extra calories from additional carbohydrates and fats.

Incomplete proteins don't have all or adequate amounts of EAAs and generally include vegetables, beans, legumes, fruits, grains, seeds, and nuts. Most vegetable-source proteins are extremely low in protein and contain significant amounts of carbohydrates and fats. Soy has an impressive amino acids profile, but is controversial as a health food due to its estrogen-mimicking effects and because it contains anti-digestion factors, including an enzyme inhibitor that blocks the action of trypsin and other enzymes needed for protein digestion. Fermented non-GMO soy products, such as tempi, miso, and soy sauces, help overcome the digestive issues related to soy and can be a healthy addition to one's diet. It is important to note that the vast majority of soy produced in the world today is genetically modified (GMO) and should be avoided.

Another important note on soy. Lecithin is a vitally important nutrient of what makes up a substantial portion of the fats in the brain. Numerous products contain soy lecithin, but not all soy lecithin is created equal. Lecithin is sold as a nutritional supplement and an emulsifying nutrient that helps different ingredients mix well and keep from separating. Soy lecithin ranges from junk food to superfood, depending on its level of purity and whether or not it is derived from genetically modified soy. The lecithin you want is a high phosphatide ultra pure (98 percent oil free) non-GMO soy lecithin, which is a superfood that contains virtually no soy protein. Sunflower lecithin is expected to be widely available in the near future and may prove to be an even better option.

Fruits contain only trace amounts of protein.

So, if you're a vegetarian, does this mean you can't get complete protein? No, we address this in my section on vegetarianism that follows.

Vegetarians frequently suffer from EAA deficiencies as well as deficiencies of omega-3 EPA/DHA, vitamin B12, vitamin D, and other vital nutrients. Vegetarians must be very educated about nutrition, food combining, nutritional supplements, and have to work much harder to get all the nutrients they need to survive, not to mention to thrive.

It seems clear that people have a difficult time getting enough high quality protein with meals and the majority of people need additional protein. Most people, including children, adults, vegetarians, and all active people could benefit from a plant-based functional superfood protein powder that combines organic brown rice protein and yellow pea protein with an amino acids profile that has been optimized with specific amino acids (giving it the strength of egg and whey proteins but from all vegetarian sources), plus digestive enzymes (to maximize digestibility) and gut healthy soluble rice fiber, prebiotics, and microencapsulated probiotics. These components work in concert to maximize protein utilization, while enhancing the digestive system and minimizing postprandial (after a meal) glycemic response that is known to rapidly convert to body fat and cause cellular damage after every high calorie meal.

Keep in mind that just because a food or supplement's amino acids profile looks favorable, there are factors that can minimize the speed of digestion. For example, when one eats a steak, it can take days before it is fully digested; therefore, amino acids are released during an extended period of time. In addition, most people do not properly chew their food, which means it takes even longer to digest. Researchers have even attempted to account for the variability of digestion speed by assigning various foods with what is called a Protein Digestibility Corrected Amino Acids Score.[70] Not all researchers agree with this method of rating proteins, but it can be a useful tool. Protein powders are among the most highly digestible forms of protein. The bottom line is that people need more high quality protein, particularly plant-based protein, and protein powders are a convenient means of getting the amounts needed. The right whey protein can be a good option for people who are not sensitive to dairy products; however, I believe that for daily use plant protein is easier on the body. (See Protein Powders and the Four Corners Shopping List.)

Food	Protein grams
1 ounce beef, fish, poultry	7
4 ounces chicken meat, cooked	35
3.5 ounces chicken breast	30
Average chicken thigh	10
Average chicken drumstick	11
Average chicken wing	6
1 large egg	6
1 egg white	4
4 ounces milk	4
4 ounces low fat yogurt	6
3 ounces tofu, firm	13
1 ounce cheese	7
1/2 cup low fat cottage cheese	14
1/2 cup cooked kidney beans	7
1/2 cup lentils	9
1 ounce nuts	7
2 tablespoons peanut butter	8
1/2 cup vegetables	2
1/2 cup of most grains/pastas	2

Our Daily Requirement of Protein

A large and growing body of research suggests that the United States government's proposed levels of protein intake are far below what is optimal for Super Health, for weight optimization, not to mention athletic performance. Most people could benefit from increasing their protein intake and decreasing carbohydrate consumption.

As recommended by the Food and Nutrition Board of the United States National Academy of Science, the recommended daily allowance (RDA) for protein is 0.8 grams protein per kilo (2.2 pounds) of body weight per day for adults, regardless of age. However, according to the United States Department of Agriculture, "When caloric ranges appropriate for normal healthy adults are considered, the rec-ommended protein intake ranges from 1.4 to 2.0 grams of protein per kilo (2.2 pounds) of body weight per day."[71] "The apparent dis-crepancy between the RDA and the recommendations of the USDA expert committees on actual dietary intake of protein can be resolved by *considering the RDA as the minimal acceptable intake and the dietary recommendations as reflecting the optimal protein intake.* When viewed in this light, it is clear that, contrary to popular belief, *expert recom-mendations for protein intake range from as low as 1.2 to 2.0 grams of protein per kilo (2.2 pounds) of body weight per day.*"[72]

In fact, in a 2005 Dietary Reference Intake report,[73] the Food and Nutrition Board reported *no known upper limit of safety for protein in-take as there is for carbohydrates and fats.* "More importantly, most stud-ies that set out to evaluate the potential adverse effects of higher protein intake actually documented the reverse—namely that higher protein intakes were beneficial on the system being studied. Thus the primary metabolic benefit of increased protein intake in the elderly is related to the stimulation of muscle protein synthesis, *positive effects on virtually all body systems may be expected in the absence of deleterious effects.*"[74]

In practical terms, a 170-pound active person should get between 50 and 100 percent of his weight in grams of protein per day, depend-ing on his objectives. This works out to be between 85 grams and 170 grams of protein per day. This person, assuming reasonable activity levels, might need as much as 150 grams per day or 50 grams per meal. Considering the myriad of benefits of higher protein intake and the compelling evidence that it is safe, it seems wise to err to the larger daily amounts even for less active and elderly people.

Therefore the Super Health Diet recommendation for daily high quality protein intake for most people is 1.1 grams to 2 grams per kilo of body weight, or in plain English 0.5 to 0.9 grams per pound of body weight per day with a strong preference toward the high end of that range. The more active you are, the higher side of the range; however, new research suggests that even overweight sedentary individuals require significantly higher protein intake than previously believed.[75] While on a low calorie diet, it is important to maintain protein levels within the high side or above these ranges to help stave off muscle loss.[76] Additionally, no one should be sedentary by choice, so if you can move, get moving.

Higher protein intake also promotes fullness, is thought to increase energy expenditure via thermogenesis, and helps to stabilize blood sugar levels.[77] High protein levels tend to limit regain of weight after dieting.[78] Let's be clear, the Super Health Diet does not advocate stuffing yourself with meats to obtain optimal protein levels. It is my opinion that high protein functional superfoods, including optimized plant protein powders and essential amino acids supplements, are essential to weight optimization and to Super Health.

Contrary to conventional thinking, higher protein diets can be healthy and beneficial for most of us, and even somewhat higher quality protein diets may be better for those with kidney dysfunction. Conventional thinking is that protein intake greater than 1.2 grams of protein per kilo (2.2 pounds) of body weight per day in individuals with renal (kidney) disease contributes to the deterioration of kidney function. As a result, a lower protein diet has been recommended as a method to prevent exacerbation of kidney damage by hyperfiltration and hypertension in type 2 diabetics suffering from renal (kidney) disease.[79] Even in the circumstance of renal disease, however, evidence of a beneficial effect of a low protein diet is questionable. In a recent long-term follow-up of 585 patients with renal disease given either 0.58 or 1.3 grams of protein per kilo (2.2 pounds) of body weight per day, no beneficial effects of the low protein diet could be demonstrated.[80] Thus, limitation of protein intake on the basis of possible adverse effects on renal function is not warranted with the possible exception of people who are likely to develop kidney failure as a result of diabetes, hypertension, or polycystic kidney disease.[81]

The renal dialysis unit in Edinburgh, England, states: "In the past a low protein diet was often recommended to slow down the steady deterioration of kidney function that occurs in some patients. We don't advise this anymore. Instead we are recommending a controlled protein diet (not low, not high; 0.8 to 1g protein per kg of ideal body weight)."[82]

Each case of renal disease is a little different, and while I would not go so far as to make a universal recommendation, it seems clear that higher protein levels are indicated. I know of no such research in this area, but it would seem that the strategic use of plant-based protein powders and essential amino acids could be beneficial in patients with renal disease.

A 2008 study led by Dr. Robert Wolfe goes a long way toward dispelling the controversies about virtually all dangers thought to be associated with high protein diets.[83] It concluded that the risks of high protein diets have been greatly exaggerated. Concerns about potential detrimental effects of increased protein intake on bone health, renal (kidney) function, neurological function, and cardiovascular function are not founded in scientific studies. In fact, many of these factors are improved in the elderly through ingesting elevated quantities of protein. The study was primarily about protein and amino acids in the elderly; however, protein requirements of post-pubescent youth, active adults, athletes, and the elderly appear to be quite similar, with athletes being at the top of the range. Sedentary individuals require less protein, often much less, but they require far few calories in general.

Other physiological processes can also potentially benefit from increased protein intake, including improved bone health,[84] maintenance of energy balance,[85] cardiovascular function,[86] and wound healing.[87] Benefits of increased protein intake include improved function and quality of life in the healthy elderly, but also the ability of hospitalized elderly patients to recover from disease and trauma such that health outcomes are improved and cost of care is decreased.[88]

For individuals on a high protein diet, it would seem prudent to add a simple urine test to your semi-annual blood-testing regimen. From a realistic and practical prospective, the microalbumin to creatinine ratio is probably the easiest and best test for assessing early renal dysfunction. The micro doesn't really have much to do with it; it merely means they have found a way to measure very small (micro) amounts of albumin, and they compare them to the amount of creatinine in the same urine specimen. The test to get is the ACR or albumin/creatinine ratio available at www.labtestsonline.org.

If you can have success in reversing age-related sarcopenia (progressive loss of lean muscle mass) in the elderly using protein and essential amino acids, without exercise, as Dr. Wolfe's study demonstrated, imagine the possibilities with exercise. This is good news for the rest of us.

The Stealth Technique of Preloading with Essential Amino Acids

The Stealth Technique is an advanced technique within the Super Health Diet whereby essential amino acids are ingested and absorbed into the bloodstream within minutes without provoking a significant endocrine response—primarily blood sugar and insulin. Unlike EAAs, all proteins require digestion, and even though protein powders are among the most digestible proteins, they nonetheless tend to provoke some level of insulin response. Interestingly, Dr. Wolfe demonstrated that insulin response was higher when nonessential amino acids were added in addition to EAAs. Insulin response is extremely important in muscle protein synthesis; however, ideally one would limit insulin surges to around mealtimes and post workout.

> The fundamental mechanism by which dietary protein affects muscle and other physiological processes is the stimulation of muscle protein synthesis by the absorbed amino acids.
>
> DR. ROBERT WOLFE

The Stealth Technique of preloading a meal with EAAs is the most efficient and practical means of increasing blood levels of EAAs and thus increasing lean muscle mass and lean body mass while optimizing metabolism and supporting numerous other biological processes. This is important for the overweight or obese person who wants to optimize their weight or for the athlete who wishes to enhance performance.

The primary purpose for consuming protein is to obtain EAAs that have a myriad of biological functions in the body. The most potent, bioavailable, and usable form of amino acids are free-form amino acids that are immediately usable by the body because, unlike proteins, they do not have to be broken down through the digestion process. *Free-form amino acids are the most efficient and expensive form of "protein" powder, but are cost effective because they are two to three times more potent and more efficient than protein powders due to being more rapidly absorbed (most protein sources are comprised of 30 to 50 percent EAAs, and the body primarily absorbs EAAs from protein).*

In fact, consider the following statement for everyone from athletes to diabetics, from the super healthy to the health challenged: *"Muscle protein synthesis is stimulated by a single dose of 15 grams of essential amino acids to a greater extent than any anabolic hormone tested, including testosterone,[89] insulin,[90] and growth hormone."*[91] There is actually a legal substance that can be more effective than banned substances if you know how to use it.

Therefore, the Stealth Technique allows peak levels of EAAs to be already circulating in the blood when the mealtime insulin surge comes. The EAAs can then immediately be used by the body to synthesize (manufacture) muscle protein and other metabolic activities without having to catabolize (tear down) muscle tissue or having to wait for ingested proteins to be digested. The Stealth Technique is analogous to having a gun fully loaded and also having an extra bullet in the chamber, allowing more rapid initial firing. Think of the insulin response as the trigger that fires the bullet in the chamber.

When preloading EAAs, it is important to take the EAAs with water only to avoid a premature spike in insulin.

In addition to sufficient protein intake, adding the Stealth Technique before any or all of your meals and at bedtime is one of the highest impact things one can do to maintain or gain muscle mass and lean body mass even while dieting, fasting, or sleeping. Remember, gaining muscle and lean body mass does not necessarily mean getting bigger. It also means a stronger heart, lungs, and other organs. Think of it as exchanging fat for muscle.

A study led by Dr. Robert Wolfe suggests that "A mixture of EAAs formulated to maximally stimulate muscle protein synthesis can be given before meals without affecting either satiety or the metabolic response to the subsequent meal."[92] Free-form amino acids enter the bloodstream substantially faster than amino acids from any protein source. The ideal EAA blend should have an optimized amino acids profile with the combined advantages of each of the best-known animal sources of protein (milk, egg, whey isolate, lean buffalo, and lean beef) along with optimized levels of leucine.

Protein powders can be used to preload a meal when EAAs are not available, but not without affecting insulin levels, satiety, and meta-bolic response to the subsequent meal. In some cases, such as dieting, this is okay, because preloading with protein powder counts toward the protein content of the subsequent meal and reduces appetite.

Additionally, EAAs may be taken with low or moderate protein meals to enhance essential amino acids intake, such as with a vegetarian meal or a Micro Fast. Recent studies substantiate that the acute stimulatory effect of EAAs or protein intake on muscle protein synthesis (manufacture) translates to improvement in lean body mass, strength, and function in the elderly.[93] For example, *supplementation of the normal diet with a mixture of 10 to 15 grams of essential amino acids (which is roughly equivalent to the amount of EAAs in approximately 30 grams of high quality protein) twice per day increased lean body mass, strength, and functional test scores even in healthy elderly subjects without any alteration in normal dietary intake or exercise.*[94] It is interesting to note that high quality protein, such as whey or beef, stimulates muscle protein synthesis in direct proportion to the amount of essential amino acids per dose of protein.[95] (See the Four Corners Shopping List and Smart Meals and SuperSmoothie Recipes for product information.)

The FUEL Fast and Micro Fast

Two other extraordinary techniques for detoxification, more rapid weight optimization, and general well-being are the FUEL Fast and the Micro Fast. These techniques are two of the most effective ways to accomplish the Four Corners of Superfood Nutrition guidelines outlined earlier in this chapter. Fasting, which we have discussed in some detail earlier in this book, is an extremely powerful technique with numerous known health benefits, including rapid weight loss. Fasting ranges from doing without food to simply eliminating certain things you normally eat for a time (i.e., fasting breads or sugar). The biggest downside to traditional water fasting, juice fasting, vegetable fasting, etc., is significant muscle loss. We have discussed the importance of maintaining muscle mass earlier in this chapter. Muscle loss is extremely unhealthy and very difficult to replace. It results in an accumulation of body fat that is diametrically opposed to the intended health benefits of fasting. If you are going to fast, make sure you are obtaining the benefits you are attempting to gain. The key is to incorporate the Four Corner of Superfood Nutrition within your fast, therefore assuring you are getting everything your body needs even while fasting, including optimal protein levels. This can be accomplished without hunger or cravings.

You can "fast" (do a FUEL Fast or Micro Fast instead of eating a meal) a single meal or every meal, depending on your goals. It can be helpful to think of each meal as either a fast or not. Most people can maintain or lose weight using the Four Corners of Superfood Nutrition at between 1,500 to 1,800 optimized calories per day, assuming they are getting everything their body needs, including enough protein. This works out to 500 to 600 calories for each of three meals per day. For example, you could eat a meal in a restaurant that is 1,500 or more calories or choose to fast that meal with 100 to 600 calories, using the techniques called "Micro Fast" or "FUEL Fast" described below. Every meal you properly fast allows you to bank more calories to be divided during your other meals or allows you to create a calories' deficit to maximize weight loss while supporting muscle mass and metabolic function.

The FUEL Fast involves "fasting" or replacing one or all of your meals (three meals per day with five to six hours in between is generally best) with a broad-spectrum, nutrient-dense high-protein SuperSmoothie that is low in calories, rich in broad-spectrum antioxidants, low in sugar and glycemic response, and contains healthy fats. Essentially, it is using a functional SuperSmoothie to provide virtually every known essential nutrient combined with known superfoods in a highly digestible Super-Smoothie. Any meals not being replaced with a SuperSmoothie should be what we call a "Smart Meal," including a clean source of protein and a wide variety of broad-spectrum organic vegetables and some organic fruit (in moderation), nuts, and seeds. (See SuperSmoothie Recipes and Smart Meal Recipes.)

The Micro Fast or Micronutrient Fast is essentially an ultra low calorie Four Corners of Superfood Nutrition fast to replace one or more meals, using only "micronutrients," which are vitamins, minerals, antioxidants, phytonutrients, essential amino acids, essential fatty acids, prebiotics, and probiotics instead of "macronutrients," which are protein, carbohydrates, and fats. One exception is that carbohydrates will be in the form of fruits or vegetables, because the micronutrient of carbohydrates is sugar, which we want to minimize. The micronutrient from carbohydrates that we do want is soluble fiber. Technically, "micro ingredients" could mean nutrients in micrograms, but for our purposes it means nutrients derived from macronutrients totaling about 100 to 200 calories per meal yet supplying everything the body needs.

Instead of a meal, you would have a small amount of fibrous low glycemic carbohydrates (fruits or vegetables, such as one half to a whole banana or an apple or green salad, depending on activity level), along with an optimized essential amino acids supplement, a broad-spectrum antioxidant essential fatty acids EPA/DHA/GLA/Vitamin D/Vitamin A/Vitamin E+ supplement, a broad-spectrum micro multivitamin, mineral, antioxidant, phytonutrient, prebiotic, probiotic supplement, and potentially a soluble fiber supplement along with drinking plenty of water. The Micro Fast can also be accomplished by making a Micro SuperSmoothie. (See Micro SuperSmoothie Recipes or a Vegetarian Smart Meal plus above recommended supplements.)

The Micro Fast is ideal during lighter activities, including light exercise. Once you have become accustomed to Micro Fasting, you can do higher levels of physical activities by simply adjusting your intake of low glycemic carbohydrates to fuel the activity. Micro fasting can also be done within a FUEL Fast by replacing a SuperSmoothie with a Micro Super-Smoothie.

Protein Powders

Protein powders are important additions to our diets. They come in three basic forms: isolates, hydrolysates, and concentrates from various sources, including dairy, goat, egg, rice, pea, hemp seed, and soy. Protein isolates contain up to 90 percent protein, while concentrates are up to 80 percent protein. Hydrolysates are isolates or concentrates that have been enzymatically predigested via a process called hydrolysis, which can result in a bitter taste. As in basic nutrition, animal-derived protein powers are generally more acidic and more inflammatory than vegetable-derived protein powders. Animal protein powders generally have a better protein profile than plant-derived protein powders; however, there is at least one plant-derived protein powder that has been scientifically blended and optimized with specific amino acids and enzymes.

Protein concentrates are generally the cheapest protein powders, followed by isolates, and hydrolysates are the most expensive.

Many people have a difficult time with dairy, egg, and soy protein due to allergies or intolerances. Pasteurized dairy is widely considered to be unhealthy with a higher likelihood of intolerance to milk protein, casein, and lactose. My recommendation is to minimize pasteurized dairy, milk protein, and casein concentrates in favor of higher quality whey isolates. Soy also has a higher risk of intolerance, and its use remains controversial. My recommendation is to avoid unfermented soy and soy protein powders as a daily food and to avoid whole egg protein powders in general due to heat damaged fats. Egg white protein powders can be a good protein source if you tolerate eggs well and are okay with the somewhat bitter taste. My preference is an optimized blend of brown rice, yellow pea protein powder, with added amino acids, fiber, probiotics, enzymes, and vitamin C, and optimized EAAs powder. (See the Four Corners Shopping List and Micro Smoothie Recipes.)

People often say they take a particular protein powder because they like the taste. However, I am not aware of any protein powder that has a naturally pleasant taste, as they all tend to be naturally bland and even somewhat chalky. This is where you can get into trouble, because many unhealthy and potentially dangerous ingredients are routinely added to enhance the taste experience. *If you are buying a protein powder because you like the taste, there is a high likelihood that it contains ingredients you should not be putting into your body in the name of health.* You can go into the largest nutrition store in your city and look at dozens of different brands of protein powders and may or may not be able to find a single one that does not contain potentially unhealthy ingredients we will discuss in more detail next. Protein powders can be made to taste great using natural ingredients, such as xylitol, tagatose, erythritol, mannitol, stevia, and real cocoa powder.

There are good reasons to have carbohydrates and even sugar, such as during workouts; however, before consuming any protein powder, be diligent in reading nutrition labels to be sure the manufacturer did not add unwanted additional calories with sugars and other high glycemic carbohydrates (sucrose, fructose, maltodextrin, etc.) or other controversial and potentially dangerous ingredients, such as artificial sweeteners (aspartame-known excitotoxin, sucralose-chlorinated sugar, acesulfame-K, which contains the known carcinogen methylene chloride). If a food, protein powder, or supplement contains these ingredients or contains GMOs (genetically modified organisms), artificial flavors, colors, or preservatives, *DO NOT CONSUME IT* and keep searching till you find a healthy alternative. It is also important to avoid ingredients such as damaged and unhealthy fats, including most vegetable oils, all hydrogenated oils, powdered eggs, and powdered milk. Again, if a protein powder or meal replacement contains any of these ingredients, please strongly consider if you should take it at all, but *DO NOT* use it as a daily staple.

> **If you are buying a protein powder because you like the taste, there is a high likelihood that it contains ingredients you should not be putting into your body in the name of health.**

Vegetarianism, Protein, and Vital Nutrients

I strongly believe in the power of a plant-based diet and understand why some people want to be vegetarians. Just about everyone could benefit from eating more fresh vegetables and fruits (in moderation). Most people today who call themselves vegetarians are not true vegetarians, because they also eat some kinds of animal protein, such as eggs or fish. There is a lot of evidence that suggests a modified vegetarian diet that includes clean animal sources of protein is extremely healthy. Combining the Bible's Old Testament vegetarian guidelines in Genesis 1:29 with the clean meats (a.k.a. Kosher guidelines in Leviticus 11) may well be the long-sought-after fountain of youth.

Most vegetarians have multiple nutrient deficiencies, including protein. They often rely on low protein sources that do not provide enough of the right combinations of essential amino acids to allow them to thrive. Many vegetarians end up eating grains instead of meats, which further exacerbates the problems. Educated vegetarian food combining can provide a good mix of EAAs but generally necessitates far too many carbohydrates into their diet. Blindly mixing various foods is not ideal. Most vegetarians are not strict and also eat eggs, dairy, and/or fish, which can go a long way toward supplying much needed protein, EAAs, and other vital nutrients, such as fish oil EPA/DHA.

However, for just about everyone, especially strict vegetarians, to obtain Super Health, it is my belief that functional superfoods, such as optimized plant protein powders and essential amino acids, are critical to health and longevity. A word of caution: Infants, children, and young adults should not consume strict vegetarian diets or be on long-term calorie-restricted diets because it can stunt their growth and cause long-term health problems. Neither should pregnant and nursing mothers.

Food is a double-edged sword. The combining of various plant foods from different categories (vegetables, grains, legumes, nuts, and seeds) can still result in a suboptimal amount of protein, varied amounts of EAAs, and unhealthy levels of carbohydrates. Mindlessly or methodically combining of various plant foods generally does not ensure optimal amounts of EAAs. It is critical for strict vegetarians to supplement with optimized plant protein powders and EAAs. (See the Four Corners Shopping List and Smart Meals and SuperSmoothie Recipes for product information.)

Meal Timing and Proteins—Three or Six Meals Per Day?

While I focus on "meal frequency" in Chapter 13, many studies have examined the benefits of nutrient timing, and most people seem to believe that six multiple meals per day are better than three larger meals in terms of nutrient utilization and maximal muscle protein synthesis. The theory is that multiple meals help maintain a constant anabolic state (muscle building) that blocks muscle protein catabolization (breakdown) and delivers a constant stream of amino acids and other nutrients into the blood. There are studies that support both sides of this issue. However, a recent study examined muscle protein synthesis, using various levels of infused (delivered directly into the bloodstream via IV) EAAs. The researchers found that muscle protein synthesis spiked, then returned to baseline even when amino acids were continually infused. They concluded that providing low to moderate levels of amino acids, then allowing adequate time between infusions of subsequent doses of amino acids provided the greatest result.[96]

It would appear from this and other studies that elevating EAAs around mealtime, then allowing time between meals for digestion provides for improved amino acids sensitivity and efficiency in muscle protein synthesis. This makes sense, because normal digestion rates of six to 10 grams per hour begin about one hour after the protein is consumed, depending on the digestibility of the protein source. Thus, a meal with 40 grams of protein is generally digested during a five- to six-hour period, while other longer acting proteins and more slowly digested proteins such as red meats can take even longer.[97] Therefore, the body remains in an anabolic state for at least five or six hours after a meal (if not much longer), and eating more frequently does not appear to offer benefit with the exception of EAAs. Because EAAs don't require a digestion process, EAAs taken between meals have been shown to offer significant benefit, even though protein from a previous meal is still digesting (see Stealth Technique).[98] One exception to eating just three meals per day without snacks might be for the athlete needing to achieve a much greater caloric intake. They may not be able to eat as many calories in three meals as six and are better able to digest more frequent meals.

Eating too often appears to cause amino acids insensitivity and can work against increases in muscle mass. In a related study, researchers found that protein oxidation by the liver decreased by 16 percent in a group given three meals versus six meals.[99] Providing a constant stream of amino acids seems to reduce the body's sensitivity to the amino acids. Providing three separate spikes of amino acids around three evenly spaced meals provides the best opportunity to maintain maximum sensitivity for muscle protein synthesis. Applying the Stealth Technique to preload a meal with EAAs about five hours subsequent to the start of a previous meal helps ensure the body remains in an anabolic (muscle building) state and allows ample time to maximize EAA sensitivity.

Another study demonstrated that eating three whole food meals per day plus taking EAAs between meals generated a greater muscle protein synthesis than the three meals alone.[100] Additionally, researchers observed that the EAA supplement generated an anabolic response even when given between meals. Incredibly, the effects of the EAAs were not blunted, even though the previous meal that included protein was still being digested. Neither were the anabolic effects of the meal blunted by the EAAs. This information strongly reinforces two things: the power of the "Stealth Technique," and that Grandma was right—eat three square meals per day with no snacks! Unless, of course, the snacks are EAAs.

> Muscle protein synthesis is stimulated by a single dose of 15 grams of essential amino acids to a greater extent than any anabolic hormone tested, including testosterone, insulin, and growth hormone.

Healthy Weight Gain

A discussion of weight optimization would be incomplete without mentioning healthy weight gain. While the overwhelming majority of people are most interested in losing weight, there are millions of people who either are or believe they are underweight, because of genetics or illness or eating disorders. And there are many reasons why some athletes want to gain weight. My two eldest sons, Kyle (17) and Austin (15), are high school quarterbacks and have successfully used this system to maximize their muscle mass and to get the most out of their growth spurts. Kyle has gained 45 pounds of lean body mass over the past year and a half, and Austin is on the same path. One important aspect here is that in addition to protein, it is important to focus on increasing healthy fats. Austin adds olive oil to his high protein SuperSmoothies. (See Healthy Fats and SuperSmoothie recipes.)

Healthy weight gain uses the same principles as healthy weight loss, but increases the volume of food—primarily protein and healthy fats—and changes the timing slightly to minimize muscle catabolism while still allowing time between meals for proper digestion and the optimization of amino acids sensitivity. It is important to follow the meal timing principles presented in this book. To gain lean body mass, I recommend eating either three meals with five to six hour spacing between meals or four meals per day with four-hour spacing between meals. Four meals allow you to consume more calories, but that is not necessarily important as long as you are getting enough protein and healthy fats. It is very important to use the Stealth Technique of preloading each meal with 15 grams of EAAs approximately 30 minutes before each meal and taking 20 grams of long-acting protein from a high fiber plant-based protein powder at bedtime. EAAs are ideal for preloading; however, if EAAs are not available, use 20 grams of high quality protein one hour before mealtime. Carbohydrate intake should be enough to adequately fuel whatever activity in which you are engaged. However, over fueling with carbohydrates will result in an underweight person with a fat belly. It is also important to increase the intensity of your workouts and never miss having a post workout protein/carbohydrate recovery drink within 45 minutes of finishing your workouts.

Protein intake is of paramount importance. For maximum gain of muscle, take protein at the highest recommended levels mentioned in this chapter while also significantly increasing your consumption of healthy fats, including nuts, nut butters, seeds, oils (see Four Corners of Superfood Nutrition). Protein and EAAs powders are extremely important in healthy weight gain, because trying to obtain optimal protein intake from continuous back-to-back meat meals can be a huge stress to the body and harmful over time, and vegetable sources of protein are not concentrated enough.

Chapter Summary

- Proteins are the basic building blocks of the human body and one of the key nutrients in the human diet.
- Proteins are made up of essential and nonessential amino acids.
- Building and maintaining lean muscle is critical for weight optimization, and inadequate protein intake can result in muscle catabolism (loss).
- Not all protein is alike, and plant and animal protein have differing amino acid profiles (a gram is not necessarily a gram).
- The Recommended Daily Allowance (RDA) of protein is the *minimal*, not the optimal, level of protein needed for daily functioning.

- Contrary to conventional thinking, high protein diets can be healthy and beneficial, even higher protein diets for those with kidney dysfunction.
- Protein intake must be maintained at optimal levels or even increased when calorie intake is reduced. While on a low calorie diet, it is important to maintain protein levels within the high side or above these ranges to help stave off muscle loss.
- Using the Stealth Technique of preloading with EAAs, the FUEL Fast, and the Micro Fast can exponentially increase your speed toward Super Health and lifelong weight optimization.
- The right EAAs are a legal substance that can be more effective than banned substances if you know how to use it. Muscle protein synthesis is stimulated by a single dose of 15 grams of essential amino acids to a greater extent than any anabolic hormone tested, including testosterone, insulin, and growth hormone.
- Protein powders can be great sources of protein, but amino acid profiles matter and beware of the other ingredients.
- Vegetarians need extra vigilance in their supplementation of protein and other vital nutrients.
- Eating more frequent meals may not result in expedited weight optimization.

THE
SUPER
HEALTH
DIET

Golden
Keys
to Unlock
Lifelong
Vitality

Smart Meals, SuperSmoothie Recipes, Micro SuperSmoothies, Alternative Superfood Recipes

You can increase your protein intake and eat smarter meals at the same time. Select from the columns below to put together a tasty Smart Meal that has between 35 to 50 grams of protein (protein amounts in grams = g). The goal is to eat between 50 and 90 percent of your body weight in grams per day with a preference toward the higher end of the range. For instance, a 170-pound person might need 100 to 150 grams of protein a day. You will find most of these foods, Functional Superfoods, and supplements in the Four Corners Shopping List and in my book *Super Health: 7 Golden Keys to Unlock Lifelong Vitality* and at www.livingfuel.com. A more comprehensive list of foods and protein amounts is in my book *Living the Seven Golden Keys to Lifelong Vitality*.

I'll share seven examples of meals with at least 35 grams of protein after you read the food protein charts. The examples will help you put together your own delicious, fun, and protein-filled meals. Buy organic food products whenever possible. Avoid purchasing food that has been genetically modified (GMO).

Getting up to the Super Health Diet recommended daily protein levels of 0.5g to 0.9g per pound of body weight per day can be challenging without overeating meats. Vegetarians will find it much more difficult to reach these recommended protein levels, since animal meats are among the highest protein sources. Vegetarians must be well educated in food combining of various plant foods from different categories—vegetables, grains, legumes, nuts, and seeds—to achieve greater balance in essential amino acids. Strict vegetarians are at extreme risk of overeating carbohydrates because most plant foods that contain protein also contain even greater amounts of carbohydrates.

I recommend that just about everyone, especially vegetarians, supplement their diets with high protein functional foods, including protein and essential amino acids powders, and, at a minimum, take an antioxidant essential fatty acids supplement daily.

Use this chart to build your Smart Meals around food combinations that provide the amount of protein you are trying to achieve each meal.

Vegetables, Beans, Legumes	Nuts & Seeds	Fruit	Meats
Lentil beans, 1/2 cup, cooked (9g)	Peanuts, 1/4 cup (9g)	Prunes, 1 cup, uncooked (5g)	Chicken breast, cooked, 3 oz. (24g)
Black beans, 1/2 cup, cooked (7.6g)	Brazil nuts, 1/4 cup (5g)	Figs, 1 cup, dried, uncooked (5g)	Turkey breast, cooked, 3 oz. (24g)
Garbanzo beans, 1/2 cup, cooked (7.3g)	Cashews, 1/4 cup (5g)	Avocado, 1 cup, sliced (3g)	Halibut, cooked, 3 oz. (23g)
Lima beans, 1/2 cup, cooked (7.3g)	Almonds, 1/4 cup (5g)	Blackberries, 1 cup, raw (2g)	Sardines, in water, 3 oz. (22g)
Kidney beans, 1/2 cup, cooked (7.6g)	Walnuts, 1/4 cup (5g)	Peach, large, with skin (2g)	Salmon, wild caught, cooked, 3 oz. (19g)
Split peas, 1/2 cup, cooked (8g)	Pecans, 1/4 cup (2.5g)	Papaya, large, raw (2g)	Grouper, cooked, 3 oz. (21g)
Potato, large, cooked (7g)	Chia seeds, 1/4 cup (8g)	Raspberries, 1 cup, raw (1g)	Cod, cooked, 3 oz. (19g)
Asparagus, raw, 1 cup (3g)	Pumpkin seeds, 1/4 cup (8g)	Kiwifruit, large, raw (1g)	Mackerel, cooked, 3 oz. (20g)
Beets, raw, 1 cup (1g)	Flaxseeds, 1/4 cup (8g)	Blueberries, 1 cup, raw (1g)	Bison, rib eye, broiled, 3 oz. (25g)

Green pepper, raw, 1 cup (1g)	Watermelon seeds, 1/4 cup (7.5g)	Strawberries, 1 cup, raw (1g)	Beef, porterhouse steak, 3 oz. (20g)
Kale, raw, 1 cup (1g)	Sesame seeds, 1/4 cup (6g)	Pear, large, raw (1g)	Beef, top sirloin, broiled, 3 oz. (26g)
Romaine lettuce, 1 cup shredded (1g)	Sunflower seeds, 1/4 cup (6g)	Banana, large, raw (1g)	Beef, tip round, roasted, 3 oz. (24g)
Artichoke, large, raw (5g)	Pistachios, 1/4 cup (6g)	Orange, large, raw (1g)	Lamb, sirloin chops, cooked, 3 oz. (18g)
Sweet potato, large, cooked (4g)	Nut butters, 2 tsb (8g)	Apple, with skin (1g)	Venison, tenderloin, broiled, 3 oz. (25g)

Dairy	**Grains**	**Other**
Large egg, poached (6g)	Wheat germ, crude (27g)	Coconut milk, 1 cup (5g)
Egg, hard-boiled, (6g)	Buckwheat, 1 cup (23g)	Almond milk, 1 cup (1g)
Soft cheeses, 1 oz. (6g)	Quinoa, cooked, 1 cup (8g)	Rice milk, 1 cup (1g)
Medium cheeses, 1 oz. (8g)	Brown rice, 1 cup, cooked (5g)	Spinach salad – loaded, 1 serving (22g)
Hard cheeses, 1 oz. (10g)	Rye bread, 1 slice (3g)	Bison stew, 4 oz., cooked (28g)
Goat milk, 1 cup (9g)	Oatmeal, rough cut, 1 cup (6g)	Lentil & turkey sausage soup, 1 cup, cooked (12g)
Cow milk, 1 cup (8g)	Bread, oat bran, 1 slice (3g)	Chicken & spinach soup, 1 cup, cooked (12 g)
Cottage cheese, 1 cup (27g)	Bread, wheat germ, 1 slice (3g)	Buckwheat pasta & turkey meat balls, 1 cup, cooked (30g)
Yogurt, 1 cup (9g)	Bread, cracked-wheat, 1 slice (2g)	Hummus snack wrap, 4 oz. (30g)

Seven Smart Meal Examples

Quiche—broccoli, cheddar, red pepper, onion, 1/4 pie pan (15g)
Quinoa—1/2 cup cooked (4g)
Green leafy salad (large) with vinaigrette (2g)
Chia seeds—1/8 cup (4g)
Blueberries—1/2 cup (.5g)
Goat milk—1 cup (9g)
Total of 34.5 grams of protein

Chicken breast—1 breast (30g)
Lima beans—1/2 cup cooked (7.5g)
Green leafy salad (large) with vinaigrette (2g)
Sweet potato—1/2 large, cooked (3.5g)
Cashews—1/8 cup (2.5g)
Coconut milk—1 cup (5g)
Total of 50.5 grams of protein

Salmon, Atlantic, wild caught, cooked, 1/2 fillet (39g)
Eggs—1/2 hard-boiled (3g)
Green leafy salad (large) with vinaigrette (2g)
Lentil beans—cooked, 1/2 cup (9g)
Rice milk—1 cup (1g)
Total of 54 grams of protein

Bison—top round, 1" steak, broiled (54g)
Loaded spinach salad—baby spinach, eggs, beets, carrots,
chopped pecans, 1/2 serving (11g)
Figs—1/2 cup, dried, uncooked (2.5g)
Herb tea—1 cup (0g)
Total of 67.5 grams of protein

Bison stew meat, carrots, garlic salt, onions, onion powder, cooked
tomatoes, pepper, water, basil leaves, potatoes, celery stalks,
6 oz. serving (42g)
Green leafy salad (large) with vinaigrette (2g)
Brown rice—1/2 cup, cooked (2.5g)
Papaya—1/2 large (1g)

Goat milk—1 cup (9g)
Total of 56.5 grams of protein

Turkey breast—3 oz. cooked (24g)
Lentil soup—lentils, water, onions, chopped celery, butter, bay leaf, sugar, thyme, mustard seeds, chopped carrot, chopped garlic, parsley, lemon juice, turkey sausage, 1 cup (12g)
Green salad (large) with vinaigrette (2g)
Pecans—1/4 cup (2.5g)
Strawberries—1/2 cup (.5g)
Coconut milk—1 cup (1g)
Total of 42 grams of protein

Chicken and spinach soup—chicken, chopped onion, sliced celery sticks, crushed garlic, potatoes, spinach, olive oil, cream, 1 cup (12g)
Green salad (large) with vinaigrette (2g)
Avocado—1/2 cup (1.5g)
Cottage cheese—4 oz. (13g)
Brazil nuts—1/4 cup (5g)
Raspberries—1/2 cup (.5g)
Goat milk—1 cup (9g)
Total of 43 grams of protein

SuperSmoothie Recipes

A team of organic chefs cannot put together a more nutritious meal than a SuperSmoothie (a high protein superfood smoothie). A SuperSmoothie is a super meal that will most likely be the most nutritious meal you have ever had with more calcium and vitamin D than milk, more potassium than bananas, more resveratrol than wine, more protein than a half dozen egg whites, more fiber than oatmeal, more vitamins, minerals, broad-spectrum antioxidants and phytonutrients than 10 servings of fruits and vegetables, plus a multivitamin and more prebiotics and friendly bacteria than 10 cups of yogurt. It is simply the most effective and convenient means of accomplishing all four elements of the Four Corners of Superfood Nutrition in a single meal.

When you finish the meal from the recipe of your choice, you will feel energetic and not be hungry for five to six hours.

Some of the most common feedback we get from people on the Super Health Diet is dramatic improvements in the way they look and feel, including energy levels, digestion, elimination, hair, skin, nails, muscle tone, and body fat levels.

Whole meal SuperSmoothies range from approximately 300 to 600 total calories, depending on the ingredients added to the 300-calorie base SuperSmoothie. The total calories can be increased as desired by adding other healthy fats, carbohydrates, and protein.

I recommend everyone, particularly taste- and texture-sensitive people, begin this program by making SuperSmoothies in a blender. Additionally, I strongly encourage you to make an investment in your Super Health lifestyle by purchasing a super blender such as a BlendTec (www.blendtec.com) or Vitamix (www.vitamix.com).

The nutritional foundation of all these SuperSmoothie recipes is LivingFuel Functional Superfoods and supplements, including LivingFuel SuperBerry Ultimate, SuperBerry, SuperGreens, SuperEssentials Aminos, SuperEssentials Omega 3EDA+ and SuperEssentials Multi-Vitamin, Mineral, Antioxidant, Phytonutrient, Prebiotic, Probiotic. For more information see the Four Corners Shopping List or www.livingfuel.com or call 1-866-580-FUEL(3835).

K.C.'s Ultimate Fast Food

1 scoop LivingFuel SuperBerry Ultimate
1 scoop LivingFuel SuperGreens
2 scoops LivingFuel LivingProtein
16 oz. spring water

Shake in blender bottle (Use of a super blender is recommended for first time SuperSmoothie drinkers and taste-and texture-sensitive individuals, such as children.)
Also take SuperEssentials Omega 3 EDA+ daily

Monica's SuperSmoothie

1 scoop LivingFuel SuperBerry Ultimate
1 scoop LivingFuel SuperGreens

1 scoop LivingFuel LivingProtein
1 tbsp. LivingFuel CocoChia Snack Mix
Splash organic cranberry juice
2 oz. organic coconut milk
10 oz. spring water
4 ice cubes
Mix in blender until smooth
Also take SuperEssentials Omega 3 EDA+ daily

17-year-old Kyle's Simple SuperSmoothie

1 scoop LivingFuel SuperBerry Ultimate
1 scoop LivingFuel SuperGreens
1 scoop LivingFuel LivingProtein
12 oz. spring water
Mix in shaker bottle

15-year-old Austin's SuperSmoothie

2 scoops LivingFuel SuperBerry Ultimate
1/3 medium banana
2 oz. organic orange juice
2 tsp. olive oil
1/2 cup ice
12 oz. spring water
Mix in blender until smooth (Use of a super blender is recommended
for first time SuperSmoothie drinkers and taste-and texture-sensitive
individuals, such as children.)
Also take SuperEssentials Omega 3 EDA+ daily

13-year-old Sarah's SuperSmoothie

1 1/2 scoops LivingFuel SuperBerry Ultimate
1/4 cup of fresh organic raspberries
1/4 cup of fresh organic strawberries
2 oz. organic orange juice
8 oz. spring water
Mix in blender until smooth
Also take SuperEssentials Omega 3 EDA+ daily

8-year-old Gracie's SuperSmoothie

1 rounded scoop LivingFuel SuperBerry Ultimate
2 oz. chocolate almond milk
2 oz. vanilla almond milk
1/2 cup ice
4 oz. spring water
Mix in blender until smooth
Also take SuperEssentials Omega 3 EDA+ daily

4-year-old Joshua's SuperSmoothie

1 scoop LivingFuel SuperBerry Ultimate
1/2 scoop LivingFuel LivingProtein
6 oz. spring water
2 oz. organic orange juice
Mix in shaker bottle or blender
Also take SuperEssentials Omega 3 EDA+ daily

SuperBerry Plus SuperSmoothie

1 scoop LivingFuel SuperBerry Ultimate
2 scoops LivingProtein
1/2 cup fresh or frozen organic blueberries
1/3 banana
1/2 cup unsweetened organic vanilla almond milk
1 tbsp. LivingFuel CocoChia Snack Mix
12 oz. spring water
3 ice cubes
Mix in blender until smooth
Also take SuperEssentials Omega 3 EDA+ daily

SuperGreens Cucumber Delight SuperSmoothie

1 scoop LivingFuel SuperGreens
1 scoop LivingFuel LivingProtein
1/2 medium organic cucumber
1/2 small organic gala apple

1/2 cup unsweetened vanilla organic almond milk
3 ice cubes
1/2 cup spring water
Mix in blender until smooth, adjust water to desired consistency
Also take SuperEssentials Omega 3 EDA+ daily

Tropical SuperSmoothie

1 scoop LivingFuel SuperBerry Ultimate
1 scoop LivingProtein
1/2 medium banana
2 tbsp. LivingFuel CocoChia Snack Mix
8 organic almonds
1/4 frozen mango
12 oz. spring water
Mix in blender until smooth
Also take SuperEssentials Omega 3 EDA+ daily

Zach's SuperSmoothie

1 scoop LivingFuel SuperBerry Ultimate
1 scoop LivingProtein
1 cup fresh juiced organic carrots
1/2 cup organic red seedless grapes
3 ice cubes
12 oz. spring water
Mix in blender until smooth
Also take SuperEssentials Omega 3 EDA+ daily

Katie's Morning SuperSmoothie

1 scoop LivingFuel SuperBerry Ultimate
2 scoops LivingProtein
1/3 frozen banana
1 cup unsweetened organic almond milk
1 tsp. organic vanilla
2 oz. organic orange juice

3 ice cubes
12 oz. spring water
Mix in blender until smooth
Also take SuperEssentials Omega 3 EDA+ daily

Florida LivingProtein SuperSmoothie

3 scoops LivingProtein
1/2 cup fresh Florida organic orange juice (fresh squeezed if possible)
1/2 medium banana
3 ice cubes
12 oz. spring water
Mix in blender until smooth
Also take SuperEssentials Omega 3 EDA+ daily

Almond Green SuperSmoothie

2 scoops LivingFuel SuperGreens
1 scoop LivingProtein
2 tbsp. creamy organic almond butter
1/2 banana
3 ice cubes
12 oz. spring water
Mix in blender until smooth
Also take SuperEssentials Omega 3 EDA+ daily

Ultimate SuperGreens SuperSmoothie

2 scoops LivingFuel SuperGreens
1 scoop LivingProtein
1 cup fresh organic raw spinach
1/2 medium organic cucumber
5–10 seedless organic red grapes
2 medium organic fresh carrots
3 ice cubes
12 oz. spring water
Mix in blender until smooth
Also take SuperEssentials Omega 3 EDA+ daily

Spicy SuperGreens SuperSmoothie

2 scoops LivingFuel SuperGreens
1 dash organic cayenne pepper (adjust to taste)
16 oz. spring water
Mix in shaker bottle
Also take SuperEssentials Omega 3 EDA+ daily
More recipes and information are available at www.livingfuel.com.

Micro SuperSmoothie Recipes—Ultra Low Calorie Four Corners Meals

1 scoop (15g) of LivingFuel SuperEssentials Aminos
Mixed with spring water in shaker
Plus, eat 1/2 to 1 banana, depending on activity level
Also take LivingFuel SuperEssentials Multi-Vitamin-Mineral-Antioxidant-Phytonutrient and SuperEssentials Omega 3 EDA+

Banana Berry Micro SuperSmoothie

1 scoop (15g) LivingFuel SuperEssentials Aminos
1/2 cup fresh or frozen organic blueberries
1/2 banana
1/2 cup unsweetened vanilla almond milk
16 oz. spring water
3 ice cubes
Mix in blender until smooth
Also take LivingFuel Super Essentials Multi-Vitamin-Mineral-Antioxidant-Phytonutrient and SuperEssentials Omega 3 EDA+

Cucumber Delight Micro SuperSmoothie

1 scoop (15g) LivingFuel SuperEssentials Aminos
1/2 medium organic cucumber
1/2 small organic Gala apple
1/4 cup organic apple juice
3 ice cubes
1/2 cup spring water

Mix in blender until smooth, adjust water to desired consistency
Also take LivingFuel SuperEssentials Multi-Vitamin-Mineral-Antioxidant-Phytonutrient and SuperEssentials Omega 3 EDA+

Tropical Micro SuperSmoothie

1 scoop (15g) LivingFuel SuperEssentials Aminos
1/2 banana
2 tbsp. CocoChia Snack Mix
1/4 frozen mango
12 oz. spring water
Mix in blender until smooth
Also take LivingFuel SuperEssentials Multi-Vitamin-Mineral-Antioxidant-Phytonutrient and SuperEssentials Omega 3 EDA+

Carrot-Apple Micro SuperSmoothie

1 scoop (15g) LivingFuel SuperEssentials Aminos
6 skinned organic carrots or 1 cup fresh juiced organic carrots
1/4 cup apple organic apple juice or 1/2 cup organic apple
5 ice cubes
16 oz. spring water
Mix in blender until smooth
Also take LivingFuel SuperEssentials Multi-Vitamin-Mineral-Antioxidant-Phytonutrient and SuperEssentials Omega 3 EDA+

Orange Vanilla Micro SuperSmoothie

1 scoop (15g) LivingFuel SuperEssentials Aminos
1/2 frozen banana
1 cup unsweetened almond milk
1 tsp. organic vanilla
2 oz. organic orange juice
3 ice cubes
12 oz. spring water
Mix in blender until smooth
Also take LivingFuel SuperEssentials Multi-Vitamin-Mineral-Antioxidant-Phytonutrient and SuperEssentials Omega 3 EDA+

Florida LivingProtein Micro SuperSmoothie

1 scoop LivingProtein
1 scoop (15g) LivingFuel SuperEssentials Aminos
1/2 cup fresh Florida organic orange juice (fresh squeezed if possible)
1/2 medium banana
3 ice cubes
12 oz. spring water
Mix in blender until smooth
Also take LivingFuel SuperEssentials Multi-Vitamin-Mineral-Antioxidant-Phytonutrient and SuperEssentials Omega 3 EDA+

Alternative Superfood Recipes

SuperBaby Formula

Start with a glass baby bottle with the silicone nipple hole cut slightly larger. Add 1 to 4 oz. of coconut milk or coconut milk powder. Add heated purified water and whisk with a fork to break up any clumps. Add cooler purified water to achieve desired consistency and temperature. Add 1/8 to 1/2 scoop of LivingFuel SuperBerry Ultimate or SuperBerry Original or SuperGreens (blend the dry powder beforehand in a coffee bean grinder to blend down the chia seeds). Stir with a fork and then shake. Serve with plenty of smiles and snuggles!

Super Soups: Tomato Brisk and Split Pea Soups

Mix, stir in or blend one scoop of LivingFuel SuperGreens per bowl of cold soup or after it is warmed. Heat to taste but don't boil.

Super Avocado Supreme

Mix one scoop of LivingFuel SuperGreens with one ripe Hass avocado, one organic whole tomato, 1/2 chopped organic sweet onion, one tablespoon extra virgin olive oil, juice from one whole organic lemon, plus pepper, sea salt, Tabasco, and other seasonings to taste. Mash the avocado and mix in the above ingredients. Chill and serve with almond crackers or other healthy equivalents, or eat it alone as a complete and balanced meal or snack.

Super Apple Sauce

Mix 1 scoop of LivingFuel SuperBerry into a bowl of apple sauce. Sprinkle in 1 tablespoon of CocoChia snack mix.

SuperBerry Yogurt

Mix 1 scoop of LivingFuel SuperBerry into a bowl of yogurt. Sprinkle in 1 tablespoon of CocoChia snack mix.

SuperBerry Oatmeal

Mix 1 scoop of LivingFuel SuperBerry into a bowl of steel cut oats. Sprinkle in 1 tablespoon of CocoChia snack mix.

More information and videos on LivingFuel Functional Superfoods and supplements, including SuperEssentials Aminos, SuperEssentials Multi, and SuperEssential Omega 3EDA+, are available at www.living-fuel.com.

Chapter 12

Anti-Aging Benefits of Eating the Four Corners Way

Make [food] simple and let things taste of what they are.
CURNONSKY

In the Introduction to my book *Super Health: 7 Golden Keys to Unlock Lifelong Vitality*, I wrote about the 2004 film *Super Size Me*, in which Morgan Spurlock embarks upon a month-long, three-meal-a-day "Mac Diet" (McDonald's food only). Prior to the experiment, Spurlock, a 30-something, 6'2", 185-pound man, was healthy, physically active, and consumed a reasonable 2,500 calories a day. Thirty days later, he was eating more than 5,000 calories a day and suffering from depression, rapid mood swings, high blood pressure, low sex drive, and symptoms of addiction. He had gained 24.5 pounds, his cholesterol shot up 65 points, and his body fat average jumped from 11 to 18 percent. After just two weeks on the diet, all three of the physicians with whom Spurlock consulted encouraged him to abandon the diet, as he was showing signs of having seriously compromised his liver. They were astonished to discover that a fast-food diet could wreak so much havoc in the body so quickly.

Spurlock's culinary adventure illustrates well the dangers of a diet that is high in trans fats, calories, and oxidative stress, and exacerbated by processed dead foods and lack of exercise—the classic sedentary American lifestyle. Although his was an extreme experiment, Spurlock had set out to answer his own question, "Why are Americans so fat?" It didn't take long to figure it out. It's abundantly clear that we cannot fool the human body. We reap what we sow.

It reminds me of the Pottenger Cat Study conducted by physician and researcher Francis M. Pottenger Jr., M.D., between the years of 1932 and 1942. Pottenger, who had successfully treated patients with asthma, emphysema, tuberculosis, and allergies by putting them on a diet of raw butter, cream, and eggs, decided to experiment to determine the effects of heat-processed food versus a raw food diet involving cats.

In one study group, the cats ate only raw meat and raw milk, while in the other groups they ate some raw meat mixed with pasteurized milk and cooked meat. During the 10 years of study, Pottenger discovered that only the all-raw group maintained good health generation after generation—with good quality bone structure, easy pregnancies, few parasites, and gentle dispositions.

The groups whose diet included pasteurized milk and cooked meat developed numerous diseases, frail bones, weakened ligaments, facial deformities, harbored parasites, and had difficult pregnancies. Both male and female cats exhibited shifts in disposition—the males becoming timid and the females more aggressive compared to those on the raw diet. After only three generations, young animals died before reaching adulthood and stopped reproducing.

While Pottenger never stated that a one-to-one comparison could be made between his findings in cat nutrition and his findings in human nutrition, it is a testament to the potential consequences of a diet without the proper nutrients. Just as was true of the consequences of Morgan Spurlock's refined, highly sweetened convenience foods and overall terrible diet, Americans are experiencing an epidemic of degenerative diseases as a result of consuming the wrong foods—much of which could be countered by a diet based upon the Four Corners of Superfood Nutrition.

As you read on in this chapter, keep in mind that the very same processes that are at the root of many if not all human diseases—*oxidation, inflammation, glycation,* and *angiogenesis,* or "the Big Four" as I call them—are also at the root of obesity, which is at the root of numerous diseases. It is bordering on miraculous that a system of eating as simple as the Four Corners of Superfood Nutrition can help regulate all of these potentially destructive processes.

I also want to note that three of the Big Four normally have beneficial roles within the body. The possible exception is glycation, for which I am unaware of any health benefits.

Oxidation and Inflammation

In "Corner #3—Consume High Antioxidant Superfoods and Supplements," I presented the relationship of *oxidation* and the destructive role of *free radicals* in the production of degenerative diseases in the body, as well as how excessive fat tissue in the body increases the oxidative stress. The role of broad-spectrum antioxidants was presented as the primary deterrent to these violently destructive molecules that attack the genetic machinery inside the DNA molecule. We have also seen that a large body of research suggests that chronic *inflammation* is a major cause of aging and many degenerative diseases, and being overweight is a major contributor to chronic inflammation.

AGE: The Damaging Process of Glycation

In my book *Super Health*, I said that I believed that in five years *glycation* might be as well known as *oxidation*. Now, five years later, few people are aware that as you age your structural proteins are typically being slowly damaged by a process known as *glycation*, which is another damaging factor of equal standing with free radicals in oxidation and inflammation. To gain a basic understanding of glycation, consider that proteins are formed from amino acids and are essential for life, because they serve two critical roles. First, proteins provide structure for the body, such as collagen, which accounts for approximately one-third of your body's total protein. It is found in skin, muscles, organs, and vascular structures and provides elasticity and cohesion to these structures. Second, proteins provide function in the form of enzymes that enable all life-sustaining biochemical reactions to occur within your body. Meanwhile, sugar, a simple carbohydrate, provides needed energy for your cells. When properly controlled and running smoothly, proteins and sugars interact without causing damage to the body.

> What is food to one man may be fierce poison to others.
>
> LUCRETIUS

Unfortunately, though, if during this process a sugar molecule (carbohydrate) attaches itself or cross-links with a protein molecule, the result is the formation of a nonfunctioning glycated protein structure called Advanced Glycation End products, or AGEs, which significantly alter the structure and function of proteins.[101] It is ironic that the acronym is AGE, because it really is an accelerated aging process. This process is known as the Maillard or browning reaction and was first noted during the heating of foods in the presence of sugars. AGEs bind to a specific receptor for advanced glycated end products (RAGE), which is located on cells of the immune system (macrophages and T-cells), cells lining the blood vessels (endothelium), and vascular smooth muscle cells. The binding of AGE to the receptor, RAGE, results in damaging effects on those cells.

> Food, one assumes, provides nourishment; but Americans eat it fully aware that small amounts of poison have been added to improve its appearance and delay its putrefaction.
>
> JOHN CAGE

While AGEs are destructive enough on their own, their interaction with free radicals causes even more havoc in the aging human body. Many researchers suggest that oxidative stress may be involved in AGE formation and that, in a vicious cycle, AGEs may induce even more oxidative stress. In fact, most AGEs that accumulate in proteins are produced under oxidative conditions. As these AGEs and free radicals accumulate in cells and tissues, molecular damage and degradation down to the level of DNA increase, leading to many of the conditions associated with growing old. A growing body of scientific evidence theorizes that AGEs and similar molecules, such as advanced lipoxidation end products, or ALEs (the products of lipids cross-linking with sugars), are significant contributors to many common pathological processes leading to conditions such as Alzheimer's disease, cancer, heart disease, type 2 diabetes, kidney disorders, atherosclerosis, high blood pressure, stroke, visual impairment, and skin disorders.[102]

Because proteins are present throughout the body, it makes sense that the destructive capacity of AGEs is vast. Understanding how to prevent the formation of AGEs is critical to slowing the aging process and reducing the risk for degenerative diseases.

Two Primary Sources for AGEs

There are two primary sources for AGEs. The first source is the food we eat. The browning of food is a cooking technique that helps to give desirable flavor to food. It is achieved by heating or cooking sugars with proteins in the absence of water, and in this process AGEs are formed. Since grains, vegetables, fruits, and meat all have proteins, this browning effect is an indication of AGEs. It is estimated that 30 percent of food-borne AGEs are absorbed when ingested.

The second source for AGEs happens inside your body through normal metabolism and aging. Carbohydrates, either simple or complex, are absorbed by your body to affect your blood sugar levels. Most of your blood sugar goes to providing the energy your body needs to properly function. However, a small proportion of your blood sugar binds to proteins in your blood and creates AGEs, which can lead to many types of dysfunction, including autoimmunity.

Because of chronically elevated blood sugar levels, diabetics have consistently faced the added challenge of AGEs. Unfortunately, this problem has also become a significant issue for the general population. *During the past 30 years, sugar consumption has increased dramatically. Simple sugars such as fructose and galactose undergo glycation at about 10 times a higher rate than glucose. Most sweeteners today are approximately 50 percent fructose or a fructose derivative.*

Add to this the complication of inflammation. Inflammation increases with weight gain, and weight gain promotes inflammation. Sugar is the greatest inflammatory substance in our diet, but trans fats are not far behind. Trans fats promote inflammation by blocking the receptors that normally switch your metabolism on and off. The result is a vicious cycle of metabolic lethargy and increased insulin resistance.[103] Medical evidence suggests that obesity-related insulin resistance may be due, in part, to chronic inflammation.[104] The C-reactive protein (hs-CRP) blood test is the best method for measuring the body's general level of inflammation. It does not, however, identify the cause of inflammation.

Inhibiting the formation of AGEs and associated molecules is thus an essential part of any anti-aging protocol. According to a paper on how AGEs affect aging, "Inhibition of AGE/ALE formation is a reasonable target for life-span extension for several reasons. First, if damage to protein reflects damage to DNA, then inhibition of AGE/ALE formation…should limit damage and mutation in DNA, leading to an increase in maximum life span. Second, accumulation of AGE/ALEs in proteins is associated with a number of age-related, chronic diseases… inhibition of AGE/ALE formation might delay the progression pathology in these diseases, thereby improving the quality of life in old age…. A third consideration is that inhibition of AGE/ALE formation might also limit secondary oxidative damage to biomolecules."[105]

Uncooked and Cooked Foods

Cooked foods and sugar are the primary contributors to glycation. The Four Corners of Superfood Nutrition is an anti-inflammatory, antioxidant, and anti-glycation diet. If you follow my guidelines, it will go a long way in your fight against the Big Four—glycation, inflammation, oxidation, and angiogenesis.

Regarding these, *I recommend eating at least one half of your diet as uncooked or minimally cooked live foods, mostly vegetables.* While it may be impossible to totally avoid foods cooked at high temperatures, it is possible to reduce exposure by changing the way food is prepared. Consider steaming, boiling, poaching, stewing, stir-frying, or using a slow cooker. These methods not only cook foods with a lower amount of heat, but they create more moisture during the cooking process. Water or moisture can help delay the browning reaction associated with higher temperature cooking. Marinating foods in olive oil, cider vinegar, garlic, mustard, lemon juice, and dry wines can also help.

Avoid foods cooked at high temperature, such as fried, barbecued, broiled, or cooked in the microwave. Remember that any food, *not just meat,* exposed to extreme high heat can scorch the natural sugars in food and create fat-inducing toxins. Foods often cooked with high heat include many prepackaged foods that have been preserved, pasteurized, homogenized, or refined, such as the usual suspects—dried milk, dried eggs, white flour, cake mixes, dairy products, including pasteurized milk, and canned or frozen precooked meals.

Interestingly, diabetics were studied to assess the difference between consuming a diet high in foods cooked at higher temperatures compared with foods cooked at lower temperatures. After six weeks, diabetics consuming the foods cooked at lower temperatures lost weight, and their blood glucose levels dropped. The group eating foods cooked at higher temperatures did not lose weight and had increased blood glucose levels. The number of calories and amounts of carbohydrates, proteins, and fats consumed were the same in both groups.[106]

Carnosine

Fortunately, we have easy access to a safe, well-tolerated dietary supplement—carnosine—that helps protect against the ravages of oxidative damage while inhibiting the formation of AGEs. Naturally present in high concentrations in human brain and skeletal muscle tissue, carnosine has been shown in multiple studies to inhibit lipid peroxidation and free radical-induced cellular damage. Additional evidence suggests that carnosine may help protect the brain against oxygen deprivation,[107] delay the impairment of eyesight with aging,[108] and extend the life span of mammals.[109] In addition, scientists have now shown that carnosine can effectively inhibit AGE formation and protein cross-linking.[110]

> All I ask of food is that it doesn't harm me.
>
> MICHAEL PALIN

By protecting against both free radical-generated oxidative damage and AGE-generated cellular toxicity, carnosine helps to counteract numerous potentially harmful biochemical processes associated with aging. Its diverse effects offer support for the aging brain and cardiovascular system. Carnosine's remarkable spectrum of health benefits makes this versatile nutrient an essential component of any anti-aging and weight loss program.

Choose Anti-inflammatory Foods

A study that was epublished on May 6, 2009, showed that Japanese individuals who were on a low carbohydrate diet could reduce AGEs levels in otherwise healthy overweight and obese subjects.[111] They demonstrated that serum AGEs can be reduced by a low carbohydrate diet intervention on weight loss, a change that correlates with the reduction in triglycerides.

The Four Corners of Superfood Nutrition is low sugar, low glycemic, and loaded with a broad spectrum of antioxidants. It helps regulate and quench the destructive hyper-aging fire of the Big Four. You can slow down your aging process and help stave off heart disease, cancer, and diabetes. Within my diet, here are the specifics regarding glycation and anti-inflammation.

Proteins. Follow my list of recommendations for proteins, with an emphasis on lean poultry, eggs, fish, nuts, legumes, seeds, and high quality protein powders and free-form essential amino acid supplements. Red meats may trigger inflammation, so restrict the fatty red meats and preferably choose leaner cuts of meats and include grass-fed beef, bison, venison, and other game meats.

Carbohydrates and Fiber. Most of your carbohydrates should come from vegetables and some fruits and a small part from the grains that I have in the Super Health Diet food lists. Minimize bread, cereal, and pasta in your diet. Vegetables and fruits also offer excellent dietary fiber, and a high fiber diet can help reduce inflammation. Berries are a great food choice, especially blueberries, cranberries, raspberries, and strawberries, which are packed with anti-inflammatory phytochemicals and antioxidants. The quercetin found in apple and red onion skins has strong anti-inflammatory properties. Other exceptional sources of healthy nutrient-dense carbohydrates are fresh vegetable juices and grain grasses, such as barley grass, rye grass, and wheat grass.

Fats and Oils. I've already made it clear that the right types of fats in your diet will impact your health and weight loss in a positive way, but keep in mind that the omega-3 essential fatty acids I've written about are very powerful anti-inflammatory agents. They are found in cold water oily fish, walnuts, chia seeds, flaxseeds, and pumpkin seeds. Adding omega-3 fatty acid supplements from fish oil or and flax oil (to a lesser extent) may also help reduce inflammation. Olive oil is another type of oil that has been shown to reduce inflammation.

Healthy Beverages. Follow the advice I've given in this book regarding what you drink every day, remembering that the simplest and best form of water is purified spring water. Other good fluid sources include herbal teas. Naturally sparkling waters can be healthy and fun but are not to be relied on for hydration. SoDelicious brand coconut milk or Almond Breeze almond, rice, and oat milks are good options. (See Four Corners Shopping List.)

Capsaicin (from cayenne pepper), green tea, ginger, turmeric, cocoa, probiotics (*Lactobacillus acidophilus, Bifidobacterium bifidum*), bromelain and proteolytic enzymes (taken on an empty stomach), and the anti-aging chemical resveratrol are all good for reducing inflammation. Ginkgo, green tea polyphenols, grape seed extract, milk thistle, rosemary, N-acetylcysteine, lipoic acid, and coenzyme Q10 help prevent oxidative stress and, as is true of many antioxidants, can help offset inflammation and glycation.

Preventing the Problems of Angiogenesis

Angiogenesis, the natural growth of new capillary blood vessels in the body for healing and reproduction, completes my Big Four. Our bodies control angiogenesis by producing a precise balance of growth and inhibitory factors in healthy tissues. If, however, the balance is disturbed, it produces abnormal blood vessel growth, either excessive or insufficient, and is recognized as a common denominator shared by a myriad of diseases that includes all cancers, cardiovascular disease, obesity, arthritis, blindness, complications of AIDS, diabetes, Alzheimer's disease, and dozens of other major health conditions.

When our body is healthy, it maintains the balance of angiogenesis modulators known as angiogenesis-stimulating growth factors ("on" switches) and angiogenesis inhibitors ("off" switches). When angiogenic growth factors are produced in excess of inhibitors, the balance shifts in favor of blood vessel growth, resulting in problems. When inhibitors are present in excess of stimulators, angiogenesis is stopped. In general, angiogenesis is "turned off" by the production of more inhibitors than stimulators.

Excessive angiogenesis occurs in diseases such as cancer, obesity, diabetic blindness, age-related macular degeneration, psoriasis, rheumatoid arthritis, and many other conditions. In the case of obesity, each additional pound of body fat requires about one mile of new angiogenic vessels. In all these conditions, new blood vessels feed diseased tissues, destroy normal tissues, and in the case of cancer, the new vessels allow tumor cells to escape into the circulation and lodge in other organs (tumor metastases). Because of abnormal amounts of angiogenic growth factors, it overwhelms the effects of natural inhibitors.

Insufficient angiogenesis occurs when tissues cannot produce adequate amounts of angiogenic growth factors and is seen in diseases such as coronary artery disease, stroke, and chronic wounds. In these conditions, blood vessel growth is inadequate, and circulation is not properly restored, leading to the risk of tissue death.

Angiogenesis-based medicine—restoring the body's natural control of angiogenesis—is a new, comprehensive approach to fighting disease. By using new medical treatments that either inhibit or stimulate angiogenesis, doctors are prolonging the lives of cancer patients, preventing limb amputations, reversing vision loss, and improving general health, which is fantastic.

However, a far better route is to prevent angiogenesis problems from starting in the first place. One solution is replacing a poor diet, which is the origin of many angiogenesis issues, with a Super Health Diet. We must add to our diets the foods that boost the body's defense system and essentially eat right to prevent angiogenesis, including its profound feeding of fat in obesity. *Fat is angiogenesis-dependent, and angiogenesis inhibitors directly result in weight loss and inhibit the development of fat.*

The good news is there are numerous foods and supplements that have been shown to have significant antiangiogenesis properties. Interestingly, the same foods also have antioxidation, anti-inflammation, anti-glycation, and antiangiogenic properties. Plus, research has shown a miraculous synergy in food/nutrient combinations to be more potent than any one by itself, which has been my philosophy of Superfood Nutrition from the beginning. Living Fuel Functional Superfoods have been lab tested to be a potent regulator/inhibitor of *all* four of these processes, and I do not know of any other food or product that can make that claim. (See Shopping List or Smart Meals and Super-Smoothie Recipes for product information.)

Angiogenesis Regulating Foods

Apples
Artichokes
Blackberries
Blueberries
Bok choy
Cherries
Dark chocolate
Fish Oil EPA/DHA
Garlic
Ginseng
Grapefruit
Grapeseed oil and extracts
Green tea
Kale
Lavender
Lemons
Licorice
Lycopene
Maitake mushrooms
Nutmeg
Olive oil
Olives
Oranges
Parsley
Pineapples
Pumpkin
Raspberries
Red grapes
Red wine
Sea cucumber
Soybeans
Strawberries
Tuna
Turmeric
Tomato

Special thanks to the Angiogenesis Foundation (www.angio.org) and, in particular, Dr. William Li, for much of this information and insight into angiogenesis as well as the food list.

THE
SUPER
HEALTH
DIET

Golden
Keys
to Unlock
Lifelong
Vitality

Chapter 13

Meal Frequency, Snacks, and Eating Speed

*Another good reducing exercise consists in
placing both hands against the table
edge and pushing back.*
ROBERT QUILLEN

The debate as to whether it is better to eat three traditional meals or six small meals a day may seem like an age-old question to nutritionists, but many point back to research that began 45 years ago. Hejde and Fabry and their colleagues studied 379 men (ages 60 to 64) to see whether or not there was a difference in body fat between eating three meals per day and eating five meals per day. They observed that men who ate three meals per day had larger skin folds than the men who ate five or more meals per day.[112]

Since that time, many research studies have aimed to determine whether or not the popular dietary trend of "grazing" can influence body weight or energy intake better than eating traditional meals can. The research I have read on this issue is inconclusive. Some studies have supported one approach; other studies have supported the other. While there is a clear consensus among nutrition experts that irregular eating patterns and skipped meals can mean trouble for most of us when it comes to weight loss, there isn't anything close to a consensus on whether we are metabolically better off eating three regular meals a day or spreading that out into five or six smaller meals.

The basic idea behind grazing is that going too long without eating will cause your metabolism (how fast the body burns calories) to slow or shut down. One example of this concept is found in Jorge Cruise's book, *The 3-Hour Diet.* His plan directs you to eat breakfast within one hour of rising, eat every three hours throughout the day, and stop eating three hours before bedtime. He says this systematic method of eating increases BMR (basal metabolic rate), increases energy levels, and decreases appetite, among other healthy benefits. The reasonable and clinical-sounding explanation for this approach is the reason grazing has almost become dietary dogma in many nutrition circles.

Does Eating More Meals Stimulate Metabolism?

One argument for eating five or six small meals a day is that when the body is deprived of food for a period of time, it will switch naturally to "starvation mode." By eating every few hours, there's no question that we signal our bodies to continue to burn calories. I have used the same "starvation" premise in this book as a warning against suddenly adopting a low calorie diet. It is true that in famine situations, when our bodies are given fewer calories, they will slow our metabolism to burn whatever fat stores we already have, thus protecting us for survival. That is a good thing.

However, here's the problem regarding this argument for eating six meals a day. While it is true our bodies do respond to a prolonged fast by slowing our metabolism to conserve energy, the key word is "prolonged." As Monica Reinagel, the Nutrition Diva, has stated: "Your body doesn't go into starvation mode if you go four hours without food. In fact, it takes about *three days of fasting or serious caloric restriction* for your body to respond with any sort of metabolic adjustment." In other words, three to six hours or even longer between meals is not going to kick your body into starvation mode.

There are really two issues that are generally being bundled into a single issue in people's minds and referred to as *metabolic rate.* The two reasons most people believe eating more frequently is best are true metabolic rate and catabolism of lean body mass. Metabolic rate is basically how much energy—carbohydrates, fats, and proteins—your body is burning while at rest. Catabolism is how long the body can go without going into a catabolic state (breaking down lean body mass to be used as building blocks or fuel in the body).

Metabolism is regulated by the thyroid. The thyroid resets metabolism every few days in response to the amount of calories ingested. A slowed metabolic rate is like the car at a traffic stop that is sputtering to stay running. When one goes on a low calorie diet for several days without the right amount and proportion of essential nutrients, including protein, the thyroid will reset to "starvation mode" or a state of lower energy expenditure. The goal is to keep your metabolism running strong by optimizing nutrition even while on a low calorie diet and not signaling a metabolic slowdown.

Catabolic means to "break down" and is the opposite of *anabolic*, which means to "build up." Simplified, catabolic is when blood levels of amino acids, sugar, and other nutrients have been depleted and the body has need for fuel or repair. The body then sends hormonal signals to release stored nutrients and to break down tissues to acquire any other needed raw materials. Catabolic hormones include cortisol, glucagon, adrenaline, and other catecholamines ("fight-or-flight" hormones released by the adrenal glands in response to stress). The body feeds off itself for raw materials if they are not otherwise available.

Metabolic adjustment and catabolism serve important functions within the body; however, it is critically important for them to be optimized. You want to maximize your resting metabolic rate and minimize catabolism. Catabolism of stored fat is very desirable, but loss of muscle and lean body mass is not.

Noralyn Mills, R.D., a spokeswoman for the American Dietetic Association, states that when we feed our body at regular intervals, we send a signal to our body that it doesn't have to store calories, but when we skip meals, we affect the metabolism negatively. "But," she also specifies, "this can be accomplished with three regular meals a day for many of us." The reality is that most people would be far better off skipping a meal than eating what they typically eat.

When looking at digestion speed of various foods and how the endocrine system works best, it would seem that eating three meals per day allows for normal digestion time and optimal endocrine function.

Eating too often can cause digestive congestion and chronically higher blood sugar and insulin levels that can lead to diabetes, Syndrome X, and virtually every other disease you can name.

What About the "Thermic Effect of Food"?

Another argument for adding meals to your day regards the amount of energy that your body burns in releasing energy from your food, called "the thermic effect of food" by scientists. It is based upon the same principle that I use to argue for eating a low glycemic diet. The concept is that if you are eating a 450-calorie meal, low glycemic foods will cause your body to burn more calories than high glycemic foods in the conversion of the food into cellular energy. In this scenario, if you burn 45 calories in the process rather than 20, the body is receiving only 405 calories and 25 less because of the quality of your foods.

> **Bigger snacks mean bigger slacks.**
>
> AUTHOR UNKNOWN

But does this principle translate to meaning that if your body is constantly in the process of digesting food, it will constantly be burning calories (via the thermic effect of food). No! Karen Collins, M.S., R.D., with the American Institute for Cancer Research, noted a study that showed the basal metabolic rate (the number of calories you'd burn if you stayed in bed all day) was unaffected by differences in meal timing. In an *American Journal of Clinical Nutrition* editorial, a team of nutrition researchers concluded that whether you are practicing the three or six meal dietary pattern, weight loss ultimately comes down to "how much energy (or calories) is consumed as opposed to how often and how regularly one eats." In other words, we are back to the tried-and-true equation for weight maintenance: "Calories in, Calories out."

As far as actually increasing the calories we burn, "The only thing that has been consistently shown to increase the basal metabolic rate is exercise," says Vicki Sullivan, Ph.D., R.D., L.D., national lecturer and president of Balance, LLC. That also puts us back to proven formulas for weight loss.

Once again, it has been shown that people can lose weight for a time whether they eat one meal per day or six or more meals as long as calorie intake is reduced or exercise is increased. *We need to keep in mind that our goal is Super Health not temporary weight loss.*

What About Maintaining Sugar Levels?

You know from what I've already written in this book that I am a proponent of avoiding the highs and lows of blood sugar levels that are particularly peaked by high glycemic foods. Many people say that eating small, frequent meals helps to keep blood sugar levels steady. Sounds good, right? And sounds reasonable. But here's the problem. While it keeps your blood sugar relatively steady, it also keeps the levels steadily high, which is not what you want.

> Inside some of us is a thin person struggling to get out, but they can usually be sedated with a few pieces of chocolate cake.
>
> AUTHOR UNKNOWN

It is both normal and good for your blood sugars to rise after meals, as food is digested and converted into glucose, and then fall back to baseline as the glucose is taken up by your cells and used for energy or stored for future use. In fact, research shows that having your blood sugar closer to baseline for more of the day helps to protect you from developing diabetes. *The key is to avoid the peaks or spikes to blood sugar levels that occur when you eat high glycemic foods—*sweets, sweetened beverages, white bread, and other refined carbohydrates. Your blood sugars shoot up very quickly and then naturally come crashing down, causing you to want to eat more of the same kinds of poor food choices. It is the well paved road that so many take to type 2 diabetes today.

I've already outlined how important it is to get off this road with the right diet.

What About Snacking Between Meals?

I have addressed this topic in various ways throughout this book. Some researchers have found an association between snacking between meals and obesity. By contrast, other researchers found that increasing meal frequency was associated with lower body weight in men, but not in women. Other researchers have also suggested that larger, less frequent meals increase the risk of obesity, heart disease, and diabetes. As noted before, there's really no consensus on the research.

While proponents of frequent snacking have some positives to point to, the truth is, the more times a day you sit down to eat a meal or grab a quick snack, the more times the door swings open to overeating. And the human reality is that, when given the opportunity, most of us choose to overeat. I've seen it occur hundreds of times to those who increase the number of times they eat every day. Most of us find it almost impossible to eat a small amount at a meal or snack, and it's almost a given that our snacks will load on the calories.

On the more technical side of snacking, I have a few more points to make that you need to read carefully. Keep in mind that the metabolic impact of the low glycemic meals I advocate versus high glycemic meals is significantly different. I have shown that the rise in blood sugar and insulin output is less when the absorption of carbohydrate is delayed. For instance, when compared to a high glycemic breakfast, a low glycemic breakfast lowers concentrations of insulin, blood sugar, free fatty acids, and triglycerides after the meal and even after a subsequent standard lunch meal, which is precisely what you want. It is believed that if lower glycemic foods are consumed, which are digested and absorbed more slowly, there appears to be less metabolic advantage to spreading those foods out over smaller, more frequent meals. That would be a significant loss.[113]

One study I read looked at the impact of a snack consumed after a standard lunch but before the subjects became hungry. The researchers fed subjects a snack (400 kilocalories) at various times after a 1,300-kilocalorie lunch when they were not hungry. *The snack did not reduce the amount of food consumed at the dinner meal and did not increase the time before the subjects requested their dinner meal.* This strongly suggests that snacking when not hungry promotes increased calorie intake and weight gain over time. When rich, highly palatable foods are readily available, as is so often true of snacks, food consumption may be triggered by mealtime or pleasure and not necessarily because of hunger or the need for extra calories.[114]

In another study, eight normal weight young men were examined concerning the impact of consuming either no snack, a high protein or a high carbohydrate snack either when subjects were hungry or when they were not hungry. The subjects were given the snacks between a standard lunch and dinner and were unaware of the time. The high protein snack delayed when the evening meal was requested and eaten by 38 minutes, but it *did not reduce the energy intake* compared to when no snack was offered. In fact, energy intake from the evening meal was even slightly higher when they consumed the high protein snack compared to no snack at all. The average energy intake was higher on the day they consumed the high carbohydrate snack than when they had no snack at all or when they consumed the high protein snack, which makes sense. The authors concluded that "a snack consumed in a satiety state has poor satiating efficiency irrespective of its composition, which is evidence that snacking plays a role in obesity."[115] In other words, snacking when you are hungry does not reduce the amounts of food eaten at subsequent meals.

> **Rich, fatty foods are like destiny: they, too, shape our ends.**
>
> AUTHOR UNKNOWN

I conclude that eating six smaller meals a day or snacking is disruptive to normal metabolic, digestive, and endocrine function and will almost always push up your caloric intake.

My position is that one needs to eat three planned, well-balanced meals per day, with five or six hours between meals, and without snacking between meals or within three hours of bedtime. I am a strong advocate for learning what and how much to eat in order to avoid crashing between meals—being as careful to not overeat as to not "under fuel." This is critical to both weight loss as well as Super Health.

Maximum Metabolic Mode

For about three to four hours after you begin eating a typical meal, your body is operating in what is called a "fully fed state." Essentially, your body is operating on what you just ate. From that point your insulin levels return to pre-meal levels, and the body is fueled from stored energy that is being released in a catabolic process. I call this state *"maximum metabolic mode," which is the time when the most body fat is being burned.* This mode can continue for another 12 to 18 hours until you eat again. This is because your bloodstream contains a steady supply of essential nutrients to stave off the breakdown of lean body mass while your endocrine system is signaling for the release of stored energy. The moment you eat anything that provokes a significant rise in blood sugar, this maximum metabolic mode stops. Because of snacking and eating too frequently, most people spend little or no time in maximum metabolic mode.

There remains the issue of catabolism of muscle and lean body mass during extended periods of maximum metabolic mode. Depending on the amount and kind of protein or amino acids consumed at the previous meal, catabolism of muscle and lean body mass can begin within four to six hours. This is one situation where my "Stealth Technique" or "Micro Fast" technique of delivering essential amino acids to the bloodstream can help stave off muscle loss without disrupting the body's maximum metabolic mode. (See "The Dynamic Role of Protein in Weight Loss" chapter.)

This strongly suggests that eating three meals per day is better than six for weight optimization.

Many people say they cannot go six hours without eating for any number of reasons, and some conclude they are hypoglycemic, which is true for some. But just because someone believes they cannot go that long does not invalidate how important it is for their health and longevity. For many of these people, it is just a matter of learning to fuel properly and even training themselves to allow more time between meals. Interestingly, some people are diagnosed with hypoglycemia because of years of improper fueling, resulting in tired adrenal glands. The conventional medical approach to hypoglycemia is to eat more frequently, which tends to further exacerbate the problem—a vicious cycle for sure. The conventional medical approach to treating pre-diabetes and diabetes is equally maddening. For those of you who are dealing with these conditions, I want to tell you there is hope beyond your doctor's office. I have seen it and firmly believe that many blood sugar issues, including hypoglycemia, type 2 diabetes, and Syndrome X, can be reversed through diet and lifestyle changes.

Spacing your three meals out more can actually have some additional beneficial effects on your blood sugar and on other aspects of your health. It takes about three hours for your body to digest a meal. If you eat every two or three hours, your body will constantly be in the process of digesting food, which nutritionists call the "fed state." If, however, you don't snack or eat again, you'll go into the post-absorptive state or maximum metabolic mode after about three hours. Keep in mind that eating is one of the most taxing things we do to our bodies, and it is important to allow time for proper digestion, assimilation, and endocrine function.

Several beneficial actions happen in the post-absorptive state. First, you begin to tap into your body's stored energy reserves to run your engine. How so? Your hormone levels adjust to shift your body out of fat-storage mode and into fat-burning mode. It also reduces free radical damage and inflammation, increases the production of antiaging hormones, and promotes tissue repair. Meanwhile, your metabolic rate remains unchanged.

If you need to snack, make sure you have a snack strategy and inventory on hand. Snacking on combinations of carbohydrates and proteins, including sports drinks, protein bars, bananas, etc., are often necessary during workouts and athletic events. Otherwise, it is best to learn to fuel yourself for five to six hours without snacking as discussed earlier in this chapter and within "The Dynamic Role of Proteins in Weight Loss" chapter. In the event you need to snack, eat small portions that have a minimal effect on blood sugar and insulin levels, such as essential amino acids, protein powder, soft-boiled eggs, raw nuts and seeds (walnuts, almonds, macadamia nuts, Brazil nuts, coconut, chia seeds, and pumpkin seeds). Eat organic whenever possible.

Change Your Breakfast, Change Your Life

I have long said "change your breakfast, change your life." Most people make the biggest mistakes at breakfast, ranging from not eating to eating high carbohydrate, low protein, empty calorie foods, including breakfast cereals, breads, and juices. Their minds seem to be engrained with the thought that only certain foods are breakfast foods.

If you regularly eat these "breakfast foods," you can experience dramatic changes in the way you feel and the way you look by getting a quality blender and changing your breakfast to a high protein Super-Smoothie. If you are a person who is routinely not hungry at breakfast time, I highly recommend applying my Micro Fast technique instead of breakfast. (See the FUEL Fast and Micro Fast section within "The Dynamic Role of Proteins in Weight Loss" chapter.)

Whether you eat three or six meals a day, breakfast is still the first meal. "Getting people to eat breakfast at all would be a great improvement and is a long-standing, well-documented way to help with weight loss and weight management," says Vicki Sullivan, Ph.D. and president of Balance, LLC.

According to Lisa Most, R.D., clinical dietitian at Greater Baltimore Medical Center, your metabolism increases if you eat breakfast. British scientists found that women who skipped breakfast ate more calories during the rest of the day and also had higher fasting levels of LDL (bad cholesterol) and total cholesterol compared with the women in the breakfast-eating group. The researchers noted that skipping breakfast could lead to weight gain if the higher calorie intake was sustained.

At the 43rd Annual Conference of the American Heart Association in March 2003, a study was presented reporting that people who eat breakfast every day are less likely to be obese and diabetic. In contrast to subjects who ate breakfast twice a week or less, subjects eating breakfast every day had 35 to 50 percent lower rates of obesity and insulin resistance. Dr. Mark A. Pereira, a scientist involved in the study, stated that breakfast may reduce the risk of obesity, type 2 diabetes, and cardiovascular disease by controlling appetite and reducing the likelihood of overeating later in the day.

In 1993, the *American Journal of Clinical Nutrition* published a study reporting that food eaten early in the day generated more energy (diet-induced thermogenesis) than food eaten later in the day.[116] This study provided evidence that the body's basal metabolic rate is highest early in the day, burning off calories as energy, whereas these same calories consumed at night are more likely to be stored as fat. Based on this evidence, some physicians advocate that overweight patients should not eat anything after

7 p.m. I believe it is really important to weight optimization and Super Health to stop eating within two to three hours of going to sleep. One exception might be for those working to gain weight.

If you add proper nutrition to your pre-day routine, you won't leave yourself open to the unhealthy foods available in snack machines or in restaurants.

Eating Speed

If your mother constantly reminded you to slow down and completely chew your food, I hope for your health's sake that you followed her wise advice. Interesting research from independent sources during the past few years proposes that you can reduce your intake of calories and make a significant reduction in weight gain by implementing your mom's extraordinarily simple eating trick: *Slow it down.*

In a study published in the 2008 *British Medical Journal,* K. Maruyama and his fellow researchers examined whether eating until full or eating quickly or combinations of these eating behaviors are associated with being overweight in Japanese men and women. They found that fast eaters are significantly more likely to be overweight or obese. Additionally, those who continue eating until they feel full are also more likely to be overweight. They concluded: "Eating until full and eating quickly are associated with, and these eating behaviors combined may have a substantial impact on being overweight."[117]

In the July 2008 *Journal of American Dietetic Association,* A. M. Andrade published study results of research that "sought to compare the impact of slow and quick eating rates on development of satiation [feeling full] in healthy women." The study utilized two test groups, with each group being given large portions of food and instructions to consume as much as desired. One group was given big spoons and advised to eat quickly. The other group got small spoons and was directed to eat slowly, taking the time to chew each bite 20 or so times. The result was unmistakable: Fewer calories were consumed when the meal was eaten slowly, and feeling fuller was higher at meal completion. "Although more study is needed, this data suggests that eating slowly may help to maximize satiation and reduce energy intake within meals."[118]

One other study was published in the January 2010 *Journal of Clinical Endocrinology and Metabolism* that purposed to determine whether eating the same meal at varying speeds elicits different postprandial gut peptide (gut hormone) responses. A. Kokkinos and other researchers at the Athens University Medical School found that eating speed does affect certain hormone levels in our body, which in turn interact with the hypothalamus (an area of the brain that produces hormones that control an immense number of bodily functions) to create the feeling of hunger or fullness—specifically, the hormones PYY, GLP-1, and ghrelin. This research found that levels of both PYY and GLP-1, which cause a body to feel full, are significantly higher when a person eats slowly. It was found that ghrelin levels, which cause the feeling of hunger, were higher two hours after eating for those who ate quickly.[119] It appears that hormone levels are responsible for the fullness slow eaters feel and the hunger fast eaters feel. Bottom line: Fast eaters feel both less full after eating more food and hungrier just a couple hours after eating than do slow eaters—that's a double whammy.

You may be familiar with how much food teenage boy athletes eat. My seventeen-year-old son, Kyle, says, "I never get full; I just get tired of chewing!" Nevertheless, eating slowly may be the easiest and most effective tip that you'll ever find regarding losing weight or maintaining a healthy weight. You may have laughed in Chapter 1 when I referred to William Gladstone, who in the late 1800s promoted chewing food 32 times before swallowing, thus lessening the appetite and leading to weight loss and better health. But eating slowly is effective—you'll eat fewer calories, feel fuller after your meal, and go longer before feeling the need to eat again. How can you beat that? Take these studies and your mother's advice to heart and change your habits today!

Chapter 14

Exercise, Weight Loss, and Health

Food fuels the furnace of metabolism;
exercise stokes its fire.
MAJID ALI, M.D.

Nutrition and exercise are two of my Seven Golden Keys to Super Health and lifelong vitality. The benefits of exercise are so well known that if it were in a pill, everyone would pay anything it costs to get it. If you have been waiting around for such a magic pill that will melt the fat away and keep the weight off of your body, you've wasted enough time. The good news is that exercise is free, and some of the best exercises can be done at home and really don't take much time—only knowledge, motivation, and accountability.

And if you think that diet alone will somehow help you gain the benefits of exercise, think again. Nutrition alone can deliver weight loss, but not all the benefits of exercise. While I put a huge emphasis on superfood nutrition and restricted caloric intake, Super Health requires both superfood nutrition and smart exercise. Many dieticians and nutritionists will tell you that it's all about "calories in, calories out." They are correct in telling you that if you have a calorie deficit, you're most likely to lose weight, and vice versa, but they often miss the point about how your body actually uses calories. Weight loss is not just about calories.

Our bodies are designed to naturally burn fat and build muscle as you eat right and exercise. Our muscles burn calories 24/7. More lean muscle mass allows us to actually eat more calories without gaining weight. Your body is a gift that keeps on giving if you treat it right. It is possible to achieve a strong, healthy, beautifully shaped body that is full of energy and vitality for a lifetime. But if you're among the 50 percent of Americans who live a sedentary lifestyle, you're not giving your body a chance to function in the healthy way it was designed to function. Despite repeated warnings from the Surgeon General, the American Heart Association, and the National Center for Chronic Disease Prevention, millions of Americans are suffering from illnesses that can be prevented or improved through regular exercise.

There's a simple reason why exercise is a huge key to weight loss. *Exercise burns calories and stimulates the growth of more muscle. Nothing else will do that, although we have seen that protein also stimulates the building of muscle.* (See "The Dynamic Role of Protein in Weight Loss" chapter.)

And there's a simple reason why exercise is so key to Super Health. "Every time you work out and sweat, you stress your muscles, draining them of energy stores; you actually injure them a little bit. It's not enough to do long-term damage, but enough to stimulate repair and growth and to make muscles a little stronger. Enzymes and proteins from those muscles enter your bloodstream, where they start a powerful chain reaction of [catabolism (breaking down)], then repair, and finally growth. And what [a miraculous] process this is: The proteins that control inflammation and growth are called cytokines, and they regulate crucial metabolic pathways in almost every tissue and cell in your body.... Even moderate exercise will stimulate the good guys—growth cytokines—that will eventually overwhelm the agents of [catabolism].... Every joint, bone, organ, and even the far reaches of your brain get a dose of healthy, rejuvenating chemistry each time you sweat."[120]

Studies show that the benefits of exercise are seemingly endless. People who regularly exercise are at significantly lower risk for all manner of diseases—those of the heart in particular. They less often develop cancer, diabetes, and many other illnesses. It reduces the risk of strokes, improves lung and immune system function, increases mental vitality, and lowers blood pressure, blood glucose, cholesterol, and triglyceride levels. Increased physical activity itself improves insulin sensitivity and mimics the effect of certain anti-diabetic drugs, which can have a favorable effect on body fat contouring.[121] Exercise can dramatically lower the incidence and severity of diseases associated with aging, such as osteoporosis and muscle and bone strength loss. How's that for starters?

How about keeping off weight once you've lost it? In an article in the October 2009 *American Journal of Physiology*, Professor Paul MacLean at the University of Colorado's School of Medicine found in a study of the metabolisms of rats that when he exercised the animals by giving them a daily bout of treadmill exercise, similar to what a lot of people do, it changed their metabolism. He stated, "It lowered their hunger that they were experiencing on a daily basis. And it reduced the amount of weight gain early on, as they relapsed to obesity and ultimately lowered the body weight. So it changed their biology." In other words, the exercise program actually changed the biological drive to eat and suppressed it. MacLean says that may mean exercise can help people stay on their diet and resist the temptation to "succumb to those biological urges of hunger pains that they feel on a daily basis after they've lost weight." It only makes sense that exercise will minimize weight regain after weight loss.[122]

Significant findings published in the journal *PLoS ONE* on May 26, 2010, indicated that dieting alone may not be enough to prevent type 2 diabetes. Researcher Preethi Srikanthan of the University of California, Los Angeles, cautions that sarcopenia—loss of skeletal muscle mass and strength often found in those who are older or obese—may put individuals at risk for developing type 2 diabetes. After looking at the data on 14,528 people from the National Health and Nutrition Examination Survey III, Srikanthan and her colleagues found sarcopenia associated with insulin resistance—the root cause of diabetes—in both obese and non-obese individuals. Low muscle mass and strength was also associated with high blood sugar levels in obese people, but not in thin people. The researcher concluded that given the increasing prevalence of obesity, further research is urgently needed to develop interventions to prevent sarcopenic (muscle wasting) obesity and its metabolic consequences.

Lifelong exercise has been shown to reduce mortality and increase life expectancy. A study published in June 2009 in the journal *Neurology* found that older people who exercise at least once a week are 30 percent more likely to maintain cognitive function than those who exercise less. People who exercise feel better, as exercise causes the release of endorphins, which are the body's natural feel-good hormones. Exercise also helps remove the adrenaline that gets pumped into our bloodstream through stress, and thus it helps keep stress under control. People who exercise perform better in both work and leisure activities and enjoy life more than people who do not exercise regularly.

An article published in the August 2010 *Proceedings of the National Academy of Sciences* reveals a mechanism for exercise and calorie restriction in delaying some of the effects of aging. Dr. Joshua R. Sanes and his Harvard University colleagues stated, "The cellular basis of age-related behavioral decline remains obscure, but alterations in synapses [the connections that exist between nerve cells or nerves and the muscles that they control] are likely candidates. Accordingly, *the beneficial effects on neural function of caloric restriction and exercise, which are among the most effective anti-aging treatments known,* might also be mediated by synapses." Their research compared a synapse in young adult and aged mice. In aged synapses of mice and humans, nerve shrinkage can reduce contact with muscle receptors, leading to sarcopenia, or muscle wasting. However, mice fed a calorie-restricted diet had significant reductions in these age-associated changes. Additionally, one month of exercise partially reversed changes that had already occurred. Dr. Sanes noted, "With calorie restriction, we saw reversal of all aspects of the synapse disassembly. With exercise, we saw a reversal of most, but not all.... This research gives us a hint that the way these extremely powerful lifestyle factors act is by attenuating or reversing the decline in our synapses."[123]

> But I discipline my body and bring it into subjection...
>
> THE APOSTLE PAUL,
> 1 CORINTHIANS 9:27

Exercise throughout life is optimal, but studies have shown people in their 90s can improve strength and increase muscle mass after only two weight training sessions per week for six weeks. Clearly, it is never too late to start, and there's no excuse for couch potatoes.

Where to Start?

Before getting started with a new exercise program, I want to reiterate a couple of critically important points. First, make sure you are adequately hydrated by drinking eight to 12 glasses of water each day for several days before beginning (see "Golden Key #1—Hydration" chapter). Second, before starting any exercise program, I strongly recommend that your daily regimen of foods include fish oil, garlic, onion, hot peppers, vitamins A, D, and E, and other nutrients that help prevent unwanted spontaneous blood clots. These are the nutrients the doctors tell surgery patients not to take within a few days before surgery. In everyday health and exercise, you want free flowing blood to minimize the risk of a clot-induced heart attack or stroke. Third, get an accountability partner who will exercise with you or simply help you to keep your exercise commitments; sometimes it is as easy as hiring a personal trainer.

I firmly believe the last place people need to go to get back in shape is the first place people tend to go—the gym. Dragging your tired metabolism to the gym based on emotion is generally short lived. It is far better to first correct your metabolism through superfood nutrition and the keys presented in this book, and *you will have so much energy you will actually want to go to the gym.*

People who are committed to losing body fat are willing to engage in the effort required to take it off, and few weight loss efforts will work over the long term without the physical body movement component. The dilemma for many people is to find an exercise strategy that really works for them.

For as long as I can remember, I have heard most medical doctors and those involved in the fitness industry say that to lose weight and to have a healthy heart, we must engage in cardiovascular exercise for 30 to 60 minutes per day at a moderate intensity, preferably on most days of the week. Cardio exercise is any activity that uses large muscle groups, is rhythmic in nature, and can be maintained for a period of time—walking, running, biking, swimming, elliptical training, and rowing. This recommendation was based on the vast majority of the early exercise science research and seems to be a permanent fixture in the media and health and fitness industry today.

Before I explain three exercise systems that I believe are *far superior* to conventional exercises, as regards strength building, time, and effectiveness, my first priority is to get you started at whatever level of exercise you can perform. If you can't walk, even just lifting your arms for 10 minutes a day or lifting a one-pound dumbbell over your head 50 times will benefit you. If your health does not allow for a brisk walk outdoors, start with walking in place for five to 10 minutes and increase as you can. You must exercise. Start somewhere. If you can move something, do it!

By way of comparison, a healthy woman of 140 pounds burns about 80 calories per hour while sitting. She'll burn 240 calories an hour if she's doing a light activity, such as cleaning the house. If she is on a brisk walk or vigorously gardening, she'll burn 370 calories per hour. And if she's advanced to jogging (a nine-minute mile), she'll burn 580 calories per hour. A healthy man of 175 pounds will burn slightly more calories than a woman while doing the same activity.

Check with your doctor before starting a new exercise program, especially if you are really out of shape. If you are older than 40 and in poor health, a treadmill test is highly recommended. A physician or exercise specialist can provide this test that checks blood pressure and uses an electrocardiogram to monitor heart performance. These tests should be repeated every three years or as often as your doctor recommends. If you ever have symptoms such as chest pain or pressure, heart irregularity, or unusual shortness of breath, call your doctor immediately.

Depending on your health, I recommend that you consider walking along with learning the Super Health 7 Tiger Moves using low tension as a great starting point for exercise. It is a very doable exercise that costs almost nothing and is very simple to accomplish. Get the right equipment to help you facilitate any exercise. For instance, if you are going to walk or run, go to a shoe store that specializes in running and talk with trained personnel who can help you get what you need.

Start out slowly. If you are really out of shape, it will take time to restore your fitness. The Surgeon General advises overweight individuals to lose weight by walking for 10 minutes three times a week, gradually increasing the amount to 150 minutes a week, which means you'll burn about 525 calories. Pushing too hard can lead to damage. You just need to be consistent.

The point is to get up and get your metabolism going. Take your spouse's hand and head out the door for a comfortable walk, burn some calories, and perhaps put a little spark of romance in your day. Depending on the distance to your job, consider walking. Park your car at the farthest end from the store entrance and take a little stroll before going inside. Something as simple as climbing five flights of stairs every day significantly lowers your risk of heart disease.

To prepare and better endure your workouts, bring some spring water to keep you hydrated and protect you from mineral imbalances (see "Golden Key #1—Hydration"). Do not train too long and too hard at first. One well-known effect of exercise is that it raises oxidative stress and increases free radical production. Though exercise has been shown to improve antioxidant mechanisms, these defenses can be overwhelmed over time, and the risks of increased free radical production are well known, such as damage to DNA and a host of pathologies that are best avoided. So be sure to follow the Four Corners of Superfood Nutrition in this book and take your broad-spectrum antioxidants.

While I want to emphasize that conventional cardio training is extremely health enhancing, I should also note that it is minimally effective in burning fat and losing weight. The December 15, 2008, edition of the *International Journal of Obesity* published a paper by S. L. Gortmaker and Kendrin Sonneville of Children's Hospital Boston, noting that "there is a widespread assumption that increasing activity will result in a net reduction in any energy gap"—*energy gap* being the term scientists use for the difference between the number of calories you use and the number you consume. But Gortmaker and Sonneville found in their 18-month study of 538 students that when kids start to exercise, they end up eating more—not just a little more, but an average of 100 calories more than they had just burned.

In a study released in January 2009, researchers from Loyola University Health System and other centers compared African American women in metropolitan Chicago with women in rural Nigeria. On average, the Chicago women weighed 184 pounds and the Nigerian women weighed 127 pounds. Researchers expected to find that the slimmer Nigerian women would be more physically active. To their surprise, they found no significant difference between the two groups in the amount of calories burned during physical activity. "People burn more calories when they exercise. Thing is, they compensate by eating more," said Richard Cooper, co-author of the study and chairman of the Department of Preventive Medicine and Epidemiology.

The February 18, 2009, peer-reviewed journal *PLoS ONE* published a study by Dr. Timothy Church of the Pennington Biomedical Research Center, Louisiana State University System, and six colleagues that regarded 464 overweight women who didn't regularly exercise. The women were randomly assigned into four groups for six months—three of the groups were asked to work out with a personal trainer for 72 minutes, 136 minutes, and 194 minutes per week, respectively, while the women in the fourth group, the control group, were told to maintain their usual physical-activity routines. All the women were asked not to change their dietary habits and to fill out monthly medical-symptom questionnaires.

On average, the women in all the groups, even the control group, lost weight, but surprisingly the women who exercised with a trainer did not lose significantly more weight than the control subjects did. How is that possible? Dr. Church called it compensation. Whether because exercise made them hungry or because they wanted to reward themselves (or both), most of the women who exercised ate more than they did before they started the experiment. Or they compensated in another way, by moving around a lot less than usual after they got home.

While it's true that typical cardiovascular exercise burns calories and that you must burn calories to lose weight, this type of exercise has another effect: It can stimulate hunger. That causes us to eat more, which in turn can negate the weight loss benefits we just accrued. After we exercise, we often crave sugary calories such as a Starbuck muffin or a "sports" drink such as Gatorade, and because we've just burned off calories, we feel entitled to indulge ourselves. A standard 20-ounce bottle of Gatorade contains 130 calories. If you're hot and thirsty after a 20-minute run in summer heat, it's easy to guzzle that bottle in 20 seconds, in which case the caloric expenditure and the caloric intake are probably a wash. It is a shame to invest so much time in traditional cardio for virtually no weight loss benefits. There is a better way!

"Fitness" Trumps "Fatness"?

I am seeing more articles and studies that suggest there is little health risk to carrying a few extra pounds. The key here would be to make certain the words "a few extra pounds" are emphasized. Don't kid yourself: If you need to lose 30 to 50 pounds, you are not healthy; but I think enough studies have been done to show that it is possible to be healthy and fit with an extra five percent body weight.

Many health experts now say that measuring only an individual's BMI (Body Mass Index), which is a measurement of body fat based on height and weight, can be misleading, and I agree. One reason given is that muscle weighs more than fat, and extremely muscular individuals can actually have BMIs that classify them as overweight or even obese. BMI only works within a range of certain normal size people, and it does not work for taller and larger framed and athletic people.

There really is no perfect way to test body fat, but some are more accurate than others. Being very accurate might be important for an athlete with extremely low body fat levels to avoid getting dangerously low. The vast majority of people really don't need to know their exact body fat percentage. If you are lean, you know it, and if you're too fat for your liking, you know that too. For my purposes, I track changes in my body composition by averaging three-point caliper results (body fat calipers measure skinfolds to calculate how much fat is under the skin) and using the Navy tape method (a series of measurements that you plug into a formula). Body fat measuring devices are widely available on the Internet and at sporting goods stores. A search for body fat calipers or the Navy tape method will give you all the information you need. Remember, the exact number is less important than being able to measure the direction you are going.

> **All true health-building exercise systems prevent injury, speed healing, and are never a source of pain.**

If you surf around the Internet, you will see a lot of different recommendations for body fat percentages. Two sources I trust are from the Sports Performance Institute and the American Journal of Clinical Nutrition based on World Health Organization and National Institutes of Health recommendations. Based on what I've seen, men should strive to be from nine to 22 percent body fat and woman between 14 and 29 percent.

Increasingly, health experts say a better measure of overall health includes not only an evaluation of body fat but a test of "fitness," too. As a result of her research, cardiologist C. Noel Bairey-Merz, the director of the Women's Heart Center as well as the Preventive and Rehabilitative Cardiac Center at Cedars-Sinai Heart Institute, reported in July 2010 that "fitness" now trumps "fatness."[124] She says those who are fit are people who can walk 30 to 60 minutes without having to stop; who can climb two flights of stairs without becoming winded; or who can do some mild to moderate aerobic activity—a brisk walk or short jog, for example. Such routine exercise strengthens heart and lung function, bones and muscles, as well as how the body processes oxygen—all essential to one's fitness.

In one study, Bairey-Merz found that women who were routinely physically active and overweight were less likely to suffer heart problems than their normal weight counterparts who didn't exercise. And conversely, normal weight women who did not exercise, she says, increased their risk of cardiovascular disease.

"Just because someone is slightly overweight doesn't mean they're not healthy," says Keri Gans, a registered dietician and spokeswoman for the American Dietetic Association. Indeed, researchers and doctors are starting to understand that eating healthy foods and getting exercise can matter more than the number that appears when you step on the scale. In two related studies conducted in 2005 and 2007 and published in the *Journal of the American Medical Association*, CDC senior scientist Katherine M. Flegal found that people who are overweight (according to the BMI) are no more likely than those of normal weight to die from cancer or cardiovascular disease.

Steven Blair, a professor of exercise science at the University of South Carolina and a leading expert on the benefits of exercise among the overweight, says, "Fitness is achievable and may do more to improve health than simply losing weight." In fact, a recent study from the university tracked 2,600 people age 60 and older for a 12-year period and found that *fit overweight people outlive unfit normal weight people.*

So while people need to know they can be fit and healthy carrying a few extra pounds but not being obese, the question is where those extra pounds land. Abdominal fat is worse than fat elsewhere in the body. Geriatrician Arun S. Karlamangla is a professor and clinician at UCLA. In one study, he analyzed the health status of more than 4,000 men and women nationwide. He found that men with a waist circumference larger than their hips experienced a 75 percent increase in death rate. For women, risk increased gradually with every inch of increased waist size.

Researchers agree that belly fat is dangerous, because in essence it becomes a powerful endocrine organ that produces inflammatory cytokines and the enzyme aromatase that converts testesterone to estrogen. Abdominal, or visceral, fat increases insulin resistance, which increases levels of insulin floating around in the body, which increases the amount of glucose in the body, which eventually leads to diabetes. Diabetes increases the risk for heart attacks and strokes.

Another interesting study in 2005 showed that obese and overweight individuals suffering metabolic syndrome and type 2 diabetes showed significant health improvements after only three weeks of diet and moderate exercise, even though the participants remained overweight. Lead researcher Christian Roberts of UCLA stated, "This regimen reversed a clinical diagnosis of type 2 diabetes or metabolic syndrome in about half the participants who had either of those conditions…. *The results are all the more interesting because the changes occurred in the absence of major weight loss, challenging the commonly held belief that individuals must normalize their weight before achieving health benefits.*"[125]

Why Strength Building Is Crucial for Weight Loss

Before we look at the Super Health 7 exercise system, here's *why strength building is so crucial.* First of all, without resistance exercises, studies tell us that between the ages of 20 and 30 we begin to lose muscle, and this continues with aging. Loss of muscle slows our body metabolism, leading to fewer calories burned naturally by the body.

Keep in mind that one pound of muscle is thought to burn about 35 calories a day! So, typically, as we age, we lose muscle and gain fat simultaneously, often without noticing it. We may eat the same number of calories and just keep adding the pounds, because of the change in our body composition and progressive loss of digestive efficiency.

Think about it. In an over-simplistic world, there are 3,500 calories stored in every pound of fat. If you were to gain 10 pounds of muscle or lean body mass through exercise, you increase your metabolic rate by about 350 calories a day (10 x 35 calories). Over a period of just 10 days, those 10 new pounds of muscle will burn off one pound of body fat naturally. Think of the new you that's possible and how much better you would feel, and it all happens naturally. *Even if you add only five pounds of muscle, that's 175 extra calories burned a day and 63,875 calories or 18 pounds a year.* Moreover, when you follow the Four Corners Program, along with my other Golden Keys, you will greatly compound the results! Superfood nutrition and optimal protein intake is also a necessary component to successfully growing new muscle. (See "The Dynamic Role of Protein in Weight Loss" and "The Four Corners of Superfood Nutrition.")

> My favorite exercise was to take a bath, pull the plug, fight the current.
>
> ZIG ZIGLAR

The second reason why strength building is so crucial regards what happens when you are overweight or obese and are carrying a high percentage of body fat. Despite your body fat, your body has built up strong muscles in order to carry the extra weight. If you are able to retain all of that muscle mass while you are losing body fat, you can maintain all the benefits of the high metabolism that comes with lean muscle. However, if you only rely upon a diet, you're going to lose existing muscle mass, which is a primary reason why so many diets fail. And most cardio exercises do little to build or retain muscle mass.

I can't stress this enough. *If you lose muscle mass, your metabolism will slow.* Lean body mass burns calories day in and day out, even when you're asleep. As I explained earlier in the book, many faithful dieters lose a considerable amount of weight and are lighter for a time, but in the process they have lost so much muscle mass that it is suddenly much easier to put on body fat. Almost inevitably they end up putting back on more weight than they lost, so they launch into another diet, only to get heavier while losing more muscle mass.

The solution to this dilemma is to utilize the Super Health 7 strength training exercises to maintain your existing muscle mass while you are losing weight. Increasingly, you gain a higher proportion of lean body mass to body fat and help your body achieve its natural, God-given strength and fitness. If you're a man, those muscles will show. If you're a woman, using these exercises you absolutely will never bulk up or become muscle bound like a man because of the lower level of testosterone that women have in their systems as compared to men. You will gain strength, but your muscles will be pleasing to the eye. On the other hand, you can get ripped, toned, and add to your muscle mass in a natural-looking way that will get heads to turn.

Your goal is to keep your metabolism at its peak. If through dieting alone you lose four pounds but one pound of that is muscle, you're losing when you think you're gaining. The scale isn't lying, but you're being tricked nevertheless. Absolutely, you want to lose four pounds, but there's no reason why you need to lose muscle in the process. You've simply got to challenge your muscular system through some bodyweight resistance exercise along with following the Four Corners of Superfood Nutrition, including protein nutrition, in this book.

The third reason that strength training is essential is that it will accelerate the speed of your weight loss effort. It can as much as double the effectiveness of your weight loss program, and it is the key to the future. Some people can keep weight off just by modifying their diet alone, but keep in mind that exercise is not just about weight loss; it is about Super Health.

The fourth reason is that the Super Health 7 system of strength training delivers superb results while protecting your joints, ligaments, tendons, and muscles, in contrast to lifting weights. Your body is designed to be healthy; it's not supposed to hurt. If you use and mobilize all your joints in a natural way, as these exercises do, they will not hurt. If you're not using those joints, then you're going to lose their range of motion, which will bring on pain. Many people who say that chronic pain is related to aging are really confusing cause and effect. It's not the fact that we're aging; it's that we've stopped using our entire body.

By the way, *if you think that lifting heavy weights is essential to building muscle size, it's simply not true.* The August 2010 journal of *PLoS ONE* published a study by a team of researchers from McMaster University (Ontario, Canada) that counters this prevailing notion. Nicholas Burd and colleagues assessed the effect of resistance exercise intensity and volume on muscle protein synthesis, anabolic signaling, and myogenic gene expression, enrolling 15 men to lift light weights that represented a percentage of what the subjects could maximally lift. At 30 percent, the team observed that subjects could lift that weight at least 24 times before they felt fatigue. The researchers report that: "These results suggest that low-load high volume resistance exercise is more effective in inducing acute muscle anabolism than high-load low volume or work-matched resistance exercise modes."[126] In other words, *low tension/weight with higher volume/reps is more effective in growing muscle.*

Three Fabulous Exercise Systems

While there is much to commend with the cardio exercises noted above, I can tell you from trying almost every exercise program that has come along during the past couple of decades, nothing I have found compares to the three exercise programs that I am about to detail. When it comes down to the amount of time, effectiveness, cost, and long-term benefits, I am certain you will reap the same rewards that I have from them. I utilize these systems in my daily workouts.

The Super Health 7 Tiger Moves

When you read *strength training,* did you visualize the massive, hulking bodybuilders who are still trying to embody what Arnold Schwarzenegger looked like in his prime? Rest assured, that's not what I mean. I'm talking about an amazing isoflexion and body-weight resistance exercise system that doesn't require a gym or expensive exercise equipment, can be done anytime and anyplace, and will not damage your joints or tendons. It is a perfect system for everyone from the weekend warrior to being an addition to the training regimen of a world-class athlete.

John Peterson is a friend of mine and, in my opinion, is today's Charles Atlas. He is a walking encyclopedia on the history of physical fitness. John's personal story in *Pushing Yourself to Power* is truly inspiring. The fact that he is in his late 50s yet is one of the most physically fit men I know is amazing enough. But the fact that he contracted polio in 1956, which left his legs dreadfully misshapen, and was the target of a bully's torture is the stuff of legends.

John developed his system of resistance and high tension isometrics by taking *the best of the best* exercises from the Masters of Physical Fitness and integrating them into one comprehensive program. The exercises I present in detail in my book *Super Health* are my favorite 10 exercises from the vast number of exercises in John's extensive system. These few exercises combined with the other systems I mention below are enough to keep you super fit without the gym. To see my series of TV interviews with John Peterson doing some of these exercises called "Super-Fit Without the Gym," go to www.LivingFuel.TV.

> **Exercise is a small price to pay for a healthy body and a healthy attitude.**
>
> MAC ANDERSON

In my book *Super Health*, I have detailed with exacting descriptions and photographs the Seven Tiger Moves. Repetition for repetition, these exercises deliver at least as many benefits as virtually any other form of exercise, even if you are dealing with sports injuries and in poor physical shape, and in less than 20 minutes per day. They help develop muscle, slim the body, and build a powerful and beautifully developed physique.

Many exercise systems can actually cause more pain and injury than benefit. It is possible for free weights and exercise machines to tear muscles and stress joints. Too much of these wrong methods can make you feel far older than your actual years.

The Seven Tiger Moves are completely natural. The secret to the system, said John McSweeney, is "nothing more than contracting and extending your muscles with *great tension* while thinking into them.

Tigers and lions stretch their entire body with a tension so great that their limbs actually quiver. The tiger's stretch is so powerful that it actually builds incredible strength and muscle. The inner resistance produced by the tension builds muscle fibers as much as the external resistance produced by weight or machines. However, since the resistance is perfectly controlled at all times throughout the entire range of motion, there is no jerking, no compression, and no harm to the body."

Because many of you already own a copy of my *Super Health* book, I refer you to the Exercise chapter there. If you don't have my book, I recommend you purchase a copy, as it provides the Seven Tiger Moves and the Big Three as well as several other body-weight exercises and more information on the benefits of exercise. The Seven Tiger Moves use "isoflexion," a combination of isometrics and movement that is truly extraordinary. If you want to know more about isometrics, I highly recommend John Peterson's book *Isometric Power Revolution*, which is the most comprehensive book on isometric contraction I have ever seen. The power of isometrics—powerfully contracting the muscle in an isolation hold—lies in being taught how to do them correctly, and no one does it better than John.

One thing I really like about the Super Health 7 exercises is they promote both strength and flexibility, which are both incredibly important.

Band Training

Another system I use for strength and flexibility is the SuperFlex bands system, using various sizes of next generation high tech rubber bands. These bands are terrific for stretching and increasing flexibility and preventing injuries. They are also an excellent way to increase speed, quickness, and explosiveness. David Herman, the SuperFlex founder, has been implementing these bands into professional athlete's workout programs for years and achieving remarkable results. Learn more at www.SuperFlexBands.com.

Sprint Interval Training

In accordance with an excellent research paper by Mark J. Smith, Ph.D., one of my colleagues on the Nutrition Advisory Board of the

Titleist Performance Institute, there is a cutting-edge trend in fitness called Sprint Interval Training (SIT) or High Intensity Interval Training (HIIT) that has shown itself to be far superior to typical cardio exercises in terms of weight loss and endurance. When I first heard about it, it was more than I could believe. I was told that if I was doing a total of 60 minutes of low to moderate exercise, such as on a treadmill, four times a week, I could gain an even greater cardio benefit by doing four high intensity workouts per week that involve four 1-minute all-out effort exercises for a total of 16 minutes per week. In other words, four minutes was better than 60.

After I asked myself, "How can this be?" I read several compelling studies that convinced me that it was worth examining and trying. What I found made so much sense that I wondered why I hadn't thought of it. If you talk with fitness experts, they tell us that our bodies are made up of almost an equal ratio of two types of muscle tissue—slow-twitch aerobic muscles, such as you use when you're walking, and fast-twitch anaerobic muscles, such as you use when you sprint or jump.

Consequently, when we go for a brisk walk, we only use about half of our muscles, which are very energy efficient. But if we sprint, we use both our aerobic and anaerobic muscles, and you know from experience that those sprint muscles demand a huge amount of energy, even after we stop. The super effort drains our oxygen and energy level and requires that we re-oxygenate our blood and cool down after all the extra heat that was generated.

And here's the good news. For an added benefit, the body reenergizes itself by metabolizing fat to refill what's been used, and it burns even more fat because we've accelerated our metabolism for hours after we've worked out—the increased calorie burning effect can last from four to up to 36 hours afterward. After a typical cardio session, it doesn't take our body long at all to get back to its pre-exercise level. But because of the boost in metabolism, studies confirm that HIIT can help people lose weight faster than people doing typical cardio exercises.

Another huge benefit is that as you are able to increase the intensity of your exercises, the caloric output accelerates exponentially, and your body increases the production of all the hormones and enzymes that help metabolize fat stores as well as stimulate the repair and growth of your body, thereby slowing down the aging process. You'll look younger and feel younger!

If you are giving your body the right nutrition, HIIT is a variable rate cardio exercise system that creates muscle growth that is essentially a metabolic engine, increasing your overall metabolism, but it does not dramatically increase one's appetite as is true of conventional cardio. You won't see your weight loss benefits get wiped out by an increase in eating.

Intensity Beats Length and Frequency

It took no time for me to come to believe that intensity of workout is more important than the length and frequency of workout.

Dr. Mark Smith says it best: "It is now clear from recent research that high intensity interval training trumps low to moderate intensity training virtually every time. This is true for a whole host of health benefits, including cardiovascular health and fat loss, the most common concerns for why people engage in an exercise program in the first place. Whenever researchers have compared these two types of training regimens side by side, the high intensity interval training has always produced more favorable results, often dramatically so.

"This is also true when working with an older population or even with individuals already suffering from cardiovascular disease. A recent study published in *Circulation*, a journal published by the American Heart Association, reported dramatic superior benefits of interval training compared to moderate continuous training in elderly patients with stable prior heart failure. Not only did the patients in the interval training group have a greater improvement in their aerobic capacity (or 'cardio' capacity) as compared to those in the moderate training group (46 percent versus 14 percent), but they also improved a number of other parameters that improved the health of their heart."

A typical HIIT workout will only take 20 minutes and increase

> Those who think they have no time for bodily exercise will sooner or later have to find time for illness.
>
> EDWARD STANLEY

your metabolism for many hours afterward. The most effective exercise intervals that allow for the greatest effort can be as short as 20 seconds and should not be more than 60 seconds. You'll be amazed by what you can accomplish in an extremely short window of time, which is what I love about it.

sprinter

marathon
runner

It doesn't take a trained eye to see the difference between the effects of moderate intensity, long duration exercise (marathon runner) and high intensity interval training (sprinter). One depletes muscle mass while the other enhances it.

So how do you start an interval training program? All it takes is a long stairway and a 20-second "burst" (a fast walk or moderate run) that you accumulate 12 minutes worth during a week. You can do the same up a steep hill or on a stationary bike with high resistance. If you have access to a running track, after a thorough warm-up, sprint for 30 seconds, then rest for 90 seconds (a light jog or brisk walk should do it). Repeat this sequence for the desired number of intervals, usually six to eight per workout. You can mix up your HIIT training by using this approach while biking, swimming, rowing, jumping rope, jumping jacks, weightlifting, or virtually any other exercise you enjoy. Taking a spin or indoor cycling class is a great example of HIIT.

Personally, I like to do what I call heavy weight bag boxing flurries combined with sprints. While focusing on breathing, I punch a heavy weight bag as quickly and solidly as I can for 100 punches, then wait to get my breath back. Then I do 100 sprint steps on one of my favorite exercise devices, called the Xiser sprint stepper (www.xiser.com), then get my breath back and do another round and so on.

Another favorite of mine is to stretch and go for a run, using the first few minutes to warm up. Then I sprint for 50 to 100 steps, followed by a jog or walk for up to twice the steps that I sprinted (getting my breath back), then do it again. I generally do this at least 10 times during a short run of two miles or less.

Here are some samples of workouts that can help you get started.

Beginner Level

Start with a 10-minute warm-up of walking or exercise that gets your heart rate up about 50 percent, then begin your first interval. Each bullet point is considered an interval.

- 20 jumping jacks as fast as you can do them in good form
- 30 seconds cranking a bike as fast as you can go
- 25 jumps with a jump rope
- If you're fit enough, run 20 paces

Week 1: After warming up, perform five intervals with two
minutes rest in between

Week 2: Increase to eight intervals

Week 3: Increase to 10 intervals

Week 4 and beyond: Each week, either increase the length or the intensity of the intervals

Intermediate Level

Start with a five-minute warm-up of brisk walking or any moderate pace exercise that gets your heart rate up about 50 percent, then begin your first interval.

- 100 jumps or one minute with jump rope, five times (two minutes rest in between)
- One minute of your hardest effort on a bike, five times (two to four minutes easy spin to recover)
- Two minutes pushing hard on an elliptical, then two minutes off, five times
- Sprint half of one straight on a track five times, walk one lap to recover
- Increase the treadmill incline to highest level and keep speed constant at 2–2.5 mph for one to two minutes, five times (drop incline to recover)

Weeks 1 and 2: Twice per week as described above

Weeks 3 and 4: Increase to eight intervals

Week 4 and beyond: Increase to 10 intervals and/or increase speed/intensity of each interval

Advanced Level

Same warm-up as the Intermediate Level. Your intervals need to be all-out, as hard as possible, with extra focus on as perfect form as possible.

- Ten 100-meter sprints (walk the curve to recover, plus an extra lap at the end)
- Five 50-yard hill sprints, walk down to recover
- Five sets of 10 burpees (squat-thrust with jump) with one lap walk or slow jog-in-place recovery

Focus on maintaining excellent form while increasing speed and intensity each week.

To read Dr. Mark Smith's fascinating research on HITT or SIT, go to www.xiser.com/downloads.php and click on the "Sprint Interval Training—"It's a HIIT" download.

Chapter 15

The Seven Golden Keys to Weight Optimization and Super Health

*The poorest man would not part with health
for money, but the richest would gladly
part with all their money for health.*
C. C. COLTON

Julie is your typical working mom who also runs a household that includes three children, a husband, and one dog. Her job is very stressful, and even with two incomes, their family is just making ends meet. All three kids have a host of allergies, and Julie can't remember when she last got a good night's rest. When she was married 15 years previous, she was 5'2" and weighed 125 pounds. Today, she is 5'2" and weighs 235 pounds. Instead of examining her entire lifestyle and diet, Julie blames her husband and the pressures of raising a family for her weight gain. She believes her problem is emotional, not dietary. And it's killing her slowly and surely, pound by pound.

Julie loves meat and cooks it for her family at almost every meal. She doesn't realize that the farmer who raised the meat in her refrigerator gave his steers a synthetic steroid hormone designed to generate rapid weight gain on less food, and she's unaware that the residues of the drug are still working when she and her family eat it. The same is true of drug residues from the pork, chicken, and other meat, plus dairy products, she's ingested every day for years. Drugs designed to artificially stimulate the animals' appetites are now in her system, and she wonders why she can't seem to stop eating. Julie literally feels hungry *all the time.*

She also has type 2 diabetes, which is not a surprise as 90 percent of people with type 2 diabetes are obese. Type 2 diabetes occurs when glucose cannot enter body cells. Sometimes called "adult onset diabetes," it is typically diagnosed among middle-aged, overweight, inactive people.

Julie is addicted to sugar and doesn't realize it. Despite her family's protests, she rigidly avoids cookies, cake, and ice cream, but doesn't realize that most of the processed food she buys (because she doesn't feel she has the time to cook "real food") contains large amounts of sugar in the form of corn syrup and trans fats, which increase the body's production of sugar. From the ketchup to the canned beans, it's almost in every can in her cupboards. One of the reasons she likes the taste of processed food is because it is loaded with salt and sugar.

She is not alone in her dependency on soda pop to give her little boosts of energy, getting a whopping 13 teaspoons of sugar in the form of high fructose corn syrup for every can consumed. Americans drink, on average, 46 to 56 gallons of soda per year. The trouble with eating refined sugar in large amounts (the average person consumed almost 63 pounds of high fructose corn syrup in 2001 according to the U.S. Department of Agriculture, and Americans typically consume about 150 pounds of sugar in total per year) is that it stresses the body and, among other things, forces the body to use up large amounts of essential B vitamins. Soft drinks contain high amounts of phosphorus as well, using up the mineral potassium. Potassium is necessary for healthy skin and stable blood pressure. A deficiency of potassium can in turn cause a deficiency of the mineral calcium that is needed for relaxed muscles and strong bones. So it's no wonder Julie's body aches all the time and she finds it hard to fall asleep.

Julie knows she should get some exercise, but she's too tired all the time to even think twice about it. She knows she should drink a lot of water, but she almost never does—coffee and soda rule her day—and their house water tastes bad.

She is caught in a vicious downward cycle that drains the body of health and vitality and opens the door to more disorders. It didn't happen overnight, but it slowly stripped her body of its ability to defend itself. And her husband is in the same boat, and the kids are following close behind.

Super Health and Weight Loss Are Interrelated

If you read my first book, *Super Health: The Seven Golden Keys to Unlock Lifelong Vitality*, you realize that my emphasis on the Super Health Diet and exercise are two of the seven foundational, life-giving principles that saved my wife from being a patient for life with depression, anxiety, and pharmaceuticals. It can equip you to live the long and vibrant life your Creator intended for you. *It is truly a whole person approach for physical, mental, emotional, and spiritual renewal that will unleash the energy, health, and fitness that your body and spirit have been waiting for.*

> **Do not be deceived. God cannot be mocked. A man reaps what he sows.**
>
> THE APOSTLE PAUL, GALATIANS 6:7

In this book, we have dealt with Golden Keys #2—Nutrition and #3—Exercise. Because this book's main focus is weight optimization, I will only cover the absolute basics of the other five Golden Keys—proper hydration, managing stress, controlling and eliminating environmental toxins, achieving restorative sleep, and meditation and prayer. I would be remiss to not bring attention to these other major areas of your life that have a profound impact on your health and weight. I encourage you to get a copy of *Super Health* to get the expanded version of these keys.

Many people excel in one or more of the Golden Keys, but few people are firing on all cylinders. In fact, we find that most people are not doing very well in four of the seven Keys. After discovering the Seven Keys, when my wife, Monica, and I looked back on her health crisis, we realized that she was doing poorly in all seven. It was no wonder she crashed.

Because these Keys are interrelated, it is critically important to address all seven areas for physical, emotional, and spiritual renewal. For example, Julie's poor nutrition (Key #2) is having an impact on the quality of her sleep (Key #5), puts stress on her body (Key #4), and introduces a constant stream of toxins into her body (Key #6). Correspondingly, improvements made in any of the Keys will positively affect the others because we are one person—mentally, physically, and spiritually. It can't be any other way. We reap what we sow on all levels of our health.

If you start with a few changes, you'll notice immediate improvements in your physical and emotional well-being. For instance, if you watched only half as much television as you do now, you might lose weight. That's the conclusion of a study published in the December 14/28, 2009 issue of the *Archives of Internal Medicine.* Researchers at the University of Vermont assessed the TV watching time of 36 adults during the course of three weeks—the participants' average TV watching time was almost five hours a day. Twenty of their subjects were given a device that turned off the television after they had watched half as many hours as they normally did. Another 16 study participants served as a control group. The group that had their TV-time cut in half burned 119 more calories per day than they did before the study. The researchers suggested that small changes in daily habits that cut only 100 calories per day "could prevent the gradual weight gain observed in most of the population."

If you follow through and implement these Seven Keys on a daily basis, you will have a new lifestyle of Super Health. This complete lifestyle program is safe and simple and will not only help optimize your weight, but they will enhance performance, increase energy, and nurture overall health. You'll find yourself increasingly able to reclaim your God-given body to its fullest potential, including finding the answers you need for permanent weight loss.

If you have not read *Super Health*, I recommend that you do so. The book is jam-packed with information on each of these seven Keys that you won't find in one source anywhere else. While I see nutrition and exercise as critically important in the battle with weight gain, if you disregard the importance of these other five Keys, you'll find even your best efforts to be sabotaged as you seek to reclaim your God-given body and to enjoy its fullest potential.

Monica and I have done numerous TV shows on these keys, and you can watch some of them at www.LivingFuel.TV.

Take your time learning about these miraculous Keys to Super Health. Implement changes a little at a time, and each one will lead to other improvements. Remember, baby steps in the right direction truly are monster steps toward Super Health.

Golden Key #1—Hydration

In an age when man has forgotten his origins
and is blind even to his most essential
needs for survival, water along with other
resources has become the victim of his
indifference.
RACHEL CARSON

Of all the needs of the body for health, the air we breathe is at the top of the list and water is right behind it. Our body is comprised of about 75 percent water, and water is involved in virtually all internal bodily processes, including digestion, absorption, circulation, and excretion. Believe it or not, water is our main source of energy. It adjusts the body's temperature and rids the body of toxins. Although we can go for a month or more without food, we won't last a week without water. Yet the vast majority of us *do not get enough water* to obtain optimal health and freedom from disease. We neglect our body, which is often in a chronic state of dehydration and crying out for water to fortify thirsty cells and systems. In ignoring the signs, we may be doing ourselves irreparable damage.

Water maintains homeostasis, or balance, in the cells, where everything is working correctly. Watery solutions help dissolve nutrients and carry them to all parts of your body. Through chemical reactions that can only take place in a watery solution, your system turns nutrients into energy or into materials it needs to grow to repair cells. Water is used for every enzyme process that governs the nerve chemicals, and therefore every thought and action, every chemical process, and therefore every function in the body.

Think of these benefits the next time you drink a glass of sparkling pure water with ice and a slice of lemon. That water flushes the kidneys and liver, enabling them to remove toxins from your body. It helps maintain energy levels, increases the efficiency of your immune system, and keeps your skin looking good and feeling soft. And it reduces the risk of developing kidney stones and gallstones as well as headaches.

Every good weight loss program recommends drinking water as a means of distinguishing true hunger from false "hunger pangs." It also aids and improves digestion. While being well hydrated, our volume of food intake then decreases dramatically, and so do our cravings. In addition, with sufficient water intake, we tend to hunger after proteins rather than fattening carbohydrates.

The Right Amounts of the Right Water

Unfortunately, most of us take water and the essential process of drinking it for granted. According to a survey conducted at Rockefeller University, most people fall short of the well-known recommendation to drink eight to 12 eight-ounce servings a day. Although almost 75 percent of Americans are aware of the recommendation, only 34 percent consume this amount. Incredibly, 10 percent do not drink water at all. By contrast, Americans drink an average of almost six servings a day of caffeinated beverages, such as coffee and soda that can actually cause the body to lose water.[127]

> **Water is life's mater and matrix, mother and medium. There is no life without water.**
>
> ALBERT SZENT-GYORGYI

The most common signs of dehydration are dry skin, muscle cramps, constipation, fatigue, and headaches. Thirst is not necessarily a reliable sign that our body needs water. When you feel thirsty, you are probably already in the initial stages of dehydration. From early adult age our sense of thirst begins to dull. This is why we need to drink water regularly, whether we feel thirsty or not.

Another important factor is to make certain that we drink the *right* water, because hydration is a very important factor in fighting acid waste accumulation, as it neutralizes and flushes toxins and acidic waste from our bodies. As an acid-clearing mechanism, water makes the interior of our cells alkaline. Ideally, the water we drink should have an alkaline pH of 7.0 or higher. Anything with a pH of 7.0 or higher is alkaline, whereas anything with a pH of less than 7.0 is acidic by definition. Much of the water available on the market today (including tap water) is lower than 7.0, sometimes much lower, which means that it is acidic. The best way to achieve a proper level of alkalinity (or non-acidity) is either through drinking mineral water or filtered water that either results in alkaline pH or ionizes and electrically charges the water to ensure alkaline pH. Ionization improves the water's absorption and movement through the aquaporin (a family of related proteins that reside in cell walls) channels of the cells, ultimately resulting in proper intracellular hydration.

The Myth of Pure Water

Making certain that the water we consume offers the least toxins is a must as we begin an active program of serious and long-term rehydration and weight loss. For instance, drinking water with fluoride can cause weight gain, and conversely, changing to spring or filtered water can affect weight loss.

You've probably read or heard ads for bottled waters telling you that your water must be "pure" rather than be merely clean and healthy. Marketers convince people that nothing but H2O should be in their water, which has led some people to drink distilled water and then take mineral supplements that contain the same minerals that have been removed from the water!

Don't be fooled. While it's true that distillation removes more contaminants than any other purification method, and active carbon filters can be used to eliminate other remaining contaminants, some impurities still remain. Another purification method is reverse osmosis (RO), where water molecules are forced through a rubber membrane, leaving impurities behind. But gases, some chemicals, and some bacteria can beat this technique, too.

Dr. Michael Mascha, the author of *Fine Waters: A Connoisseur's Guide to the World's Most Distinctive Bottled Waters*, states, "There is no such thing as pure water. It's a myth. Natural water has mineral content. By removing minerals, water becomes acidic and aggressive, meaning it will seek to replace the minerals removed. Water treated by either distillation or RO will become acidic upon contact with the air. Airborne carbon dioxide reacts with the water, taking the place of the removed minerals or contaminants.... Clean, healthy water does not have to be pure. In fact, the waters with the most epicurean interest contain minerals and trace elements."

Tap water is detrimental to your health. The trick is getting water from the source to you with as minimal contamination as possible. From an environmental and economic perspective, the top water priority should be to correct the water that comes from our taps. In my book *Super Health*, I recommend several water filtration systems, including shower filters, that remove the fluoride, chlorine, other chemicals, metals, and bacteria from our water. Shower filters are among the least expensive and most important filters, because your skin drinks water. These range from the Ionizer Plus Water Micro-Filtration and Naturally Filtered, which also restore the pH balance of the water, to carbon filters, such as Brita and PUR. Keep in mind that while drinking pure water is critically important, it is also important to shower or bathe in pure water, because your skin is your largest organ, and bathing in it is not much different from drinking it.

So which purification system is right for you—reverse osmosis, ionization, distillation, desalination, filtration, sedimentation, ultra violet purification? Each of these processes has their benefits; however, none of them are ideal as the single best option. The amount of choices out there and making sense of the confusing claims the manufacturers and distributors are making can be maddening. The reality is that no commercially available water purification system has been shown to remove pharmaceutical and personal care pollutants (PPCPs), and few systems actually remove fluoride and chloramines (a combination of ammonia and chlorine).

Water filtration companies are notorious for giving you a huge list of compounds that their system removes. When you are speaking to a sales rep about a filtration system, ask them to show you, not tell you, that their system removes fluoride and chloramines and PPCPs (which none of them remove). I have been doing a lot of research on this subject during the past five years, and we will soon be doing a report on this evolving subject at LivingFuel.TV.

Virtually any water purification system is better than no filtration system. *If you don't have a filter, you are the filter.* So if all you can afford are sink filters or pitcher filters, purchase name-brand versions. I am not a fan of the Zero Water filters because their angle is to remove total dissolved solids (TDS), which seems misleading. TDS is not generally considered a primary pollutant (it is not deemed to be associated with health effects). It is used as an indication of aesthetic characteristics of drinking water and as an aggregate indicator of the presence of a broad array of chemical contaminants. The most common TDS chemicals are calcium, phosphates, nitrates, sodium, potassium, and chloride. These are hardly a health hazard.

The bottom line is that it is best to drink spring water that has never been polluted in the first place, which has become increasingly difficult in today's world. By far the best water comes from a deep spring or aquifer, and like a fine wine, the older the water source the better. Some of the best water sources are thousands of years old. Imagine being able to bless our health today by drinking from the same sources that Jesus did.

The vast majority of bottled waters come in plastic bottles, in spite of the fact that there is a known tendency for small amounts of the plastic in these bottles to leach out into the water itself. The safest type of bottle to drink water from is glass or stainless steel. When you must use plastic, look for the plastic bottles that appear clear as glass. This clear plastic bottle will have a triangle stamped at the bottom with a number 1 in it, symbolizing that the plastic is a PET or PETE. This plastic is thought to be the "least worst" plastic, although there are a couple of biodegradable plastic bottles on the market, such as corn-derived plastic, but the jury is still out as to whether they might contain potentially harmful chemicals.

Not all bottled waters are created equal…far from it. Whenever possible, choose spring water, not drinking water or purified water, and stay with recognized national brands. More bottled waters claim springs as their origin than any other type of source. Spring waters vary widely in their mineral composition and TDS level, both of which are influenced by the geology of the local area. Some springs naturally

carbonate the water. The best tasting spring water comes from a protected, free-flowing spring and is treated as little as possible during the
bottling process.

The actual definition of spring water is controversial. Geologists
characterize it as water flowing through the surface of the earth with no
help from machines. But water from a well drilled next to the spring can
also be considered spring water by the U.S. Food and Drug Administration on these conditions: If a hydraulic link between the spring and the
borehole can be shown, the water from both the well and the spring are
chemically identical, the borehole does not prevent the spring's natural
flow, and the well does not open the aquifer to surface water.

Interestingly, I would rarely if ever recommend some of the large
national and international companies, such as Nestlé, which owns
Zephyrhills and Poland Springs brands, as companies that truly care
about your health. However, companies such as Nestlé have higher
standards than are required, and they test their water dozens of times
per day to avoid potential liability that could result from selling tainted
water. The result is that we can feel pretty good that the water is pure.
Be careful when you pick up these same brands, as they also offer purified city water as drinking water in addition to spring water. Water
bottle brands that you should only drink if you have no other choices
include waters from the major soft drink companies sold under the
labels Dasani and Aquafina. Both companies have admitted they are
selling repurified tap water. Lastly, don't drink private label brand water
bottles unless you have no other options. Again, always choose spring
whenever possible.

Among the hundreds of different brands of bottled water, there
is a vast range in quality. Here are some products I've researched and
recommend as healthy and safer bottled water choices:

- *Mountain Valley Spring Water* (glass bottle)—www.mountainval-
  leyspring.com. This company is the one spring water I am aware
  of that offers five-gallon glass bottles for your water dispenser.
  Typical five-gallon water bottles are made from #7 plastic, which
  is thought to be among the worst of the plastics for water. It does

not matter how good the water is in typical #7 plastic five-gallon water bottles, because toxins will leach into the water.

- *VOSS Artesian Water* (glass bottle)—www.vosswater.com. Voss is now also sold in #1 clear plastic bottles. Whenever possible, choose the glass bottles for home and office use. Voss glass bottles can be cleaned and refilled with spring or purified water. If glass bottles are not available, it is best to choose a spring water that is bottled in #1 PET plastic that is higher in pH, above 7, such as Fiji, as this helps minimize chemicals leaching from the plastic.
- *Penta Water* claims to be ultra purified even from PPCPs, using state-of-the-art proprietary processes, and that their water is energized to provide antioxidant activity. They claim that no other water is pure. I have not been able to find evidence to validate their claims; however, if this is true, it is a tremendous accomplishment and might justify the high price of this water. This water is only available in #1 plastic bottles.
- Trinity water made similar claims as Penta; however, Trinity is apparently no longer being produced due to an internal legal battle.

Water and Effective Weight Loss

If your grandmother told you that drinking more water might promote weight loss, she was right. In August 2010, at the 240th National Meeting of the American Chemical Society (ACS) in Boston, scientist Brenda Davy, Ph.D., of Virginia Tech said in a statement to the media: "We are presenting results of the first randomized controlled intervention trial demonstrating that *increased water consumption is an effective weight loss strategy.* We found in earlier studies that middle aged and older people who drank two cups of water right before eating a meal ate between 75 and 90 fewer calories during that meal. In this recent study, we found that during the course of 12 weeks, dieters who drank water before meals, three times per day, lost about five pounds more than dieters who did not increase their water intake."

Previous research had suggested that drinking water before meals reduces the intake of calories, but until now, there has never been the scientific "gold standard" evidence from a randomized, controlled clinical trial comparing weight loss among dieters who drank water before meals to dieters who did not drink the extra water.

Healthy Weight Optimizing Hydration Tips

- Sip water all day long.
- Drink water when you first get up in the morning to correct dehydration produced while you slept.
- Minimize all drinks with sugars and artificial sweeteners, including juices and sports drinks, and if you do have one of these, drink a glass of water before it. In the U.S., this alone could reduce your total calorie intake by as much as 15 percent.
- *Drink sports drinks only during training and competition that require maximum effort,* such as football, basketball, strength training, long distance endurance sports, etc.
- Minimize alcoholic beverages.
- Add a little lemon or lime juice to your water.
- Many cultures believe it is best to drink water at room temperature or cool but not really cold, as ice cold water can compromise digestion.
- Use glass bottles whenever possible and never save and reuse plastic bottles, because plastic breaks down over time (see Golden Key #6).
- With exercise, the American College of Sports Medicine suggests that you ensure proper hydration by beginning with a large drink, about 16 ounces, two hours before going out to exercise.
- *Discover teas (lightly caffeinated or decaffeinated)*—organic green, white, black, red, and herbal, as they are a great way to drink more water.

Eliminate All "Empty Calorie" Beverages

When it comes to weight loss, what you drink may be more important than what you eat. According to results published in the April 1, 2009, issue of the *American Journal of Clinical Nutrition* and based on research at the Johns Hopkins Bloomberg School of Public Health, researchers examined the relationship between beverage consumption among adults and weight change. They found that weight loss was positively associated with a reduction in liquid calorie consumption and liquid calorie intake had a stronger impact on weight than solid calorie intake.

Benjamin Caballero M.D., Ph.D., senior author of the study, stated, "Both liquid and solid calories were associated with weight change; however, only a reduction in liquid calorie intake was shown to significantly affect weight loss during the six-month follow-up. A reduction in liquid calorie intake was associated with a weight loss of 0.25 kg at six months and 0.24 kg at 18 months. Among sugar-sweetened beverages, a reduction of one serving was associated with a weight loss of 0.5 kg at six months and 0.7 kg at 18 months. Of the seven types of beverages examined, *sugar-sweetened beverages were the only beverages significantly associated with weight change.*"

"Changes in the consumption of diet drinks and alcoholic beverages," added Liwei Chen, M.D., Ph.D., lead author of the study, "were inversely associated with weight loss, but were not statistically significant. Our study supports policy recommendations and public health efforts to reduce intakes of liquid calories, particularly from sugar-sweetened beverages, in the general population."

It is not surprising that the consumption of liquid calories from beverages has increased in parallel with the obesity epidemic. Consumption of carbonated soft drinks in the United States exploded during the past 40 years and has more than doubled since 1971. People today are consuming 15+ percent of their daily calories via "empty calorie" beverages (soda, juices, sports drinks, coffee drinks, etc.), which now account for more than one out of every four beverages consumed in America.

Carbonated drinks are the single biggest source of refined sugars in the American diet. These contain carbohydrate calories that have virtually no nutritional value and aren't nearly as satisfying as solid food. Regular soft drinks, juice boxes, and sports drinks provide children and young adults with hefty amounts of refined sugars, usually in the form of high fructose corn syrup and calories. Even diet sodas may replace more nutritious foods and beverages and decrease consumption of various nutrients. Children are including these types of beverages as a foundation of their daily lifestyle, and consuming these liquid calories, however tasty, can lead to a shortened life of obesity and disease. We so often hear that "Junior" won't eat his food, then we find out that he drinks the sugar-laden commercial beverages all day long.

Removing the calories that offer the least amount of nutrition will help in your efforts to lose weight. Cut the least satisfying and least nutritious calories first, then move on. Even so-called healthy drinks that are thought to be a better option for weight loss can bring along extra calories as well.

When reading your drink labels, the most important things to look at are carbohydrate calorie count and total sugars. A can of non-diet soda can have from 160 to 180 calories (virtually all from sugars) in it, whether it's been sweetened with high fructose corn syrup or something else. Enhanced water can have 125 calories from carbs, mostly, if not all, from sugars; sweetened tea may have 210 calories from carbs, mostly, if not all, from sugars, and fruit juice may have 190 calories from carbs, mostly, if not all, from sugars. In the end, it's the number of carbohydrate calories that really counts. Artificial sweeteners are not the answer. You will notice that very few diet soda drinkers are losing weight. Your best drink choice is to move more toward zero calorie, all natural water and unsweetened herbal teas or herbal teas sweetened with low calorie natural sweeteners such as stevia, TheraSweet, xylitol, tagatose, or erythritol.

One additional fact to consider: Drinks that contain alcohol or caffeine, such as coffee, highly caffeinated teas, or soft drinks, increase the loss of water from the body in urine. This can leave the body dehydrated. Replace these drinks with lightly caffeinated or non-caffeinated herbal and fruit teas or coffee substitutes made with barley, rye, chicory, or dandelion. Substitute diluted fruit juices in sparkling water or herbal cocktail drinks for alcoholic drinks.

In my book *Super Health*, I wrote in detail about all the toxins in conventional coffee and how acidic it is. It is called "The Coffee Story."

By that time, I had stopped drinking coffee, which I liked very much. Finally, I invented a liquid Arabica coffee concentrate that has all the benefits of traditional coffee without all the problems. A few drops in water creates the smoothest and most delicious cup of coffee you've ever had. It is called SuperCoffee.

Reducing or eliminating these hidden and unnecessary calories and replacing them with fresh water and unsweetened herbal teas not only is an effective weight loss strategy, but it can increase the years of your life and the life of your years.

Golden Key #4—Stress

His heart was behaving in that strange way
again, like a madly bouncing ball, beating
the breath out of his body.
HELEN HUDSON

Simply put, stress is synonymous with change and refers to anything that causes us to react to a physical, emotional, social, or spiritual stimulus. As we adjust to the continual fluctuations and startling threats that are a part of life, the effects can be emotional as well as physical, negative as well as positive. Stress can be good or bad for you, depending on the stressor and whether you react or respond to it. Stresses that are exciting can be positively stimulating, such as athletic competition. Anything that causes change in our lives causes stress. Even good change, such as falling in love or a promotion at work, can be stressful, but imagined change (worry and fear) can be extremely stressful. Science tells us that chronic worry and fear have devastating consequences to our health. The accumulation of stressors, whether good or bad, if intense enough, will ultimately cause physical disorders.

Stress comes in all shapes and sizes. There is emotional stress, such as a disagreement with a friend or grief about a loss. There are physical stresses, such as illness or a lack of sleep or pushing our body to extremes. There are external stresses, such as climatic extremes and environmental toxins. Also there are internal stresses, such as anxiety about a speech or fear of punishment. Hormonal shifts and allergic responses are stresses. Relentless work pressure, financial worries, excessive caffeine, alcohol consumption, smoking, and unresolved traumas from the past—all of these are stresses, and they can exact a grim toll on our body and our psyche.

The physical symptoms include thyroid gland malfunctions, high blood pressure, itchy skin rashes, decreased resistance to infection, flus and colds, gastrointestinal problems, such as ulcers, cramps, diarrhea, colitis, and irritable bowel, fatigue, hair loss, jaw pain, irregular heartbeat, palpitations, shortness of breath, obscure aches and pains, insomnia, and tension headaches. Emotional symptoms include depression, moodiness, nervousness, irritability, frustration, memory problems, cognitive impairment, lack of focus, substance abuse, phobias, overreactions, and anxiety attacks (panic).

The National Institute of Mental Health reports that 19 million Americans between the ages of 18 and 54 are afflicted by anxiety- and stress-related illnesses per year.[128] The effects of stress are profound. They impact not only our susceptibility to disease, but they also affect the progression of disease and our ability to recover from it. In fact, virtually every major physical disorder is caused by, or greatly exacerbated by, stress, from migraine headaches to asthma. The toll it takes on the body is every bit as severe as smoking, obesity, and genetic predisposition.

Stress and Weight

The hormone *cortisol* plays an important role in regulating blood sugar, energy production, inflammation, the immune system, and healing. If you have too little cortisol, you may suffer from fatigue, chronic fatigue, exhaustion, and Addison's disease. If your adrenal glands are producing too much cortisol, such as happens when one is under prolonged stress (a.k.a. repetitive stress), you may develop conditions such as weight gain, especially around the abdomen, depressed immune function with all of the consequences, accelerated aging, and stomach ulcers.

Emerging studies suggest a link between central obesity—marked by abdominal fat and a high waist-to-hip ratio—and elevated cortisol levels. One such study examined healthy premenopausal women, half of whom demonstrated central fat distribution as determined by a high waist-to-hip ratio, and half of whom did not.[129] All the women participated in three sessions of psychosocial challenges on four consecutive days to gauge and measure their reaction to stress. Women with higher waist-to-hip ratios experienced the laboratory challenges as more threatening, performed more poorly on them, and reported more chronic stress. These women also secreted more cortisol than women with lower waist-to-hip ratios. The investigators noted that central fat distribution is related to greater psychological vulnerability to stress and cortisol reactivity.

In a study published in 2004, researchers examined the relationship between stress levels, cortisol, and abdominal obesity in obese women, half of whom had a binge-eating disorder.[130] The researchers found a positive correlation between high stress and cortisol levels and central obesity, noting, "hyperactive HPA axis due to stress raises cortisol, which may contribute to binge eating and abdominal obesity."

Clearly, there is an intimate relationship between stress, cortisol levels, and overall health. Lowering cortisol levels may thus offer support for healthy weight management and prevent negative health outcomes associated with central obesity.

Good Stress / Bad Stress

When you simplify it, there are basically two kinds of stress. Bad stress (or *distress*) occurs when unresolved stress is prolonged and not dealt with in a positive way. Good stress (called *eustress*) compels us into action and results in greater awareness, emotional intelligence, and resiliency. Meeting a goal, problem solving, excelling in competition, working through a conflict with a coworker, and even grief can be important learning experiences that enrich and broaden our lives.

Without the challenges of daily life, we cannot mature and become complete human beings in a healthy way. Instead of eliminating stress, we need to learn how to *manage* it and increase our tolerance for it by following the Super Health Seven Keys!

The benefits of stress management are pervasive and profound. Stress management can help lower blood sugar as well as our risk for heart disease; and it can make us less susceptible to colds and flu as well. It can reduce violence, accidents, and poor job performance. It allows us to rebound faster (both physically and mentally). It can literally alter our appearance, taking pounds off our body and years off our age—increasing our longevity and dramatically improving our overall quality of life.

Stress Management

Stress management techniques and nutritional supplements can help you manage stress and lower cortisol to promote optimal health and longevity. The following techniques can help support a healthy response to stress.

- *Attitude and Positive Self-Talk.* A positive attitude, particularly rooted in faith (see Golden Key #7), directly correlates with an increased ability of the immune system to fight pathogens. There are numerous biblical scriptures that promote a positive attitude and speak of not doubting or worrying. One such scripture states, "Finally, brethren, whatever is true, whatever is honorable, whatever is right, whatever is pure, whatever is lovely, whatever is of good repute, if there is any excellence and if anything is worthy of praise, dwell on these things" (Philippians 4:8). The ability to handle stress positively and proactively in everyday life can alleviate the constant activation of the endocrine system. Studies have shown that optimists tend to have better coping skills and to rely on more supportive social networks, which gives them a greater capacity for growth and positive reinterpretation of negative events. Stress management doesn't mean eliminating stress. It means changing how we react to it so that we don't feel overwhelmed by it. If we believe a situation is too overwhelming and we can't cope with it, that stress can damage us. There are several attitudinal modifications that can help us monitor and manage stress whenever it rears its ugly head: Acknowledge the stress, decide what you can change, gauge and monitor your emotional and physical reaction to stress, build your physical reserves, and give yourself a day of rest and relaxation.
- *Exercise.* The most effective techniques for fighting stress are the Seven Golden Keys, including regular and effective exercise and optimal nutrition. Exercise, particularly HIIT (see Chapter

14), causes the brain to release natural endorphins (neurotransmitters in the brain that have pain-relieving properties akin to morphine). Exercise also is a detoxifier, useful in removing the byproducts of the stress response. Remember…*regular exercise* is more important than intense exercise. Working ourselves into a state of exhaustion while exercising can actually intensify feelings of anxiety, while regular, moderate exercise lowers anxiety and relaxes the body (Golden Key #3). HIIT training or 30 to 45 minutes of both anaerobic (resistance training) and aerobic (jogging, cycling) every other day will make a difference.

- In 2004, research conducted and published in the *Proceedings of the National Academy of Sciences* by Nobel Prize winner Elizabeth H. Blackburn and colleagues at the University of California, San Francisco (UCSF), revealed the negative impact of stress on telomeres in people who are exposed to chronic psychological pressures. Telomeres are pieces of DNA that cap and protect the ends of chromosomes, which play a significant role in cellular aging. On May 26, 2010, in the online journal *PLoS ONE*, Dr. Blackburn and her associates published the findings of a current study that demonstrate *a protective effect for brief periods of exercise against stress-induced damage.*

  UCSF Department of Psychiatry associate professor Elissa Epel, Ph.D., who was one of the lead investigators, stated, "Telomere length is increasingly considered a biological marker of the accumulated wear and tear of living, integrating genetic influences, lifestyle behaviors, and stress. Even a moderate amount of vigorous exercise appears to provide a critical amount of protection for the telomeres."

  Noted psychologist and lead author of the research, Eli Puterman, Ph.D., added, "At this point, we have replicated previous findings showing a link between life stress and the dynamics of how cells age. Yet we have extended those findings to show that,

> Therefore do not worry about tomorrow, for tomorrow will worry about itself. Each day has enough trouble of its own.
>
> JESUS, MATTHEW 6:34

in fact, there are things we can do about it. If we maintain the levels of physical activity recommended, at least those put forth by the Centers for Disease Control and Prevention [an average of 75 minutes of vigorous activity per week], we can prevent the unyielding damage that psychological stress may have on our body."

- *Talk It Out.* Many people who suffer from chronic stress and anxiety have benefited from traditional talk therapy. This can be with a psychologist, a minister, a counselor, or even a wise and trusted friend. Research has shown that when individuals talk about a tragic or stressful event, they show an elevated immune response and are generally healthier than those who are emotionally inhibited and nondisclosing. Therapy has been shown to decrease the number of sick days and to lower health care costs. In turn, individuals with an effective social support network have also been shown to have stronger immune abilities.

- *Dietary Options and Supplements.* One of the chief problems with the body's stress response has to do with the "auto-oxidation" of the very stress hormones that our body naturally releases in order to help us deal with the stress. What this means is that our stress hormones *themselves* can become oxidized once they are released by our adrenal glands, which means they then go on to create a cascade of dangerous free radicals within the body. This is one of the main reasons why chronic stress is such a killer—because of all the excess free radicals that are produced by the very release of these stress hormones. This is where antioxidants, such as full-spectrum Vitamin E, the essential mineral selenium, and serotonin can be of tremendous help (see Corner #3—Consume High Antioxidant Superfoods and Supplements). One warning: Do not self-prescribe supplements if you are taking prescription drugs. For further recommendations on supplements, check out my book *Super Health.*

- *Specific Supplements to Reduce High Cortisol Levels.*
Vitamin C: 1,000 to 3,000 mg/day
Fish oil: 1 to 4 grams of combined EPA/DHA per day
Vitamin D3: 2,500 to 5,000 IU per day followed by 25-OH

Vitamin D blood test within 90 days—preferred blood levels 50 to 70 mg/ml

Phosphatidylserine: 300 to 800 mg/day

Rhodiola rosea: 100 to 200 mg/day, standardized extract

Ginseng: 100 to 300 mg/day, standardized extract

Ginkgo biloba: 100 to 200 mg/day, standardized extract

DHEA: 25 to 50 mg/day (should be monitored by your physician)

l-tryptophan: 500 mg three times per day on an empty stomach and 1,000 to 2,000 mg at bedtime

- *Breathing and Relaxation.* When facing a stressful situation, relaxation and deep breathing exercises deliver immediate and direct benefits to the body, including lowering our heart rate and blood pressure and improving our sleep. Relaxation and creative visualization exercises, aromatherapy, meditation, and prayer—all of these techniques relax the mind and spirit, allowing us to feel and think better. Fifteen to 30 minutes daily are essential to reducing stress levels.

- *Make Fun and R&R a Priority.* How many of us often choose to overwhelm our spirits and minds with noisy and often negative clutter, from cell phones to television to the Internet. We need to take a break from our hectic, technology-driven schedules and stop taking life so seriously. Why not find ways to nurture yourself. Go for a long walk or replenish our spirits with a good book or an afternoon playing with our children. Schedule a massage. Take a luxurious bath—it's a cheap mini-vacation. Light some candles and listen to your favorite Mozart concerto. Plant some flowers, draw a picture, or enjoy a leisurely meal with some friends. Learn to laugh. Creative activities, such as expressive writing or "journaling," have been shown to reduce stress and alleviate the symptoms of asthma and rheumatoid arthritis in patients with these chronic illnesses.

- *Make it a practice to have more fun and laugh and smile every day.* The Bible declares that "a merry heart does good, like medicine, but a broken spirit dries the bones" (Proverbs 17:22). It is well known in the scientific community that laughter is not only an effective stress reliever, but can be heart healthy. Research presented at the American College of Sports Medicine's 56th Annual Meeting in May 2009 examined the role of a good laugh as it relates to health and showed that it improves both vascular function and "arterial compliance," the amount of blood that moves through the arteries at a given time. Additionally, many research studies have shown that smiling releases endorphins (the feel-good hormone), natural painkillers, and serotonin, relieves stress, boosts the immune system, and lowers blood pressure.

- *Prayer and Meditation.* Turning to God during periods of apprehension and worry is important because we learn to trust in God's power rather than ourselves. It is easy to get caught up in the materialism and egocentrism of our lives today. Spirituality gives us a broader perspective. While prayer provides a place of respite and calm during trying times, it also is an intimate conversation with God that allows us to see beyond our everyday realities and concerns, putting our stresses and anxieties into proper perspective. For more information, see Golden Key #7.

THE
SUPER
HEALTH
DIET

Golden
Keys
to Unlock
Lifelong
Vitality

Golden Key #5—Sleep

Sleep that knits up the ravelled sleave of care
The death of each day's life, sore labour's bath
Balm of hurt minds, great nature's second course,
Chief nourisher in life's feast.
WILLIAM SHAKESPEARE

Sleep is one aspect of our daily routine that many of us take for granted…until we have a couple nights in a row of either not enough sleep or interrupted sleep. It is without a doubt one of the most important aspects of our daily routine as far as the maintenance of health and prevention of disease is concerned. After all, sleep is when the body regenerates itself, thereby making it ready for a whole new day of activity. The heartbeat and breathing rate slow down, blood pressure falls, muscles relax, and the overall metabolic rate of the body decreases. Sleep gives our body a chance to rebalance itself and restores energy to the body, particularly to the brain and nervous system, having a major impact on every cell in our body.

Simply put, people who sleep well feel better, look younger, live longer, and are more energized and motivated throughout their day.

When the body is deprived of sleep, even a little bit, one's overall degree of health can easily become compromised without one even knowing it. When you wake up tired, you feel irritated through the day. Combine a lack of sleep with high stress at your job, caring for a newborn or a sick child, a heavy class load at school, or going through menopause, and we start to feel like a basket case. You can't "burn the candle at both ends" and not pay a price.

Regularly catching only a few hours of sleep speeds up the aging process, as it can hinder metabolism and hormone production in a way that is similar to the effects of aging and the early stages of diabetes.

Chronic sleep loss may lead to depression and anxiety and speed the onset or increase the severity of age-related conditions, such as type 2 diabetes, high blood pressure, obesity, and memory loss. Sleep debts are sort of like stress.

Sleep is not a luxury. It is crucial, and chronic sleep deprivation is dangerous. Sleep is an essential key to Super Health. Make it a priority in your life. Many people go to bed late and get up early to exercise to try to be healthy, but the reality is that in many cases those people would be better off to sleep more and exercise less. Obviously, it is best to do both. But that is how important a good night's sleep is.

If you feel you are among the sleep deprived, you are among a large group. According to the National Commission on Sleep Disorders, one in three Americans does not get enough sleep. Other experts estimate the number of chronically sleep-deprived people in this country to be closer to one in two (about 100 million people).[131]

Sleep deprivation has been a wartime torture practice since the dawn of war itself. When a person is forced to stay awake, they will eventually crack. Sleep is an invaluable commodity, yet we seem to give it up for any reason at all, whether to watch a game or just out of habit.

Why Sleep Quality Is Critical

It behooves us to do everything possible to ensure that we get as much sleep as our bodies naturally require, which for most adults is between seven and eight and a half hours per night. The average American sleeps roughly six to seven hours a night. A little more than a century ago, before electricity, people were sleeping about one and a half to two and a half hours longer because they worked harder, went to bed at dark, and woke up at light. Many people sleep less as they get older, which can be an indication of a compromised hormone production, including melatonin and growth hormone (GH or HGH).

There is no magic number for how many hours of sleep you need, because every individual's requirements are different. You need as much sleep as you need to feel rested in the morning. If you don't feel refreshed, you won't be able to function at peak efficiency throughout the following day.

One of the most critical parts of the sleeping process is the REM sleep. This is the stage of sleep in which people dream, and when they dream, their eyes dart about underneath their eyelids, as though they are watching the events of a dream. While there is much about the phenomenon of dreaming that is not understood, this is the time when most of the psychological stressors of the mind and body are dealt with.

Accordingly, anything that interferes with REM sleep is bound to cause problems the next day. A large number of substances are known to interfere greatly with REM sleep, including alcohol, benzodiazepine tranquilizers (such as Valium), prescription and over-the-counter sleep medications, caffeine, and other mood-altering drugs. This can ultimately become catastrophic for the person who is regularly deprived of REM sleep, since the accumulated sleep deficit can manifest in ways such as suddenly falling asleep at anytime during the day (also known as narcolepsy). Even getting up in the middle of the night to go to the bathroom can interfere with the quality of sleep.

> **Insomnia is a gross feeder. It will nourish itself on any kind of thinking, including thinking about not thinking.**
>
> CLIFTON FADIMAN

Insomnia—the Enemy of Sleep

One of mankind's oldest complaints and the greatest enemy of restful sleep is the plague of insomnia, or habitual sleeplessness. For a wide variety of reasons, many people just can't get to sleep at night or can't fall back to sleep if they wake up. It affects one of ten Americans (approximately 40 million) and about 30 percent of healthy seniors.[132] Failure to get an entire night's sleep on most nights during a one-month period is considered chronic insomnia and threatens the well-being, productivity, and safety of all who suffer with it.

One cause of insomnia that affects about 20 million Americans is sleep apnea. The person with apnea actually stops breathing altogether for about 10 seconds at a time while they are asleep. When the breathing stops, the level of oxygen in the body drops, then the person wakes up with a start, and the breathing resumes. This phenomenon may occur up to 200 times a night, and it's not a surprise they wake up feeling exhausted. Sleep apnea is associated with an increased risk of high blood pressure, heart attack, congestive heart failure, stroke, and type 2 diabetes.

Unfortunately, there are no truly good remedies for either snoring or sleep apnea, as sleep medicine is in its infancy. Nevertheless, it is critical to work toward optimal health by addressing all of the Super Health Seven Keys. Sometimes these issues will resolve themselves once food intolerances are addressed and optimal fitness and body weight are obtained. Conventional medical approaches address symptoms and rarely get to the root of the problem. Sleep apnea is extremely serious and can be a death sentence if it is not taken seriously.

One conventional route is to first go through a formal sleep study, in which a person sleeps in a controlled environment, where they are constantly being monitored for various abnormalities. Once these abnormalities are documented, you will generally be given two surgical options and a device called Continuous Positive Airway Pressure (CPAP) or Bilevel Positive Airway Pressure (BiPAP)—masks you wear while you sleep that keep your airway open through continuous air pressure.

Neither of these are good long-term options. Do everything you can to resolve the cause of the problem, such as losing weight and eliminating foods that are causing inflammation. One great technique is doing the FUEL Fast for four to seven days. When you start eating your normal diet, you will often notice that certain foods don't make you feel good, and these are often the source of problems with sleep, including snoring. Pasteurized dairy, sugar, and gluten are often found to be at the root of these issues, so another option is to eliminate these and see if it helps.

Sleep and Weight

A study in the December 2004 issue of *PLoS (Public Library of Science) Medicine* investigated the link between sleep duration and two appetite-regulating hormones—leptin and ghrelin. Leptin levels rise when you experience a calorie surplus, making you feel full.[133] Percent levels, on the other hand, rise in response to a calorie shortage, stimulating your appetite. This new study found that short sleep duration is not only associated with increased BMI, but also with reduced leptin levels and elevated ghrelin levels, which could—in theory—lead to weight gain.

Another study from the University of Chicago in the December 2004 issue of the *Annals of Internal Medicine* supported these findings.[134] In this study, 12 men slept in a laboratory setting for 10 hours two consecutive nights and for four hours two consecutive nights, with a six-week buffer period between. The participants completed questionnaires to assess their hunger and appetite, and the researchers measured levels of leptin and ghrelin in the participants' blood. They found that sleep restriction was associated with an 18 percent decrease in leptin, a 28 percent increase in ghrelin, a 24 percent increase in hunger, and a 23 percent increase in appetite—especially for calorie-rich and high carbohydrate foods. Eve Van Cauter, Ph.D., professor of medicine at the University of Chicago, stated, "It provides biochemical evidence connecting the trend toward chronic sleep curtailment to obesity and its consequences, including metabolic syndrome and diabetes."

> Sleep is the golden chain that ties health and our bodies together.
>
> Thomas Dekker

More recent studies that were both reported on in June 2010 further highlight the relationship between sleep and appetite. In a controlled experiment, 12 young men reported feeling hungrier before both breakfast and dinner after sleeping only four hours a night compared to eight. The result? They ate on average 600 additional calories.[135] In another study that lasted seven years with more than 7,000 men and women aged 40 to 60 (an age at which many of us put on unwanted pounds), researchers found that about one-third of women who reported sleep problems gained weight, while only one-fifth of women with no sleep problems did so.[136]

A report published online in October 2010 in the *Proceedings of the National Academy of Sciences* suggests that some of the increase in obesity observed during the past several decades could be due to increased exposure to light at night and shift work, which disrupts the release of melatonin, a hormone produced by the pineal gland in the brain in response to darkness. "Light at night is an environmental factor that may be contributing to the obesity epidemic in ways that people don't expect," observed study co-author and Ohio State University professor of neuroscience and psychology Randy Nelson. "Societal obesity is correlated with a number of factors, including the extent of light exposure at night."

Dr. Nelson and his colleagues evaluated the effects of nighttime light exposure in mice. The animals were exposed to 24 hours of constant light, to a standard light-dark cycle consisting of 16 hours of light and 8 hours of darkness, or to 16 hours of daylight and 8 hours of dim light, which models environmental light pollution experienced by those living in industrialized nations. As early as one week after the onset of treatment, a greater increase in body mass was observed among mice exposed to constant light and those exposed to a cycle of daylight and dim light compared to animals that received standard light-dark exposure. At four weeks these groups showed impaired glucose tolerance. "Although there were no differences in activity levels or daily consumption of food, the mice that lived with light at night were getting fatter than the others," noted lead author and OSU doctoral student Laura Fonken.

Interestingly, to produce more eggs, chickens are often kept in an environment with the lights on all the time to "trick" them into thinking it is daytime. One wonders what other effects this might have?

While sleep deprivation alone cannot explain the increasing prevalence of overweight and obesity, it appears to be a significant factor, now supported by physiologic evidence.

Natural Remedies to Help With Sleep

- *Melatonin* is a neurohormone, which is released by the pineal gland from within the center of the brain when one is asleep. The pineal gland is influenced by the amount of light seen by our eyes each day, and production of the hormone is cyclical. Melatonin helps to make us drowsy and helps regulate REM sleep. Scientists have found increased blood levels of stress hormones in people with chronic insomnia, suggesting that these individuals suffer from sustained, round-the-clock activation of the body's system for responding to stress.[137] Melatonin helps produce a substance called arginine vasotocin, which inhibits an adrenal gland stress hormone called cortisol. Cortisol has multiple functions, including protein, carbohydrate, and fat metabolism. Cortisol production is increased during periods of stress, causing the body to feel agitated. Immune functioning is also improved when cortisol production is cut back.[138]

There is an important caveat that must first be heeded before this natural melatonin production can take place. It is now known that optimal melatonin production can only take place in total darkness. Even a tiny nightlight or the light from an alarm clock can greatly interfere with natural melatonin production. This being the case, you can either make sure that you are sleeping in a pitch black bedroom, or you can use the very handy "eye pillows" that are available through a variety of outlets. They block all light from entering the eyes, and in the process, they ensure that the greatest amount of melatonin will naturally be produced within the brain, but darkness is the best. One way that many people have found to improve their sleep is to take melatonin in supplement form.

- *Create a sleep sanctuary.* Make your bedroom comfortable and quiet, with beautiful drapes and pleasant, peaceful pictures. Create a place where when you enter, you immediately feel relaxed and peaceful. When you sleep, keep your bedroom completely dark to ensure maximum melatonin production. Wear ear plugs if you are easily awakened by small noises. Invest in a comfortable bed. If it is too quiet, listen to a recording of nature sounds or soft music. Find a temperature that is most conducive to your sleeping—many people find that cool temperatures help to find a restful sleep. Don't allow the air to get stuffy. Keep the air circulating with a fan in your bedroom.

- *Exercise.* Nothing has been shown to improve sleep quality as effectively as regular exercise. It relieves stress and leads to relaxation. But don't work out within three hours before going to bed, because your metabolism needs time to slow down.

- Another terrific natural remedy for sleep disorders is the calming amino acid *l-tryptophan*. Tryptophan is now available in the U.S. without a prescription. If you have trouble getting tryptophan itself, you can get the next best thing, which is known as 5HTP.

- *Valerian.* Many people like to take the herb known as *valerian* before sleeping, because it does indeed induce a state of drowsiness in most individuals, probably because it binds in the same brain receptors that Valium and other benzodiazepines do.

- *Do not eat or drink anything within two to three hours before sleeping.* Late eating can disrupt hormone production and late drinking can cause you to disrupt sleep by going to the bathroom in the middle of the night.

- Relax with a bath. Consider socks: warm feet = deep sleep. Establish normal sleep patterns and stick with them. Stay away from caffeine after lunch. And wind down before going to bed.

- Make improvements in each of the Super Health Seven Keys as each can affect sleep.

- *Embarking on the Four Corners Program of Superfood Nutrition* is probably the single best step you can do to help improve the quality of your sleep. By changing your diet for the better, the body will naturally begin to operate more naturally, including detoxifying the toxic substances that help to keep us up at night. This is what internal toxins do—they prevent sleep because they disrupt the entire brain and its concomitant neurological functioning. Moreover, by providing your body with the many natural substances that it needs to operate at peak efficiency, through superior nutrition, you will naturally encourage your brain and body to operate normally for a change, and this can naturally result in far better sleep patterns. Moreover, by providing your body with the many natural substances that it

> Without enough sleep, we all become tall two year olds.
>
> JoJo Jensen

needs to operate at peak efficiency, through superior nutrition, you will naturally encourage your brain and body to operate normally for a change, and this can naturally result in far better sleep patterns.

THE
SUPER
HEALTH
DIET

Golden
Keys
to Unlock
Lifelong
Vitality

Golden Key #6— Environmental Hazards

> *As crude a weapon as the caveman's club, the chemical barrage has been hurled against the fabric of life—a fabric on the one hand delicate and destructible, on the other miraculously tough and resilient, and capable of striking back in unexpected ways.*
> RACHEL CARSON

Without becoming paranoid or obsessive about environmental hazards, the reality is that we all face them every day and in almost countless ways. Polluted air, contaminants in the water, food additives and preservatives, and pesticides and herbicides are only a few issues on an extensive list. Gradually, over time we have been exposed to steadily increasing numbers of toxic poisons—asbestos, formaldehyde (in particle board, plywood, paints, and plastics), vinyl chloride, and radioactivity—which can compromise our immune system and lead to disease. It is crucial that we educate ourselves regarding environmental hazards and effect change in our own homes to counteract and prevent them from doing their damage. The key is to avoid the hazards we can while keeping our bodies and immune systems strong so we can deal with the constant barrage of the hazards we cannot avoid.

Given the heavy, sometimes frightening, implications of environmental pollution and toxins, it is easy to feel helpless. The magnitude of the problem may seem overwhelming, but it is not insurmountable. We all have the capacity to affect change on a personal level. It may sound overly simple, but the first place to begin making changes is in our homes. It is important that you are aware of the environment around you, and that you make changes to the things you can control. This will give your body the best possible chance of success.

In my book *Super Health*, I deal with the complex science that explains environmental hazards in an in-depth style that space does not allow me to cover in this book. However, here are a number of practical ways you can safeguard yourself and your family within your own home.

Plastics

Plastic is everywhere and used in everything, and yet few of us understand how toxic it really is. For instance, as a consumer of water and any other beverage that is bottled in plastic, you need to know that plasticizers leach into the water over time as the flexible, malleable plastic degrades while sitting in hot warehouses. Even with #1 PET recyclable plastic, which is generally considered the safest *single-use* plastic bottle choice, there has been some research to suggest that long-term storage of beverages in PET containers may increase the levels of DEHP, an endocrine disrupting phthalate and a probable human carcinogen. Therefore, experts recommend this water not be stored for long periods of time, and that the containers *never be kept for reuse.*

Whenever possible, use glass for drinking and storage containers, ceramic or stainless steel cooking implements and storage products, such as lead-free Corning Ware, and Pyrex containers. Other steps to take include buying your water in glass water bottles, use cellophane or waxed paper for packing your children's lunches, and do not allow the dentists to put plastic sealant on your children's teeth. And ask the butcher to wrap your meats in paper not plastic. It is ironic that we pay huge premiums for organic meats wrapped in plastic.

Fluoride and Weight Loss

While I note several warnings regarding the effects of fluoride in my book *Super Health*, I need to also point out that fluoride in drinking water is known to suppress thyroid function, and reduced thyroid function causes weight gain. Chapter 8 in this book shows the direct correlation between the health of the thyroid and weight loss.

According to the U.S. National Research Council, "Evidence of several types indicates that fluoride affects normal endocrine function or response; the effects of the fluoride-induced changes vary in degree and kind in different individuals. Fluoride is therefore an endocrine disruptor in the broad sense of altering normal endocrine function or response, although probably not in the sense of mimicking a normal hormone."[139]

The effectiveness of the potential of fluoride to impair thyroid function is shown by the fact that up until the 1970s, European doctors used fluoride to reduce the activity of the thyroid gland for patients with hyperthyroidism, at doses from 2 to10 mg/day. Today, many people who live in fluoridated communities are ingesting 1.6 to 6.6 mg/day of fluoride. There is widespread concern that these current levels of fluoride exposures may be playing a role in the widespread incidence of the more common hypothyroidism (underactive thyroid) in the U.S. As I note in Chapter 8, hypothyroidism is a serious condition with a diverse range of symptoms, including fatigue, depression, weight gain, hair loss, muscle pains, increased levels of "bad" cholesterol (LDL), and heart disease.

> Give a man a fish, and he can eat for a day. But teach a man how to fish, and he'll be dead of mercury poisoning inside of three years.
>
> CHARLES HAAS

With water fluoridation, we are forcing people to drink what has been a thyroid-depressing medication that could, in turn, serve to promote higher levels of hypothyroidism (underactive thyroid) in the population, and all the subsequent problems related to this disorder.

Perfumes and Beauty Products

Up to 400 different toxic chemicals are used in a single perfume manufactured today, and today's fragrances are 97 percent synthetic chemicals. Today, man-made fragrance chemicals are used in everything from cleaning materials and toys to garbage bags and kitty litter. The fragrance industry is a self-regulated industry, and the unhappy truth is that 84 percent of these chemical ingredients have never been tested for human toxicology or have been tested only minimally.[140] An

EPA study found that 100 percent of the perfumes examined in its study contained toluene, a known mutagen and sensitizer that can easily accumulate in the body. Toluene not only triggers asthma attacks, it is known to produce asthma in previously healthy people.[141] Fragrance can impact the brain and nervous system along with the immune system. There are numerous organic essential oils on the market today with natural scents, such as lavender, that can be used as wonderful perfumes and colognes.

Look for completely natural hair and skin products, with organic ingredients and devoid of synthetics or petrochemicals. There are a wide variety of companies that make natural personal care products. Two of my favorites are Aubrey Organics and Bert's Bees. Organic products are now available, including hair care, shaving products, makeup and facial care formulations derived from live plants, pure essential oils, trace minerals, and antioxidants. Natural personal care products are often less expensive than their best known chemically laden counterparts.

Food-borne Bacteria and Other Concerns

E. coli is a source of well-recognized food-borne bacterial infections. The specific strain of E. coli known as "O157:H7" can release a powerful toxin that attacks the lining of the intestine. An extraordinarily resilient microbe that is easy to transmit, E. coli is also difficult to eradicate. It is resistant to acid, salt, and chlorine. It can last weeks in moist environments. It survives freezing and heat of up to 160°F. A small uncooked particle of hamburger can contain enough of the pathogen to kill a human. Other significant concerns related to food include mold, mycotoxins, fungus, and parasites. My book *Super Health* explains the steps you can take to safeguard yourself regarding these. A helpful website is the Partnership for Food Safety Education at www.fightbac.org.

From Heavy Metals to VOCs

There are numerous other environmental toxins related to your home that you can control. High concentrations of exposure to heavy metal, such as the use of mercury in silver amalgam dental fillings and in many vaccinations, including flu shots, should be avoided. It should be noted that the FDA mandated that mercury be removed from vaccinations, so mercury was largely replaced with aluminum, which is still a health risk. Flu shots are exempt from having to remove mercury. Indoor air pollutants, such as pollen, pet dander, dust mites, cockroaches, and tobacco and cooking smoke particles, can cause asthma attacks as well as itchy eyes, sneezing, and runny noses. Additionally, VOCs (volatile organic compounds), a major contributor to ozone, are also an air pollutant, two to five times more prevalent in indoor air than outdoor air because they are present in many household products, including our carpets, paints, deodorants, cleaning fluids, cosmetics, air fresheners, and more. Even the electromagnetic waves transmitted by cell phones and other electrical devices (portable phones, microwaves) can damage our cells. And if you are living with someone who smokes, insist that he or she smoke outside—secondhand smoke has strong links to lung cancer.

Vaccines

Be informed and make your own decisions. Vaccinations are a very controversial issue that I address in detail in *Super Health*, and it is imperative that you do your own research and take responsibility for your own health. In my opinion, the world's leading authorities on this subject are bestselling author Dr. Sherri Tenpenny (http://drtenpenny.com) and Barbara Loe Fisher of the National Vaccine Information Center (www.nvic.org), which is the oldest and largest consumer organization advocating the institution of vaccine safety and informed consent protections in the mass vaccination system. We have done programs on this subject that you can watch at www.LivingFuel.TV.

Medical Radiation

Radiation is another hidden danger that is well known to damage DNA, yet the vast majority of people are blissfully unaware of it. The younger you are, the greater the risk, although there is no safe radiation dose. Lifetime exposure to all sources of radiation is thought to be a root cause of cancer and numerous other diseases, yet most people simply have unnecessary radiation tests done just because the doctor wants them. X-ray is the least of the problem, except that they add up during a lifetime. Dental x-rays are about 16 times the radiation of a typical x-ray. CT scans, CAT scans, and PET scans have huge radiation doses that produce up to 500 times the radiation of a chest x-ray. A woman getting 30 MRIs during a lifetime has the radiation equivalent of being within a few miles of the explosion of an atomic bomb. This is why an expert scientific panel changed the mammography recommendation from every year after 40 years old to every other year after 50 years old. There are often imaging tests that are far safer than the one being prescribed, including MRI, ultrasound, and thermography. Again, you must do the research in advance and take your health into your own hands. We have done programs on this topic that you can watch at www.LivingFuel.TV.

Problems in the Food Supply

Did you know that manufacturers routinely put chemical additives and preservatives into our foods to increase shelf life? Or that according to the EPA, 60 percent of herbicides, 90 percent of fungicides, and 30 percent of insecticides are known to be carcinogenic? Pesticide residues have been detected in 50 to 90 percent of U.S. foods, increasing our risk for cancer, Parkinson's disease, miscarriage, birth defects, nerve damage, and more.[142] Or did you know that food irradiation is used to extend the shelf life of our foods by eliminating or controlling pests, sprouting, and rapid ripening, which is highly dangerous for the individuals performing this process as well as also dangerous to those consuming the irradiated foods? Or that GMOs (genetically modified, altered, and biotechnical designed foods) have exploded onto the marketplace (most soy, cotton, and canola are genetically modified, in addition to half of the corn produced) and bring a very real health concern related to whether eating these genetically manipulated foods will lead to increased risk of disease?

The growing consensus among scientists is that small doses of pesticides and other chemicals can cause lasting damage to human health, especially during fetal development and early childhood. Scientists now know enough about the long-term consequences of ingesting these powerful chemicals to advise that we minimize our consumption of pesticides.

Beyond that, a study with rats shows that long-term exposure to the agricultural pesticide Atrazine, one of the most commonly used herbicides to control grasses and weeds worldwide, *causes weight gain* in animals fed normal diets and obesity in those fed high fat diets.[143] These health conditions can lead to diabetes, and they may be triggered by damage to critical structures in cells responsible for making energy. The results suggest a mechanism to explain prior studies that found an association between areas of the United States with heavy Atrazine use and high obesity prevalence.

> There's so much pollution in the air now that if it weren't for our lungs there'd be no place to put it all.
>
> ROBERT ORBEN

Other studies of Atrazine have shown that, depending on Atrazine's administered dose, exposure of male rats during the early postnatal or peripubertal periods can result in alterations in endocrine function.[144] My point to referring to this research is that pesticides, herbicides, and other household chemicals have a negative effect on the endocrine system and lead to weight gain. Excess body fat leads to inflammation in the body and estrogen dominance and further weight gain.

Research by the Environmental Working Group (www.ewg.com) has found that people who eat five fruits and vegetables a day from the Dirty Dozen™ list that follows consume an average of 10 pesticides a day. Those who eat from the 15 least contaminated conventionally grown fruits and vegetables ingest fewer than two pesticides daily. The data used to create these lists is based on produce tested as it is typically eaten (meaning washed, rinsed, or peeled, depending on the type of produce). Rinsing reduces but does not eliminate pesticides. Peeling helps, but valuable nutrients often go down the drain with the skin.

An easy solution to safer foods is to eat only whole, natural organic foods. Organic foods by definition must be free from all genetically modified organisms and produced without artificial pesticides and fertilizers and from an animal raised without the routine use of antibiotics, growth promoters, or other drugs. The Organic and Natural foods industry has exploded and made it much easier for people in busy populated cities to obtain clean whole foods that have not been processed (or perhaps just moderately processed).

While there has not been a huge number of research studies comparing the nutrient levels of organic and conventional crops, the data I have studied shows that organic crops have a higher nutrient level or lower toxic level in 56 percent of the comparison while conventional crops were better only 37 percent of the time. And through the number of nutrients in the crops that have been studied, the average organic crop has approximately 10 to 20 percent higher nutrient levels than a comparable conventional crop. Studies showed that organically fed animals had less illness, better recovery from illness, better testes condition and greater sperm motility in males, greater egg production in females, better fertility, fewer stillbirths and perinatal deaths, and better survival of young—all indicators of health status.[145] This, in my opinion, tells me there are unquestionably enough nutritional benefits for the consumer to buy organic whenever possible.

Another tip is to avoid most fortified or enriched foods as well as processed foods, which are the foods most likely to have genetically modified ingredients. Read labels—if a label lists ingredients such as corn flour and meal, dextrin, starch, soy sauce, margarine, and tofu, there is a good chance that it has come from genetically modified corn or soy. And look closely at produce stickers. These stickers on fruits and vegetables contain different PLU (Price Look Up) codes depending on how the item was grown. The PLU code for conventionally grown produce consists of four numbers prefaced with the number 4; organically grown produce has five numbers, prefaced by the number 9; and genetically modified produce has five numbers prefaced by the number 8. Keep in mind that we want to minimize our exposure to toxins, including agricultural chemicals; however, sometimes you have to just eat your vegetables when organic is not an option. When organically grown is not available, it is a good idea to opt for the product on the Clean 15 list below or at least choose the varieties of fruits and vegetable that you don't eat the skin, which is the part that came in contact with the chemicals.

Dirty Dozen™—Buy These Organic

Celery	Bell peppers
Peaches	Spinach
Strawberries	Kale
Apples	Cherries
Blueberries	Potatoes
Nectarines	Grapes (imported)

Clean 15—Lowest in Pesticides

Onions	Cabbage
Avocado	Eggplant
Sweet corn	Cantaloupe
Pineapple	Watermelon
Mangoes	Grapefruit
Sweet peas	Sweet potato
Asparagus	Honeydew melon
Kiwi	

The Importance of Detoxification in Weight Optimization

Our bodies naturally detoxify 24/7 as part of a normal process. Detoxification is one of the body's most basic subconscious functions that eliminates and neutralizes toxins through every cell, system, and organ of the body, including the colon, kidneys, liver, lungs, lymphatic system, and skin.

With the toxins found in today's air and water and in the food we eat, especially in junk food, our bodies can become overwhelmed. The Standard American Diet, or "SAD," of too much sugar, carbohydrates, damaged fats and trans fats, caffeine, alcohol, and factory farmed animal fat and protein combined with household and lawn and garden chemicals radically changes our internal balance.

Body systems and organs that were once capable of cleaning out unwanted substances are now completely overloaded to the point where toxic material remains inside our tissues, causing a cascade of issues that includes weight gain. Our bodies try to protect us from these hazardous toxins by storing them in various places, particularly in fat cells and in the colon, often coating them with mucus and fat in an attempt to correct the imbalance or prevent an immune response. This excess mucus can cause significant weight gain that will not come off until the hazardous substances are detoxified from the body through detoxification diets or herbal cleansing programs.

The human body has several systems for detoxifying the wide array of pesticides and other foreign compounds that are found in our environment as well as eliminating the toxic end products of naturally occurring metabolic processes produced within the body.[146] Provided the systems are functioning well, the detoxification process will occur quickly and without undue damage to the body. However, as with many bodily processes, the efficiency of these systems may be diminished with declines in general health as we age. This highlights the importance of Superfood Nutrition, combining the most powerfully known nutrients with superfoods and maintaining ample supplies of antioxidants and other liver-protective nutrients in the body.

Detoxification diets are important for everyone, but of particular importance in situations of degenerative disease, diabetes, and autoimmune diseases. It is vital to periodically remove all toxins from your diet and get off of your normal nutritional treadmill by completely stopping the intake of offending foods for a few days and instead do a super clean Four Corners liquid diet. The detox regimen I practice and recommend is called the FUEL Fast, which you can read about in the "Superfood Nutrition" chapter.

While a variety of nutrients act to enhance detoxification and as essential cofactors in detoxification, four have been found to directly enhance it: curcumin, chlorophyllin, wasabi, and broccoli extract.

Curcumin, a phytonutrient derived from the Indian spice turmeric, the main ingredient in curry, is one of the most effective anti-mutagens. A member of the ginger family, turmeric has a reputation for quelling inflammation and healing various maladies ranging from ulcers to upset stomach to arthritis and has been shown to have numerous cardiovascular benefits, in part because it reduces total cholesterol levels and inhibits LDL (low density lipoprotein) oxidation. Researchers have discovered that curcumin can also help protect against the multitude of mutagens in our environment that are often a direct link to cancer development.[147] As I discuss elsewhere in this book, hot peppers also assist in fat burning.

Chlorophyllin, a sodium/copper derivative of chlorophyll, has the benefit of being water soluble, allowing it to be transported easily in the blood. It also has anti-carcinogenic properties. Several studies have demonstrated chlorophyllin's effectiveness. In an experiment with bacteria, the nutrient was added to petri dishes containing substances that normally produce mutations, such as fried beef, fried pork, cigarette smoke, coal dust, and diesel emission particles.[148] Chlorophyllin inhibited mutagenicity by a minimum of 75 percent and by as much as 100 percent.

Wasabi, the green, pungent horseradish usually served with sushi, is a member of the cruciferous family of vegetables, which includes cabbage, broccoli, cauliflower, bok choy, horseradish, and ten other plants. These vegetables contain high levels of glucosinolates, a group of compounds that are converted to isothiocyanates. Wasabi is one of the most potent sources of isothiocyanates among all plant species. A Japanese study found that allyl isothiocyanate has significant antioxidant actions, particularly against the superoxide radical.[149] According to the authors, this phytochemical also has an inhibitory effect on the growth of food poisoning bacteria and fungi and showed anti-mutagenic activity against a common carcinogen found in broiled fish and meat. Wasabi supplementation is highly recommended.

Broccoli is another plentiful source of glucosinolates, which are converted enzymatically into isothiocyanates. In the body, the isothiocyanates boost production of several detoxification enzymes, enhance antioxidant status, and protect animals against chemically induced cancer.[150] As a result, nutritionists recommend consuming broccoli and similar vegetables at least three times a week. Concentrated extracts of broccoli enable you to boost your intake of these beneficial compounds even more.

Increasing your consumption of greens and spices can be Super Healthy.

THE
SUPER
HEALTH
DIET

Golden
Keys
to Unlock
Lifelong
Vitality

Golden Key #7—Meditation and Prayer

*The man who kneels to God can
stand up to anything.*
LOUIS EVANS JR.

We have seen the importance of our physical and mental health in the first six Golden Keys, which dealt primarily with the body and soul. Now we move on to the inner man, the human spirit, and meditation and prayer as the key to our spiritual health. God created you as a three-dimensional person; that is, you have a spirit (wisdom, consciousness, and commune), a soul (mind, will, and emotions), and a body (bone, blood, and flesh). He created us with a destiny to fulfill, but many of us live our lives disconnected from Him. Many of the afflictions and symptoms of depression, alienation, and many other disorders that we deal with are the result of having lost our connection with God.

Science has recognized the existence of body, soul, and spirit, and in part due to recent advancements in the science of human genetics, scientists continue to call into question major elements of Darwin's Theory of Evolution. As a result, the Theory of Intelligent Design has gained significant traction in the global scientific community. I have always thought that the theory that says out of nothing came something, and out of that something came everything, was a little on the weak side. In my book *Super Health: Seven Golden Keys to Unlock Lifelong Vitality*, I discussed the scientific evidence supporting meditation and prayer. More and more studies have been published showing the miraculous power of these timeless practices.

It is important to note a legitimate scientific principle called placebo.

A placebo is a phony drug or treatment designed to convince a patient that he or she is receiving care for their condition, and the results are compared to patients receiving various real treatments. Placebos are foundational to scientific research, and it is well known that the placebo effect is a real clinical effect that must be accounted for. Interestingly, in an article published on MedPageToday.com in December 2010, the placebo effect has been demonstrated to work even in patients who realize they are taking a placebo. We have discussed earlier in this book that virtually any diet can work for a while. This is similar to a placebo effect. Any time a person rightly or wrongly believes that something is going to work for them, it often does work for a time. *Real power to effect change in your circumstances is when you apply your belief to something that is actually true.*

My wife and I are Christian ministers who love and respect people of all religions. Meditation and prayer are at the root of virtually all religions with the possible exception of the religion of sports fanaticism. In numerous research studies, meditation and prayer have demonstrated remarkable and statistically significant power to reduce stress and effect change in human life. With so much research behind it, thinking people can no longer simply reject it out of hand. No matter what you believe, you have a duty to yourself to know why you believe what you believe. Don't just believe a certain way because someone told you to or because it was the way you were taught. The truth can stand the test. And it is the Truth that will set you free.

Throughout history many great thinkers, including Galileo Galilei, Isaac Newton, J.R.R. Tolkien, and C. S. Lewis, were Christians. As an atheist, C. S. Lewis is said to have become a Christian trying to disprove the Bible.

The Bible tells us in Jeremiah 33:3, "Call to me, and I will answer you, and show you great and mighty things, which you know not."

We are also promised in Deuteronomy 4:29, "To seek the Lord your God, and you will find Him if you search for Him with all your heart and all your soul."

In today's relentless world, there is never enough time, money, or breaks from the pressures. Between juggling a career, a family, hobbies, and public duties, countless demands scream for our attention and can cause anxiety. If they reach our heart, they destroy our peace, overwhelm our emotions and minds, and can easily escalate into health problems at every level.

But in the midst of all this commotion, God is speaking to us, "Be still, and know that I am God" (Psalm 46:10). Have we stopped to listen? Can we hear Him? "How?" you may ask. Through meditation and prayer. The Lord is asking us to quiet our soul, to sit at His feet, and listen to Him. He wants to be our friend, and He wants to spend time with us.

Meditation and prayer are by far the most important of the Seven Keys, because we were created to know and love God and to have fellowship with Him in this life…and for eternity. Living in a loving relationship with God as our Father, we receive the gracious blessings of the children of God. As we deepen our relationship with Him, and God becomes our best friend, the more profound of an impact He will naturally have on our life and health.

Meditation and prayer involves a two-part process of communicating with our Lord. Meditation prepares our spirit, soul, and body to speak and listen to God, and prayer is the act of speaking with God. What happens within our spirit has a profound effect on our whole being.

Through meditation and prayer, we take the time to get alone with Him, for only His presence will fulfill the desires of our spirit. He longs for us…waits for us to come to Him with all our heart. He knows that many of the life issues we are trying to deal with will vanish when we know Him as our heavenly Father. He wants to meet our deepest needs. But the yearning within will only be satisfied when we find God, and He cannot be found in the midst of noise and restlessness.

Meditation

Meditation is simply concentrating and focusing on several words or a single sentence on a persistent and intense basis. It incorporates and utilizes all the sensory processes, especially visualization, for an extended period of time. The ultimate purpose is to develop a deeper understanding of it.

Christian meditation differs from Eastern meditation in these ways. Eastern meditation focuses on emptying the mind, withdrawing from reality, and results in a loss of personal identity; Christian meditation focuses on filling the mind with an awareness of God's presence, knowing God in reality, and results in gaining our true identity in Jesus Christ. Eastern meditation recognizes no objective truth and is dependent upon the person's ability to meditate; Christian meditation recognizes the Word of God as the only standard for truth and a dependency on the Holy Spirit to accomplish God's purposes in us. Eastern meditation has no goal outside of the experience itself, whereas the goal of Christian meditation is a greater love for God and others. The greatest commandment is: "Thou shalt love the Lord thy God with all thy heart, and with all thy soul, and with all thy strength, and with all thy mind; and thy neighbor as thyself" (Luke 10:27).

> **But his delight is in the law of the Lord, and in His law He meditates day and night.**
>
> KING DAVID,
> PSALM 1:2

Meditation and Prayer Tips

1. Find a quiet, solitary place.
2. Relax. Sit quietly in a comfortable position. Close your eyes. Deeply relax all your muscles. Breathe slowly and naturally, and as you do, repeat your focus word, phrase, or prayer silently to yourself as you exhale.
3. Listen to instrumental Christ-centered worship music.
4. Let the intrusive thoughts come and go.
5. Focus on inspirational thoughts, such as "God will make a way where there is no way!"
6. Visualize Jesus as the Good Shepherd to whom you go when you are distressed or frightened.
7. Be comfortable physically.
8. Make it a habit (establish regularity and consistency). Many people prefer early morning, as this is often the most solitary and uncomplicated time of day. Because our bodies and minds naturally gravitate toward rituals, you will be able to move into meditation with greater ease if you are habitual in your practice.

Prayer

"And when He had sent the multitudes away, He went up on the mountain by Himself to pray. Now when evening came, he was alone" (Matthew 14:23). If Jesus Christ made it a regular priority to be alone in prayer, do we really think we can do without it? We must have our times of being alone with our Father if we would have our heart filled with peace and our mind opened to the daily revelation that God gives to those who love Him. Make it a pattern for your life as well.

Get alone and quiet your spirit and soul. Learn to love the silence, for it is in solitude with God where you learn to depend on Him alone. Reflect upon God and His wondrous personality. Give Him the opportunity to show Himself to you and to do all that He says He'll do for you. To *hope* in God, to *rest* in the Lord, to *wait* on Him, to *know* Him—these express the purpose and joy of prayer.

You can talk with God, telling Him of your joys and hopes and desires, and receive back His answers to your own heart. In prayer God comes to us and calms our fears, gives us His perspective on our lives, and grants us understanding of the things that please Him. To know God in the personal experience of His presence and love is life indeed.

Eight Prayer Principles

1. Ask forgiveness for anything you have said or done to displease God, including judging others, and forgive and release all judgments against everyone who has wronged you. Unforgiveness of others will block the fullness of God's will for your life. It is like drinking a cup of poison and expecting it to hurt someone else. You will be judged as you judge others. "Therefore you are inexcusable, O man, whoever you are who judge, for in whatever you judge another you condemn yourself; for you who judge practice the same things. But we know that the judgment of God is according to truth against those who practice such things. And do you think this, O man, you who judge those practicing such things, and doing the same, that you will escape the judgment of God? Or do you despise the riches of His

goodness, forbearance, and longsuffering, not knowing that the goodness of God leads you to repentance?" (Romans 2:1–4).

2. Give thanks and praise to God. Open the eyes of your soul to the person and majesty of God as your Father.

3. Read the Bible. Open His timeless Book and hear His gentle voice speaking to you. Study to show yourself approved by God.

4. Meditate on the Word of God. His Word will breathe life into you with power, His truths will be inscribed on your heart, and you will find His secrets to living a fulfilled life.

5. Pray for others. Keep a list of the prayer needs of others and offer them to God.

6. Pray for yourself. In the Psalms, David talked to God about how he was feeling, and so should you. His prayer life dealt with the real issues he was facing, and so should yours.

7. Keep a list of your needs and the desires of your heart and ask God to meet them. Meditate and listen for the still small voice of God.

8. "Cast your burden upon the Lord and He will sustain you; He will never allow the righteous to be shaken" (Psalm 55:22).

If you have read this chapter and wonder if there is more truth for you to explore, please consider the following scriptures. "For God so loved the world that He gave His only begotten Son, that whoever believes in Him should not perish but have everlasting life" (John 3:16). That Son, Jesus, said; "I am the way, the truth, and the life. No one comes to the Father except through Me" (John 14:6). God's invitation to you is "that if you confess with your mouth the Lord Jesus and believe in your heart that God has raised Him from the dead, you will be saved" (Romans 10:9).

ENDNOTES

1. http://agingcenters.org/docs/resHigh8.pdf

2. http://www.reuters.com/article/newsOne/idUSTRE50863H20090109

3. http://abcnews.go.com/Health/WellnessNews/Story?id=791
    1505&page=1

4. http://www.prweb.com/releases/2005/03/prweb223760.htm

5. Skov AR, Toubro S, Rønn B, Holm L, Astrup A. Randomized trial of
    protein vs carbohydrate in ad libitum fat reduced diet for the treatment
    of obesity. Int J Obes Relat Metab Disord 1999;23:528-536.

    Brehm BJ, Seeley RJ, Daniels SR, D'Alessio DA. A randomized trial
    comparing a very low carbohydrate diet and a calorie-restricted low fat
    diet on body weight and cardiovascular risk factors in healthy women. J
    Clin Endocrinol Metab 2003;88:1617-1623.

    Foster GD, Wyatt HR, Hill JO, et al. A randomized trial of a low
    carbohydrate diet for obesity. N Engl J Med 2003;348:2082-2090.

    Samaha FF, Iqbal N, Seshadri P, et al. A low carbohydrate as compared
    with a low fat diet in severe obesity. N Engl J Med 2003;348:2074-
    2081.

    Yancy WS, Olsen MK, Guyton JR, Bakst RP, Westman EC. A low
    carbohydrate ketogenic diet versus a low fat diet to treat obesity and
    hyperlipidemia: a randomized, controlled trial. Ann Intern Med
    2004;140:769-777.

    Volek J, Sharman M, Gómez A, et al. Comparison of energy-restricted
    very low carbohydrate and low fat diets on weight loss and body
    composition in overweight men and women. Nutr Metab (Lond)
    2004;1:13-13.

    Due A, Toubro S, Skov AR, Astrup A. Effect of normal fat diets, either
    medium or high in protein, on body weight in overweight subjects: a
    randomized 1-year trial. Int J Obes Relat Metab Disord 2004;28:1283-
    1290.

    Gardner CD, Kiazand A, Alhassan S, et al. Comparison of the Atkins,
    Zone, Ornish, and LEARN diets for change in weight and related risk
    factors among overweight premenopausal women: the A to Z Weight
    Loss Study: a randomized trial. JAMA 2007;297:969-977. [Erratum,
    JAMA 2007;298:178.]

    Shai I, Schwarzfuchs D, Henkin Y, et al. Weight loss with a low
    carbohydrate, Mediterranean, or low fat diet. N Engl J Med
    2008;359:229-241.

6. Noakes M, Keough JB, Foster PR, Clifton PM. Effect of an energy-restricted, high protein, low fat diet relative to a conventional low fat, high carbohydrate diet on weight loss, body composition, nutritional status, and markers of cardiovascular health in obese women. Am J Clin Nutr 2005;81:1298-1306.

McLaughlin T, Carter S, Lamendola C, et al. Effects of moderate variations in macronutrient composition on weight loss and reduction in cardiovascular disease risk in obese, insulin-resistant adults. Am J Clin Nutr 2006;84:813-821.

McMillan-Price J, Petocz P, Atkinson F, et al. Comparison of 4 diets of varying glycemic load on weight loss and cardiovascular risk reduction in overweight and obese young adults: a randomized controlled trial. Arch Intern Med 2006;166:1466-1475.

Das SK, Gilhooly CH, Golden JK, et al. Long-term effects of 2 energy-restricted diets differing in glycemic load on dietary adherence, body composition, and metabolism in CALERIE: a 1-y randomized controlled trial. Am J Clin Nutr 2007;85:1023-1030.

Lecheminant JD, Gibson CA, Sullivan DK, et al. Comparison of a low carbohydrate and low fat diet for weight maintenance in overweight or obese adults enrolled in a clinical weight management program. Nutr J 2007;6:36-36.

7. Foster GD, Wyatt HR, Hill JO, et al. A randomized trial of a low carbohydrate diet for obesity. N Engl J Med 2003;348:2082-2090.

Due A, Toubro S, Skov AR, Astrup A. Effect of normal fat diets, either medium or high in protein, on body weight in overweight subjects: a randomized 1-year trial. Int J Obes Relat Metab Disord 2004;28:1283-1290.

Das SK, Gilhooly CH, Golden JK, et al. Long-term effects of 2 energy-restricted diets differing in glycemic load on dietary adherence, body composition, and metabolism in CALERIE: a 1-y randomized controlled trial. Am J Clin Nutr 2007;85:1023-1030.

Stern L, Iqbal N, Seshadri P, et al. The effects of low carbohydrate versus conventional weight loss diets in severely obese adults: one-year follow-up of a randomized trial. Ann Intern Med 2004;140:778-785.

Dansinger ML, Gleason JA, Griffith JL, Selker JP, Schaefer EJ. Comparison of the Atkins, Ornish, Weight Watchers, and Zone diets for weight loss and heart disease risk reduction: a randomized trial. JAMA 2005;293:43-53.

Luscombe-Marsh ND, Noakes M, Wittert GA, Keough JB, Foster P, Clifton PM. Carbohydrate restricted diets high in either monounsaturated fat or protein are equally effective in promoting fat loss and improving blood lipids. Am J Clin Nutr 2005;81:762-772.

Keogh JB, Luscombe-Marsh ND, Noakes M, Wittert GA, Clifton PM. Long-term weight maintenance and cardiovascular risk factors are not different following weight loss on carbohydrate-restricted diets high in either monounsaturated fat or protein in obese hyperinsulinemic men and women. Br J Nutr 2007;97:405-410.

8. Ornish D, Scherwitz LW, Billings JH, et al. Intensive lifestyle changes for reversal of coronary heart disease. JAMA 1998;280:2001-2007. [Erratum, JAMA 1999;281:1380.]

Barnard ND, Cohen J, Jenkins DJ, et al. A low fat vegan diet improves glycemic control and cardiovascular risk factors in a randomized clinical trial in individuals with type 2 diabetes. Diabetes Care 2006;29:1777-1783.

Turner-McGrievy GM, Barnard ND, SciAlli AR. A two-year randomized weight loss trial comparing a vegan diet to a more moderate low fat diet. Obesity (Silver Spring) 2007;15:2276-2281.

9. Due A, Toubro S, Skov AR, Astrup A. Effect of normal fat diets, either medium or high in protein, on body weight in overweight subjects: a randomized 1-year trial. Int J Obes Relat Metab Disord 2004;28:1283-1290.

Shai I, Schwarzfuchs D, Henkin Y, et al. Weight loss with a low carbohydrate, Mediterranean, or low fat diet. N Engl J Med 2008;359:229-241.

Turner-McGrievy GM, Barnard ND, SciAlli AR. A two-year randomized weight loss trial comparing a vegan diet to a more moderate low fat diet. Obesity (Silver Spring) 2007;15:2276-2281.

Toubro S, Astrup A. Randomized comparison of diets for maintaining obese subjects' weight after major weight loss: ad lib, low fat, high carbohydrate diet v fixed energy intake. BMJ 1997;314:29-34.

McManus K, Antinoro L, Sacks F. A randomized controlled trial of a moderate fat, low energy diet compared with a low fat, low energy diet for weight loss in overweight adults. Int J Obes Relat Metab Disord 2001;25:1503-1511.

10. http://content.nejm.org/cgi/content/full/360/9/859

11. Bray GA, Greenway FL (1999). Current and Potential Drugs for Treatment of Obesity: Table 19: Clinical trials with metformin for the treatment of obese diabetics. Endocrine Reviews 20 (6): 805–87. Doi:10.1210/er.20.6.805. PMID 10605627. http://edrv.endojournals. org/cgi/content/full/20/6/805/T19. Retrieved 2006-08-07

12. Leigh C. Serotonin and the Biology of Bingeing. *Eating Disorders: A Reference Sourcebook.* In: Lemberg R. Ed., Oryx Press; 1998:51.

13. Breum L, Rasmussen MH, Hilsted J, Fernstrom JD. Twenty-four-hour plasma tryptophan concentrations and ratios are below normal in obese subjects and are not normalized by substantial weight reduction. Am J Clin Nutr. 2003 May;77(5):1112-8.

   Brandacher G, Hoeller E, Fuchs D, Weiss HG. Chronic immune activation underlies morbid obesity: is IDO a key player? Curr Drug Metab. 2007 Apr;8(3):289-95.

14. Cavaliere H, Medeiros-Neto G. The anorectic effect of increasing doses of L-tryptophan in obese patients. Eat Weight Disord. 1997 Dec;2(4):211-5.

15. Maeda H, Hosokawa M, Sashima T, Funayama K, Miyashita K. Fucoxanthin from edible seaweed, Undaria pinnatifida, shows antiobesity effect through UCP1 expression in white adipose tissues. Biochem Biophys Res Commun. 2005 Jul 1;332(2):392-7.

16. www.mayoclinic.com/health/weight loss/HQ01160.

17. Abate N, Haffner SM, Garg A, Peshock RM, Grundy SM. Sex steroid hormones, upper body obesity, and insulin resistance. J Clin Endocrinol Metab. 2002 Oct;87(10):4522-7.

   Vermeulen A, Kaufman JM, Goemaere S, van Pottelberg I. Estradiol in elderly men. Aging Male. 2002 Jun;5(2):98-102.

   Marin P, Krotkiewski M, Bjorntorp P. Androgen treatment of middle-aged, obese men: effects on metabolism, muscle and adipose tissues. Eur J Med. 1992 Oct;1(6):329-36.

18. Villareal DT, Holloszy JO. Effect of DHEA on abdominal fat and insulin action in elderly women and men: a randomized controlled trial. JAMA. 2004 Nov 10;292(18):2243-8.

19. Abbott RD, Launer LJ, Rodriguez BL, et al. Serum estradiol and risk of stroke in elderly men. Neurology. 2007 Feb 20;68(8):563-8.

   Dunajska K, Milewicz A, Szymczak J, et al. Evaluation of sex hormone levels and some metabolic factors in men with coronary atherosclerosis.

Aging Male. 2004 Sep;7(3):197-204.

Wranicz JK, Cygankiewicz I, Rosiak M, Kula P, Kareba W. The relationship between sex hormones and lipid profile in men with coronary artery disease. Int J Cardiol. 2005 May 11;101(1):105-10.

20   Jankowska EA, Rozentryt P, Ponikowska B. Circulating estradiol and mortality in men with systolic chronic heart failure. JAMA. 2009 May 13;301(18):1892-901.

21.   Somers V, Davison D, Singh P, Huyber C, Lopez-Jimenez F, Jensen M. Modest Visceral Fat Gain Causes Endothelial Dysfunction in Healthy Humans. J Am Coll Cardiol, 2010; 56:662-666, doi:10.1016/j.jacc.2010.03.063.

22.   Jacobs EJ, Newton CC, Wang Y, Patel AV, McCullough ML, Campbell PT, Thun MJ, Gapstur SM. Waist Circumference and All-Cause Mortality in a Large U.S. Cohort. Arch Intern Med. 2010;170(15):1293-1301.

23.   Li S, Zhao JH, Luan J, Ekelund U, Luben RN, et al. (2010) Physical Activity Attenuates the Genetic Predisposition to Obesity in 20,000 Men and Women from EPIC-Norfolk Prospective Population Study. PLoS Med 7(8): e1000332. doi:10.1371/journal.pmed.1000332.

24.   Huang AJ, Subak LL, Wing R, West DS, Hernandez AL, Macer J, Grady D. For the Program to Reduce Incontinence by Diet and Exercise Investigators. Arch Intern Med. 2010;170(13):1161-1167.

25.   Roy Walford, *Beyond the 120 Year Diet* (New York: Four Walls Eight Windows, 2000), pp. 45-59.

26.   Ahmed T, Das Sai K, Golden J, Saltzman E, Roberts S, Meydani S. Calorie restriction enhances T-cell-mediated immune response in adult overweight men and women. The Journals of Gerontology. Series A, Biological sciences and medical sciences 2009;64(11):1107-13.

27.   Yamasa T, Ikeda S, Koga S, et al. Evaluation of glucose tolerance, postprandial hyperglycemia and hyperinsulinemia influencing the incidence of coronary heart disease. Intern Med. 2007;46(9):543-6.

28.   Henry RR, Wiest-Kent TA, Scheaffer L, Kolterman OG, Olefsky JM. Metabolic consequences of very-low-calorie diet therapy in obese non-insulin-dependent diabetic and nondiabetic subjects. Diabetes. 1986 Feb;35(2):155-64.

Larson-Meyer DE, Heilbronn LK, Redman LM, et al. Effect of calorie restriction with or without exercise on insulin sensitivity, beta-cell function, fat cell size, and ectopic lipid in overweight subjects. Diabetes Care. 2006 Jun;29(6):1337-44.

Bodkin NL, Ortmeyer HK, Hansen BC. Long-term dietary restriction in older-aged rhesus monkeys: effects on insulin resistance. J Gerontol A Biol Sci Med Sci. 1995 May;50(3):B142-7.

Gumbs AA, Modlin IM, Ballantyne GH. Changes in insulin resistance following bariatric surgery: role of caloric restriction and weight loss. Obes Surg. 2005 Apr;15(4):462-73.

Nakai Y, Taniguchi A, Fukushima M, et al. Insulin sensitivity during very-low-calorie diets assessed by minimal modeling. Am J Clin Nutr. 1992 Jul;56(1 Suppl):179S-81S.

29. Heilbronn LK, de Jonge L, Frisard MI, et al. Effect of 6-month calorie restriction on biomarkers of longevity, metabolic adaptation, and oxidative stress in overweight individuals: a randomized controlled trial. JAMA. 2006 Apr 5;295(13):1539-48.

30. Emral R, Koseoglulari O, Tonyukuk V, et al. The effect of short-term glycemic regulation with gliclazide and metformin on postprandial lipemia. Exp Clin Endocrinol Diabetes. 2005 Feb;113(2):80-4.

Deutsch JC, Santhosh-Kumar CR, Kolhouse JF. Efficacy of metformin in non-insulin-dependent diabetes mellitus. N Engl J Med. 1996 Jan 25;334(4):269-70.

Charles MA, Eschwege E. Prevention of type 2 diabetes: role of metformin. Drugs. 1999;58 Suppl 1:71-3.

31. Ahima RS, Lazar MA. Adipokines and the peripheral and neural control of energy balance. Mol Endocrinol. 2008 May;22(5):1023-31.

32. Walford RL, Harris SB, Gunion MW. The calorically restricted low-fat nutrient-dense diet in Biosphere 2 significantly lowers blood glucose, total leukocyte count, cholesterol, and blood pressure in humans. Proc. Natl Acadamy Sci USA. 1992 Ded 1;89(23):11533-7.

33. Bjornholt JV, Erikssen G, Aaser E, et al. Fasting blood glucose and under estimated risk factor for CVD. Diabetes Care. 1999 Jan;22(11):45-9.

34. Brand-Miller JC, Holt S, Pawlak DB, McMillan J. Glycemic Index and Obesity. Am J Clin Nutr. 2002 July;76(1):281S-5S.

35. Stephen Holt, M.D., *Combat Syndrome X, Y and Z* (Newark: Wellness Publishing, 2002), p. 32.

36. Stephen Holt, M.D., Lecture, "Combating Syndrome X and Enhancing

Low Carb Diets" (Washington, D.C.: Natural Products Expo East/ Organic Products Expo—BioFach America, October 15, 2004).

37. Despres JP, Lemieux I. Abdominal obesity and metabolic syndrome. Nature. 2006 Dec 14;444(7121):881-7.

    Bodary PF, Iglay HB, Eitzman DT. Strategies to reduce vascular risk associated with obesity. Curr Vasc Pharmacol. 2007 Oct;5(4):249-58.

38. Williams MJ, Williams SM, Milne BJ, Hancox RJ, Poulton R. Association between C-reactive protein, metabolic cardiovascular risk factors, obesity and oral contraceptive use in young adults. Int J Obes Relat Metab Disord. 2004 Aug;28(8):998-1003.

39. Stephen Holt, M.D., Lecture, "Combating Syndrome X and Enhancing Low Carb Diets" (Washington, D.C.: Natural Products Expo East/ Organic Products Expo—BioFach America, October 15, 2004).

40. Cheryle Hart, M.D. and Mary Kay Grossman, *The Insulin-Resistance Diet* (Sylmar, CA: NTC Publishing Group, 2001), pp. 67-81.

41. Deborah S. Romaine and Jennifer B. Marks, *Syndrome X: Managing Insulin Resistance* (New York: Harpertorch, 2000), pp. 157-181.

42. Keijzers GB, De Galan BE, Tack CJ, Smits P. Caffeine Can Decrease Insulin Sensitivity in Humans. Diabetes Care. 2002 Feb;25:364-369.

43. Kromhout D, Bloemberg B, Seidell JC, Nissinen A, Menotti A. Physical activity and dietary fiber determine population body fat levels: the Seven Countries Study. Int J ObeS Relat Metab Disord. 2001 Mar;25(3):301-6.

44. Liu S, Willett WC, Manson JE, et al. Relation between changes in intakes of dietary fiber and grain products and changes in weight and development of obesity among middle-aged women. Am J Clin Nutr. 2003 Nov;78(5):920-7.

45. Ludwig DS, Pereira MA, Kroenke CH, et al. Dietary fiber, weight gain, and cardiovascular disease risk factors in young adults. JAMA. 1999 Oct 27;282(16):1539-46.

46. Karhunen LJ, Juvonen KR, Flander SM, et al. A psyllium fiber-enriched meal strongly attenuates postprandial gastrointestinal peptide release in healthy young adults. J Nutr. Apr2010:140(4):737-44.

47. Luo W, Cao J, Li J, He W. Adipose tissue-specific PPARgamma deficiency increases resistance to oxidative stress. Exp Gerontol. 2007 Nov 21.

48. Ziccardi P, Nappo F, Giugliano G, et al. Reduction of inflammatory

cytokine concentrations and improvement of endothelial functions in obese women after weight loss over one year. Circulation. 2002 Feb 19;105(7):804-9.

49. Yin J, Xing H., et al. 2008. Efficacy of berberine in patients with type 2 diabetes mellitus. Metabolism 57(5): 712-717.

50. Mas E, Woodman RJ, Burke V, Puddey IB, Beilin LJ, Durand T, Mori TA. The omega-3 fatty acids EPA and DHA decrease plasma F(2)-isoprostanes: Results from two placebo-controlled interventions. Free Radical Research. Published online ahead of print, doi: 10.3109/10715762.2010.492830.

51. Young D, Talukdar S, Bae EU, Imamura T, Morinaga H, Fan W, Li P, Lu WJ, Watkins S, Olefsky JM. GPR120 Is an Omega-3 Fatty Acid Receptor Mediating Potent Anti-inflammatory and Insulin-Sensitizing Effects. Cell, Volume 142, Issue 5, 687-698, 3 September 2010.

52. Dulloo AG, Duret C, Rohrer D, et al. Efficacy of a green tea extract rich in catechin polyphenols and caffeine in increasing 24-h energy expenditure and fat oxidation in humans. Am J Clin Nutr. 1999 Dec;70(6):1040-5.

53. Dulloo AG, Seydoux J, Girardier L, Chantre P, Vandermander J. Green tea and thermogenesis: interactions between catechin-polyphenols, caffeine and sympathetic activity. Int J Obes Relat Metab Disord. 2000 Feb;24(2):252-8.

54. Wong RHX, Howe PRC, Buckley JD, Coates AM, Kunz I, Berry NM. Acute resveratrol supplementation improves flow-mediated dilatation in overweight/obese individuals with mildly elevated blood pressure. Nutrition, Metabolism & Cardiovascular Diseases. 02 August 2010 (10.1016/j.numecd.2010.03.003).

55. Matsumoto T, Miyawaki C, Ue H, Yuasa T, Miyatsuji A, Moritani T. Effects of capsaicin-containing yellow curry sauce on sympathetic nervous system activity and diet-induced thermogenesis in lean and obese young women. J Nutr Sci Vitaminol (Tokyo). 2000 Dec;46(6):309-15.

56. Ohnuki K, Niwa S, Maeda S, Inoue N, Yazawa S, Fushiki T. CH-19 sweet, a non-pungent cultivar of red pepper, increased body temperature and oxygen consumption in humans. Biosci Biotechnol Biochem. 2001 Sep;65(9):2033-6.

57. Joo JI, Kim DH, Choi JW, Yun JW. Proteomic Analysis for Antiobesity Potential of Capsaicin on White Adipose Tissue in Rats Fed with a High Fat Diet. J. Proteome Res., 2010, 9 (6), pp 2977–2987, April 1, 2010.

58. Andrew L. Stoll, *The Omega-3 Connection* (New York: Simon & Schuster, 2002), p. 116.

59. Jolly CA, Muthukumar A, Avula CP, Troyer D, Fenandes G. Life Span Is Prolonged in Food-Restricted Autoimmune-Prone (NZB x NZW)F(1) Mice Fed a Diet Enriched with (n-3) Fatty Acids. Journal Nutrition. Oct2001;131(10):2753-60.

60. Li JJ, Huang CJ, Xie D. Anti-obesity effects of conjugated linoleic acid, docosahexaenoic acid, and eicosapentaenoic acid. Mol Nutr Food Res. 2008 Jun;52(6):631-45.

61. Makhoul Z, Kristal AR, Gulati R, Luick B, Bersamin A, Boyer B, and Mohatt GV. Associations of very high intakes of eicosapentaenoic and docosahexaenoic acids with biomarkers of chronic disease risk among Yup'ik Eskimos. Am J Clin Nutr 2010 91: 777-785; First published online January 20, 2010. doi:10.3945/ajcn.2009.28820.

62. Melanson SF, Lewandrowski EL, Flood JG, Lewandrowski KB. Measurement of organochlorines in commercial over-the-counter fish oil preparations: implications for dietary and therapeutic recommendations for omega-3 fatty acids and a review of the literature. Arch Pathol Lab Med. 2005 Jan;129(1):74-7.

63. Laidlow M, Holub BJ. Effects of supplementation with fish oil-derived n-3 fatty acids and linolenic acid on circulating plasma lipids and fatty acid profiles in women. Am J Clin Nutr. Jan2003;77:37-42.

64. Neubronner J, Schuchardt JP, Kressel G, Merkel M, von Schacky C, Hahn A. Enhanced increase of omega-3 index in response to long-term n-3 fatty acid supplementation from triacylglycerides versus ethyl esters. European Journal of Clinical Nutrition. Published online ahead of print, doi: 10.1038/ejcn.2010.239.

65. www.nutraingredients-usa.com/Industry/Supplements-can-fill-health-gaps-say-dietitians/?c=dmCIFMv2LEYRCPB8TXpTIQ%3D%3D&utm_source=newsletter_daily&utm_medium=email&utm_campaign=Newsletter%2BDaily

    www.news-medical.net/news/20091210/Registered-dietitians-recommend-vitamins-and-supplements-for-improved-bone-health.aspx

    www.lifesupplemented.org/supplements/healthcare_professionals_impact_study/physicians.htm

    www.lifesupplemented.org/supplements/healthcare_professionals_impact_study/nurses.htm www.lifesupplemented.org/articles/news/nurse_practitioners_to_patients_can_we_talk.htm

66. Dickinson A, Boyon N, Shao A. Physicians and nurses use and recommend dietary supplements: report of a survey. Nutr. J. 2009 Jul 1;8:29.

67. Sareen S. Gropper, Jack L. Smith, James L. Groff, *Advanced Nutrition and Human Metabolism* (Wadsworth Publishing).

68. Chumlea WC, Baumgartner RN, Vellas BP. Anthropometry and body composition in the perspective of nutritional status in the elderly. Nutrition 1991;7:57e60.

69. Wolfe RR. Regulation of muscle protein by amino acids. J Nutr2002;132:3219Se24S.

70. http://jn.nutrition.org/cgi/content/full/130/7/1865S.

71. 2005 Dietary guidelines for Americans. 6th ed. Washington, DC: US Department of Health and Human Services; 2005.

72. Robert R. Wolfe, et al. Optimal protein intake in the elderly. Clinical Nutrition (2008), doi:10.1016/j.clnu.2008.06.008.

73. Institute of Medicine. Dietary reference intakes for energy, carbohydrate, fiber, fat, fatty acids, cholesterol, protein and amino acids. Washington, DC: National Academy Press; 2005.

74. Robert R. Wolfe, et al. Optimal protein intake in the elderly. Clinical Nutrition (2008), doi:10.1016/j.clnu.2008.06.008.

75. Layman DK. Protein quality and quantity at levels above the RDA improves adult weight loss. Journal of Am. Coll. Nutr. (2004) 23(6):635-8].

76. Westerterp-Plantenga MS. The significance of protein in food intake and body weight regulation. Curr Opin Clin Nutrition Metabolic Care. (2003) 6(6):635-8.

77. Laymen DK, Braum JI. Dietary protein impact on glycemic control during weight loss. Journal Nutrition. (2004) 134(4):968S-73S.

78. Weserterp-Plantenga MS, et al. High protein intake sustains weight maintenance after body weight loss in humans. Int Journal Obesity Related Metabolic Disorders. (2004) 28(1):57-64.

79. Brenner BM, Lawler EV, Mackenzie HS. The hyperfiltration theory: a paradigm shift in nephrology. Kidney Int 1996;49:1774e7.

80. Levey AS, Greene T, Sarnak MJ, Wang X, Beck GJ, Kusek JW, et al. Effect of dietary protein restriction on the progression of kidney disease:

long-term follow-up of the Modification of Diet in Renal Disease (MDRD) Study. Am J Kidney Dis 2006;48:879-88.

81. Walser M. The relationship of dietary protein to kidney disease. In: Liepa GH, editor. Dietary proteins: how they alleviate disease and promote better health. Champaign: American Oil Chemists Society Monograph; 1992. p. 168e78.

82. http://www.edren.org/pages/edreninfo/diet-in-renal-disease/diet-for-the-failing-kidney-and-ckd.php

83. Robert R. Wolfe, et al. Optimal protein intake in the elderly. Clinical Nutrition (2008), doi:10.1016/j.clnu.2008.06.008.

84. Dawson-Hughes B. Calcium and protein in bone health. ProcNutr Soc 2003;62:505e9.

85. Wilson MM, Purushothaman R, Morley JE. Effect of liquid dietary supplements on energy intake in the elderly. Am J ClinNutr 2002;75:944e7.

86. Hu FB, Stampfer MJ, Manson JE, Rimm E, Colditz GA, Speizer FE, et al. Dietary protein and risk of ischemic heart disease in women. Am J Clin Nutr 1999;70:221e7.

87. Stratton RJ, Ek AC, Engfer M, Moore Z, Rigby P, Wolfe RR, et al. Enteral nutritional support in prevention and treatment of pressure ulcers: a systematic review and meta-analysis. Ageing Res Rev 2005;4:422e50.

88. Schurch MA, Rizzoli R, Slosman D, Vadas L, Vergnaud P, Bonjour JP. Protein supplements increase serum insulin-like growth factor-I levels and attenuate proximalfemur bone loss in patients with recent hip fracture: a randomized, double-blind, placebo-controlled trial. Ann Intern Med 1998;128:801e9.

89. Ferrando AA, Tipton KD, Doyle D, Phillips SM, Cortiella J, Wolfe RR. Testosterone injection stimulates net protein synthesis but not tissue amino acid transport. Am J Physiol 1998;276:E864e71.

90. Biolo G, Fleming GRYD, Wolfe RR. Physiologic hyperinsulinemia stimulates protein synthesis and enhances transport of selected amino acids in human skeletal muscle. J Clin Invest 1995;95:811e9.

91. Yarasheski KE, Zachwieja JJ, Campbell JA, Bier DM. Effect of growth hormone and resistance exercise on muscle growth and strength in older men. Am J Physiol 1995;268:E268e76.

92. Paddon-Jones D, Sheffield-Moore M, Aarsland A, Wolfe RR, Ferrando AA. Exogenous amino acids stimulate human muscle anabolism without

interfering with the response to mixed meal ingestion. Am J Physiol 2005;288:E761e7.

93. Solerte SB, Gazzaruso C, Schifino N. Metabolic effects of orally administered amino acid mixture in elderly subjects with poorly controlled type II diabetes mellitus. Am J Cardiol 2004;93:A23e9.

94. Boersheim E, Bui QU, Tissier S, Kobayshi H, Ferrando AA, Wolfe RR. Amino acid supplementation improves muscle mass, strength and physical function in elderly. Clin Nutr April 2008;27(2):189e95.

95. Tipton KD, Elliott TA, Cree MG, Wolf SE, Sanford AP, Wolfe RR. Ingestion of casein and whey proteins result in muscle anabolism after resistance exercise. Med Sci Sports Exerc 2004;36:2073e81.

    Symons TB, Schutzler SE, Cocke TL, Chinkes DL, Wolfe RR, Paddon-Jones D. Aging does not impair the anabolic response to a protein-rich meal. Am J Clin Nutr 2007;86:451e6.

96. Bohe J., et al. Human muscle protein synthesis is modulated by extracellular, not intramuscular amino acids availability: a dose-response study. Journal Physiology (2003) 552: 315-324.

97. Layman DK. Protein quality and quantity at levels above the RDA improves adult weight loss. J American College of Nutrition (2004) 23(6 Supplement):631S-636S.

98. Paddon-Jones D, et al. Exogenous amino acids stimulate human muscle anabolism without interfering with the response to mixed meal ingestion. American Journal of Physiological Endocriniol Metabolism (2005) 288(4):E761.

99. Chumlea WC, Baumgartner RN, Vellas BP. Anthropometry and body composition in the perspective of nutritional status in the elderly. Nutrition 1991;7:57e60.

100. Paddon-Jones D, et. al. Exogenous amino acids stimulate human muscle anabolism without interfering with the response to mixed meal ingestion. American Journal of Physiological Endocriniol Metabolism (2005) 288(4):E761-7.

101. Baynes JW. The role of AGEs in aging: causation or correlation. Exp Gerontol. 2001 Sep;36(9):1527-37.

102. DeGroot J. The AGE of the matrix: chemistry, consequence and cure. Curr Opin Pharmacol. 2004 Jun;4(3):301-5.

    Harding JJ. Viewing molecular mechanisms of ageing through a lens. Ageing Res Rev. 2002 Jun;1(3):465-79.

Onorato JM, Jenkins AJ, Thorpe SR, Baynes JW. Pyridoxamine, an inhibitor of advanced glycation reactions, also inhibits advanced lipoxidation reactions. Mechanism of action of pyridoxamine. J Biol Chem. 2000 Jul 14;275(28):21177-84.

Vlassara H. Advanced glycation in health and disease: role of the modern environment. Ann NY Acad Sci. 2005 Jun;1043:452-60.

Baynes JW. The Maillard hypothesis on aging: time to focus on DNA. Ann NY Acad Sci. 2002 Apr;959:360-7.

Takeuchi M, Yamagishi S. TAGE (toxic AGEs) hypothesis in various chronic diseases. Med Hypotheses. 2004;63(3):449-52.

103. Phinney SD. Fatty acids, inflammation, and the metabolic syndrome. Am J Clin Nutr. 2005 Dec;82(6):1151-2.

104. Xu H, Barnes GT, Yang Q, et al. Chronic inflammation in fat plays a crucial role in the development of obesity-related insulin resistance. J Clin Invest. 2003 Dec;112(12):1821-30.

105. Baynes JW. The role of AGEs in aging: causation or correlation. Exp Gerontol. 2001 Sep;36(9):1527-37.

106. Vlassara H, Cai W, Crandall J, Goldberg T, Oberstein R, Dardaine V, et al. (2002). Inflammatory mediators are induced by dietary glycotoxins, a major risk factor for diabetic angiopathy. Proc Natl Acad Sci USA 99:15596-15601; erratum in Proc Natl Acad Sci USA 100:763, 2003.

107. Boldyrev AA, Stvolinsky SL, Tyulina OV, et al. Biochemical and physiological evidence that carnosine is an endogenous neuroprotector against free radicals. Cell Mol Neurobiol. 1997 Apr;17(2):259-71.

108. Wang AM, Ma C, Xie ZH, Shen F. Use of carnosine as a natural anti-senescence drug for human beings. Biochemistry (Mosc.). 2000 Jul;65(7):869-71.

109. Yuneva MO, Bulygina ER, Gallant SC, et al. Effect of carnosine on age-induced changes in senescence-accelerated mice. J Anti-Aging Med. 1999;2(4):337-42.

110. Dukic-Stefanovic S, Schinzel R, Riederer P, Munch G. AGES in brain ageing: AGE-inhibitors as neuroprotective and anti-dementia drugs? Biogerontology. 2001;2(1):19-34.

Guiotto A, Calderan A, Ruzza P, Borin G. Carnosine and carnosine-related antioxidants: a review. Curr Med Chem. 2005;12(20):2293-315.

Hipkiss AR, Michaelis J, Syrris P. Non-enzymatic glycosylation of the dipeptide L-carnosine, a potential anti-protein-cross-linking agent. FEBS Lett. 1995 Aug 28;371(1):81-5.

Hipkiss AR. Carnosine, a protective, anti-ageing peptide? Int J Biochem Cell Biol. 1998 Aug;30(8):863-8.

Gallant S, Semyonova M, Yuneva M. Carnosine as a potential anti-senescence drug. Biochemistry (Mosc.). 2000 Jul;65(7):866-8.

111. Gugliucci A., Kotani K, Taing J, Matsuoka Y, Sano Y, Yoshimura M, Egawa K, Horikawa C, Kitagawa Y, Kiso Y, Kimura S, Sakane N. Ann Nutr Metab. 2009;54(3):197-201.

112. Fabry P, et al. 1964. The frequency of meals: Its relation to overweight, hypercholesterolemia and decreased glucose tolerance. Lancet, 2 (7360), 614-5.

113. Jenkins DJA, Wolever TMS, Ocana AM, et al. Metabolic effects of reducing rate of glucose ingestion by single bolus continuous sipping. Diabetes 1990; 39:1339-46

114. Marmonier C, Chapelot D, Louis-Sylvestre J. Metabolic and behavioral consequences of a snack consumed in a satiety state. Am J Clin Nutr 1999;70:854-66.

115. Marmonier C, Chapelot D, Fantino M, Louis-Sylvestre J. Snacks consumed in a nonhungry state have poor satiating efficiency: influence of snack composition on substrate utilization and hunger. Am J Clin Nutr 2002;76:518-28.

116. Laville M, Cornu C, Normand S, Mithieux G, Beylot M & Riou JP. (1993) Decreased glucose-induced thermogenesis at the onset of obesity. Am J Clin Nutr. 57;851-856.

117. http://www.ncbi.nlm.nih.gov/pubmed/18940848.

118. http://www.ncbi.nlm.nih.gov/pubmed/18589027.

119. http://www.ncbi.nlm.nih.gov/pubmed/19875483.

120. Chris Crowley and Henry S. Lodge, M.D., "Young at Heart," *Reader's Digest,* February 2005, pp. 88-90.

121. Hawley JA, Lessard SJ. Exercise training-induced improvements in insulin action. Acta Physiol (Oxf). 2008 Jan;192(1):127-35.

122. Srikanthan P, Hevener AL, Karlamangla AS (2010). Sarcopenia Exacerbates Obesity-Associated Insulin Resistance and Dysglycemia: Findings from the National Health and Nutrition Examination Survey III. PLoS ONE 5(5): e10805. doi:10.1371/journal.pone.0010805.

123. Valdez G, Tapia JC, Kang H, Clemenson GD, Gage FH, Lichtman JW, and Sanes JR. Attenuation of age-related changes in mouse neuromuscular synapses by caloric restriction and exercise. PNAS published ahead of print August 2, 2010, doi:10.1073/pnas.1002220107.

124. http://www.npr.org/templates/story/story.php?storyId=128267723.

125. Roberts CK, Won D, Pruthi S, Kurtovic S, Sindhu RK, Vaziri ND, and Barnard RJ. Effect of a diet and exercise intervention on oxidative stress, inflammation, MMP-9, and monocyte chemotactic activity in men with metabolic syndrome factors. J Appl Physiol 100: 1657-1665, 2006. First published December 15, 2005; doi:10.1152/japplphysiol.01292.2005 8750-7587/06.

126. Burd NA, West DWD, Staples AW, Atherton PJ, Baker JM, et al. Low-Load High Volume Resistance Exercise Stimulates Muscle Protein Synthesis More Than High-Load Low Volume Resistance Exercise in Young Men. PLoS ONE 5(8): e12033; doi:10.1371/journal.pone.0012033.

127. "Americans Relate Water to Well-Being, but Most Don't Get Their Fill; Survey Shows 33 Percent of What Americans Drink Can Cause Dehydration," The Rockefeller University, New York, for the International Bottled Water Association, New York, May 30, PRNewswire.

128. "Anxiety Disorders Research at the National Institute of Mental Health: NIMH," National Institute of Mental Health, NIH Publication No. 99-4504, printed 1999.

129. Epel ES, McEwen B, Seeman T, et al. Stress and body shape: Stress-induced cortisol secretion is consistently greater among women with central fat. Psychosomatic Med. 2000 Sept;62(5):623-32.

130. Gluck ME, Geliebter A, Lorence M. Cortisol stress response is positively correlated with central obesity in obese women with binge eating disorder (BED) before and after cognitive-behavioral treatment. Ann NY Acad Sci. 2004 Dec;1032:202-7.

131. Dr. Gayle Olinekova, *Power Aging* (New York: Thunder's Mouth Press, 1998), p. 54.

132. Balch and Balch, *Prescription for Nutritional Healing,* Third Edition, p. 473.

133. Taheri S, Lin L, Austin D, Young T, Mignot E. Short sleep duration is associated with reduced leptin, elevated ghrelin, and increased body mass index. PloS Medicine. 2004;1(3).

134. Spiegel K, Tasali E, Penev P, Van Cauter E. Sleep curtailment in healthy young men is associated with decreased leptin levels, elevated ghrelin levels, and increased hunger and appetite. Annals of Internal Medicine. 2004;141:846-850.

135. Brondel L, Romer MA, Nougues PM, Touyarou P, and Davenne D. Acute partial sleep deprivation increases food intake in healthy men. Am J Clin Nutr 2010 91:1550-1559.

136. Lyytikäinen P, Lallukka T, Lahelma E, and Rahkonen O. Sleep problems and major weight gain: a follow-up study. International Journal of Obesity advance online publication 8 June 2010; doi: 10.1038/ijo.2010.113.

137. Laidlow M, Holub BJ. Effects of supplementation with fish oil-derived n-3 fatty acids and linolenic acid on circulating plasma lipids and fatty acid profiles in women. Journal of Clinical Endocrinology & Metabolism. Aug2001;86:3787-3794.

138. Olinekova, *Power Aging*, p. 58.

139. National Research Council. (2006). Fluoride in Drinking Water: A Scientific Review of EPA's Standards. National Academies Press, Washington, D.C. p 223.

140. Nicholas A. Ashford and Claudia S. Miller, *Chemical Exposures: Low Levels and High Stakes* (Hoboken, New Jersey: John Wiley and Sons, 1998).

141. "Making Sense of Scents," Citizens for a Toxic-Free Marin, P.O. Box 2785, San Rafael, CA. 94912-2785, 1996. Repeated exposure to toluene can damage bone marrow, as well as the liver and kidneys, slow reflexes, and at the very least cause headaches and trouble concentrating. (Betty Bridges. Fragrance: Emerging Health and Environmental Concerns. Flavour and Fragrance Journal. Volume 17, Issue 5, 2002, 361-371.)

142. Dr. Joseph Mercola, "How to Avoid the Top 10 Most Common Toxins."

143. Lim S, Ahn SY, Song IC, Chung MH, Jang HC, Park KS, Lee KU, Pak Y, and Lee HK. 2009. Chronic exposure to the herbicide, atrazine, causes mitochondrial dysfunction and insulin resistance. Public Library of Science, one doi:10.1371/journal.pone.0005186.

144. Rosenberg BG, Chen H, Folmer J, Liu J, Papadopoulos V, Zirkin BR. Gestational exposure to atrazine: effects on the postnatal development of male offspring. Journal of Andrology, Vol. 29, No. 3, May/June 2008.

145. Worthington V. Effect of Agricultural Methods on Nutritional Quality:

A Comparison of Organic with Conventional Crops. Alternative Therapies, Volume 4. 1998:58-69.

146. Liska DJ. The detoxification enzyme systems. Altern Med Rev. 1998 Jun;3(3):187-98.

147. Dashwood RH. Use of transgenic and mutant animal models in the study of heterocyclic amine-induced mutagenesis and carcinogenesis. J Biochem Mol Biol. 2003 Jan 31;36(1):35-42.

148. Ong TM, Whong WZ, Stewart J, Brockman HE. Chlorophyllin: a potent anti-mutagen against environmental and dietary complex mixtures. Mutat Res. 1986 Feb;173(2):111-5.

149. Kinae N, Masuda H, Shin IS, Furugori M, Shimoi K. Functional properties of wasabi and horseradish. Biofactors. 2000;13(1-4):265-9.

150. Shapiro TA, Fahey JW, Wade KL, Stephenson KK, Talalay P. Chemoprotective glucosinolates and isothiocyanates of broccoli sprouts: metabolism and excretion in humans. Cancer Epidemiol Biomarkers Prev. 2001 May;10(5):501-8.

LIVINGFUEL
THE LEADER IN SUPERFOOD NUTRITION

SuperFood Snacks

Living Fuel's CocoChia Sustained Energy Bars and **CocoChia Snack Mix** are delicious and nutritious—a great choice for athletes, those with active lifestyles, dieters, children, and diabetics alike. Crafted with raw and organic superfoods, they're great-tasting, low-glycemic, and made with the superfoods coconut, chia seeds, chocolate, and almonds. *Living Fuel's CocoChia products contain clean, smart fats, fiber, and protein that your body needs for Super Health!* Choose the Original CocoChia Bar, the Double Chocolate CocoChia Bar, or our CocoChia Snack Mix.

Original CocoChia Bars (Box of 12 Bars)
Sustained energy, smart fats, and plant fiber with clean all-natural raw and organic ingredients. The original CocoChia bar!

Double Chocolate CocoChia Bars (Box of 12 Bars)
All the smart fats and fiber of the Original CocoChia Bar, raw and organic ingredients, plus a double coating of yummy low-glycemic dark chocolate.

CocoChia Snack Mix (Box of 12 Packets)
Our delicious blend of shredded raw organic coconut and raw whole chia seeds—a remarkably healthy and tasty low-glycemic snack fuel! *Now in convenient individually wrapped single-serving packets.* Twelve 24.5g servings per box. Also available in a large 490g bulk bag with 20 servings.

TO LEARN MORE:
1-866-580-FUEL(3835)
www.LivingFuel.com

LIVINGFUEL
THE LEADER IN SUPERFOOD NUTRITION

SuperEssentials™

SuperEssentials™ Omega—*quite possibly the most important supplement on earth.* SuperEssentials Omega is the most sophisticated antioxidant essential fatty acids complex available today. It contains Omega 3 EPA and DHA, Omega 6 GLA, potent levels of all-natural full-spectrum Vitamin E (tocotrienols, tocopherols), and the powerful antioxidants Vitamin A, Vitamin D, and Astaxanthin. 120 softgel capsules per bottle.

Pure Essential Omega 3 EPA and **DHA** essential fatty acids from sardines and anchovies caught in pristine cold waters.

Protective crucial Omega 6 GLA from borage seed oil

Powerful antioxidants Vitamin A & D from cold water fish

Superior proprietary blend of full-spectrum all-natural Vitamin E (tocotrienols and tocopherols)

Superior powerful all-natural carotenoid Astaxanthin

Easy to swallow buffalo gelatin capsules

Also...

SuperEssentials™ Aminos

SuperEssentials™ Multi

TO LEARN MORE:
1-866-580-FUEL(3835)
www.LivingFuel.com